"This edited volume is a very welcome contribution to 1 _____ business, peace and development. With both theoretical an_____ different parts of the world and various topics, it offers fo___ ___ _____ and insights relevant to a range of audiences, including researchers, policy-makers, activists, managers, investors and staff of international (non-)governmental organizations. I hope it will draw further attention to this topic that is so important for business and society, and for local populations in particular, and that deserves more dedicated and in-depth investigation."

Professor Ans Kolk, University of Amsterdam

"If PEACE coins the optimal environment for the human potential to flourish, business surely has an instrumental role to play. But, as this important book sets out, business "doing good" or avoiding doing harm, does not necessarily add up to peace. Business does not exist in a vacuum, but in an interlinked symbiosis with society, conditioned on trust and public confidence. This supports well the broadened mindset now evolving in sophisticated business leadership. We call it businessworthy leadership. As business seeks to adjust to the complexity, volatility and risks of conflicts deriving from the simultaneous acceleration of technology, globalization and climate change, we must bring the front lines of academic thinking and business together to inform mindsets and action that enhance peace. This book is an important contribution. This book demonstrates the need for system thinking, analysis, strategic engagement and a longer-term approach. It presents some strong corporate perspectives and empirical reflections."

Per Saxegaard, Founder, Business for Peace Foundation

"Though war and peace are matters of state, business cannot adopt a disinterested posture when it comes to operating or investing in conflict zones. Armed conflict is a business risk. But beyond the immediate financial implications, it raises fundamental issues of corporate citizenship: when is a company complicit in conflict or its causes? Could it alleviate the ills of war? Should it withdraw from a conflict zone or stay put, for what reasons and under what kind of operating guidelines? Rarely are there clear-cut answers, but rather difficult dilemmas requiring well-informed decision-making and a firm moral compass calibrated by the limits of what is possible. Conducting business in a war situation puts the spotlight on the boundary between realism and idealism. This book is an intellectual tool for CEOs and investors facing armed conflict or situations where they can help prevent conflict."

Carlos Joly, Co-Chair of Expert Group on the UN Principles of Responsible Investment and fellow, Cambridge Institute for Sustainability Leadership

"The role of business in peacebuilding has been the subject of active discussion (and some controversy) over the past two decades. The adoption of SDG 16 has further fueled this issue. However, much of the discussion and analysis has been at the theoretical and (arguably) rhetorical level. The contributions in this book cast a critical eye to this body of work and bring to life real-world examples of where business has contributed to peace and where real challenges still lay."

Reg Manhas, Senior Vice President, External Affairs, Kosmos Energy

BUSINESS, PEACEBUILDING AND SUSTAINABLE DEVELOPMENT

The intersection of business, peace and sustainable development is becoming an increasingly powerful space, and is already beginning to show the capability to drive major global change. This book deciphers how different forms of corporate engagement in the pursuit of peace and development have different impacts and outcomes. It looks specifically at how the private sector can better deliver peace contributions in fragile, violent and conflict settings and then at the deeper consequences of this agenda upon businesses, governments, international institutions and not least the local communities that are presumed to be the beneficiaries of such actions. It is the first book to compile the state-of-the-field in one place and is therefore an essential guide for students, researchers, policy-makers and practitioners on the role of business in peace.

Without cross-disciplinary engagement, it is hard to identify where the cutting edge truly lies, and how to take the topic forward in a more systematic manner. This edited book brings together thought leaders in the field and pulls disparate strands together from business ethics, management, international relations, peace and conflict studies in order to better understand how businesses can contribute to peacebuilding and sustainable development.

Before businesses take a deeper role in the most complicated and risky elements of sustainable development, we need to be able to better explain what works, why it works, and what effective business efforts for peace and development mean for the multilateral institutional frameworks. This book does just that.

Jason Miklian is a Senior Researcher at the Peace Research Institute Oslo and a postdoctoral fellow in business and peacebuilding at the Centre for Development and the Environment (SUM), University of Oslo.

Rina M. Alluri is Senior Researcher at the University of Zurich Geography Department and co-founder and consultant at the World Habitat Research and Creativity Network (WHRC).

John E. Katsos is an Associate Professor of Management at the American University of Sharjah, UAE.

BUSINESS AND PEACEBUILDING

The *Business and Peacebuilding* series seeks to deliver applied and theoretical knowledge of the complex and shifting role of the private, corporate and civil-society sectors in enhancing peacebuilding. This series is designed to encourage cross-disciplinary approaches and to break down research silos, showcasing perspectives on business and peacebuilding through a broad array of strategies and delivery mechanisms. These may include: corporate social responsibility, business and human rights, socially responsible investment, participation in the United Nations Sustainable Development Goals, environmental, social and corporate governance guidelines, leadership studies, supply chain management, conflict-sensitive business practice, and indigenous studies.

Recognizing that effective peace action is contingent upon comprehensive understanding of local context, *Business and Peacebuilding* also encourages exploration of bottom-up approaches including topics such as: entrepreneurship and innovation, indigenous perspectives, area and comparative studies, community and inequality impacts, Small and Medium Enterprises (SMEs), private-public partnerships and business-civil society partnerships for peacebuilding.

Editors:

Jason Miklian
Edwina Pio
Eric Schockman

Books in the series:

Business, Peacebuilding and Sustainable Development
Editors: Jason Miklian, Rina M. Alluri and John E. Katsos

BUSINESS, PEACEBUILDING AND SUSTAINABLE DEVELOPMENT

Edited by Jason Miklian, Rina M. Alluri and John E. Katsos

Routledge
Taylor & Francis Group

LONDON AND NEW YORK

First published 2019
by Routledge
2 Park Square, Milton Park, Abingdon, Oxon OX14 4RN

and by Routledge
52 Vanderbilt Avenue, New York, NY 10017

Routledge is an imprint of the Taylor & Francis Group, an informa business

British Library Cataloguing in Publication Data
A catalogue record for this book is available from the British Library

Library of Congress Cataloging-in-Publication Data
A catalog record has been requested for this book

ISBN: 978-0-367-17503-0 (hbk)
ISBN: 978-0-367-17506-1 (pbk)
ISBN: 978-0-429-05722-9 (ebk)

Typeset in Bembo
by Taylor & Francis Books

CONTENTS

ILLUSTRATIONS

FOREWORD

In 1999, as I was starting my first writing on business and peace, there were not many sources to rely upon. To be sure, the notions that trade and economic development fostered peace were echoed by leaders of most liberal democracies and further traced back to philosophers such as Kant, Montesquieu, and (as this volume's Introduction suggests) even Hobbes. Yet, there was very little about how these engines of trade and economic development – businesses – contribute to peace.

Of course, some organizations, such as Rotary International have advocated for a role for business in fostering peace for a century. At the turn of the century, the United Nations was just announcing its Global Compact, which put it on a path to recognize the role of business in a positive, problem-solving direction, culminating in the Sustainable Development Goals. In 1999, however, I was left to examine anthropological studies (such as David Fabbro's 1978 *Peaceful Societies*) or primatological research, (such as Frans de Waal's 1989 *Peacemaking Among Primates*) and cobble together a very interdisciplinary (albeit unusual) argument from those sources along with Hawaiian history to argue for a "corporate makahiki:" a time for business to focus on peace. To put it mildly, some of integrations I attempted were a stretch.

In 2000, Jane Nelson's *The Business of Peace,* Raymond Kelly's anthropological study *Warless Societies* and Virginia Haufler's *A Public Role for the Public Sector* added more to chew upon so that, with my University of Michigan colleague, Cindy Schipani, we decided to host a conference with the unwieldy title: Corporate Governance, Stakeholder Accountability, and Sustainable Peace. Many of our colleagues thought we had lost our minds and warned us that we risked destroying our careers by pursuing such an oddball topic. We couldn't even find speakers who would even experiment with the ideas to fill out the schedule for our November 2001 event.

Then 9–11 happened and everything changed. People wanted to respond in some way – any way – to the idea that there might be something people – in our case, at a business school – could do to lessen violence. Our conference was not about terrorism, but that really didn't matter. What mattered was that issues of peace and violence became very important. For us, that led to articles, a book, special issues of law journals, more conferences and a growing body of scholarship that found itself meeting similarly minded scholars and practitioners alike who were experimenting with these ideas around the world.

In our 2003 book, *The Role of Business in Fostering Peace*, we formulated a simple set of practices businesses could do to foster peace:

(1) provide economic development,
(2) support rule of law,
(3) contribute to a sense of internal and external community, and
(4) track-two diplomacy.

In looking in this volume, one can see these themes continue to have currency, which is gratifying. What is more gratifying, however, is the sophistication of the arguments being presented by a new generation of scholars who have taken to this field. Back in 2001, Cindy and I (two legal scholars) were clear that while we were presenting a *prima facie* case (a legal term denoting that there was enough evidence to force a trial on a topic, but not necessarily decide the merits of the case), we did not ourselves believe that we had proven that business could really impact peace by a preponderance of the evidence, let alone beyond a reasonable doubt. We challenged – and often begged – other scholars to contribute their expertise to meet these evidentiary challenges.

The scholars in this volume have met that burden. Throughout this book, by case studies, empirical analysis, integration with other fields of studies, and augmentation of theories that business can make a positive contribution to peace.

The theoretical part of this volume provides very helpful integrations with other peace-related fields. This has always been at the core of business and peace research and my expectation will always need to be augmented. Peace, after all, is a complex subject. So too is business. Those affected (and who affect) each of these are numerous leading to multiple approaches to the topic. One of the hallmarks of this field to date is how willing scholars from different disciplines have been to drop their guard to explore new ways of thinking. This section of the book is very much in keeping with that exemplary tradition, providing new ways to "sync" theoretical approaches to business and peace with disciplines that have something to say about the topic.

Similarly, this field will continually need insights as to practical developments and activities. Times change. What might be a business strategy in 1970 might look very different in an Internet Age. Given the multiple variables impacting peace in a given region, case studies, investigative research, and comparative assessments provide examples for practice and also provide the foundation for future theoretical development. Here again, this volume features such real-world insight essential for the field.

Finally, untethered businesses will not create peace by itself. There must be policy dimensions. That includes policies that businesses themselves develop and it also includes public policies that thwart violent-risking conduct and nudge businesses toward more peaceful interactions. These aspects are also helpfully explored in this volume.

All of this amounts to a pleasing and fitting set of affairs, 20 years on, and indeed, this field of business and peace continues to grow and develop around the world. I have many hopes for this field and, indeed, for these scholars, some of whom have been my students. I believe that this field, led by these scholars and other organization's such as (but not limited to) Per Saxegaard's Business for Peace Foundation, will be able to further the activities of business fostering peace so that it is embraced as an accepted way of life such as environmental sustainability is today.

Twenty-five years ago, as I was starting my first tenure-track job, I winced at the reality that environmental scholars were widely unwelcomed in business schools, frequently derided, and rarely supported. Today, it is impossible to walk down the corridor of any business school in the world without seeing the school's touting of its environmental awareness and commitment. My sense is that the field of business and peace may be another 15 years away from this level of acceptance and integration, but I think it will happen, especially given the quality of scholarship in this volume.

If this does come to fruition, then my challenge and hope will be for scholars in this field to show how an ambivalent social construct can find its normative compass to direct itself toward peace and away from violence and apply those lessons to other such institutions. Music, sports, film, religion, and other cultural forces as well are, like business, ambivalent. An easy out when talking about any of them is to note that, well, it (music, sports, film, religion, business etc.) acts in violent or at least problematic ways. While this is true, the observation contributes little other than to make others aware that these social constructs have a dark side.

The question is normative: how do we identify those traits that lead to a positive good and what can any social construct (again, music, sports, film, religion, business, etc.) do to orient itself toward the admirable? This is a normative task, yet it need not become bogged down in philosophical disputation. If we agree that peace (albeit not in a Carthaginian style) is good, then identifying those practices that lead to it suggests they have normative content. In that sense, the contributions to this volume may not be explicitly normative in a philosophical sense, but they are so in a thoroughgoing way. It is important to bear this in mind, both for business and peace studies, as well as for the ways in which studies like this can contribute to the peacebuilding actions of other social constructs.

Leaving those future possibilities to the side, I welcome this volume and the fine scholars who have contributed to it and I express my admiration to those scholars and to the editors for taking on this effort to advance not just the field of business and peace, but more importantly, the well-being of humanity.

Timothy L. Fort, PhD, JD
Eveleigh Professor of Business Ethics
Professor of Business Law and Ethics
Kelley School of Business
Indiana University

WHAT'S OLD IS NEW AGAIN

> In [war] there is no place for industry, because the fruit thereof is uncertain, and consequently no culture of the earth, no navigation nor use of the commodities that may be imported by sea, no commodious building, no instruments of moving and removing such things as require much force, no knowledge of the face of the earth; no account of time, no arts, no letters, no society, and, which is worst of all, continual fear and danger of violent death, the life of man solitary, poor, nasty, brutish, and short. (Thomas Hobbes, The Leviathan)

In the face of war, life is hell. Nearly 400 years ago, Hobbes considered it reduced to one that is "solitary, poor, nasty, brutish and short," and one could argue that little has changed since. Most of us have come across the final line of this quote before, but Hobbes also advocated for the clear role of industry – or as we might say today, business – in the creation and maintenance of a stable and functional society. Just as war can lead to economic and societal breakdown, business and peace are intertwined and can be mutually supportive of each other in a healthy society, creating the joint space, opportunity and potential to grow and develop.

From the days of the British East India Company, the integral yet complex role of business in society is well-worn scholarly ground. Business can grow societies, and they can exploit them. Trade can bring states together, and it can trigger wars. Firms can use either peace or conflict as a window to profit. But beyond the time when eminent scholars thought that the only true social responsibility of a business was to grow its profits (Friedman 1970), today the sheer power and scale of businesses in fragile parts of the world combined with a growing societal demand for them to be positive, socially aware actors has opened new paths to peace.

Thus, the field of business and peace has emerged, exploring components of the assertion that businesses have a role to play in maintaining and promoting peace and societal development in conflict-affected or otherwise fragile parts of the world. This vision promises that businesses can flourish alongside society, and that this relationship is both reciprocal and mutually beneficial. Beyond contributing to academic debates on issues such as corporate governance, conflict sensitivity or the role of business in peacebuilding, business and peace research also tries to offer practical solutions to companies and investors on how to enhance peace in a pragmatic, justifiable and perhaps even replicable way.

The shared corpus of work across disciplines that has been published over the past 15 years is now becoming recognizable as a field distinct from the current 'home' fields such as political science, sustainability, economics, sociology, international business, law, and philosophy. But while empirical and theoretical reflections on business and peace have proliferated over the past decade, this has often taken place within research silos that are not in sync with one another. The lack of research continuity is partly due to a dearth of central texts that serve as reference points for the field. This book seeks to be such a reference point.

This book is a multi-disciplinary and cross-disciplinary exploration of business and peace, and intends to be a guiding reference point for future work on the topic. It has three sections that intend to contribute to this aim: *theoretical advances, business and peace in practice,* and *emerging peace policy.* The volume brings together top scholars and practitioners across the fields of business ethics, management, peacebuilding, philosophy, human rights, international law, development studies, and international relations. Perhaps more importantly, the contributions aim to not only speak to one field or the other but across them, showing how scholarship on business and peace can and should cut across disciplines to maximize its power and value. The chapters in this book retain the interdisciplinary essence that is so vital to the development of the field.

Two overarching questions that drive this volume are: How can the private sector better deliver peace contributions in fragile, violent and/or conflict settings? And what are the deeper consequences of this agenda for businesses, governments, international institutions and not least local communities that are presumed to be the beneficiaries of such actions? This volume also explores relationships between political stability/fragility, ethical business activity and economic opportunity through research-supported good practices by business for sustainable peace. Further, business-related issues for international relations practitioners are explored, including management and policy frameworks in the context of the limitations for peace promotion by businesses in post-conflict zones. To show how businesses function as development actors, this volume deciphers how different forms of corporate engagement in the pursuit of peace and development have different impacts and outcomes. In the process, we bridge the intersection of peace and sustainable development means for businesses in practice, and how international organizations like the United Nations are helping frame business action and opportunity in conflict-affected areas.

In this introductory chapter, we sketch out major theories on business and peace before introducing the book's structure and contributions. First, the main research-based business and peace assertions are examined, highlighting three forces that drive these assertions: motivation, integration, and effectiveness. Next, we explore recent developments and critiques of these prevailing theories, with emphasis on business efforts for peace through the United Nations Sustainable Development Goals (SDGs). We then outline the structure of the book, uniting the main themes of the field through our thematic sections. Business leaders, peace practitioners, researchers and scholars, and students will all find value in these pages.

State of the art in business and peace

Business and peace scholarship can to date largely be housed within three approaches: 1) theoretical perspectives and debates on the 'potential' of business to contribute to peace; 2) business-perspective approaches that look at the impacts of conflict upon business and the rationales for how and why businesses engage in peacebuilding; and 3) practitioner perspectives of how business has contributed to peacebuilding in a practical way.

First, much theoretical literature has sought to craft theories of change related to private sector enhancement of peace and to properly categorize the types of activities that might – based on prevailing theories in fields such as economics, political science, management, and psychology – help to enhance peace (Oetzel et al. 2009; Forrer and Katsos 2015; Westermann-Behaylo et al. 2015; Iff and Alluri 2016b; Miklian 2017). This is supported by guiding policy documents that have proposed roles and responsibilities of business-conflict affected contexts (UN Global Compact 2010; OECD 2011). This literature is the core of the business and peace field, where scholars, practitioners and policymakers are engaging with and building upon one another's work. One fundamental challenge throughout the literature lies in the attempts to define 'peace' itself, a multi-faceted and deeply complex concept whose definitional slipperiness has made building theory on this topic an onerous endeavor. For our purposes, we consider 'peacebuilding' to include strategies, processes and activities that aim to reduce and prevent the recurrence of violence by addressing the root causes of conflict (Boutros-Ghali 1992; Lederach 1997) through, for example, reconciliation and justice, socio-economic foundations, security and political framework. Thus, peacebuilding by business incorporates those sets of activities explicitly designed to forward such aims.

'Peacemaking' and 'peacekeeping' are often conceived of as straight-forward concepts, but the boundaries of 'peacebuilding' – especially in its interactions with development – are more fluid. Here, businesses can set out intentionally to make peace more likely in society by, for example, helping parties settle disputes and helping maintain peace after a peace accord. Corporate culture and operations are considered peacebuilding when they model non-violence (Forrer and Fort 2016), and most firms see peacebuilding as a long-term and incremental endeavor. This approach shares much with the idea of being 'businessworthy' (Business for Peace Foundation n.d.), but practitioners often find this incremental approach to be reductive in nature as peace cannot be reduced to the sum of its parts (e.g. Ganson,

Chapter 1). Peacebuilding also need not be in a conflict zone. Ethical business conduct could occur anywhere and still be labeled peacebuilding insofar as it incrementally enhances peace through culture and operations (Fort 2015).

Rooted in Fort and Schipani's (2004) seminal work, Oetzel et al.'s (2009) review of the business and peace literature reviews the four ways that business can promote peace: promoting economic development, engaging in track-two diplomacy, enhancing rule of law, and promoting a sense of community. The notion that business promotes economic development is a basic tenant that can be traced to Adam Smith, and economic development in this context is business doing what it does naturally: creating value for shareholders (Friedman 2009), employing local workers (Milliken et al. 2015), transferring valuable technology (Spencer 2008), and making foreign direct investments (Buckley 2014; Getz and Oetzel 2009). By focusing on its core business, business helps reduce prospects for violent conflicts. Multinational companies increasingly enter developing and conflict-affected economies to deliver greater global growth gains (Haufler 1997; Borensztein et al. 1998). But as developing countries have a 40 per cent risk of returning to violence whereas others have only a 9 per cent risk (Collier et al. 2008), such environments necessitate a greater level of engagement with peace and conflict dynamics. Still, even modest increases in economic growth can reduce the likelihood of reversion to conflict (Collier 2007), especially when accompanied by peace-positive management practices (Milliken et al. 2015).

The broader 'liberal economic peace' argument – that increased trade between states raises the likelihood for peaceful interaction – remains a robust point of assessment in relations between bordering states and for global trade openness (Pyun and Lee 2016). However, this positive connection is conditional. Several studies (e.g. Midtgard et al. 2017; Chisadza and Bittencourt 2016; Sorens and Ruger 2015) find that the relationship between economic opening and reduction of intrastate conflict is null at best and potentially negative, meaning that rapidly opening states might find themselves *more* susceptible to internal conflict (Miklian 2019). Rapid economic opening can also serve to entrench conflict elites and encourage conflict against minority groups (Barkemeyer and Miklian 2019). Studies have yet to show a clear peace benefit from economic opening alone, even as it retains its popularity in business and international financial institutional circles as a rationale for rapidly entering new markets.

Businesses are also assumed to help deliver peace by promoting rule of law through third-party standards such as international codes of conduct (Emmelhainz and Adams 1999; Kolk and Tuldere 2002) and engaging in conflict risk assessments before entering and while operating within conflict countries (Anderson et al. 2010; Iff et al. 2010; Guaqueta 2008; O'Neill 2008). By adopting principles of external valuation, companies can advance the rule of law within countries by binding themselves to more stable international norms. This is often called 'hard trust,' indicating the need for stakeholders to know that companies are bound by legally enforceable mechanisms that compel them to follow rules of operations (Bies et al. 2007). Examples of external valuations include International Organization for Standardization (ISO) 26000, the UN Global Compact, the UN Guiding Principles on Business and Human Rights (sometimes referred to as the Ruggie Principles), and the International Labor Organization's labor standards. Principles of external valuation not only set a model of behavior that engenders social and economic justice but also are a way for business to contribute to peace (by setting examples of good citizenship).

Business-peace legal arguments often center in discussions of nonbinding (or lightly binding) multilateral regulation of business. One example is the Responsibility to Protect (R2P) doctrine, covered extensively in an edited volume by Forrer and Seyle (2016). R2P and other such frameworks include arguments for firms to understand why they should be involved, arguments to the international community for why firms should be incorporated, and arguments to the scholarly and practitioner communities about why this is an important and emerging area worthy of deeper study. Underpinning such frameworks are normative elements that can be considered to be relatively stable within the Global North and its promoted multilateral institutions; but the application and prioritization of norms is shifting. This process will accelerate as new actors like China begin to assert more influence over international and multilateral bodies at the expense of those like the United States and United Kingdom that have taken a more inward turn. To illustrate, we can see how the twinned notions of risk of and engagement with local communities is being reframed by Global South firms in conflict and crisis regions (cf. Dittgen 2015) encouraging more local peace engagement by those firms in an effort to build operational security. Another way forward is to follow the conclusion of Fort (2007): business engagement is unlikely to enhance peace unless it is ethical.

Recently, scholars have brought expansions and nuance to Oetzel et al. (2009), but without challenging its core (e.g. Westermann-Behaylo et al. 2015; Forrer and Katsos 2015; Miklian 2017). For instance, Forrer and Katsos (2015) noted that it was precisely in grey areas between formal war and peace where businesses (and indeed any actors) may have the greatest impact on peace. In response, they develop a triadic construct that presents countries as existing in three basic conditions – war, buffer condition, and peace – that has several advantages for businesses to understand how they can best promote peace. The buffer condition also allows businesses to better integrate addressing structural violence (Galtung 2006) in their peacebuilding operations, even as such settings retain many of the traits of violence and the war economy even after war or limited war has ceased (Ballentine and Nitzschke 2005), in particular in levels of informal and black-market activity. Buffer economies, for instance, often have high levels of black economic output because the government monopolizes the formal economy, forcing anti-government groups to use the informal and black economies to fund their activities (Fearon 2004; Winer and Roule 2003). In such settings, consumption and investment decline and there is mass movement of people as either refugees or internally displaced persons (IEP 2014). Social, political, and economic processes are hindered, and prospects for sustainable growth and development are reduced. All of these factors prevent business from operating efficiently.

In sum, cutting-edge research over the previous decade has improved our understandings of on the complex relationships between business, peace and development, and we know significantly more about several key tenants of the potential for private sector contributions to peace and development (e.g. Ganson and Wennmann 2016; Iff and Alluri 2016b; Miklian 2017a). National firms are more likely to be successful than multinationals in local peace and development (Miklian and Bickel 2017), firms can enjoy reputational rewards for peacebuilding action in fragile local communities that can be just as valuable as traditional mitigation of reputational risk measures (Oetzel and Breslaurer 2015), business-development partnerships show significant promise in specific circumstances (Miklian and Bickel 2017), and the investment community is an interested but underutilized asset for peacebuilding and development aims (Reichberg and Syse, Chapter 10).

The business-perspective literature views how businesses conceptualize and operationalize societal issues of peace and development, most typically for their direct areas of operation. These studies tend to coalesce around a core question: Why do firms want to develop a peacebuilding presence? Beyond strategic motivations, firms are encouraged to become peace actors through internal and external incentives. Internal factors include aspirations for pro-peace actions to project positive corporate cultures and the impression of a virtuous firm; the belief that corporations can go beyond 'responsibilities' to personally sponsor peace action; and the mindset amongst leadership of international firms in particular that profit motivations alone are insufficient and firms must also try to make a positive difference to society. These aspirational thrusts can come from shareholders, boards, or management training, and mandate action to attempt to facilitate peace. Beyond idealistic motivations alone, the emerging mindset that business should serve a higher purpose than profit generation is driving political engagement and local policy advocacy as peacebuilding.

Most business-oriented literature has sought to ascertain the perceptions of managers – primarily at multinational enterprises (MNEs) – operating in conflict (Darendeli and Hill 2015; Oetzel and Getz 2012). These approaches are generally underpinned in either the corporate social responsibility or risk literatures, and attempt to understand how firms navigate through conflict, and in some cases make active attempts to build peace in a way mutually beneficial to themselves and local societies. Other major theories study why companies and their leaders pursue peace promotion (Fort 2015). Companies can contribute to peace using one of three aims: peacemaking, peacekeeping, and peacebuilding (Fort 2015). Companies promoting peace fall into one of three categories: peace entrepreneurs, instrumental businesses, and unintentional contributors to peace. (Fort 2015).

Other business-oriented perspectives explore how business 'fits' into local society in conflict contexts, particularly in how business can contribute to a sense of community and enhance social cohesion (Dworkin and Schipani 2007; Fort and Schipani 2004). Management theorists are perhaps most familiar with the notion of contributing to a sense of community as it is embedded within the literature on corporate social responsibility (CSR) (Aguilera and Rupp 2005; Davies et al. 2003; Freeman and McVea 2001). By taking all stakeholders into account, rather than just owners of the firm (Freeman 1984), businesses can obtain their 'social license' to operate in a foreign country (Gunningham et al. 2003). This is especially important for reducing operational risks in conflict-sensitive regions (Oetzel and Getz 2012). Milliken et al. (2015) also note the importance of incorporating employee voice into management of companies in conflict-affected regions as an important way to enhance the sense of community.

For firms with active peacebuilding portfolios, the role of 'who' is usually filled by the CEO, typically a founder with an activist mindset (Fort 2015), and the role of the CEO is essential in business-peace success (Fort 2015). Gender, tenure, and education of the CEO influence the degree of peace action (Huang 2013), as CEO-led peacebuilding initiatives are often presented through individual ethics or 'moral leadership' (Skubinn and Herzog 2016; Liu and Baker 2016). Preliminary evidence shows that firms who pay CEOs for CSR activities have more robust CSR mandates (Hong et al. 2016), and it is plausible that the same holds for incentivizing peacebuilding if business leaders also see themselves as transformed into 'peace leaders' in conflict settings of operation (Ledbetter 2016; Miller 2016). Following, Golan-Nadir and Cohen (2016) explore the notion of businesspersons as 'policy entrepreneurs' for peace in the Israel-Palestine conflict, highlighting the incremental successes of such initiatives at a time of political deadlock.

How businesses integrate peacebuilding within their corporate structures is more complicated. Beyond compartmentalizing the CSR sphere or allowing for an activist CEO to see peacebuilding as a pet project, institutional change is harder to implement. While most firms that engage in conflict areas recognize the need to engage in 'peace,' few see their role as integral to peacebuilding, and most see peacebuilding as the primary responsibility of the state. For example, Rettberg (2016) defines the multiple strategic goals of security, social change philosophy, and profit-making that business leaders confront as tripartite elements of 'need, creed, and greed' that can institutionalize deeper corporate peace involvement.

Different kinds of businesses can also be peace enhancing. Peace entrepreneurs are those companies and leaders who set out to make some intentional contribution to peace. It is an essential aspect of the firm's DNA and they seek ways to use their operations to contribute to peace. Peace instrumentalists are more likely to use corporate diplomacy (Fort 2015; Westermann-Behaylo et al. 2015). Instrumentalists make a rational calculation that companies perform better in peacetime, and take action that align the firm's strategic interests with society's peace interests. The investment community is increasingly aware of negative business impact, and is increasingly developing social development and conflict-sensitive markers in investment decisions. Finally, 'unconscious peacebuilders' contribute to peace without awareness of it by using self-perceived ethical business conduct that also happens to correlate with peace contribution (Joras 2009).

External encouragement for businesses to become peacebuilders has also grown. International non-governmental organizations (NGO) increasingly facilitate space for business-peace ventures, and the UN encourages firms to help vulnerable societies. Epitomizing the shift is the UN Guiding Principles on Business and

Human Rights (UNGPs) initiative, the first global standard on how businesses should protect universal human rights. The belief is that if companies comply with this and other (often sector-specific) international human rights standards (e.g. the UN Voluntary Principles on Security and Human Rights and the Extractive Industry Transparency Initiative), they will ipso facto contribute to peace – even though such initiatives fall outside the scope of what most academics and practitioners consider 'peacebuilding.' It may also have punitive components, as ongoing UN Human Rights Council sessions are working to draft a "legally binding instrument to regulate, in international human rights law, the activities of transnational corporations and other business enterprises" (UNHRC 2016: 1). Thus, a failure to sign on may constitute a future reputational and even legal risk for engaged firms. While the UNGPs can be considered a cutting-edge business-peace framework, the progressive push for deeper business-peace activities is ultimately defined by political will.

While peacebuilding scholars have been debating the lessons of the last conceptual wave, the corporate sector itself has been exploring new ideas, including Political CSR, conscious capitalism, Creating Shared Value initiatives and corporate citizenship (Carroll 2015). The debate has even entered the virtual realm, exploring how businesses can promote "cyber peace" (Shackelford 2016) or use social media for societal benefit (Martin-Shields 2016). Technology and innovation might also improve the incorporation of peace into existing sustainable development initiatives (Miklian and Hoelscher 2018). Examples include green energy and biogas along the Israel/Palestine border (Teller 2016); mobile peacebuilding apps in Rwanda (Spillane 2015) and Afghanistan (Lindberg and Torjesen 2013); the Souktel digital alert systems to improve school safety in Gaza (CDAC Network 2012); information and communication technology infrastructures in developing countries (Martin-Shields 2016); and violence monitoring and mapping apps in Kenya (Ríos and Espiau 2011). Similarly, start-up cultures may also improve prospects for peace and security (Koltai 2016), particularly in base-of-the-pyramid (Prahalad and Hart 2002) or entrepreneurship (Mair and Marti 2006) frameworks.

Third, the practitioner perspective studies how business has contributed to peacebuilding in a practical way. This subfield is growing rapidly, focusing on empirical cases of private sector actors in conflict zones (e.g. Katsos and Forrer 2014; Berdal and Wennmann 2013; Guaqueta 2008; Nelson 2000). It is rarely rooted in or in reference to business and peace theory, as perhaps expected given the practitioner approach and focus upon better guidance and best practices. Rather, it often is derived from other disciplines such as political science or development studies with a tangential link to business and peace.

Most practitioner studies attempt to contribute to an overarching question of: What is effective business-peace action, and how can it complement our understandings of effective peacebuilding? Of course, effectiveness is itself contextual and multi-faceted, influencing future risk/reward calculations of these actions for businesses. As one example, business can engage in track-two diplomacy. Track-two diplomacy is usually defined as informal, nonbinding negotiations that are explicitly intended to reduce conflict through face-to-face meetings (Diamond and

McDonald 1996; Westermann-Behaylo et al. 2015), but it also refers to any time corporations act as brokers between sides in a conflict with explicit engagement in the political process (Galtung 1996; Ramsbotham et al. 2011; Montville 1991; Oetzel et al. 2009). Business can engage in conflict resolution through NGO partnerships that help to alleviate the causes of conflict (Kolk and Lenfant 2015; Oetzel and Doh 2009; Westley and Vredenburg 1991), participation in global multilateral agreements (Oetzel et al. 2007), and direct informal negotiations between the two sides engaged in active conflict (Lieberfeld 2002). Westermann-Behaylo et al. (2015) have further suggested that multinationals could have greater influence on peace through the pursuit of corporate diplomacy.

There is growing evidence that the presence of business actors in mediation and negotiation positively correlates with peace progress (Iff and Alluri 2016a). What is less clear is if the business community provides a unique 'value added' in such negotiations, or if their presence is merely a side effect of the establishment of more inclusive peace processes, which may be the true determining factor for peace durability (Paffenholz 2015). For example, the business community has been involved to some degree over the past 20 years in Colombia's peace negotiations with the FARC insurgency, for reasons of both self-interest and national altruism, with their degree of involvement often based upon a calculation of reputational risk and opportunity as likelihood for a deal ebbed and flowed (Rettberg et al. 2019). Here, business was involved in an ultimately successful peace process, but we still do not know the strength of relationships between business participation and peace negotiation success.

A rapidly growing set of qualitative studies have also attempted to explain how businesses can promote local peace. Of particular mention is Local Business, Local Peace (International Alert 2006), which showcased examples from the world over. Other ethnographic-based research shows how entrepreneurial tourism in Rwanda (Alluri 2009), community development in Fiji, Papua New Guinea, and South Africa (McEwan et al. 2017), sports (Collison et al. 2016), and community projects in Colombia (Miklian and Bickel 2017) have developed distinctive programs, practices, and partnerships that enhance peace. These and other studies tend to show a positive relationship between community engagement by business and the impact (or the perception of impact) of that engagement on peace, but with varied metrics for 'impact' and varied actors assessed for such, and no meta-studies yet done, no firm conclusions can yet be drawn.

Several emerging issues also temper the broadest claims of the literature. First, development and peacebuilding projects are highly dependent upon local governments for success. Second, local development initiatives may have little measurable or immediate peace impact. Impact itself is also conditional on local political dynamics (Lujala et al. 2016). What then are 'legitimate' business-development contributions to peace? Researchers and scholars have spent the past decade trying to answer this question. Practitioners and consultants have often ignored the question of legitimacy entirely. In addition, development scholars disagree about which development actions generate sustainable peace. Despite attempts to provide clarity (e.g. Mueller-Hirth 2017), many firms continue to avoid engagement on peace issues for this reason.

Businesses can also unintentionally generate conflict through missteps created through poor understanding of the consequences of their policies and practices (Westermann-Beyhalo et al. 2015). More problematically, conflicts and insecurity events that spur firms to societal improvement in their operational areas often generate only development initiatives like building schools or hospitals, which do not inherently generate peace or mitigate root causes of conflict (CDA 2014). Attempts to address root causes of conflict can also meet substantial resistance from national stakeholders, who often hold divergent views on what 'peace' and 'development' mean (McNulty 2014). There are also considerable variations in peacebuilding practice across different business sectors, in different conflict settings, and within different divisions or country offices of firms themselves. Thus, guidance documents such as "Conflict-Sensitive Business Practice" (International Alert 2006) and the "Guidance on Responsible Business in Conflict-Affected and High-Risk Areas" (UN 2010) are two examples of resources available to firms to assess and manage risk when negotiating complex peace issues in conflict regions of operation.

Conflict-sensitive business practices (CSBP) have thus emerged as a key business-peace research arena (Ford 2015; Handschin et al. 2016), providing some of the richest engagement between researchers and businesses. Legal obligations, especially 'do no harm' principles, figure robustly into this knowledge stream. This is largely due to corporate budgets committed to due diligence. CSBPs also constrain conflict drivers, while not necessarily promoting peace. CSBPs allow firms to recognize opportunities and adapt activities toward peace promotion without necessarily promising peace as a result. While CSBPs may constrain conflict drivers, their focus on security and stability might perpetuate the status quo. Melin (2016) argues that the private sector must be more engaged in conflict resolution because of its political role in society. Alternatively, Widger (2017) argues that firms most interested in corporate 'good governance' are unlikely to challenge governments on core national identity issues. Larger firms are aware of the value of incorporating sustainable development into their strategy (e.g. Oyevaar et al. 2016). Peacebuilding and conflict resolution are often seen as too political or too complicated to warrant deeper engagement. Research can make a larger impact by showing the 'business case' for peace promotion. This may help firms justify incorporating peace into their sustainable development initiatives.

Engaging in each of these research streams is fundamental to the furtherance of business and peace as an interdisciplinary field. What has been missing thus far, and what this book addresses, is a perspective that unites these streams yet is rooted firmly in the established business and peace literature. We feel that the most promising thematic forward avenue would be to explore an agenda that businesses, peace practitioners, and academics are all assigning high priority: the United Nations SDGs.

Business, peace and the SDGs

The UN SDGs are perhaps the most ambitious multilateral undertaking ever attempted – an effort to reconstruct the bottom of global society by eliminating the world's worst inequalities and injustices. The UN considers the private sector to be an essential partner in this agenda. In 2015, UN Secretary General Ban Ki-Moon said, "we are counting on the private sector to drive success in the SDGs, (and) we call upon all businesses to apply their creativity and innovation to solving sustainable development challenges" (Ban 2015). Today, over USD 2 trillion in projects and investments is benchmarked to sustainable social investments (including the Government Pension Fund Global in Norway), and another USD 20 trillion is directed to do the same through guiding language within large pension funds. These figures are growing rapidly, driven by a new generation of investor that demands more socially responsible companies to invest in. They incorporate over 20,000 companies that are formal signatories to peace and sustainable development initiatives around the world. In short, corporate engagement in the SDGs represents a mind-bogglingly large and powerful undertaking, but we still know little about what actually works regarding how the private sector can help build peace and sustainable development in fragile and conflict contexts.

In fact, the question of if businesses should be peace actors is increasingly considered regressive, as typified by arguments for business to be an agent of world benefit (Haski-Leventhal 2015). Related research has suggested that changing corporate structures can help integrate peace in corporate sustainable development initiatives (e.g. Banks 2016; Franca et al. 2017). A key argument is that private sector intervention is preferable to government inaction, especially as regards SDG Goal 16: Peace, Justice and Strong Institutions (Sharma 2015). Goal 16 aims to "Promote peaceful and inclusive societies for sustainable development, provide access to justice for all and build effective, accountable and inclusive institutions at all levels," but even those most inclined to support the SDGs warn that it is "hard to quantify" peace and justice goals, and regarding the how, "the challenges seem overwhelming" for businesses to help the most fragile and in need states (DNV-GL 2016: 74).

New findings also question whether business initiatives for peace and development are an unqualified good. For example, economic opening after conflict or repression can be as likely to generate conflict as peace (Oetzel and Miklian 2017), business engagement in human rights is often undermined by its non-punitive 'checklist' or 'guideline' reporting nature (O'Connor and Labowitz 2017), philanthropic efforts like building schools or hospitals can lead to conflict as businesses usurp local government roles and bodies like the UN that try to engage business often offer little more than 'bluewashing' as initiatives like Business for Peace are based only in corporate self-reporting that is not independently verified (e.g. Miklian and Bickel 2017). Most businesses (and their managements) are skittish about direct peace action, viewing it as the provenance of government (Ganson and Wennmann 2016).

As an example of this volume's thematic value, Business and Human Rights (BHR) frameworks are an emerging set of initiatives for engendering business compliance with human rights standards to reduce conflict drivers and/or enhance peacebuilding efforts. Decisions and actions by businesses that have an adverse human rights impact may, especially where violations are systematic, also affect peace dynamics (IHRB 2011; Ford 2015). This is so both in terms of failure to prevent business-sourced violations (including through supply chains), and the lack of avenues for resolving associated grievances. Following, normative frameworks on human rights impact are well established relative to efforts to measure impacts on 'peace' and 'inclusivity' (and associated institution-building). A poor human rights culture is presumed to inhibit peacebuilding and development as framed by the SDGs, so mapping business performance against human rights standards might help address our problems in isolating whether and when business actors or actions help or hinder peacebuilding (Bailey et al. 2015).

The question, then, is whether existing BHR initiatives are adapted both to the wider challenge of helping achieve relevant business and peace targets, and to the research challenge of knowing whether and how business (or business-oriented) actions and initiatives may be contributing to those achievements. This volume thus presents new scholarship on which BHR initiatives are the most viable, well-subscribed, effective and legitimate in generating human rights outcomes that are SDG-positive. Prevailing studies also tend to rely on assumptions about whether formal compliance or engagement with BHR initiatives in fact contributes to more peaceful, inclusive investment or business activity. Meanwhile, an under-studied area in design and evaluation of BHR initiatives is whether these initiatives might strengthen generic state and other institutional capacity or responsiveness.

With firms increasingly realizing that they cannot remove themselves from the political contexts in which they operate, actors like the World Bank and UN are pushing the private sector to engage in local peace and development as a duty. Following, the private sector itself has made a massive commitment to the SDGs in mission statements and through the investment community. The SDGs are thus the most important framework for firms today to present and operationalize their social works. They provide a multitude of avenues for positive change, and directly target the private sector's role in peace and development. Goal 16, speaking to peace, justice and strong institutions, is of particular interest due to its cross-cutting nature: other Goals are presumed to be peace-positive, and unfulfilled Goals are assumed to generate injustice, conflict, and repression as socio-economic conditions in conflict and crisis regions correlate strongly with SDG priority targets. Moreover, in these areas, businesses can have the most direct impact on local livelihoods, far above that of government. In conjunction with Goal 8 (Work and Economic Growth) and Goal 9 (Industry, Innovation and Infrastructure), Goal 16 envisions a specific role for the private sector as a potential foundational engine for peace and development – but only if it acts in a 'responsible' and 'sustainable' way.

A common critique of Goal 16 is that it incorporates lofty targets that are idealistic yet complicated to implement. There are few metrics for success (or corporate promotion of such), little guidance on implementation of targets, and a lack of engagement with the business community on the integral yet undefined role that they are presumed to play in ensuring the success of Goal 16 in practice on key issues including corruption, bribery, human rights and global governance. More concerning is the fact that many of Goal 16's 12 Targets rest upon 'common sense' but lightly tested (or even untested) assumptions of the relationships between economic development and peace, and promote activity that has generated conflict under certain conditions. In this sense, the SDGs are a meaningful advancement in business-peace study and practice, providing the first workable framework for business engagement in peace and sustainable development.

However, any work that wishes to explore the deeper mechanisms that underpin such interactions must go beyond the sum of these parts. An astute reader may already see a fundamental missing piece to the above: applications of sound theory to provide more effective policy guidance to businesses, practitioners and policymakers regarding how the private sector can make a meaningful and durable contribution to peace and sustainable development. Such guidance is already being sought out by companies and social impact investors – but aside from a loose set of 'best practice' documents, nothing exists to help contextualize individual corporate actions for peace, or to help scholars across disciplines to place business and peace scholarship in a meaningful way that encourages forward engagement.

Structure of the book and contributors

This book aims to fill precisely these gaps, and is thus structured in three complementary sections: *Theoretical advances in business and peace; Business, peace and development in practice*; and *Emerging policy for peace and sustainable development by business*. Each section brings together works by senior scholars on business, peace and development dynamics, and each chapter specifically aims to provide cross-disciplinary value.

Part I: Theoretical underpinnings

This section explores several existing theoretical gaps in the relationships between peace and violence, political stability/fragility, ethical business activity and economic opportunity. While the emerging literature on business and peace is growing, we see several key areas where new contributions are needed: in more critical perspectives of this new literature stream; in taking the literature beyond existing component- and categorization-driven approaches, and better incorporating ethics and human rights into the core of the business-peace approach, across fields. The four works in this section attempt to contribute to such gaps, offering research-supported cutting-edge theoretical studies in business roles for the purpose of sustainable peace.

First, Head of the Africa Centre for Dispute Settlement at the University of Stellenbosch Business School *Brian Ganson* dives deep into the nature of business-peace scholarship in "Business and peace: a need for new questions and systems perspectives," showing how there is likely no one set of business activities that can be characterized as unambiguously peace-positive. Instead, the manner of peace action by business and the context in which their actions unfold that may be more determinative of their impact. Ganson unites business-peace literature with that of the peacebuilding community to highlight this schism, showing how decades of work by peacebuilders and development practitioners in conflict zones to achieve at this understanding should be utilized by business-peace actors. Beyond a 'state of play' analysis, this chapter explores gaps between these communities to invite and guide further research and strategic thinking across fields that use systems approaches of analysis.

Florian Wettstein is Director of the Institute for Business Ethics at the University of St. Gallenand *Judith Schrempf-Stirling* is Associate Professor of Responsible Management at the University of Geneva. Their chapter "Business, peace, and human rights: a political responsibility perspective" brings the deep body of work on BHR to the business management literature, where there has been thus far little engagement. The chapter provides a foundation from which to derive human rights obligations for corporations and reflect on some of the persistent conundrums that have characterized the discussion on BHR in the past, such as the dichotomy between hard vs. soft law approaches to corporate accountability, domestic (foreign direct liability) vs. global approaches (treaty for BHR), or the role of leadership and corporate culture for the implementation of corporate human rights responsibility. Adopting a business ethics lens instead of the dominant legalistic perspective can open new ways of looking at some of these issues and thus guide us to different conclusions as they are currently discussed in the BHR literature. The chapter concludes with investigation of how a business ethics perspective on BHR can open up new avenues for our thinking on business and peace.

Last, *Gearoid Millar* is a Lecturer in Sociology at the Institute for Conflict, Transition, and Peace Research at the University of Aberdeen. His chapter "The messy business of peace amid the tyranny of the profit motive: complexity and culture in post-conflict contexts" argues that the complexity of local social, political, economic and cultural settings can derail even the most promising business-peace projects planned with the best of intentions. Millar presents a critical perspective on the forces driving business engagement in peacebuilding today, as market-driven interventionary mechanisms are theorized to provide a variety of peace-promoting benefits considered necessary to support still fragile post-conflict states. However, they can also have negative consequences including resource depletion, environmental degradation, labor abuse, increased inequality, minority marginalization, and conflict. While such problems can be framed as a result of predatory corporate practices, this chapter highlights more subtle reasons for such dynamics. Arguing that voluntary guidelines for conflict-sensitive investments and even well-meaning commitments to CSR processes can fail to avoid generating new conflict promoting dynamics, this chapter argues for a thorough commitment to understanding local complexity and the implications of intervention, which, in turn, requires very different skill sets and very different timelines for operations.

Part II: Perspectives on the corporate side

A key need for business-peace scholarship is in the development of new interdisciplinary and cross-disciplinary empirical work that can better contextualize how specific business actions for peace manifest within local populations. This section offers three chapters that do just that. The following explorations of business-peace activities in conflict-affected areas present their findings in ways intended to speak to business managers, practitioners and scholars alike. Here we include relevant case studies both in terms of 'best practice' and in terms of disasters to avoid. These chapters offer new ways to conceptualize commonly used concepts, including that of a 'peace dividend,' what constitutes a 'peace contribution by business,' and what 'conflict-sensitive business practice' really means on the ground.

Kogod International Business Professor at American University *Jennifer Oetzel* and Senior Manager for Strategic Partnerships at the Alliance for Peacebuilding *Stone Conroy* explore the cutting edge of government-corporate policy partnerships in their chapter "Furthering business efforts to reduce social risk and promote peacebuilding: the potential of social impact bonds (SIBs)." For the private sector to consciously engage in peacebuilding efforts, this chapter argues that managers must be able to quantify their firms' efforts to promote peacebuilding - a challenging task since it is not always clear what actions promote the outcomes that further peace and not all efforts toward peace building can be quantified, especially in the short-term. A relatively new financial tool for addressing this challenge is the social impact bond. SIBs, originally developed in the United Kingdom in 2010, are financial contracts between private sector funders, a public entity (whether local, regional or national), and often a non-profit organization, to improve social outcomes. Gains for investors accrue when a given social venture is successful. Public sector savings are passed onto private sector funders as returns on investment. The purpose of this chapter is to analyze how SIBs are used in peacebuilding, identify challenges for adoption, and to explore several specific ways where these bonds have been applied to peace and sustainable development.

Jolyon Ford, Associate Professor at Australia National University (ANU) School of Law, maps the mandatory and voluntary mechanisms and schemes that exist, in the context of the emphasis put on corporate due diligence in the 2011 *UN Guiding Principles on Business and Human Rights.* 'Business and peace' scholarship can sometimes attribute too much assumed significance to corporate action or agency in shaping peace or conflict dynamics, generally and in specific situations. Nevertheless, in some contexts and sectors, corporate decision-making and management practices on environmental, social and governance (ESG) issues can significantly impact prospects for sustainable and inclusive peace. This chapter explores one ESG vector (human rights), the emergence of corporate due diligence and other procedural mechanisms for managing human rights risk and impact, and the importance – for peace processes – of these frameworks for direct corporate operations and indirect supply-chain impacts relating to fragile states or situations.

Associate professor of International Relations at Universidad de los Andes (Bogota, Colombia) *Angelika Rettberg* and *Jason Miklian*'s chapter "From war-torn to peace-torn? Mapping business strategies in transition from conflict to peace in Columbia" takes as a starting point that the literature on the relationship between the private sector, armed conflict, and peacebuilding has extensively analyzed how companies adapt to unstable contexts, what risks they face and how they are tackled, and the degree to which expected peace dividends serve as motivation for companies to engage in peacebuilding. However, while the importance of the private sector for war-to-peace transitions is clear, little has been said about the specific strategies adopted by companies in transition periods. How do companies prepare for peace? What choices do they face? How essential is the role of the CEO or owner? What unique strategies do firms take to adapt to political change? This chapter builds theory on business strategies in times of transition from conflict to peace, as well as their role within broader government peacebuilding aims. This chapter identifies four types of business strategies for peace (operational, political, philanthropic, public relations). The authors explore these strategies through choices of firms operating in Colombia to suggest five new research strands that have the potential to integrate strategy and risk calculations into a testable study of business-peace relationships.

Part III: Empirical reflections

Beyond developing theory and our empirical knowledge base, molding such findings into a better understanding of what governments and businesses do (and intend to achieve) through business and peace is a naturally emerging cross-field activity. Here, we present four chapters that examine management and policy frameworks in the context of peace by businesses in post-conflict zones. Beyond grandiose promises of 'disrupting poverty' by 'bringing mutual development' in a 'win–win' manner or the like, these chapters explore the more direct and specific operational markers that require firms to spell out the benefits of their business-peace activities. Considering peacebuilding context as determinative of effectiveness, these chapters unite in their understanding of policy on business-peace having limitations until the nature of 'effectiveness' is better problematized – both for peace, and more broadly, for sustainable development itself.

Associate Professor of Management at the American University of Sharjah *John E. Katsos* argues in "'The only hope left': Differences between multinational and local company peacebuilding activities in Syria and Iraq," that active war zones alter the ability of business to enhance peace, but do not destroy the connection entirely. The governments of Syria and Iraq have faced off against the so-called "Islamic State of Iraq and Syria" ("ISIS") since its declaration in 2014. During that time, ISIS has taken over large swaths of territory in both countries. Based on over 100 interviews conducted over 2 years, this contribution examines the policies, trade-offs, threats, and opportunities for business to enhance peace that came with ISIS assaults on both countries. Interviews with business owners, managers, government officials, and international policymakers shed light on the similarities and differences of dealing with ISIS as a force de jure controlling the territory.

Andrea Iff, Policy Advisor at the Swiss Agency for Development Cooperation and *Rina M. Alluri*, Senior Researcher at the University of Zurich argue that local business actors have the potential to play a positive role in peacebuilding in different contexts. In the cases of Sri Lanka and El Salvador, it was during the mediated peace processes where local business actors played a relevant role in actively lobbying for a peaceful resolution to conflict. This contribution to the economic 'peace dividend' provides insights into how business actors can play a role in mediation processes. However, the long-term impact of those engagements are rarely assessed. This chapter analyzes the role that local business actors have played in peace processes in Sri Lanka and El Salvador, while providing critical reflections into the role of business once a peace process has been successful but also once a peace process has failed. It provides both theoretical and empirical insights into how local businesses face both opportunities and challenges to contributing to peacebuilding.

From CDA Collaborative Learning Projects, Senior Program Manager *Sarah Cechvala* and Associate Director of Advisory Services *Ben Miller* bring an expert practitioner perspective with "Practicing business and peace? Considerations overheard in the field." In this chapter, they consider how contemporary discussions of the private sector's contributions to peace are prone to presenting effective pro-peace actions as a menu of options to choose from according to preference or, in some cases, according to the types of conflict that exist in the society outside of the company. These discussions leave unexplored the conditions under which those options can be used as templates for meaningful and plausible action by company staff in the field. Conditions of fragility and conflict in operational environments, however, impose upon companies a broad range of external constraints, pressures, and requirements that make certain approaches to business activity difficult, risky, or even impossible. More particularly, they create a range of practical problems and dilemmas that threaten to suck companies into local conflicts. This chapter's evidentiary base consists of dialogues with company staff to resolve conflict issues and develop practical approaches to conflict-sensitive business operations. This chapter presents learning from these sources as a vehicle for exploring the practical challenges that constrain companies' actions and ability to act constructively in the interests of peace. These real-world examples serve as a foundation for the chapter's broader contention that much of the published work on business and peace has only limited utility for corporate practitioners, and that the literature's claims to describe the realities of corporate operations are inflated.

Greg Reichberg and Henrik Syse, both Research Professors and political philosophers at the Peace Research Institute Oslo, explore the under-studied investment community in their chapter "Norges Bank Investment Management: A New Actor for Peace?" Norges Bank Investment Management (NBIM) manages the world's most valuable sovereign wealth fund, with USD 900 billion in assets. The Fund has investments worldwide in nearly 9,000 companies, and NBIM has increasingly emphasized a commitment to fostering sustainable business practices on the part of the companies in its portfolio. The avoidance of negative social impacts (in particular human rights violations) forms a core aspect of NBIM's stated mandate as a universal investor (namely an investor in a wide range of industries and regions). NBIM will likely establish a closer linkage between beneficial social impacts and peace, notably by discouraging firms in its portfolio from causing harmful social impacts. Issuing guidelines for such conflict-sensitive business practice, and perhaps even divesting from firms that fail to observe acceptable practice in this domain, could eventually become part of NBIM's mandate. This chapter explores the openings for such an approach within NBIM's institutional framework.

This book is explicitly designed to be both a reader that provides a window into the many facets of business-peace-development interactions, and a source of inspiration for students and scholars who will see many under-explored yet highly impactful topics to study. Thus, we see this work as holding value for the following four audiences:

- Instructors, dissertation advisors and students: they can identify ways in which courses on topics such as peacebuilding, BHR, business management ethics and CSR can integrate the area of business and peace into their curriculum. Courses on CSR, social investment, business ethics, international law and regulation, corporate governance, and other social impact-relevant elements will all find this work of deep value. In addition, students of development studies, international relations, political science and similar will find the work to be an ideal window into the varied roles of the private sector in peace and development, bridging a fundamental gap between these fields and business/management.
- Business leaders and private sector partners (e.g. companies, business associations): they can acquire concrete examples from sector leaders on how to integrate peacebuilding into their activities while learning from challenges that businesses have faced when operating in conflict-affected contexts.
- Researchers (e.g. think tanks, independent scholars): they can identify theoretical and empirical areas which have established relevant findings as well as gaps that need to be filled in the future. This holds both for comparative work as well as empirical case study assessments.
- Practitioners (INGOs, IGOs, NGOs, governments): they can access concrete, empirical examples that demonstrate ways that leading practitioners have engaged with businesses in order to help them support peacebuilding.

We trust that they will find in this work useful challenges to received wisdom, a window on the complexity of the business and peace landscape, and inspiration for further research and practice.

References

Aguilera, R. V. and Rupp, D. E. (2005) "Putting the S Back in Corporate Social Responsibility : a Multi-Level Theory of Social Change in Organizations," *Academy of Management Review*, 32(3), pp. 836–863.

Alluri, R. (2009) "The Role of Tourism in Post-conflict Peacebuilding in Rwanda." *Swisspeace Report Working Paper #2/2009*.

Anderson, J., Markides, C. and Kupp, M. (2010) "The Last Frontier: market creation in conflict zones, deep rural areas, and urban slums," *California Management Review. University of California Press Journals*, 52(4), pp. 6–28. doi:10.1525/cmr.2010.52.4.6.

Bailey, R. and Ford, J. (2015) *Investing in Stability: Can Extractive Sector Development Help Build Peace?*London: Chatham House.

Ballentine, K. and Nitzschke, H. (2005) "The Political Economy of Civil War and Conflict Transformation," *Berghof Research Center for Constructive Conflict Management.*

BanKi-Moon (2015) *Address to the UN Business Forum.* New York: United Nations. September 25.

Banks, H. (2016) "The Business of Peace: Coca-Cola's Contribution to Stability, Growth, and Optimism," *Business Horizons.* doi:10.1016/j.bushor.2016.03.018.

Barkemeyer, R. and Miklian, J. (2019) "Responsible Business in Fragile Contexts: Comparing Perceptions from Domestic and Foreign Firms in Myanmar," *Sustainability* 11(3): 598.

Berdal, M. and Wennmann, A. (eds) (2013) *Ending Wars, Consolidating Peace: Economic Perspectives.* London: Routledge.

Bhoutros-Ghali, B. (1992) *An Agenda for Peace.* New York: United Nations. A/47/277.

Bies, R. J., Bartunek, J. M., Fort, T. L. and Zald, M. N. (2007) "Corporations as Social Change Agents: Individual, Interpersonal Institutional, and Environmental Dynamics," *Academy of Management Review*, pp. 788–793. doi:10.5465/AMR.2007.25275515.

Borensztein, E., De Gregorio, J. and Lee, J. (1998) "How Does Foreign Direct Investment Affect Economic Growth," *Journal of International Economics*, 45(1), pp. 115–135. doi:10.1016/S0022-1996(97)00033-0.

Buckley, P. J. and Ghauri, P. N. (2004) "Globalisation, Economic Geography and the Strategy of Multinational Enterprises," *Journal of International Business Studies*, 35(35), pp. 81–98. doi:10.1057/palgrave.jibs.8400076.

Business for Peace Foundation. (n.d.) *Being Businessworthy.* Retrieved March 15, 2019, from http://businessforpeace.no/about-us/being-businessworthy/

Carroll, A. B. (2015). "Corporate Social Responsibility: The Centerpiece of Competing and Complementary Frameworks," *Organizational Dynamics*, 44(2), 87–96.

CDA Collaborative Learning (2014) *Business for Peace: Understanding and Assessing Corporate Contributions to Peace.* Paper presented at the UN Global Compact's Business for Peace conference.

CDAC Network (2012) "UNESCO Uses Souktel Online Messaging System: Case Study: Sending SMS Emergency Alerts to Families in Gaza," Retrieved March 16, 2019, from http://www.cdacnetwork.org/tools-and-resources/i/20140725102754-chkn3.

Chisadza, C. and Bittencourt, M. (2016) "Globalisation and Conflict: Evidence from sub-Saharan Africa," *Economic Research Southern Africa Working Paper 634.*

Collier, P. (2007) "Post-Conflict Recovery : How Should Policies be Distinctive?" *Centre for the Study of African Economies.*

Collier, P., Hoeffler, A. and Soderbom, M. (2008) "Post-Conflict Risks," *Journal of Peace Research*, 45(4), pp. 461–478. doi:10.1177/0022343308091356.

Darendeli, I. S. and Hill, T. L. (2015) "Uncovering the Complex Relationships Between Political Risk and MNE Firm Legitimacy: Insights from Libya," *Journal of International Business Studies*, 47(1), pp. 68–92. doi:10.1057/jibs.2015.27

Davies, G., Chun, Rosa, da Silva, Rui Vinhas and Roper, Stuart. (2003) "Corporate Reputation and Competitiveness," *Corporate Reputation Review.* doi:10.1057/palgrave.crr.1540185.

Diamond, L. and McDonald, J. W. (1996) *Multi-track Diplomacy: A Systems Approach to Peace.* Sterling, VA: Kumarian Press.

Dittgen, R. (2015) "Of Other Spaces? Hybrid Forms of Chinese Engagement in Sub-Saharan Africa," *Journal of Current Chinese Affairs*, 44(1): 43–73.

DNV-GL (2016). "Future of Spaceship Earth: Will the Sustainable Development Goals be Reached?" Oslo: DNV-GL.

Dworkin, T. and Schipani, C. (2007) "Linking Gender Equity to Peaceful Societies," *American Business Law Journal*, 44(2), pp. 391–415.

Emmelhainz, M. and Adams, R. J. (1999) "The Apparel Industry Response to 'Sweatshop' Concerns: A Review and Analysis of Codes of Conduct," *Journal of Supply Chain Management*, 35, pp. 51–57. doi:10.1111/j.1745-493X.1999.tb00062.x.

Fearon, J. D. (2004) "Why Do Some Civil Wars Last So Much Longer than Others?" *Journal of Peace Research*, 41(3), pp. 275–301. doi:10.1177/0022343304043770.

Forrer, J. J. and Katsos, J. E. (2015) "Business and Peace in the Buffer Condition," *Academy of Management Perspectives*, 29(4), pp. 438–450. doi:10.5465/amp.2013.0130.

Forrer, J. J. and Fort, T. L. (2016) "The PACO Index," *Business Horizons*. doi:10.1016/j.bushor.2016.03.017.

Franca, C. L., Broman, Goran, Robert, Karl-Henrik, Basile, George and Trygg, Louise (2017) "An Approach to Business Model Innovation and Design for Strategic Sustainable Development," *Journal of Cleaner Production*, 140(1), pp. 155–166.

Freeman, R. E. (1984). "Strategic Management: A Stakeholder Theory," *Journal of Management Studies*, 39(1), 1–21.

Freeman, R. and McVea, J. (2001) "A Stakeholder Approach to Strategic Management," *SSRN Electronic Journal*, (January). doi:10.2139/ssrn.263511.

Friedman, M. (1970). "The Social Responsibility of Business is to Increase its Profits," *New York Times Magazine*, September 13.

Friedman, M. (2009) *Capitalism and Freedom*. Chicago, IL: University of Chicago Press.

Ford, J. (2015) "Perspectives on the Evolving 'Business and Peace' Debate," *Academy of Management Perspectives*, 29(4), pp. 451–460. doi:10.5465/amp.2015.0142.

Forrer, J. and Seyle, C. (eds) (2016) *The Role of Business in the Responsibility to Protect*. Cambridge: Cambridge University Press.

Fort, T. L. and Schipani, C. A. (2004) "The Role of Business in Fostering Peaceful Societies," *The Role of Business in Fostering Peaceful Societies*. Cambridge: Cambridge University Press, pp. 11–40. doi:10.1017/CBO9780511488634.

Fort, T. L. (2007) "The Times and Seasons of Corporate Responsibility," *American Business Law Journal*, 44(2), pp. 287–329. doi:10.1111/j.1744-1714.2007.00038.x.

Fort, T. L. (2015) *The Diplomat in the Corner Office: Corporate Foreign Policy*. Stanford, CA: Stanford University Press.

Galtung, J. (1996) *Peace by Peaceful Means: Peace and Conflict, Development and Civilization*. London: PRIO and SAGE Publications.

Galtung, J. (2006) "Twenty-Five Years of Peace Research: Ten Challenges and Some Responses," *Theories of International Relations vol. 2*, 22(2), pp. 38–61.

Ganson, B. and A. Wennmann (2016) *Business in Fragile States: Confronting Risk, Preventing Conflict*. London: IISS Publications.

Getz, K. A. and Oetzel, J. (2009) "MNE Strategic Intervention in Violent Conflict: Variations Based on Conflict Characteristics," *Journal of Business Ethics*, 89(Suppl. 4), pp. 375–386. doi:10.1007/s10551-010-0412-6.

Golan-Nadir, N. and Cohen, N. (2016). "The Role of Individual Agents in Promoting Peace Processes: Business People and Policy Entrepreneurship in the Israeli-Palestinian Conflict," *Policy Studies*, 2016, pp. 1–18.

Guaqueta, A. (2008) "Occidental Petroleum, Cerrejon, and NGO Partnerships in Colombia: Lessons Learned," *Responsible Corporate Citizenship and the Ideals of the United Nations Global Compact*, pp. 381–402. Notre Dame, IN: University of Notre Dame Press.

Gunningham, N., Kagan, R. and Thornton, D. (2003) *Shades of Green: Business, Regulation, and Environment*. Stanford, CA: Stanford University Press.

Handschin, S., Abitbol, E. and Alluri, R. (eds) (2016) "Conflict Sensitivity: Taking it to the Next Level," *swisspeace Working Paper 2*.

Haski-Leventhal, D. (2015) "Editorial: My David Cooperrider Moment: Business as an Agent of World Benefit and Peace," *Business, Peace and Sustainable Development*, 5(4), pp. 3–6.

Haufler, V. (1997) *Dangerous Commerce: Insurance and the Management of International Risk*. Cornell, NJ: Cornell University Press.

Hobbes, T. (2006). *Leviathan*. Chicago: A&C Black.

Hong, Bryan, Li, Frank and Minor, D. (2016) "Corporate Governance and Executive Compensation for Corporate Social Responsibility," *Journal of Business Ethics*, 136(1), pp. 199–213.

Huang, S. K. (2013) "The Impact of CEO Characteristics on Corporate Sustainable Development," *Corporate Social Responsibility and Environmental Management*, 20, pp. 234–244.

Iff, A. and Alluri, R. M. (2016a). "Business Actors in Peace Mediation Processes," Business and Society Review, 121(2),pp. 187–215.

Iff, A. and Alluri, R. M. (2016b). "Business Contributions to Peacebuilding: Exploring the Evidence," *Business, Peace and Sustainable Development*, 8, pp. 7–33.

Iff, A., Sguaitamatti, D., Alluri, R. M., Kohler, D. (2010) "Money Makers as Peace Makers: Business Actors in Mediation Processes," *swisspeace Working Paper 2*.

Institute for Economics and Peace (IEP) (2014). *Global Peace Index*. Geneva: IEP.

Institute for Human Rights and Business (2011) "From Red to Green Flags: The Corporate Responsibility to Respect Human Rights in High-risk Countries." London: IHRB.

International Alert (2006) *Local Business, Local Peace: The Peacebuilding Potential of the Domestic Private Sector*. Banfield, J., Gunduz, C. and Killick, N., (eds). London, UK: International Alert.

Joras, U. (2009) "Motivating and Impeding Factors for Corporate Engagement in Peacebuilding," *swisspeace Working Paper 1*.

Katsos, J. E. and Forrer, J. (2014). "Business practices and peace in post-conflict zones: lessons from Cyprus," *Business Ethics: A European Review*, 23(2), 154–168.

Kolk, A. and Tuldere, R. Van (2002) "Child Labor and Multinational Conduct: A Comparison of International Business and Stakeholder Codes," *Journal of Business Ethics*, pp. 291–301.

Koltai, S. (2016) *Peace Through Entrepreneurship: Investing in a Startup Culture for Security and Development*. Washington DC: Brookings.

Ledbetter, B. (2016) "Business Leadership for Peace," *International Journal of Public Leadership*, 12(3), pp. 239–251.

Lederach, J. P. (1997) *Sustainable Reconciliation in Divided Societies*. Washington DC: USIP Press.

Lieberfeld, D. (2002) "Evaluating the Contributions of Track-two Diplomacy to Conflict Termination in South Africa, 1984-90," *Journal of Peace Research*, 39(3), pp. 355–372.

Lindberg, Y. and Torjesen, S. (2013) "Mobile Phones Build Peace," *Stanford Social Innovation Review*, August 15.

Liu, Helena and Baker, C. (2016) "Ordinary Aristocrats: The Discursive Construction of Philanthropists as Ethical Leaders," *Journal of Business Ethics*, 133(2), pp. 261–277.

Lujala, Paivi, Rustad, Siri and Kettenmann, S. (2016) "Engines for Peace? Extractive Industries, Host Countries and the International Community in Post-conflict Peacebuilding," *Natural Resources*, 7(3), pp. 1–21.

Mair, J. and Marti, I. (2006) "Social Entrepreneurship Research: A Source of Explanation, Prediction, and Delight," *Journal of World Business*, 41(1), pp. 36–44.

McEwan, C., Mawdsley, E., Banks, G. and Scheyvens, R. (2017) "Enrolling the Private Sector in Community Development: Magic Bullet or Sleight of Hand?" *Development and Change*, 48(1), pp. 28–53.

MacNulty, R. (2014) "Reflections on the Importance of Business for Peace in 21st-Century Peacebuilding," *Business, Peace and Sustainable Development*, 4, pp. 113–122.

Martin-Shields, C. (2016) "Communicating Stability," *Business, Peace and Sustainable Development*, pp. 50–65.

Melin, M. (2016) "Business, Peace and World Politics: The Role of Third Parties in Conflict Resolution," *Business Horizons*, 59(5), pp. 493–501.

Midtgard, Trude, Vadlamannati, K. C. and de Soysa, I. (2017) "Economic Liberalization Via IMF Structural Adustment: Sowing War or Reaping Peace?" *Review of International Organization*, 9(1), pp. 1–28.

Miklian, J. (2017) "Mapping Business-Peace Interactions: Five Assertions for How Business Create Peace," *Business, Peace and Sustainable Development*, 10(1), pp. 3–24.

Miklian, J. (2019) "Contextualising and theorising economic development, local business and ethnic cleansing in Myanmar," *Conflict Security and Development*, 18(1), pp. 55–79.

Miklian, J. and Bickel, J. P. M. (2018) "Theorizing Business and Local Peacebuilding Through the 'Footprints of Peace' Coffee Project in Rural Colombia," *Business and Society*. https://doi.org/10.1177%2F0007650317749441

Miklian, J. and Hoelscher, K. (2018) "A New Research Approach for Peace Innovation," *Innovation and Development*, 8(2), pp. 189–207.

Miller, W. (2016) "Toward a Scholarship of Peace Leadership," *International Journal of Public Leadership*, 12(3), pp. 216–226.

Milliken, F. J., Schipani, C. A., Bishara, N. D. and Prado, A. M. (2015) "Linking Workplace Practices to Community Engagement: the Case for Encouraging Employee Voice," *Academy of Management Perspectives*, 29(4), pp. 405–421. doi:10.5465/amp.2013.0121.

Mills, R. and Fan, Q. (2006) "The Investment Climate in Post-Conflict Situations," World Bank Institute.

Montville, J. (1991) "Transnationalism and the Role of Track-two Diplomacy," Thompson, Scott W. and Jenson, Kenneth M. (eds) *Approaches to Peace: An Intellectual Map*. Washington DC: United States Institute of Peace.

Mueller-Hirth, N. (2017) "Business and Social Peace Processes: How Can Insights from Post-conflict Studies Help CSR to Address Peace and Reconciliation?" Vertigans, S. and Idowu, S. (eds.) *Corporate Social Responsibility*. London: Springer.

Nelson, J. (2000) *The Business of Peace, the Private Sector as a Partner in Conflict Prevention and Resolution*. Prince of Wales Business Leaders Forum.

O'Connor, C. and Labowitz, S. (2017). *Measuring Human Rights Performance for Investors*. New York: NYU Stern.

OECD (2011) "Due Diligence Guidance for Responsible Supply Chains of Minerals from Conflict-Affected and High-Risk Areas." Paris: OECD.

Oetzel, J. and Breslauer, M. (2015) "Editorial: The Business and Economics of Peace: Moving the Agenda Forward," *Business, Peace and Sustainable*. Greenleaf Publishing in association with GSE Research.

Oetzel, J., Getz, K. A. and Ladek, Stephen. (2007) "The Role of Multinational Enterprises in Responding to Violent Conflict : A Conceptual Model and Framework for Research," *American Business Law Journal*, 44(2), pp. 331–358.

Oetzel, J. and Doh, J. P. (2009) "MNEs and Development: A Review and Reconceptualization," *Journal of World Business*, 44(2), 108–120.

Oetzel, J. and Getz, K. (2012) "Why and How Might Firms Respond Strategically to Violent Conflict?" *Journal of International Business Studies*, 43(2), pp. 166–186. doi:10.1057/jibs.2011.50.

Oetzel, J. and J. Miklian (2017) "Multinational Enterprises, Risk Management, and the Business and Economics of Peace," *Multinational Business Review* 25(4), pp. 270–286.

Oetzel, J., Getz, K. A. and Ladek, Stephen. (2007) "The Role of Multinational Enterprises in Responding to Violent Conflict : A Conceptual Model and Framework for Research," *American Business Law Journal*, 44(2), pp. 331–358.

Oetzel, J., Westermann-Behaylo, M., Koerber, C., Fort, T. L. and Rivera, J. (2009) "Business and Peace: Sketching the Terrain," *Journal of Business Ethics*. Netherlands: Springer, 89 (SUPPL. 4), pp. 351–373. doi:10.1007/s10551-010-0411-7.

O'Neill, D. A. (2008) "Impact Assessment, Transparency and Accountability – Three Keys to Building Sustainable Partnerships Between Business and its Stakeholders," Williams, Oliver F. (ed) *Peace Through Commerce: Responsible Corporate Citizenship and the Ideals of the United Nations Global Compact*. Notre Dame, IN: University of Notre Dame Press.

Oyevaar, Martin, Vazquez-Brust, Diego and van Bommel, H. (2016) *Globalization and Sustainable Development: A Business Perspective*. London: Red Globe.

Paffenholtz, Thania (2015) "Can Inclusive Peace Processes Work? New Evidence from a Multi-year Research Project." Inclusive Peace and Transition Initiative Policy Brief. Geneva: Graduate Institute of Geneva.

Prahalad, C. K. and Hart, S. (2002) "The Fortune at the Bottom of the Pyramid," *Strategy +Business*, 26(2), pp. 1–24.

Pyun, Ju Hyun and Lee, J. (2016) "Does Trade Integration Contribute to Peace?" *Review of Development Economics*, 20(1), pp. 327–344.

Ramsbotham, O., Woodhouse, T. and Miall, H. (2011) *Contemporary Conflict Resolution* (Third Edition). Cambridge: Polity.

Rettberg, A. (2016) "Need, Creed, and Greed: Understanding Why Business Leaders Focus on Issues of Peace," *Business Horizons*, 59(5), pp. 481–492.

Rettberg, A., Median, D. and Miklian, J. (2019) "Corporate Strategies to Assist Post-Conflict Peacebuilding in Colombia," *PRIO: PRIO Paper* 2019(1).

Ríos, P. and Espiau, G. (2011) "New Trends in Peace-Building: Another Form of Social Innovation," *International Catalan Institute for Peace, Working Paper No. 2011/2*.

Schouten, P. and Miklian, J. (2018). "The Business–peace Nexus: 'Business for Peace' and the Reconfiguration of the Public/Private Divide in Global Governance," *Journal of International Relations and Development*. doi:10.1057/s41268-018-0144-2.

Shackelford, S. J. (2016). "Human Rights and Cybersecurity Due Diligence: A Comparative Study," *University of Michigan Journal Law Reform*, 50, 859.

Sharma, A. (2015) "Who Leads in a G-Zero World? Multi-nationals, Sustainable Development and CSR in a Changing Global Order," *Washington International Law Journal*, 24, pp. 589–602.

Skubinn, R. and Herzog, L. (2016) "Internalized Moral Identity in Ethical Leadership," *Journal of Business Ethics*, 133(2), 249–260.

Sorens, J. and Ruger, W. (2015) "Globalisation and Intrastate Conflict: An Empirical Analysis," *Civil Wars*, 14(4), pp. 381–401.

Spillane, J. (2015) "ICT4P: Using Information and Communication Technology for Peacebuilding in Rwanda," *Journal of Peacebuilding and Development*, 10(3), pp. 97–103.

Teller, Yair (2016) "The Business of Peace through Green Energy: The HomeBiogas Story." Ensemble video, 01:25:42. Retrieved from: https://ensemble.dickinson.edu/Watch/CboQZ2Yln0aTelVNwofA_Q

UN Global Compact (UNGC) (2010) *Guidance on Responsible Business in Conflict-affected and High-risk Areas*. New York: UNGC.

United Nations Human Rights Council (UNHRC) (2016) "Open-ended Intergovernmental Working Group on Transnational Corporations and Other Business Enterprises with Respect to Human Rights." Meeting October.

Westermann-Behaylo, M. K., Rehbein, K. and Fort, T. L. (2015) "Enhancing the Concept of Corporate Diplomacy: Encompassing Political Corporate Social Responsibility, International Relations, And Peace Through Commerce," *Academy of Management Perspectives*, 29(4), pp. 387–404. doi:10.5465/amp.2013.0133.

Westley, F. and Vredenburg, H. (1991). "Strategic Bridging: The Collaboration Between Environmentalists and Business in the Marketing of Green Products," *The Journal of Applied Behavioral Science*, 27(1), pp. 65–90.

Widger, T. (2017) "Visions of Philanthronationalism: The (In)equities of Corporate Good Governance in Sri Lanka," *Contemporary South Asia*. Retrieved from https://doi.org/10.1080/09584935.2016.1203861.

Winer, J. M. and Roule, T. J. (2003) "Follow the Money: The Finance of Illicit Resource Extraction," Bannon, Iain and Collier, Paul (eds) *Natural Resources and Violent Conflict. Options and Actions*, pp. 161–214. Washington DC: The World Bank.

PART I

Theoretical underpinnings

1

BUSINESS AND PEACE

A need for new questions and systems perspectives

Brian Ganson

The roots of the mobilization of business for peace

Numerous international initiatives provide evidence of the persistent attention paid over the past decades to the potential for private sector roles in peacemaking and peacebuilding – that is, 'the range of activities that are undertaken by non-state groups explicitly to end violent conflict and establish the conditions for lasting peace' (Anderson and Olson, 2003, p. 8). Already in 2002, an International Labour Organization (ILO) report could note that, 'The private sector is increasingly being seen as an important partner on conflict prevention, and resolution' (Muia, 2003, p. 2). The Rev. Leon Sullivan and United Nations Secretary General Kofi Annan had, in 1999, announced the Global Sullivan Principles to 'advance the culture of peace,' (Tully, 2005, p. 174), building on the 1977 Sullivan principles for ethically conducting business and promoting positive change in apartheid South Africa; the UN Global Compact held its first multi-stakeholder dialogue on 'The Role of the Private Sector in Zones of Conflict' in 2001 (Shoji, 2012, p. 139). Since then, any number of analyses, guidance notes, and multi-stakeholder platforms supported by the World Bank Group, World Trade Organization, ILO, OECD, various UN agencies, and private initiatives such as the Business for Peace Foundation have posited that business can, in the words of the UN Global Compact's 2010 *Guidance on Responsible Business in Conflict-affected and High-risk Areas*, 'make a positive long-lasting contribution to peace and development' (UNGC and PRI, 2010, p. 2).

To some extent, business and peace is simply a special case of long-standing international discourse and policy concerning the role of the private sector within development broadly construed. In the contemporary period, the International Finance Corporation of the World Bank Group was founded in 1956 on the 'firm conviction that the most promising future for the less developed countries was the establishing of good private industry' (Tenney and Salda, 2014, p. 119). Over time, this perceived value in the mere presence of a robust private sector shifted towards advocacy for a more intentional role by business in development, shaped by a period of exploration of private sector solutions to problems which had seemed difficult or impossible for public sector actors to solve. By the time we arrive at the Busan Partnership for Effective Development Cooperation, for example, established by representatives of developing and developed countries at the fourth High-Level Forum on Aid Effectiveness in 2011, international policy articulated 'the central role of the private sector in advancing innovation, creating wealth, income and jobs, mobilising domestic resources and in turn contributing to poverty reduction' (Busan High Level Forum on Aid Effectiveness: Proceedings, 2011, p. 25). The Partnership therefore commits 'to enable the participation of the private sector in the design and implementation of development policies and strategies to foster sustainable growth and poverty reduction' (Ibid., p. 26).

More pronounced focus on the private sector and peace emerged in part from a period of reflection on the world's civil wars, and on the challenges (and sometimes abject failure) of international policy and practice towards post-conflict stabilization and peacebuilding. A relatively large number of studies explored the intersection of the private sector, development and peace (e.g. Collier and Sambanis, 2002; Guimond, 2007; Naudé, 2007; Shankelman, 2007). These often advance prescriptions for the better harnessing of the private sector for post-conflict development (e.g. Aaronson et al., 2008; Bagwitz et al., 2008; Banfield, 2007; Collier, 2006; Ersenkal and Wolf Fellow, 2007; Gündüz and Klein, 2008; Hudon and Seibel, 2007; IFC/FIAS-GTZ-BMZ, 2008; SEEP, 2007; Spilsbury and Byrne, 2007; Stabilization Unit, 2008a; USAID, 2009; USAID, 2007). A subsequent wave of scholarship underlined that fragile and conflict-affected states were not meeting any of the Millennium Development Goals, punctuated by the World Bank's review of the link between conflict and development in its *World Development Report 2011: Conflict, Security and Development* (World Bank, 2011). In the wake of these and other works,

> MNCs and state-owned firms alike have increasingly been drawn into the discussion as the UN, World Bank and other international organizations have reported on success stories of public-private partnerships worldwide that try to stimulate peaceful development through poverty reduction, socio-economic growth, and security provision.
>
> *(Miklian and Schouten, 2014)*

As evidenced by the 2011 World Development Report's unabashedly positive view on private sector contributions to 'security, justice and jobs' (World Bank, 2011, p. xii) in fragile and conflict-affected contexts, arguments for the proposition that the private sector is an under-utilized development and peacebuilding actor are strongly influenced by the liberal economic tradition. As early as 1884, the political economist John Stuart Mill claimed that 'it is commerce which is rapidly rendering war obsolete, by strengthening and multiplying the personal interests which are in natural opposition to it' (Mill, 1848, p. 582). Thomas Friedman captured the contemporary reincarnation of this thinking in his 1990 Golden Arches Theory of Conflict Prevention – 'No two countries that both had McDonald's had fought a war against each other since each got its McDonald's' (Friedman, 1990, p. 248) – updated in 2005 to the Dell Theory of Conflict Prevention – 'No two countries that are both part of a major global supply chain, like Dell's, will ever fight a war against each other as long as they are both part of the same global supply chain' (Friedman, 2005, p. 421). Thus, much of the business and peace rhetoric tends to take as axiomatic, as asserts the Freedom of Investment process – an intergovernmental forum on investment policy hosted since 2006 by the OECD Investment Committee – that 'international investment spurs prosperity and economic development' (OECD, 2014), and thereby contributes to peace.

Even the concept of business as an intentional actor for peace is not particularly new. Wharton Business School professor Howard V. Perlmutter, writing during the great post-war expansion of the multinational enterprise in the 1960s, named 'the senior executives engaged in building the geocentric enterprise … the most important social architects of the last third of the twentieth century.' They offered 'an institutional and supra-national framework which could conceivably make war less likely, on the assumption that bombing customers, suppliers and employees is in nobody's interest' (Perlmutter, 1969, pp. 9–10). The first issue of the *Journal of World Business*, in 1966, similarly argued that business is an unmatched force for peace (Brown, 1966, p. 6). Within this worldview, as asserts the UN Global Compact's Business for Peace platform, there is 'effectively no contradiction between maximized long-term financial performance and positive contributions to peace and development' (UNGC and PRI, 2010, p. 6), positioning business as a natural peacebuilding actor. At least between those inclined to view the private sector favorably, we can therefore trace a fair amount of continuity in perceptions about business and peace across the decades, if not centuries.

What may be distinctive in contemporary discourse, however, may be the focus by traditional peacebuilding actors – including the United Nations agencies, defense actors, and international non-governmental organizations – on mobilizing private sector actors as peacebuilders. As enshrined in the UN Global Compact, businesses should be committed to 'peace' and incorporate conflict sensitivity into their day-to-day business practices (UNGC and PRI, 2010). In the US,

> the Defense Department's 2010 Quadrennial Defense Review (QDR), the State Department's inaugural Quadrennial Diplomacy and Development Review (QDDR), and the 2010 U.S. National Security Strategy (NSS) acknowledge the importance of according the business sector a major role in solving strategic challenges and fostering peace; leveraging the core competencies of the private sector in problem solving; tapping the business sector's ingenuity and innovation in both processes and outcomes; using public-private partnerships as vehicles to institutionalize anticorruption measures; and providing tangible peace dividends, such as jobs, income, wealth, and services.
>
> *(Forrer, Fort and Gilpin, 2012)*

Businesses operating in fragile environments are now expected to become full 'partners in broader peacemaking and peacebuilding assessment, planning and execution'. (Ganson, 2014, p. 128).

Any number of initiatives by traditional peacebuilding actors then attempt to put these principles into action. International Alert, for example, works with companies under the belief that 'they can help a country turn its back on conflict, and move towards lasting peace' (International Alert, 2005). An entire literature is emerging around the 'business case' for more constructive engagement of companies in fragile and conflict-prone environments (e.g. Franks et al., 2014; Goulbourne, 2003; Henisz, Dorobantu, and Nartey, 2014) in an attempt to motivate business contributions to peaceful development, and it is probably safe to say that attempts to create public–private partnerships to address pressing issues related to conflict and peace are now the norm rather than the exception within UN agencies. In perhaps the most prominent call to action, UN Secretary General Ban Ki-Moon launched the United Nations Global Compact 'Business for Peace' platform, aiming to 'mobilize high-level corporate leadership to advance peaceful development through actions at the global and local levels' (UNGC, 2013b, p. 41).

A menu of roles for business in peace

If the assertion is made that international businesses can and should be called upon as peacebuilders, then the question arises as to how they can do so. There are a growing number of meta-studies of the literature of business and peace, resulting in a variety of maps of the arguments made for how business does, could or should advance peace in what is now a substantial body of academic and policy work. For example:

- Most recently, Miklian (2017) documents widespread assertions that (1) economic engagement facilitates a peace dividend; (2) encouraging local development facilitates local capacities for peace; (3) importing international norms improves democratic accountability; (4) firms can constrain the drivers or root causes of conflict; and (5) undertaking direct diplomatic efforts with conflict actors builds and/or makes peace. He explores how 'motivational drivers for deeper and more comprehensive business engagements into peace and justice arenas' (Ibid., p. xx), the ways in which 'businesses integrate peacebuilding within their corporate structures' (Ibid., p. xx), and understanding of 'what constitutes a 'peace contribution' by business' (Ibid., p. xx) impact upon business-peacebuilding trends.
- Oetzel et al. (2010) 'focused on specific ways companies can actively engage in conflict reduction including promoting economic development, the rule of law, and principles of external valuation, contributing to a sense of community, and engaging in track-two diplomacy and conflict sensitive practices' (Oetzel et al., 2010, p. 351). Their survey notes that 'the argument arising out of the literature is not that businesses should promote peace, but that …

ethical businesses already are conducting actions that contribute to peace' and that, to be more effective peacebuilders, 'they may not have to radically transform their practices as much as one might think when first hearing about a connection between business and peace' (Ibid., p. 352).

- In between, a number of other works attempt to survey and make sense of business and peace within and across fields (e.g. Andersson, Evers, and Sjostedt, 2011; Forrer, Fort and Gilpin, 2012; Forrer and Katsos, 2015; Fort, 2015; Katsos, 2016).

From these and other treatments of business and peace, we can distill commonly promoted arguments about business as an intentional peacebuilding actor, relating these to three dynamics of conflict and peace presumed to be crucial to peace-making and peacebuilding efforts:

- *Socio-economic dynamics*, particularly as these are influenced by the resources available for peaceful development (as well as their distribution across different groups in society), and those available to conflict actors;
- *Socio-political dynamics*, including state-society relations, relationships between different groups in society, and the institutions through which these are mediated;
- *Peacemaking dynamics*, or the processes by which peace is pursued and agreed to.

We explore later in this chapter the ways in which these propositions are directly and indirectly contested and qualified in the academic and policy literature – ultimately raising serious doubts as to their general applicability – but state and describe them here in the positive form more typical of the business and peace literature:

Businesses do, can or should impact socio-economic dynamics of conflict-prone places in peace-positive ways.

A significant portion of academic literature on business and peace studies the role of business in addressing, influencing and changing the material conditions of peacemaking and peacebuilding environments. One common proposition is that, if material conditions on the ground can be changed for the better, the root causes of conflict are addressed and the incentives for conflict are reduced. (See, e.g. the 'jobs' thrust of the World Bank's World Development Report 2011). Under this argument, a company can become an intentional peacebuilding actor simply by deciding to be present in a conflict-prone place, despite risks and potential limitations on short-term returns. In this vein, one executive of a company operating in Afghanistan noted that,

> No matter what planning is done or precautions taken, working in a war zone is a nightmare. It may be important to be there all the same, because the things you build can help ordinary people. In such cases the company's work is in

fact closer to CSR than to business development, even if there is a hope that
the company will work there in the future.

(Ganson, 2013a, p. 83)

Business intentions may, however, go beyond doing business in difficult places.
Business and government actors together may arguably make it harder for conflict
actors to monetize control over resources, as attempted through, for example, the
Kimberley Process for diamonds (Kimberley Process, 2002), the Conflict Free
Minerals Initiatives in the Eastern DRC (OECD, 2015), and efforts to prevent the
sale of oil from ISIS-held areas (Stupples, 2015). Companies may apply principles
of 'do no harm' to help ensure that they do not intentionally or unintentionally
provide material support to conflict actors, for example, by paying ransoms,
extortion monies, or 'security' fees to militias or rebel groups, or by engaging
contractors or human resources with ties to armed groups – even if this means that
they may withdraw from conflict areas because they cannot remain untangled with
conflict protagonists, whether state actors (as, for example, Talisman experienced in
the Sudan) (Associated Press, 2003) or non-state actors (as AngloGold experienced
in the DRC) (Kapelus, Hamann and O'Keefe, 2005).

At the same time, businesses can be conscious of economic grievances that, it is
asserted, can be addressed at least in part through business operations. For example,
companies may create employment for ex-combatants presumed to be at high risk
for resumption of violence, as did Juan Valdez coffee growers in Colombia (Miklian, Schouten and Ganson, 2016). Through management of their presence and
operations, therefore, it is argued that businesses help decrease resources that promote conflict and increase resources that promote peace.

Businesses do, can or should impact socio-political dynamics of conflict-prone places in peace-positive ways.

State-society relations and relations across ethnic, religious or other divides are often the
focus of peacebuilding efforts, and so too the business and peace literature explores the
business nexus to such socio-political dynamics. Examples are highlighted of business
support for transparency that is intended to enable greater civil society engagement with
government, for example, Total's advocacy of EITI in Myanmar (MEITI, 2015);
business work with anti-corruption watchdogs, for example, Transparency International's partnership on OECD anti-bribery efforts with private firms (OECD, 2013b);
and business support for initiatives that create space for the voices of local government
actors and civil society, for example, the Tintaya dialogue table in Peru (Kasturi, Barton,
and Reficco, 2012), or the Business Partners for Development experiment (Business
Partners for Development, 2002). Businesses may work to support local capacities for
peace, for example, by investing in peacebuilding organizations, as did Chevron in
Partners for Peace initiatives in the Niger Delta (NDPI, 2014); and may support credible
local institutions, as did Barrick Gold's by supporting for municipal planning and service
delivery capabilities in the Dominican Republic (Ausland and Tonn, 2010).

In addition, businesses may work to make positive changes through their own operations in conflict-prone places. They may attempt to engage in fairer and more peaceful rules of engagement with communities, for example, through application of the Voluntary Principles on Security and Human Rights (Voluntary Principles, 2000). They may distribute resources through structures for dialogue and decision making meant to be more inclusive, as does Chevron through its development committees in the Niger Delta (Hoben et al., 2012). They may commit to international standards of conduct, for example, the IFC performance standards (IFC, 2012), or the Guiding Principles on Business and Human Rights (OHCHR, 2011). They may make it possible for people to come together across conflict lines in the workplace. And they may commit themselves to just processes for conflict resolution even in weak rule of law states, as did mining companies in apartheid South Africa with the formation of the Independent Mediation Service of South Africa (IMSSA) (Hirschsohn, 1996). In doing so, companies are thought to be contributing to 'islands of peace' that have the potential to create new and more positive dynamics in society (Miller et al. 2019).

Businesses do, can or should impact peacemaking dynamics *in peace-positive ways.*

While most of the business and peace literature focuses on peacebuilding – often within a framework of post-conflict recovery – the literature also examines business actors working to end active conflicts. This is in part a reflection of business leaders as key people and the business community as key constituencies in conflict and peace, leading, for example, to the role of the Bogota Chamber of Commerce in the Colombia peace process (Rettberg, 2013), the role of the Nicosia Chamber of Commerce in Cyprus (Katsos and Forrer, 2014), and the Consultative Business Movement in South Africa (Charney, 1999). Business leaders may help to engineer and play roles in Track II diplomacy, for example, as described in Aceh (Iff and Alluri, 2016). Business may also catalyze and support mediation of conflict in an area of limited government capacity, as does, for example, Chevron in Nigeria through its Partners for Peace initiative (Ganson and Wennmann, 2016). And its roles may be more mundane, providing material support such as transportation or meeting space in a peacemaking context. The argument is therefore that businesses can be facilitators and enablers for peace in society (UN Global Compact, 2015).

Assumptions rather than evidence about business and peace

In large measure, the literature posits (sometimes explicitly but more often implicitly) that the activities described above – whether investment itself, conflict sensitivity or CSR – represent contributions to peace. In much of the analysis, causal connections that are asserted about a particular business activity and peace-positive impacts are premised not on specific case evidence of peace outcomes (or lack thereof), but rather on a set of postulates from related but distinct perspectives:

- *Liberal peace*: a business's intentions may be no more than to be present in a conflict-prone place; it is argued that business advances peace by 'doing what business does,' for example, creating jobs or building infrastructure. The IFC's Conflict Affected States in Africa initiative, for example, largely conflates 'growth, job creation, peace, and stability' (IFC, 2013); the Bpeace network simply asserts, 'more jobs means less violence' (Bpeace, n.d.).
- *Conflict-sensitive business practice*: a business's intentions may be to avoid entanglement in conflict; it is argued that business advances peace by understanding its own impacts and acting proactively to not exacerbate conflict in already difficult places. The OECD Due Diligence Guidance for Responsible Supply Chains of Minerals from Conflict-Affected and High-Risk Areas, for example, purports to supply companies 'with a complete package to source minerals responsibly in order for trade in those minerals to support peace and development and not conflict' (OECD, 2013a, p. 3).
- *Business and human rights*: a business's intentions may be to understand and address the human rights impacts of its operation, and to remedy problems to which it has contributed. The Swiss Federal Department of Foreign Affairs in its publication Business, Human Rights and Peace, for example, argues that businesses have an interest in promoting peace building through, among other measures, 'respecting the rights of each and every member of society' (Ibid., p. 1).
- *Corporate social responsibility*: a business's intentions may be to apply international norms, standards and best practices even though this is not required in the conflict-prone environment; it is argued that business advances peace by acting out of enlightened self-interest. The Hague Institute's policy brief on Corporate Social Responsibility and Human Security in Fragile States: Private Sector Engagement in Peacebuilding, for example, states that, 'A Corporate Social Responsibility (CSR) framework is instrumental in guiding efforts of the private sector to contribute to human security' and thus to peace (Appiah and Jackson, 2015, p. 5).
- *Corporate philanthropy*: a business's intentions may be to help out in a place it has a significant presence; it is argued that business advances peace by providing resources that are otherwise difficult to come by in conflict-prone environments. It is asserted, for example, that 'Philanthropy heals wounds in times of need,' contributing to individual and relational transformation (Ghimire and Upreti, 2012, p. 86).

Policy and practice with regard to business and peace should ideally be driven by sound data rather than assertions or assumptions about a particular business activity and its impact on peace.

Yet building from these postulates and assumptions, decent livelihoods, the ability to accumulate capital, state revenues for service delivery and environmental sustainability, for example, are all commonly asserted to be part of 'peace-conducive economic development' of which the private sector can be part (International Alert, 2015, p. 5) – without specifying where or how these activities have contributed to peace.

Such assertions without context-specific evidence leaves the evidentiary links between company activity and peace outcomes, in the aggregate, weak. It was noted in the context of business and post-conflict reconstruction that, 'To date, there has been little work done on assessing the impact of programming' (MacSweeney, 2008, p. 11). The question of whether business efforts in fact contributed to peace often seems to be treated as an unnecessary distraction in the literature; of 15 company examples in the UN Global Compact's report on 'Responsible business advancing peace,' for example, only two report, as outcomes, any reduction in conflict or violence or increase in social cohesion to which the company activity has even arguably contributed (UNGC, 2013a). It still appears true that

> the current enthusiasm for private sector's contribution to peace is based more on eagerness to do things differently than on a strong evidence base of success stories. The empirical evidence of how businesses have influenced state- and peacebuilding processes remains marginal and at best anecdotal.
>
> *(Hoffmann, 2014, p. 4)*

Additionally, 'it is clear that a different picture emerges depending on whether the object of focus is specific corporate citizenship activities or a company's broader impacts' (Gitsham, 2007, p. 40), meaning that the focus of the business and peace literature on discrete initiatives can veil conflict impacts from a company's broader operations or very presence in a conflict-prone environment.

Given that there is certainly no consensus that business activities enumerated in the business and peace literature illustrated above will make the places in which they are carried out more peaceful, this is problematic. In the realm of socio-economic dynamics, for example, a variety of critiques make clear that the nexus between material conditions and conflict or peace are questionable, unclear, or at the very least far more complex than a simple 'input-output' model can explain (e.g. Woodrow and Chigas, 2009). In the realm of socio-political dynamics, some critics see ever-deeper involvement of businesses into fragile conflict zones as conflict-fomenting neo-colonial exploitation (e.g. Provost, Ford and Tran, 2014); others argue that the privileging of business in the peace and development space is warping international agendas in fragile states further towards corporate interests (Englebert and Portelance, 2015; Barbara, 2006), and can in fact increase grievances by further marginalizing excluded communities (Obenland, 2014). In the realm of peacemaking dynamics, oft-touted efforts, such as logistical support given by 'Tiny' Rowland for the Mozambique peace process, may be taken out of context; he was known both to have supported the liberation movement Renamo through 'protection' payments (Conciliation Resources, 1998), and has been implicated in broader engineering of conflict and commissioning of violence (Drohan, 2004). Indeed, for each of the assertions made about the positive impacts of the activities constituting mainstream business and peace, we can identify significant qualifiers and counter-assertions.

Similarly, discussions of business and peace based on assumptions rather than evidence remain largely disconnected from the literature on 'business and conflict' addressing the private sector as an agent, intentional or not, for conflict and violence. An entire body of literature holds that business is in fact a primary enabler of conflict, either through complicity (e.g. OHCHR, 2008), or through intentional exploitation of conflict for profit (e.g. Drohan, 2004). Case evidence from such disparate settings as Afghanistan (DuPée, 2012) Nigeria (Idemudia, 2010) and Colombia (Dunning and Wirpsa, 2004) indicates that operations of multinational corporations in volatile environments may even prolong or exacerbate conflict, notwithstanding explicit ambitions to bring a 'development dividend' to local populations (Schouten and Miklian, 2018).

Yet this is rarely acknowledged in the mainstream business and peace literature. The World Bank's *World Development Report 2011: Conflict, Security and Development*, for example, strongly advocates business incentives and 'a new global partnership to galvanize investments in countries and communities where high unemployment and social disengagement contribute to the risks of conflict' (World Bank, 2011, p. 31). In its treatment of the private sector across 51 pages, however, it makes no mention at all of predatory multinational companies that may exploit fragility, or the possible negative impacts of private foreign investment on conflict or violence (Ganson and Wennmann, 2016, p. 94). Similarly, a report on the 'role of mining in national economies' by the International Council on Mining and Metals – an industry association that espouses among other principles the upholding of fundamental human rights – fails to make a single reference to any negative impact of mining on national economies or local communities, even in fragile states (Ibid.) The inter-relationships of business as an agent for peaceful development when at the same time it acts as an agent of conflict – intentionally or not – remain largely unaddressed.

A profound disconnect from contemporary peacebuilding theory and practice

Perhaps most importantly, the emphasis on discrete activities presumed to be peace-positive seems profoundly disconnected from contemporary peacebuilding theory and practice. It is perhaps true that, 'Two decades ago international peacebuilding was understood as a centrally coordinated package of interventions aimed at resolving a conflict by addressing its root causes' (de Coning, 2016, p. 1), drawing from a menu of interventions that looked much like those found in the current business and peace literature. But based on hard lessons learned from failed or suboptimal interventions (e.g. Anderson and Olson, 2003) peacebuilding has since then developed in a variety of important directions:

- *Systems thinking.* Increasingly, conflict-prone environments are understood as complex systems in which institutions and power relations reinforce conflict dynamics and undermine dynamics that would support peaceful development. Because these systems 'are functioning to achieve some purpose – protecting the power and authority of a particular elite, for example – they are highly resistant to change' (Ganson and Wennmann 2016, p. 192). This means that peacebuilders must work not only on building or reinforcing positive factors (often the focus of business and peace activities), but 'also ask what factors (actors, issues, motives, resources, dynamics, attitudes, behaviors) maintain or reinforce the conflict system, who would resist movement toward peace, and why' (CDA, 2010, p. 5). Because the goal is a system that reinforces peaceful development rather than conflict and violence, they focus on the factors that are driving the evolution of the system, and that, if they were changed, would lead to a significant change in the system (Ibid., p. 8).

- *Focus on resilience of social institutions.* Another import focus is on the capacity of social institutions 'to absorb and adapt in order to sustain an acceptable level of function, structure and identity under stress' (Dahlberg, 2015). For example, the inability or unwillingness of traditional authorities in West Africa to adapt the allocation of communal land to the realities of changing demographics – which would reduce the resources controlled by current landholders – was found to be a significant contributing factor to the large numbers of young men lacking social or professional attachment, and thus their availability for recruitment into the various brutal conflicts of the region (Richards and Chauveau, 2007). Peacebuilders thus often put considerable effort into compensatory mechanisms for building social consensus to address pressing problems, sometimes under the umbrella term of 'infrastructures for peace' (e.g. Odendaal, 2013; Kumar and De la Haye, 2011).

- *Attentiveness to motivations for violence.* Violence is often treated as inevitable, as Albert Einstein wrote to Sigmund Freud, 'Because man has within him a lust for hatred and destruction' (Cramer, 2006, p. 4). Yet more than two decades of conflict research establish that violence is the result of planned, purposeful action. 'Part of the problem with much existing analysis is that conflict continues to be regarded as simply a breakdown in a particular system rather than as the emergence of an alternative system of profit, power and even protection' (Keen, 1998, p. 22). Peacebuilders have therefore come to understand that, 'Only by understanding these functions of conflict and violence can interveners identify the underlying organizational aspects and motives of conflict that need to be understood and dealt with to nurture its prevention, diffusion and resolution' (Ganson and Wennmann, 2016, p. 110).

- *Linkages of peacebuilding activities.* A 'trickle up' theory of impact – that if enough people engage in enough positive activity, peace can emerge – is implicit in the business and peace literature's menu of presumably peace-positive activities; 'contributions to peace,' often within a limited sphere, are treated as drops in the bucket that will somehow add up to systemic change. This assumption has been challenged in peacebuilding circles for some time (e.g. Chigas and Ganson, 2003); it turns out that small efforts are more often than not overwhelmed by broader systems dynamics. Peacebuilders therefore increasingly focus on a variety of critical connections among peacebuilding activities, among which the most important are linkages of individual and personal change (targeting skills, attitudes, perceptions, ideas and relationships with other individuals) to socio-political change (including governance reform as well as social norms, group behavior, and inter-group relationships), and linkages of efforts to reach broad segments of the population with efforts to reach key people (CDA, 2010).

- *Local ownership.* There is increasing acknowledgement that societies in conflict are complex, in that (1) the properties of a given conflict system cannot be understood by its component parts alone, but must be seen as a whole; that (2) small changes can have large impacts and large inputs may not affect meaningful change, as outputs of the system are not proportionate to inputs; and that (3) the system responds to a large number of dynamic factors according to the adaptations of its constituent parts, without a controlling agent (de Coning, 2016). Attempts 'to engineer specific outcomes' thus run a high risk of generating 'on-going instability, dependence and fragility' (Ibid., p. 13). There is therefore a growing emphasis among peacebuilders on the need to accompany rather than direct local actors in their own peacebuilding analysis, planning, and intervention (GPP, 2015, p. 8).

In light of these peacebuilding principles, the starting point for contemporary peacebuilding practice is a systems map of key actors and the key driving factors of cohesion and division, ideally developed by diverse local actors in dialogue with each other. This is because, as a result of highly context-specific local dynamics, 'an approach that contributes to peace in one context may be irrelevant to peace in another, and may actually worsen conflict in a third' (CDA, 2014, p. 3). Interventions are designed with reference to the systems map in ways that have some meaningful chance of altering fundamental socio-political realities in positive ways. This allows for actors – intending for their activities to be peace-positive but necessarily only taking steps on a path to peace – to move beyond rhetoric that is still common in business and peace discourse that 'the effectiveness of peace efforts is hard to measure.' Rather, understanding fundamental systems dynamics, peacebuilders can have some certainty that they are making a meaningful contribution to a broader peace if their activity is addressing key dynamics of conflict and peace, AND it also:

- Results in the creation or reform of political institutions to handle grievances in situations where such grievances genuinely drive the conflict;
- Contributes to a momentum for peace by causing participants and communities to develop their own peace initiatives in relation to critical elements of context analysis;
- Increasingly prompts people to resist violence and provocations to violence;
- Results in an increase in people's security and in their sense of security; and/or
- Results in meaningful improvement in inter-group relations (Chigas, Church and Corlazzoli, 2014).

Despite the growing evidence base for effective peace practice, and its incorporation into mainstream policy such as the OECD DAC guidance on *Evaluating Peacebuilding Activities in Settings of Conflict and Fragility* (OECD, 2012, p. 67), the business and peace literature deals with such peacebuilding principles and strategies for effectiveness only superficially, or not at all.

The high risk of suboptimal outcomes and unintended consequences

As the peacebuilding community itself needed to learn (Anderson, 1999; Anderson and Olson, 2003), there are significant risks of suboptimal outcomes and unintended consequences for peacebuilding work in the absence of the systems analyses, context-specific strategies, and attentiveness to effectiveness measures at the heart of sound peacebuilding practice:

- *'Doing good' but not building peace.* Conflict-prone environments may have many needs, among others for better health, education, employment, infrastructure, security and governance. A corporate intervention to help eradicate malaria or operate in compliance with international labor norms even where this is not required by local law – assuming they are carried out professionally and in a conflict-sensitive manner – are therefore in all likelihood positive from a social perspective. They will have only tangential impact on peace, however, in places where there is no close nexus between these issues and key drivers of conflict. In particular, evidence from development and peacebuilding practice shows that assumptions about the relationship between economic development efforts and peacebuilding are largely untested and often false (cf. Stewart, 2000; Stewart, 2008; Berman et al., 2011; Blair et al., 2012).
- *Small 'wins' that don't add up to peace.* A company may in fact undertake initiatives that, for example, increase a local community's sense of security through its efforts to help reform local policing consistent with the Voluntary Principles; its actions might additionally have a close nexus to key drivers of conflict where, for example, state-society relations are particularly tense. Ultimate effectiveness of peacebuilding work, though, is premised on it moving forward fast enough, being sustained over time, and together with other activities, being undertaken at a scale commensurate with the challenges and adequately linked to other levels of peace-positive activity in the conflict system (Anderson and Olson, 2003). Discrete initiatives must therefore be intentionally linked to other efforts if they are to make a meaningful contribution to a conflict-prone environment moving sustainably towards peaceful development.
- *Program failures.* Even if a company is working towards meaningful goals, it must make progress in a fragile environment despite complex conflict dynamics. Otherwise, the very dynamics of political fragmentation, mistrust, exclusion and grievance that make a context fragile in the first place will undermine attempts to address underlying grievances. Schools and clinics will

be constructed only to stand empty because the system is too dysfunctional to build them in the first place also won't allocate resources to run them; infrastructure projects meant to support inclusive growth will be subject to the same corrupt influences or political rivalries that inhibited inclusive economic growth before (Ganson and Wennmann, 2016). Corporate initiatives must therefore take account of, and address, potential pushback and spoilers in the system.

- *Perverse impacts.* Companies are prone to concentrate on the good they are bringing to conflict-prone places, whether measured in jobs, local procurement or tax revenues. But the introduction of new resources into resource-constrained societies more often intensifies competition between groups or actors in conflict than eases it (Zandvliet and Anderson, 2009). For every employed person in a platinum mine in South Africa, for example, it is estimated that there are 10 migrant job-seekers who remain unemployed. The dynamics of large numbers of jobless young men support 'a host of criminal and trafficking networks' which, along with contested control over allocation of jobs among the mining company, local government, traditional authorities, and competing labor unions, contributed to the tensions that led up to the Marikana massacre (Breckenridge, 2014).

It is tempting to take a rhetorical stance in favor of business doing something rather than nothing in the face of conflict and violence. But without more substantial points of intersection between business and peace and contemporary peacebuilding theory and practice – in particular the drawing of a thread from the purported peacebuilding activity to key drivers of conflict based on rigorous systems understanding – business and peace advocates will largely be unable to draw meaningful conclusions about the impacts – positive or negative – of a particular business or peace initiative in a particular place. They will rather be limited to vague assertions about business activities 'bringing mutual benefit and the advancement of peace' (UN Global Compact, 2013a, p. 4), or making 'a significant contribution to the common good' (Ibid., p. 11). And they will risk failing to contribute to peace or even doing harm, even if their intentions are to do good.

Also missing from the equation: the 'who' and the 'how'

As outlined above, the gap is already wide between the menu of activities typically enumerated in the literature as business roles for peace, and the strategies and questions grounded in systems analysis that constitute effective peacebuilding. But peacebuilding is not only a what, it is a who. Effective action is dependent not only on strategic engagement with the key drivers of conflict in a particular context, but on the place of the peacemaking or peacebuilding agent within that system. The business and peace literature also largely sidesteps a critical set of questions about the capacity and motivations for business to engage as a peacebuilding actor, and the relationships to other actors in a conflict system that enable them to accept private sector actors as such.

To the extent that it requires going beyond actions 'ethical businesses already are conducting' (Oetzel et al., 2010, p. 352), one may in the first instance question whether companies have the requisite capabilities to engage in peacebuilding. Mary Anderson, an authority on outside intervention in conflict-prone environments, noted that 'peace is not an area for amateurs' (Anderson, 2008, p. 125). For companies to effectively apply peacebuilding principles, they must

> perform accurate and up-to-date conflict analysis; establish comfortable, trusting, and transparent relationships with diverse people who may not share their values; use specialized mediation skills to identify common concerns that can unite antagonists while also respecting fundamental differences and opposing positions; and have the ability to be calm and comfortable in situations of danger, threat, and emotional and physical stress.
>
> *(Anderson, 2008, pp. 125–126)*

In what is perhaps a pronounced understatement, she concludes that these 'are not common, everyday skills found among corporate managers' (Ibid., pp. 125–126). Anderson's comments echo studies suggesting that global companies require business competencies in areas in which most managers have no background or training, including the competencies needed to deal with foreign country interests, multiple domestic and foreign pressure groups, or international conflict (Saner, Yiu and Søndergaard, 2000). It is also an incomplete answer to attempt to outsource these functions, as robust governance and management systems are required within the company, in addition to individual skills and courage (Ganson, 2014). How peacebuilding capabilities are integrated into company structures and how these impact peacebuilding effectiveness remains largely unexplored in the business and peace literature.

The question of corporate capabilities for peacebuilding goes hand in hand with the question of motivation. Typical of business and peace policy and practice is the OECD argument that 'MNEs have a strong business incentive to act responsibly' (OECD, 2008, p. 17); as noted above, the UN Global Compact for its part takes the position that there is 'effectively no contradiction between maximized long-term financial performance and positive contributions to peace and development' (UNGC and PRI, 2010, p. 6). Yet companies have long found that they could capitalize on high returns on investment despite instability (Goulbourne, 2003). Countries such as Colombia, Indonesia, Algeria and the Philippines attracted high levels of foreign direct investment (FDI) even during periods of overt armed conflict (Campbell, 2002); flows of FDI to Côte d'Ivoire remained positive during its entire civil war (MIGA, 2010), and the cases of Brazil, South Africa and Mexico highlight that FDI occurs despite high levels of criminal violence (Wennmann, 2011). Studying why direct conflict risks do not deter investment, a 2010 study by MIGA, the Multilateral Investment Guarantee Agency of the World Bank Group, found that companies across sectors, company size and geographical origin believed that business opportunities outweigh risks and that potential losses were limited

(MIGA, 2010). Business and peace policy and practice, however, largely discounts the reality that, as concluded in *The Economist*, 'For brave businessfolk, there are rich pickings in grim places' (Anonymous, 2000). With limited exceptions, (e.g. Rettberg, 2016) the literature therefore sheds less insight than it might on the actual motivations of companies taking peace-positive action, and on how the calculus of companies not taking such action might be changed.

Even a company capable and motivated to undertake peacebuilding work must still recognize that the characteristics of the company in its context determine, at least in part, the possible ways in which it can participate in peace efforts. A company operating in a conflict-prone environment becomes part and parcel of a complex system, with multiple and intricate inter-relationships among the company, its operations, its neighboring communities and the broader society (Ganson, 2013b). Companies often have close relationships with the elites whose support they cultivate, and have operations that touch on land, distribution of jobs and other benefits, and other issues of profound interest to many people. Their operations will inevitably have direct and indirect impacts on existing social tensions, on the effectiveness and legitimacy of government, and in more extreme cases on the impunity with which governments or others may violate human rights; and companies are often confronted by the unfulfilled expectations and grievances of local populations (Bardouille-Crema, Chigas and Miller, 2013). Additionally, national companies will have, in most cases, very different characteristics, relationships, entry points and histories than multinational companies with global operations (Banfield, Gunduz, and Killick, 2006). It is certainly not impossible for even the same businesses to play both positive and negative roles; mining companies in South Africa, for example, were champions for change at the national level in South Africa (Marais and Davies, 2015), even while their local operations were still focal points for violence driven by apartheid policies and practices in which the mines actively participated (TRC, 1998). Yet in the development sphere, it has been found that approaches by oil companies in the Niger Delta that try to bring benefits to communities without addressing the negative impacts of company operations 'tinker around the problem of poverty and underdevelopment in host communities' and thus have marginal impact (Idemudia, 2009, p. 111). It would not seem unlikely that the same will obtain for peacebuilding – that the full range of a company's impacts in a complex environment will shape its relationships and thus its ability to play a peace-positive role – meriting more attention in business and peace research.

Finally, it is unlikely that business actors will achieve substantial results in the domain of conflict and peace without close collaboration with other actors. Yet the interdependent facets of peacebuilding will often require professional and institutionalized support to coordinate and sustain them. Ad hoc processes convened directly by stakeholders can die from the exhaustion of planning and managing complex collaborative initiatives that are outside the core mandate or expertise of any participant (Ganson and Wennmann, 2016). Companies in particular may face resistance from local actors until they 'relinquish some measure of control over decision-making' (Laplante and Spears, 2008, p. 115). The United Nations guidance on effective mediation suggests a variety of support functions that may be

necessary to support collaboration in situations of conflict: to help build relationships of confidence where they do not sufficiently exist among local actors themselves; to facilitate across a variety of actors the participatory analysis of conflict
dynamics as well as local strengths and challenges faced in dealing with them; to
ensure the careful evaluation of strategic and tactical options for introducing new
thinking and new modes of action for conflict prevention into a fragile environment; to provide expert support for the design, management and evaluation of
conflict prevention systems; and to engage in consistent outreach to the full range
of stakeholders nationally and internationally for coherent action (UN, 2012;
UNDPA and UNEP, 2015). More generally, a 'backbone support organization'
that provides services such as neutral facilitation or mediation, technology and
communication, data collection and reporting, and administrative support is
increasingly seen as a critical enabler of complex collaborative efforts (Kania and
Kramer, 2011, p. 40). This suggests a need for further exploration of the key relationships and institutional enablers of business and peace.

A richer set of perspectives and questions

This analysis establishes a pressing need for researchers and practitioners to shift
some share of mind from the 'what' – the menu of possible business interventions
for peace that dominates the business and peace literature – to the 'who' and the
'how' of business and peace. Advocates will accelerate progress by drawing from
contemporary peacebuilding theory and practice to situate private sector actors
within a complex conflict system, understand key dynamics reinforcing conflict and
undermining attempts towards peace, and seeking entry points for positive influence.
What factors matter most in a particular place, what forces are inhibiting sufficient
coalitions for positive change from forming, and what particular advantages might
businesses have in addressing these?

Peace advocates will also move more dependably towards their goals as they
survey the full range of negative as well as positive impacts of private sector actors
in conflict environments, acknowledging and addressing tensions between business
roles and relationships in different parts and at different levels of the system. What
business interventions are perceived as most legitimate and welcome by different
actors, and why? How can business best play a peace-positive role, even as its
contributions to conflict, intentional or not, are acknowledged?

The analysis also suggests the need to move beyond the stereotyping of private
sector actors – largely as a homogenous force for bad or good, depending on the
commentator's perspective – to a more nuanced understanding of the perspectives,
interests, motives, capabilities, limitations and possibilities for action of particular business actors. Peacebuilding actors will need to work with private sector actors in the
same way they work to understand and engage other actors – even those seen to be
hostile or indifferent to peace, in governments, opposition groups, or civil society –
within conflict environments. How do we move beyond the 'coulds' and 'shoulds' of
business and peace to understand how companies in practice find the courage and

commitment to work for peace? What is the supporting infrastructure that allows cross-cutting coalitions between business and other actors to emerge and succeed?

Asking and answering these questions will require broader and deeper inquiry than that which currently typifies business and peace research, advocacy and practice. But the broad experience of peacebuilding practice suggests that, as these questions are asked and answered for particular businesses in particular conflict contexts, it will become increasingly possible to understand, conceptualize, plan, implement, and measure the effectiveness of business-inclusive strategies for peace.

References

Aaronson, H., Vubovic, B., Trebjesanin, B., and Hempfling, C. (2008). *Accelerating Sustainable Growth in Post-Conflict Serbia*. Washington, DC: USAID.

Anderson, M.B. (1999). *Do No Harm: How Aid Can Support Peace or War*. London: Lynne Rienner.

Anderson, M. B. (2008). False Promises and Premises?, in Oliver F. Williams (ed.), *Peace Through Commerce*. Notre Dame, IN: University of Notre Dame Press.

Anderson, M. B., and Olson, L. (2003). *Confronting War: Critical Lessons for Peace Practitioners*. Cambridge, MA: The Collaborative for Development Action, Inc. Retrieved from http://cdacollaborative.org/wordpress/wp-content/uploads/2016/01/Confronting-War-Critical-Lessons-for-Peace-Practitioners.pdf

Andersson, J. J., Evers, T., and Sjostedt, G. (2011). *Private Sector Actors and Peacebuilding* (Vol. Note No. 1). Retrieved from http://cdi.mecon.gov.ar/biblio/docelec/bm/ppps/N203.pdf

Anonymous. (2000). Business in Difficult Places: Risky Returns. *The Economist*, 355:8171, 85–88.

Appiah, M., and Jackson, E. (2015). *Corporate Social Responsibility and Human Security in Fragile States*. The Hague: Hague Institute for International Justice.

Associated Press (2003). Talisman Pulls Out of Sudan. Retrieved from http://news.bbc.co.uk/2/hi/business/2835713.stm

Ausland, A. and Tonn, G. (2010). *Partnering for Local Development: An Independent Assessment of a Unique Corporate Social Responsibility and Community Relations Strategy*. Johannesburg: Barrick Gold Corporation.

Bagwitz, D., Elges, Reinhold, Grossmann, H., and Kruk, G. (2008). *Private Sector Development in (Post) Conflict Situations*. Eschborn: GTZ. Retrieved from https://www.mierke.de/assets/files/Private%20Sector%20Development%20in%20%28Post-%29Conflict%20Situations%20Guidebook%20GTZ%202008.pdf

Banfield, Jessica. (2007). Business and Conflict – Options and Instruments for Government Actors. In Lalive d'Epinay, Danielle and Schnabel, Albrecht (Eds.). *Transforming War Economies*. Working Paper. Swiss Peace Foundation. Retrieved from: http://edoc.vifapol.de/opus/volltexte/2011/2442/pdf/WP3_2007.pdf

Banfield, J., Gunduz, C. and Killick, N. (eds.) (2006). *Local Business, Local Peace: The Peacebuilding Potential of the Domestic Private Sector*. London: International Alert.

Barbara, J. (2006). Nation Building and the Role of the Private Sector as a Political Peacebuilder. *Conflict, Security and Development* 6:4, 581–594.

Bardouille-Crema, D., Chigas, D. and Miller, B. (2013). How Do Our Operations Interact with the Environment? In Ganson, Brian (ed.), *Management in Complex Environments: Questions for Leaders*. Stockholm: NIR, pp. 59–85.

Berman, E., Callen, M., Felter, J. H., and Shapiro, J. N. (2011). Do Working Men Rebel? Insurgency and Unemployment in Afghanistan, Iraq, and the Philippines. *Journal of Conflict Resolution* 55:4, 496–528.

Blair, G., Fair, C. C., Malhotra, N., and Shapiro, J. N. (2012). Poverty and Support for Militant Politics: Evidence from Pakistan. *American Journal of Political Science* 57, 30–48. doi:10.1111/j.1540-5907.2012.00604.x

Bpeace (n.d.). Retrieved from www.bpeace.org/about-us.html

Brainard, L., Chollet, D., and LaFleur, V. (2007). *The Tangled Web: The Poverty-Insecurity Nexus*. Washington, DC: Brookings Institution Press. Retrieved from https://www.brookings.edu/wp-content/uploads/2016/07/toopoorforpeace_chapter.pdf

Breckenridge, K. (2014). Marikana and the Limits of Biopolitics: Themes in the Recent Scholarship of South African Mining. *Africa* 84:1, 151–161. doi:10.1017/S0001972013000624

Brown, C. C. (1966). Notes From the Editor. *Columbia Journal of World Business*, 1:1, 5–6.

Busan Fourth High Level Forum on Aid Effectiveness: Proceedings. (2011). Busan, Korea, pp. 1–252. Retrieved from: https://www.oecd.org/dac/effectiveness/HLF4%20proceedings%20entire%20doc%20for%20web.pdf

Business Partners for Development (2002). *Putting Partnering to Work: Tri-sector Partnership Results and Recommendations*. Retrieved from www.oecd.org/unitedkingdom/2082379.pdf

Campbell, A. (2002). *The Private Sector and Conflict Prevention Mainstreaming*. Ontario: Country Indicators for Foreign Policy.

CDA (2010). *Reflecting on Peace Practice Training Manual*. Cambridge, MA: CDA.

CDA (2014). Business for Peace: Understanding and Assessing Corporate Contributions to Peace. Discussion paper presented at the UN Global Compact's Business for Peace (B4P) conference, Istanbul, TurkeySeptember 29. Retrieved from http://cdacollaborative.org/wordpress/wp-content/uploads/2016/01/Business-for-Peace-Understanding-and-Assessing-Corporate-Contributions-to-Peace.pdf

Charney, C. (1999). Civil Society, Political Violence, and Democratic Transitions: Business and the Peace Process in South Africa, 1990 to 1994. *Comparative Studies in Society and History*, 41:1, 182–206.

Chigas, D. and Ganson, B. (2003). Grand Visions and Small Projects: Coexistence Effort in Southeastern Europe, in Chayes, A. and Minow, M. (eds), *Imagine Coexistence: Restoring Humanity after Violent Conflict*, 59–84. San Francisco, CA: Jossey Bass.

Chigas, D., Church, M. and Corlazzoli, V. (2014). *Evaluating Impacts of Peacebuilding Interventions: Approaches and Methods, Challenges and Considerations. CCVRI Guidance Product*. London: DFID.

Collier, P. (2006). Private Sector Development and Peacebuilding. Paper given at the conference: Private Sector Development and Peace-building – Exploring Local and International Perspectives. September. Berlin: GTZ.

Collier, Paul and Sambanis, Nicholas. (2002). Understanding Civil War: A New Agenda. *Journal of Conflict Resolution* 46:1, 3–12. https://doi.org/10.1177/0022002702046001001

Conciliation Resources. (1998). *Annual Report 1998*. London. Retrieved from www.c-r.org/resources/annual-review-1998

Cramer, C. (2006). *Civil War is Not a Stupid Thing: Accounting for Violence in Developing Countries*. London: C. Hurst & Co.

Dahlberg, R. (2015). Resilience and Complexity: Conjoining the Discourses of Two Contested Concepts. *Culture Unbound: Journal of Current Cultural Research* 7:3, 541–557. doi:10.3384/cu.2000.1525.1573

de Coning, C. (2016). From Peacebuilding to Sustaining Peace: Implications of Complexity for Resilience and Sustainability. *Resilience*. doi:10.1080/21693293.2016.1153773

Deitelhoff, N., and Wolf, K. D. (2010). *Corporate Security Responsibility: Corporate Governance Contributions to Peace and Security in Zones of Conflict.* London: Palgrave Macmillan.

Drohan, M. (2004). *Making a Killing: How and Why Corporations Use Armed Force to Do Business.* Guilford: Lyons Press.

Dunning, T. and Wirpsa, L. (2004). Oil and the Political Economy of Conflict in Colombia and Beyond: A Linkages Approach. *Geopolitics* 9:1, 81–108.

DuPée, M. (2012). Afghanistan's Conflict Minerals: The Crime-state-insurgent Nexus. *CTC Sentinal* 5:2, 11–14.

Englebert, P. and Portelance, G. (2015). The Growth-governance Paradox in Africa. *Africaplus.* Retrieved from https://africaplus.wordpress.com/2015/01/06/the-growth-governance-paradox-in-africa/

Ersenkal, E., and Wolf Fellow, J. (2007). *Field manual: Supporting Microfinance Through Grants in Post-crisis Settings.* Bethesda, MD. Retrieved from https://dai.com/sites/default/files/pubs/other/Field_Manual.pdf

Forrer, J., Fort, T., and Gilpin, R. (2012). *How Business Can Foster Peace.* New York, NY. Retrieved from www.usip.org/sites/default/files/SR315.pdf

Fort, T. L. (2015) *Diplomat in the Corner Office: How Business Contributes to Peace.* Palo Alto, CA: Stanford University Press.

Franks, D. M., Davis, R., Bebbington, A. J., Ali, S. H., Kemp, D., and Scurrah, M. (2014). Conflict Translates Environmental and Social Risk into Business Costs. *Proceedings of the National Academy of Sciences of the United States of America* 111:21, 7576–7581. Retrieved from http://doi.org/10.1073/pnas.1405135111

Friedman, T. L. (1990). *The Lexus and the Olive Tree.* New York: Anchor.

Friedman, T. L. (2005). *The World is Flat: A Brief History of the Twenty-first Century.* New York: Farrar, Straus and Giroux.

Ganson, B. (ed.) (2013a). *Management in Complex Environments: Questions for Leaders.* Stockholm: NIR.

Ganson, B. (2013b). How Do We Succeed in a Complex Environment? In Ganson, B. (ed.), *Management in Complex Environments: Questions for Leaders.* Stockholm: NIR, pp. 10–16.

Ganson, B. (2014). Business in Fragile Environments: Capabilities for Conflict Prevention. *Negotiation and Conflict Management Research* 7:2, 121–139. http://doi.org/10.1111/ncmr.12028

Ganson, B., and Wennmann, A. (2016). *Business and Conflict in Fragile States: The Case for Pragmatic Solutions.* London: International Institute for Strategic Studies.

Ghimire, S., and Upreti, B. R. (2012). Corporate Engagement for Conflict Transformation: Conceptualising the Business-Peace Interface. *Journal of Conflict Transformation & Security* 2:1, 77–100.

Gitsham, M. 2007. How Do you Measure the Impact of Corporate Citizenship at the Local Level in a Zone of Conflict? An Examination of Five Approaches to Understanding the Case of BP in Casanare, Colombia. *JCC* 28, 31–42.

Goulbourne, T. (2003). Corporate Social Responsibility: The Business Case. *International Affairs.* Ottawa, Canada. Retrieved from http://www4.carleton.ca/cifp/app/serve.php/1053.pdf

GPP, Geneva Peacebuilding Platform (2015). White Paper on Peacebuilding. Geneva: Geneva Peacebuilding Platform.

Guimond, Marie-France. (2007). Structural Adjustment and Peacebuilding Road to Conflict or Peace? Working Paper. Retrieved from: http://citeseerx.ist.psu.edu/viewdoc/download?doi=10.1.1.610.2912&rep=rep1&type=pdf

Gündüz, C., and Klein, D. (2008). *Conflict-sensitive Approaches to Value-chain Development.* microREPORT #101. Washington, DC: USAID. Retrieved from http://pdf.usaid.gov/pdf_docs/Pnady232.pdf

Henisz, W. J., Dorobantu, S., and Nartey, L. J. (2014). Spinning Gold: The Financial Returns to Stakeholder Engagement. *Strategic Management Journal* 35:2, 1727–1748. http://doi.org/10.1002/smj.2180

Hirschsohn, P. (1996). Negotiating a Democratic Order: Learning from Mediation and Industrial Relations. *Negotiation Journal* 12:2, 139–150.

Hoben, M., Kovick, D., Plumb, D. and Wright, J. (2012). *Corporate and community engagement in the Niger Delta: Lessons learned from Chevron Nigeria Limited's GMOU Process.* Cambridge, MA: Consensus Building Institute.

Hoffmann, A. (2014). From 'Business as Usual' to 'Business for Peace'? Unpacking the Conflict-sensitivity Narrative. *CRU Policy Brief* No. 28; February 2014. The Hague: Clingendael Institute.

Hudon, M., and Seibel, H. D. (2007). Microfinance in Post-disaster and Post-conflict Situations: Turning Victims into Shareholders. *Savings and Development* 31:1, 5–22. Retrieved from http://www.jstor.org/stable/25830949

Idemudia, U. (2009). Oil Extraction and Poverty Reduction in the Niger Delta: A Critical Examination of Partnership Initiatives. *Journal of Business Ethics* 90:Supp. 1, 91–116.

Idemudia, U. (2010). Rethinking the Role of Corporate Social Responsibility in the Nigerian Oil Conflict: The Limits of CSR. *Journal of International Development* 1, 833–845. http://doi.org/10.1002/jid

IFC. (2012). *Performance Standards on Environmental and Social Sustainability.* Retrieved from www.ifc.org/wps/wcm/connect/115482804a0255db96fbffd1a5d13d27/PS_English_2012_Full-Document.pdf?MOD=AJPERES

IFC. (2013). *IFC's Conflict Affected States in Africa Initiative: Final Report for CASA's First Cycle 2008–2013.* Retrieved from www.ifc.org/wps/wcm/connect/5f675b004540e75a95de9dc66d9c728b/IFC+CASA+I+Final+Report.pdf?MOD=AJPERES

IFC/FIAS-GTZ-BMZ. (2007). Conflict-Sensitive Economic Development in Conflict-Affected Countries. Washington DC, Eschborn and Bonn.

Iff, A. and Alluri, R. M. (2016). Business Actors in Peace Mediation Processes. *Business and Society Review* 121, 187–215. doi:10.1111/basr.12085

International Alert. (2005). *Conflict-sensitive Business Practice: Guidance for Extractive Industries.* London. Retrieved from www.iisd.org/pdf/2005/security_conflict_sensitive_business.pdf

International Alert. (2015). *Peace Through Prosperity: Integrating Peacebuilding into Economic Development.* Retrieved from www.international-alert.org/sites/default/files/Economy_PeaceThroughProsperity_EN_2015.pdf

Kania, J. and Kramer, M. (2011). Collective Impact. *Stanford Social Innovation Review*, Winter, 36–41.

Kapelus, P., Hamann, R. and O'Keefe, E. (2005). Doing Business with Integrity: The Experience of AngloGold Ashanti in the Democratic Republic of Congo. *International Social Science Journal* 57, 119–130. doi:10.1111/j.1468-2451.2009.00711.x

Kasturi, R. V., Barton, B. and Reficco, E. (2012). Corporate Responsibility and Community Engagement at the Tintaya Copper Mine (A). *Harvard Business School* Case 506–023, February 2006, Revised November 2012.

Katsos, J. (2016). Access and Application: Addressing the Two Major Problems in Current Business and Peace Research. *Business, Peace and Sustainable Development* 7, 3–7.

Katsos, J. E. and Forrer, J. (2014). Business Practices and Peace in Post-conflict Zones: Lessons from Cyprus. *Business Ethics European Review* 23, 154–168. doi:10.1111/beer.12044

Keen, D. (1998). Special Issue: The Economic Functions of Violence in Civil War. *Adelphi Papers*, 38:320, 1–120.

Kimberley Process. (2002). *Kimberley Process Certification Scheme.* Retrieved from www.kimberleyprocess.com/en/kpcs-core-document

Kumar, C. and De la Haye, J. (2011). Hybrid Peacemaking: Building National 'Infrastructures for Peace'. *Global Governance* 18:1, 13–20.

Laplante, L. J. and Spears, S. A. (2008). Out of the Conflict Zone: The Case for Community Consent Processes in the Extractive Sector. *Yale Human Rights and Development Law Journal* 11:1, 69–116.

MacSweeney, N. (2008). *Private Sector Development in Post-conflict Countries*. Cambridge. Retrieved from https://lra.le.ac.uk/bitstream/2381/27928/4/PostConflict_PSD_EN_rev2.pdf

Marais, N. and Davies, J. (2015). *The Role of the Business Elite in South Africa's Democratic Transition: Supporting an Inclusive Political and Economic Transformation*. Berlin: Berghof Foundation.

MEITI, Myanmar Extractive Industries Transparency Initiative (2015). *EITI Report for the period April 2013-March 2014: Oil, gas and mining sectors*. Retrieved from https://eiti.org/sites/default/files/documents/fy2013-2014_myanmar_eiti_report.pdf

MIGA (2010). *World Investment and Political Risk 2010*. Washington, DC: MIGA.

Miklian, Jason (2017) The Dark Side of New Business. *Harvard International Review*, 38(4): 66–72.

Miklian, Jason, and Schouten, Peer. (2013). Fluid Markets. *Foreign Policy*, 202: 71–75, JSTOR. Retrieved from www.jstor.org/stable/24576059.

Miklian, J., and Schouten, P. (2014). *Business For Peace: The New Paradigm of International Peacebuilding and Development*, December 14. Oslo. Retrieved from http://dx.doi.org/10.2139/ssrn.2538113

Miklian, J., Schouten, P. and Ganson, B. (2016). From Boardrooms to Battlefields: 5 New Ways that Businesses Claim to Build Peace. *Harvard International Review*, June 10. Retrieved from http://hir.harvard.edu/13494-2/

Mill, J. S. (1848). *Principles of Political Economy*. London: Hacke.

Miller, B., (2003). Cechvala, S., Ganson, B. and Miklian, J. (2019). *A Seat at the Table: Capacities and Limitations of Private Sector Peacebuilding*. Cambridge, MA: CDA.

Muia, F. M. (2003). The Private Sector in Conflict Prevention and Post-conflict Reconstruction. In Date-Bah, Eugenia, *Jobs After War: A Critical Challenge in the Peace and Reconstruction Puzzle*. Geneva: ILO.

Naudé, W. (2007). *Peace, Prosperity and Pro-growth Entrepreneurship*. Discussion Paper No. 2007/02. Helsinki: WIDER. Retrieved from https://core.ac.uk/download/pdf/6379833.pdf

NDPI, Niger Delta Partnership Initiative (2014). *The Niger Delta Partnership Initiative in Review 2010–2013*. Washington, DC: NDPI.

Obenland, W. (2014). *Corporate Influence Through the G8 New Alliance for Food Security and Nutrition in Africa*. Aachen/Berlin/Bonn/New York. Retrieved from www.globalpolicy.org/images/pdfs/GPFEurope/Corporate_Influence_through_the_G8NA.pdf

Odendaal, A. (2013). *A Crucial Link: Local Peace Committees and National Peacebuilding*. Washington, DC: United States Institute of Peace.

OECD (2008). *OECD Guidelines for Multinational Enterprises*. Paris: OECD.

OECD (2012). *Evaluating Peacebuilding Activities in Settings of Conflict and Fragility – Improving Learning for Results*. Paris: OECD. Retrieved from https://mneguidelines.oecd.org/mneguidelines_rbcmatters.pdf

OECD (2013a). *Due Diligence Guidance for Responsible Supply Chains of Minerals from Conflict-affected and High-risk Areas: Second Edition*. Paris: OECD. Retrieved from www.oecd.org/corporate/mne/GuidanceEdition2.pdf

OECD (2013b). *OECD Working Group on Bribery Annual Report 2013*. Paris: OECD. Retrieved from www.oecd.org/daf/anti-bribery/AntiBriberyAnnRep2012.pdf

OECD (2014). *Towards Open and Transparent Policies for International Investment*. Paris: OECD. Retrieved from www.oecd.org/daf/inv/investment-policy/Freedom-of-investment-info-sheet.pdf

OECD (2015). *Mineral Supply Chains and Conflict Links in Eastern Democratic Republic of Congo: Five Years of Implementing Supply Chain Due Diligence*. Paris: OECD. Retrieved from http s://mneguidelines.oecd.org/Mineral-Supply-Chains-DRC-Due-Diligence-Report.pdf

Oetzel, J., Westermann-Behaylo, M., Koerber, C., Fort, T. L., and Rivera, J. (2010). Business and Peace: Sketching the Terrain. *Journal of Business Ethics* 89:Supp. 4, 351–373. http://doi.org/10.1007/s10551-010-0411-7

OHCHR (2008). *Protect, Respect and Remedy: A Framework for Business and Human Rights*. Document no. A/HRC/8/5, April 7.

OHCHR (2011). *Guiding Principles on Business and Human Rights*. Retrieved from www. ohchr.org/Documents/Publications/GuidingPrinciplesBusinessHR_EN.pdf

Perlmutter, H. V. (1969). The Tortuous Evolution of the Multinational Corporation. *Columbia Journal of World Business* 4:1, 9–18.

Provost, C., Ford, L. and Tran, M. (2014). G8 Alliance Condemned as New Wave of Colonialism in Africa. *Guardian* (February 18).

Rettberg, A. (2013). Peace is Better Business, and Business Makes Better Peace: The Role of the Private Sector in Colombian Peace Processes. *GIGA Working Papers No. 240* (November 1). http://dx.doi.org/10.2139/ssrn.2356238

Rettberg, A. (2016). Need, Creed, and Greed: Understanding Why Business Leaders Focus on Issues of Peace. *Business Horizons* 59:5, 481–492. http://dx.doi.org/10.1016/j.bushor. 2016.03.012

Richards, P. and Chauveau, J. P. (2007). *Land, Agricultural Change and Conflict in West Africa: Regional Issues from Sierra Leone, Liberia and Côte d'Ivoire*. Paris: OECD.

Saner, R., Yiu, L. and Søndergaard, M. (2000). Business Diplomacy Management: A Core Competency for Global Companies. *Academy of Management Executive* 14:1, 80–92.

SEEP. (2007). Market Development in Crisis-Affected Environments: Emerging Lessons for Achieving Pro-Poor Economic Reconstruction. Washington DC: SEEP Network. Retrieved from: www.meda.org/resources/publications/technical/misc/58-market-deve lopment-in-crisis-affected-environments-emerging-lessons-for-achieving-pro-poor-econom ic-reconstruction/file

Shankleman, Jill. (2007). *Oil Profits and Peace: Does Business have a Role in Peacemaking?* Washington, DC: United States Institute of Peace.

Shoji, M. (2012). The United Nations Global Compact and Peace. *The Keiai Journal of International Studies*, 25, February 2012, 135–159.

Spilsbury, J., and Byrne, K. G. (2007). *Value Chain Activities for Conflict-affected Populations in Guinea*. Washington, DC. Retrieved from https://www.microlinks.org/sites/microlinks/ files/resource/files/mR90.pdf

Stabilization Unit. (2008a). Stabilisation through Economic Initiatives and Private Sector Development (PSD). Draft April. London: UK Cabinet Office Stabilization Unit.

Stewart, F. (2000). *Crisis Prevention: Tackling Horizontal Inequalities*. Oxford: Queen Elizabeth House.

Stewart, F. (2008). *Horizontal Inequalities and Conflict: Understanding Group Violence in Multi-ethnic Societies*. Basingstoke: Palgrave Macmillan.

Stupples, D. (2015). To Defeat Islamic State We Must Sever Its Oil Lifeline – Here's How. *The Conversation*, December 3. Retrieved from https://theconversation.com/to-defea t-islamic-state-we-must-sever-its-oil-lifeline-heres-how-51751

Tenney, S., and Salda, A.C. (2014). *Historical Dictionary of the World Bank*. Lanham, MD: The Scarecrow Press.

TRC (1998). Institutional Hearing: Business and Labour. In *Truth and Reconciliation Commission of South Africa Report* 4:2: 18–58. Retrieved from: http://www.justice.gov.za/trc/ report/finalreport/Volume%204.pdf

Tully, S. (2005). *International Documents on Corporate Responsibility*. Northampton, MA: Edward Elgar.

UN (2012). *Guidance for Effective Mediation*. New York: UN.

UNDPA and UNEP (2015). *Natural Resources and Conflict: A Guidance for Mediation Practitioners*. New York and Nairobi: UNDPA and UNEP.

USAID (2007) Poverty Reduction in Conflict and Fragile States: Perspectives from the Household Level, Summary of Proceedings from a Conference HeldNovember 8–9, 2006. Washington DC: U.S. Agency for International Development.

USAID (2009) *A Guide to Economic Growth in Post-Conflict Countries*. Washington DC: USAID.

UNGC (2013a). *Responsible Business Advancing Peace: Examples from Companies, Investors and Global Compact Local Networks*. New York: UNGC.

UNGC (2013b). *Leaders' Summit 2013: Architects of a Better World*. New York: UNGC.

UN Global Compact (2015). *Business for Peace*. New York: UNGC.

UNGC and PRI (2010). *Guidance on Responsible Business in Conflict-affected and High-risk Areas: A Resource for Companies and Investors*. New York: UN Global Compact and PRI.

Voluntary Principles. (2000). *The Voluntary Principles on Security and Human Rights*. Retrieved from www.voluntaryprinciples.org/files/voluntary_principles_english.pdf

Wennmann, A. (2011). The Role of Business in Armed Violence Reduction and Prevention. *International Review of the Red Cross* 94:887, 919–940.

Woodrow, P., and Chigas, D. (2009). *A Distinction with a Difference: Conflict Sensitivity and Peacebuilding. Reflecting on Peace Practice Project*. Cambridge, MA. Retrieved from http://scholar.google.com/scholar?hl=en&btnG=Search&q=intitle:A+Distinction+with+a+Difference+:+Conflict+Sensitivity+and+Peacebuilding#1

World Bank. (2011). *World Development Report 2011: Conflict, security, and development*. Washington, DC: World Bank. http://doi.org/10.1596/978-0-8213-8500-5

Zandvliet, L., and Anderson, M. B. (2009). *Getting it Right: Making Corporate Community Relations Work*. Sheffield: Greenleaf.

2

BUSINESS, PEACE, AND HUMAN RIGHTS

A political responsibility perspective

Florian Wettstein and Judith Schrempf-Stirling

Introduction

Human rights have not commonly been associated with business conduct. Rather they have been perceived as relevant only in connection with governments. As a result, not even the well-established discussions on corporate social responsibility (CSR) or corporate sustainability and the like have commonly referred to human rights in a systematic manner. Similar things can be said about peace. Establishing and maintaining peace has generally been perceived as the task of governments and international organizations, rather than as a responsibility of business. However, in both areas, recent years have heralded increasing awareness of the profound impacts that corporations can have on both human rights and peace, respectively. The two fields that emerged from this heightened awareness, BHR on the one hand and business and peace on the other, are closely related and overlapping. However, they have emerged as separate discussions linked to their own respective academic and practical communities. Despite this separation, or perhaps precisely because of it, it seems important that both discussions take note of the respective other. Based on this, the contribution at hand attempts to introduce the BHR discussion to a business and peace audience and to outline some themes and research areas of common interest. Rather than putting the emphasis on the legal aspects of BHR, which are dominating the field, we will adopt a corporate responsibility lens on the subject. This strikes us as most promising not least in regard to identifying common themes and perspectives between BHR and business and peace.

After this brief introduction, we will provide an overview of the BHR field in the second section. The third section will engage with the nature of the corporation and how it relates to corporate human rights responsibility. Here in particular, we will not engage with legal foundations. At the center of our elaborations is the social and political nature of the corporation as an institution, instead. In this vein, corporate human rights responsibility will be conceptualized as essentially a political responsibility of companies. In the fourth section, we will pick up on some select alternative themes, which derive from such a foundational perspective on corporate human rights responsibility as political responsibility. These themes may not 'make the headlines' in current BHR discussions, but strike us as important nevertheless, not least with a view on possible intersections with the business and peace discussion. The intersection with the business and peace discussion will then be explored more deeply in section five, again by applying a perspective of human rights responsibility as political responsibility. From that perspective, we will outline two themes, which emerge from our own scholarship and which strike us as promising research avenues for a closer integration of BHR and business and peace.

Business and human rights: overview

Despite BHR being closely related to the more general and much older discussion on CSR, the two are not the same, nor did BHR emerge as a logical extension or specification of CSR. Rather, BHR as an academic discussion and field emerged from legal studies, particularly those focusing on international law (Ramasastry 2015). Thus, granted that BHR has turned into an interdisciplinary research field in recent years (Schrempf-Stirling and Van Buren 2017; Santoro 2015; Wettstein 2012a), its main focus and thus its trajectory is still heavily dominated by legal perspectives on the issue. Non-legal perspectives, as a result, make up for a much smaller part of the discussion. The main disciplinary 'homes' of such non-legal perspectives are business ethics (Wettstein 2009; Arnold 2010; Cragg 2000), management studies and CSR (Preuss and Brown 2012; Giuliani and Macchi 2014; Obara 2017), as well as international relations and political science (Kobrin 2009; Karp 2014).

The academic debate on BHR traces BHR as a movement. The BHR movement is commonly perceived to have started in the mid-1990s in the context of Western oil companies – most prominent among them, Shell – getting tangled up with human rights violations committed by the Nigerian Abacha government against the Ogoni population in the Niger Delta, or large multinational sporting goods brands such as Nike being confronted with allegations of sweatshop and child labor in their factories overseas. Human rights issues in connection with business were raised before, for example, when Western businesses were called upon to resist and divest from apartheid South Africa. Some academic writers picked up on such issues and started to engage conceptually with the intersection between corporations and human rights, both from legal (Clapham 1993) and non-legal (Donaldson 1989) perspectives. However, a broader, more systematic discussion on the conceptual link between business and human rights did not emerge before mid- to late-1990s (Ramasastry 2015; Cragg, Arnold and Muchlinski 2012). Before the mid-1990s, the BHR debate in academia was "sporadic and fragmented" (Wettstein 2012a: 746) with several important, but isolated publications in the 1970s and 1980s (Munchus 1989; Post 1985; Werhane 1985). At the end of the 1980s, Donaldson (1989) published his seminal work *Ethics of International Business* which has put human rights as a foundational element for corporate conduct. It is thus regarded as one of the first milestones in the BHR debate.

While the initial BHR movement of the late 1990s was characterized by NGO investigations and activism, there was a push for institutionalization particularly at the UN level around the turn of the millennium. Two initiatives were of particular significance around that time. First, the UN Global Compact, a non-binding soft-law initiative, which was launched in the year 2000, was the first major international standard for responsible business that put human rights concerns center stage. Doing so, it not only helped advance policy and academic discussions on BHR more generally, but started to raise awareness about and develop best practices on human rights issues among thousands of signatory companies. At the same time the UN sub-commission on human rights launched an attempt to draft a legally binding framework for corporate human rights obligations. While the resulting UN Draft Norms were eventually dropped by the UN commission on human rights in 2004, the controversial discussions ensuing around the process led to the creation of the mandate of a UN special representative for business and human rights (SRSG) in 2005, for which Harvard professor John Ruggie was appointed. John Ruggie's mandate led him to publish two reports of overarching significance for the BHR movement. In his first major report, which is now known as the "UN protect, respect and remedy framework" (UN Framework) (Ruggie 2008), Ruggie outlined in broad terms the distribution of human rights responsibility between states and corporations along three pillars of human rights responsibility. While governments have a binding international-law-based duty to protect human rights, corporations ought to 'merely' respect, that is not violate, human rights. The corporate responsibility to respect human rights is one grounded in social expectations and thus not based on or meant to create new legal norms. Both states and corporations have certain responsibilities to remedy human rights as a part of their respective duty to protect or responsibility to respect. In his second major report, now known as the "UN Guiding Principles on Business and Human Rights" (UNGPs) (Ruggie 2011), Ruggie operationalized the UN Framework by outlining a number of specific guiding principles for each pillar of responsibility, establishing human rights due diligence as the main instrument to ensure corporate human rights respect.

After John Ruggie stepped down in 2011, a UN working group, consisting of five experts in the BHR field was tasked with advancing the dissemination and implementation process of the UNGPs. Many governments have since taken first steps toward the implementation of the UNGPs, namely by committing to National Action Plans on business and human rights, which have put the topic firmly on the national policy agendas. Most recently, the UN Human Rights Council has passed a petition by the governments of Ecuador and South Africa to start new negotiations for a binding treaty on business and human rights. Those negotiations started in 2015 with the creation of an open-ended working group and are ongoing.

What is characteristic and perhaps unique for the BHR field is that the lines between BHR as a movement and as an academic discussion frequently blur. While the academic discussion has followed closely the developments outlined above, it has, at the same time, always taken an active role in shaping it as well. More than in other fields perhaps, the boundaries between academic, civil-society and other non-academic domains in the BHR space are fluid with many actors moving seamlessly between these domains. Consistent with this view, the early, predominantly law-driven debate on BHR during the late 1990s and early 2000s was preoccupied with making the case for why there may be a problem to be addressed at the intersection of human rights and corporate conduct in the first place (Muchlinski 2001). That is, the discussion centered on exploring the possible legal grounds to include non-state actors more generally (Clapham 2006) and corporations more specifically (Frey 1997, Ratner 2001) as human rights duty-bearers alongside governments, on the shape and nature of corporate complicity (Clapham and Jerbi 2001) and on possible grounds for litigation in such cases of complicity (Zerk 2006; Joseph 2004). Thus, one can argue that the BHR movement developed out of a crisis with rising cases of corporate complicity in human rights violations (Ramasastry 2015) and a quest for remedying harm. In that sense, the BHR movement applied originally a backward-looking perspective and has had a negative connotation which is reflected in the description or the definition of the BHR debate in some academic scholarship.

The basic idea of corporate human rights responsibility may have come more natural to non-legal scholars doing research in fields related to responsible business. So natural perhaps, that truly foundational discussions on the grounds of corporate human rights responsibility, focused perhaps less on the grounds of such responsibilities (examples here are Donaldson 1989; Wettstein 2009; Cragg 2000), rather than on their extent (Santoro 2000, 2009; Arnold 2010; Wettstein 2012a).

The academic discussion exploded after the publication of the UNGPs both in terms of sheer quantity, as well as of disciplinary breadth (Schrempf-Stirling and Van Buren 2017). A whole body of literature on the UNGPs themselves developed, taking both critical (Deva and Bilchitz 2013; Wettstein 2015) as well as affirmative (Buhmann 2013; Jägers 2013) positions; others focused on specific aspects of the UNGPs such as human rights due diligence (Fasterling 2017; Fasterling and Demuijnck 2013), or on corporate remedy and grievance mechanisms (Thompson 2017). Yet another discussion has engaged in comparisons of the evolving BHR field to existing discussions on CSR (McCorquodale 2009; Wettstein 2012b; Ramasastry 2015). The treaty negotiations in the UN Human Rights Council have led to a stream of research both on the justification, and shape of a BHR treaty (Bilchitz 2016, De Schutter 2016, Deva and Bilchitz 2017) as well as on the role of regional and international human rights courts (Londoño-Lázaro, Thoene and Pereira-Villa 2017). Most recently, empirical research on BHR has blossomed, addressing corporations' human rights impacts on developing countries (Giuliani and Macchi 2014), the quality of their human rights due diligence processes (McCorquodale 2017), the content of their human rights policies (Preuss and Brown 2012), their responses to lawsuits in human rights litigation cases (Schrempf-Stirling and Wettstein 2017), or their sense-making in regard to human rights more generally (Obara 2017).

Corporate human rights responsibility and the nature of the corporation

As the above overview showed, BHR scholars were engaged in foundational research particularly in the formative years of the discussion. Legal scholars were looking for a legal basis from which to derive corporate human rights responsibility, both at the level of international as well as domestic law. Non-legal scholars, on the other hand, were mostly engaged in deliberating the moral and ethical foundations of such responsibilities. John Ruggie, as mentioned above, proposed a third way and grounded corporate human rights in social expectations.

Thus, both legal and non-legal BHR scholars have used human rights as the starting point of their thinking. While legal scholars derived such obligations from human rights law, non-legal scholars predominantly referred to the moral nature and foundation of human rights. Business ethics scholars, for example, have focused on ethical argumentation based on Kantian ethics (Luke 1998), Confucian ethics (Kim 2014), and social justice (Bishop 2008) to argue why business has human rights obligations. However, what few of them have done, is to connect their thinking on human rights with a foundational account of *corporations*. The nature of corporations, as the second dominant focus in the 'business and human rights' equation, has largely remained unaddressed and it remains a black-box in the BHR discussion to this day. For example, the UN Guiding Principles give little thought to the nature of the corporation and its potential implications for the derivation of respective human rights responsibilities. Instead, they build on a rather conventional, at its core, almost neoclassical view of the corporation. Corporations, in Ruggie's view, are "economic actors" with "unique responsibilities," and "while they may be 'organs of society'," they are "specialized economic organs, not democratic public interest institutions." Based on this account of corporations as specifically and uniquely economic actors, Ruggie set out to assess "the distinctive responsibilities of companies in relation to human rights" (Ruggie 2008: 16). It is not surprising that Ruggie framed the respective corporate human rights responsibilities narrowly as a merely negative duty not to violate human rights, or more generally, not to do harm. Anything beyond such a narrow account would have been difficult to reconcile with the economic paradigm guiding his view on the corporation. Similarly, unsurprising is the instrumental grounding on which he bases this responsibility. Rather than providing a moral foundation, Ruggie advances an instrumental argument based on a corporation's reputational risk and its social license to operate for why they should respect human rights. This too, is consistent with a narrow economic understanding of corporations, but appears misguided and incomplete, once we broaden our view beyond the economic dimension of companies.

Business ethics, CSR, and management scholarship have long traditions of advocating for such broader views on the corporation. In 1961 already, Dow Votaw pointed explicitly to the need to understand companies in broader than merely economic terms: "Only if we have a thorough familiarity with the corporation as a political institution, as well as an economic and social one, can we hope even to recognize the effects that it has had and will have on the rest of society." (Votaw 1961: 106).

Votaw's statement proved visionary. His insight that corporations are not only and not even predominantly economic, but inherently social institutions at their core, provided, together with other important works (Bowen 1953; Davis 1960; Frederick 1960; Carroll 1977) the foundation on which today's CSR field, including various sub-streams on corporate philanthropy, sustainability, or corporate citizenship, is built and on which it has been able to challenge mainstream management paradigms at their core. But for the purpose of this chapter perhaps even more important is his view on corporations not as social, but as *political* institutions. It would take another 45 years until a solid research tradition on this premise would emerge and it is from this tradition that the BHR field may have most to gain, particularly with regard to the framing of respective corporate human rights responsibility. Under the label 'political CSR' this sub-discussion of the broader CSR field has systematically analyzed corporations as political actors particularly in (global) environments of weak and incomplete governance (Matten and Crane 2005). Thus, a major focus of political CSR is corporations' deep involvement in today's global governance mechanisms, which calls not least for a stronger corporate engagement in public deliberation processes, their contribution to solving some of our pressing global problems, and more generally, for their active participation in new democratic will-formation processes (Scherer and Palazzo 2007). Thus, it postulates a view of corporations that stands in sharp contrast precisely to the above-stated view of corporations as private economic actors as opposed to democratic public interest institutions.

Granted that political CSR has not engaged explicitly with BHR, but the conceptualization of corporations opens an alternative path to ground and frame corporate human rights obligations. As political actors, corporations have political responsibilities. Political responsibility, according to the philosopher Iris Marion Young (2004, 2006, 2011), contrast with a more conventional understanding of responsibility as liability. Such conventional understandings are backward-looking and hold that agents are responsible for what they have caused or causally contributed to. Young argues that such liability-based accounts of responsibility are of limited use under structural conditions, that is, in societies, in which more and more harm is being produced through the complex, structural interplay of collective actions, rather than through direct, relational wrong doing. Under such conditions, causality is losing significance as a determinant of a particular agent's responsibility while social connection is gaining significance. Agents are socially connected to specific harms through structural processes, in which they take part. Political responsibility, according to Young, is thus the responsibility to transform such processes and make them more just for those to whose disadvantage the structures are working. Thus, political responsibility is essentially structural responsibility. Such responsibility, according to Young, is a function of four parameters: power (to change structures); benefit (from structural processes); collective ability (as a quintessential political ability) and interest (in changing structures). Hence, corporate human rights responsibility, understood through the lens of Youngean political responsibility, aims perhaps less at direct corporate wrongdoing and complicity (though this is a part of it as well) and more at the underlying structural processes that lead to large-scale human rights problems and the role that companies play in upholding such processes as well as the role they could play in improving them. A political responsibility lens for BHR obligations, thereby, provides the foundation for more expansive and positive corporate human rights obligations instead of the negative corporate human rights responsibilities advanced in the UNGPs.

In sum, this alternative perspective is not meant to dismiss the importance of a perspective on complicity and liability in the context of corporate human rights violations. To the contrary, such aspects are of overarching importance and legal scholars have rightly put emphasis on exploring them in detail. However, in addition to such legalistic views on BHR, a political CSR perspective on BHR can shed light on underlying structural processes and the respective political responsibilities of companies to shape and transform them. This will inevitably move the nature and form of the company to the center of the BHR discussion again and it will bring back conversations, e.g. on corporate power (Wettstein 2009), on the purpose and function of the corporation more generally, or on their historic legacy (Schrempf-Stirling, Palazzo and Phillips 2016), which have moved to the background in the recent, more 'applied' scholarship on UNGP implementation. In the following section, we will expand on three such under-researched areas in the BHR discussion.

Business and human rights: current themes and alternative perspectives

In the previous section we proposed an alternative to the backward-looking perspective with a focus on corporate wrongdoing, complicity, and liability. Our 'alternative' perspective on BHR is rooted in political CSR and management scholarship, which can complement the dominant legal perspective in the BHR field. In the following, we will briefly outline three research areas, which are connected to such a perspective and which are commonly not in the spotlight of current BHR scholarship.

Human rights and corporate power: corporate power has not played a significant role in academic discussions on BHR. This may come as a surprise to some, given the intimate link between human rights and governmental power in traditional human rights studies. However, in the 'mainstream' debate on BHR, the view on corporate power as a parameter of corporate human rights responsibility has, with some exceptions (Wettstein 2009; Wood 2012) fallen through the cracks, while the legal debate has adopted a liability perspective on BHR for which causality and contribution of an agent to a particular human rights harm is more decisive than its power and influence, ethical accounts have argued that as moral rights, human rights obligate not merely powerful governments, but all actors with potentially negative impacts on human rights. Thus, from both perspectives, a systematic inquiry into the nature and shape of corporate power seemed unnecessary. As a result, the dominant view within the BHR debate, both legal and non-legal, has adopted a limited view on corporate human rights responsibility as outlined in the UNGPs. According to this account, corporations merely have a responsibility not to violate human rights. However, such a responsibility not to do harm is neither specific to corporations nor to human rights. It is a basic moral responsibility of general nature and thus holds per se for everyone and at all times (Hsieh and Wettstein 2014). Against this background, Hsieh has argued that we ought to base our thinking on BHR, not on a moral, but on an institutional understanding of human rights. However, in such an institutional account, as he argues, power and authority are preconditions for human rights responsibility to be assigned to a specific agent. Two research issues emanate from this insight: first, do corporations indeed operate in such positions of authority? And second, what would this imply for the nature and extent of their human rights responsibility? Interestingly, John Ruggie (2017) himself has addressed the first question in one of his most recent publications. In his publication, Ruggie argues that multinational corporations in particular operate in positions of relational, structural, and discursive power and often exert a great deal of authority over their vast production networks. This insight is not new. The vast structural power of multinationals in particular has been pointed out before and connected to quasi-governmental, de facto authority (Wettstein 2009). What is new and promising, is that Ruggie's publication may kick-start a much-needed discussion on corporate power in the BHR mainstream. However, once corporate power is back on the BHR research agenda, so may be the renegotiation of corporate human rights responsibility. Power, as we saw above, is precisely one of the determinants of the Youngean account of political responsibility, which aims not at the avoidance of relational harm, but at the improvement of unjust structures. Thus, it opens a view to understand corporate human rights responsibility as a political and structural responsibility, which reaches far beyond a general responsibility to respect human rights into the domains also of protecting and realizing human rights (Wettstein 2009, 2012a).

Human rights and political CSR: As mentioned earlier in this text, human rights have not played a particularly prominent role in conventional thinking on CSR. This may not be a coincidence. On the one hand, the state-centrism that has been guiding the conventional human rights discourse has likely shaped the perception of CSR scholars on human rights and thus moved them beyond their immediate interest or focus. Furthermore, the strong association of CSR as a voluntary and inherently private responsibility of businesses (Carroll 1999; Waddock and Smith 2000) clashes with the common view of human rights as a public concern and as correlating with obligations. Thus, the very nature of human rights and human rights obligations does not sit well with the idea of CSR as an inherently voluntary affair. However, as pointed out above, the more recent discussion on political CSR may serve as a linchpin between the two fields. While we showed above that political CSR, with its focus on transnational spaces and the governance challenges they raise, and on corporations as political actors and their respective political responsibilities, offers promising links to the BHR discussion, the commensurability and the role of a human rights perspective within and for political CSR is yet to be explored. Indeed, a latent relativism and thus an implicit rejection of universal ideas like human rights has often been alleged at least for some of the more prominent accounts of political CSR. At the same time, a BHR perspective can balance out some of the perceived marginalization of government in political CSR. Granted, the BHR debate examines the role of business in human rights violations, but it equally addresses the importance of a state apparatus and government in protecting human rights and providing remedy. While global governance challenges exist and business has political responsibilities, the state also still has an important role to play (Schrempf-Stirling 2016).

Human rights governance: The quest for corporate accountability has always been at the center of the BHR field. This is reflected both in the BHR movement, in which attempts to install legally binding approaches to corporate human rights responsibility has been a recurring feature since the very beginning, as well as in the academic debate that has been dominated by legal scholarship, which is generally sympathetic to such approaches as well. This focus on hard laws and regulation stands in sharp contrast to the predominantly non-legal debates on CSR, which have commonly put their emphasis squarely on voluntary, self-regulatory approaches and spent little time reflecting on legal frameworks. Thus, the difference between CSR and BHR, as discussed above, is reflected also in the kind of policy that is proposed to advance and support the movements. In the political debates on such policy, soft- and hard-law approaches are often played off against each other for tactical reasons. Opponents of hard regulation point to the successes of soft-law and self-regulatory approaches as a more accepted and more successful alternative to legally binding measures, while proponents argue that such approaches lack effectiveness altogether unless they are backed by legal enforcement mechanisms. In contrast to such 'contrarian' views on hard and soft-law, the UNGPs propagate a smart mix of the two, seeing them not as mutually exclusive alternatives, but as complementary mechanisms, both of which having their rightful place within a holistic accountability regime. However, a closer analysis of the emerging accountability regime in the BHR space suggests that we may have to rethink the very distinction and dichotomy between soft- and hard-law entirely, and with it the standard approaches to holding corporations accountable for their human rights impacts. In certain contexts and situations, the interplay – the smart mix – between the two mechanisms transforms their very mode of operation, thus blurring the very typology of hard- and soft-law. Thus, we are dealing with a co-evolution of the two mechanisms, which we can characterize as a hardening of soft-law on the one hand and as a softening of hard law on the other. Several mechanisms can be mentioned as examples of the hardening of soft-law. For example, a number of countries have recently implemented mandatory due diligence laws, which render parts of the UNGPs mandatory at the domestic level. Thus, the implementation of such complementary laws transform the very mechanism of the UNGPs, which are designed as a soft-law initiative, but are turning into hard norms through the process of domestic regulation. Another example is the integration of human rights due diligence in supplier contracts. Turning due diligence into a contractual obligation essentially means hardening the UNGPs within a specific supplier relationship. Here too, the very mode of operation of the UNGPs changes within that relationship. Finally, the UNGPs will likely be used increasingly as interpretative tools for legislation in the BHR space. Doing so, their soft mechanism indirectly finds its way into hard law provisions. However, there are reverse processes of softening hard law as well. For example, as we showed in a recent study (Schrempf-Stirling and Wettstein 2017), 20 years of case history in human rights litigation against parent companies of foreign subsidiaries have not led to a single guilty verdict in court. Only a handful of cases were settled out of court and the vast majority was thrown out at the outset. However, what we noticed is that in almost all of those cases, the companies under investigation started reporting on human rights, offering human rights training to their employees, or signing up to soft-law initiatives during the time of the trial or shortly thereafter. Thus, while the legal process did not lead to a 'hard' outcome, it did prompt the companies to up their voluntary measures to ensure human rights respect. Thus, the hard law approach has not been useless, as some may conclude prematurely, but rather it has been softening in the litigation process.

A BHR perspective on business and peace

BHR and business and peace are closely aligned; while they are not the same, there is considerable overlap between them. Conflicts of all nature affect human rights in various ways; furthermore, where human rights are protected, the propensity of conflict is reduced. Two conclusions derive from this insight for BHR: first, when businesses operate in contexts of conflict, the probability of getting drawn into human rights violations increases dramatically; in such contexts, companies are at risk of becoming complicit in conflict-related human rights violations and thus obstructions to peace. Second, when businesses go beyond merely not harming human rights and instead engage in the pro-active protection and realization, they have the possibility to become a progressive force for peace in such conflict-ridden contexts.

The UNGPs with their framing of corporate human rights responsibility as 'do no harm' have put emphasis on the first of these two interpretations. In fact, contexts of conflict are one area on which the UNGPs put special emphasis and propose special measures particularly for host governments. Governments are called on to put forth "special policy innovations ... to prevent corporate abuse" and to "promote conflict-sensitive practices in their business sectors" (Ruggie 2008: 13–14). The UNGPs call on home states to engage at the earliest possible stage with enterprises in conflict areas, to provide adequate assistance to them in identifying and addressing the heightened risk emanating from conflict, and to deny public support and services for businesses involved in abuse, and unwilling to cooperate (Ruggie 2011: 10) Both governments and businesses are called on "to pay particular attention to the risk of sexual and gender-based violence, which is especially prevalent during times of conflict" (Ruggie 2011: 11). According to the UNGPs, companies ought to respect human rights by engaging in a process of human rights due diligence. As a risk-based process, human rights due diligence prompts companies to address contexts of heightened risk with higher priority. Thus, contexts of conflict necessarily are one of the main human rights due diligence foci of businesses and may trigger enhanced due diligence processes. One of the reasons for why conflict-related human rights impacts are of particular significance for business is the risk to face escalating human rights risks when companies' activities are linked to violence (Graf and Iff 2017:115). In order to address this 'conflict spiral', Graf and Iff (2017) advocate for the integration of 'conflict sensitivity' into standard human rights due diligence processes. While both processes focus on the avoidance of negative impacts, conflict sensitivity does not use human rights impacts as a reference frame, but negative impacts on conflict (Graf and Iff 2017: 120). As such, integrating conflict sensitivity into human rights due diligence can add an early warning dimension, which catches potential conflict-related risks before they may appear on the radar as actual human rights risks. The likelihood of escalation can thus be reduced. However, as Graf and Iff (2017: 121) point out, conflict sensitivity also includes a dimension of promoting positive impacts: "conflict sensitivity in turn is very explicitly not limited to doing no harm, but also strives for capitalizing on potentials to foster peace and social cohesion."

This last insight seems consistent also with our perspective on human rights responsibility as political responsibility as we have developed it in the previous sections. Such a perspective suggests a more expansive view on the role of corporations in regard to conflict and peace, that is, a role that cannot be captured by a perspective that is limited to due diligence. Thus, against the background of our own scholarship on business and human rights, we see two fields of investigation at the intersection of such more expansive political interpretation of human rights responsibility and the business and peace discussion, one backward-looking and one forward-looking.

Looking back – historic CSR in the context of business and peace: "Time will tell" is a popular adage that alludes to the situation that information on past incidences often emerge over time and the full truth may be known years after the incidence or perhaps never at all. This holds also for human rights violations and perhaps in particular for such violations taking place in contexts of conflict, which are often characterized by their complexity, murkiness, precarious information flows, and distortions by propaganda and misinformation campaigns. However, as knowledge about conflicts and the atrocities they can lead to emerges and increases over time, so does the awareness of corporate involvement in past conflict-related human rights violations. This raises the question of such corporations' responsibility for historic human rights violations and how they ought to deal with such involvements of previous generations of managers in the present. The legitimacy of claims against companies for past (human rights) harm can be seen as a function of the past institutional pressure to conform, their knowledge on the impact and wrongfulness of their actions at the time they occurred, the magnitude and durability of the harm, the receptivity regarding the past incidence and the respective allegations within the current context, the history and reputation of both the accused and the accuser, and the plausibility of the narrative underpinning the accusation. For harm that occurred in conflict situations, some of these elements may be of particular relevance. For example, there may be stronger institutional pressure on corporations to conform with and participate in harmful activity, which reduces their room to maneuver and mitigates responsibility. On the other hand, past harms produced in contexts of conflict are often not incidental, but ongoing, systematic and egregious, which increases the legitimacy of the claim to hold corporations accountable in the present. The receptivity of claims against companies for past harm may generally be larger if such harm occurred in the context of ongoing and severe conflict, rather than as isolated incidents – the same goes for the plausibility of the narrative supporting the allegations. A political view on corporate responsibility would suggest that a company engages pro-actively with legitimate allegations (Schrempf-Stirling, Palazzo and Phillips 2016: 710). Rather than merely managing the claims, pro-active engagement includes positive steps toward reconciliation and remedial of past harm. Such pro-active engagement then can contribute to the healing of the ongoing trauma that often characterizes post-conflict environments even decades after the harm originally occurred.

Looking forward – silent complicity and human rights advocacy: Contexts of conflict may increase the risk not only of companies becoming actively complicit in human rights abuses, e.g. by financing armed groups, but also of becoming passively linked to them by benefitting from them or merely silently standing by while events unfold within a company's sphere of influence. The UNGPs and most other international BHR initiatives and standards recognize explicitly that silence and benefit can amount to actual complicity under certain circumstances. Silent complicity, as it is commonly defined,

> suggests that a non-participant is aware of abusive action and, although possessing some degree of ability to act, chooses neither to help protect nor to assist victims of the abuse, remaining content to meet the minimal ethical requirement to do no (direct) harm.
>
> *(Kline 2005: 79)*

Not any organization's silence in the face of human rights violations amounts to silent complicity. For this to be the case, the organization needs to be in a position to mitigate or stop the abuse. What grounds the accusation of silent complicity is thus not silence per se, but the moral encouragement or support that derives from silence if it emanates from someone in a position to act. Through silent complicity, corporations contribute to the structural conditions under which human rights occur. Thus, silent complicity connects business to harm and from this connection derives a political responsibility to act. The risk of ongoing and systematic violations taking place in the vicinity of a company and thus of the company being perceived as partial and lending its support to the perpetrator is perhaps most acute in contexts and situations of conflict. If silence can turn into complicity, then what is required from a company under such circumstances is that it intervenes. The very

idea of silent complicity illustrates the implicit assumption that under certain circumstances companies may have a duty to protect human rights, which reaches
substantially beyond mere non-violation. Such contexts, and among them contexts
of conflict in particular, can politicize the silence of powerful companies: in order
to meet their responsibility to protect human rights, companies in such situations
must use their power and speak out with a view of mitigating or stopping the
abuse, that is, they have to engage in actual human rights advocacy. Corporate
human rights advocacy is one manifestation in which a Youngean understanding of
political responsibility as essentially communicative responsibility is linked with a
concern for human rights. Four criteria characterize legitimate corporate human
rights advocacy (Wettstein 2012b). First, a corporate duty to speak out and advocate for human rights should be limited to severe, ongoing, and systematic instances
of human rights abuse. It is this criterion that makes this political responsibility
particularly relevant for contexts of conflict, in which the nature of human rights
violations meets these characteristics perhaps most often. Second, corporations
should speak out in response to the concerns of the global public and of those
whose rights are being violated. That is, their decision to speak out should be
backed by broad support. In other words, there should be a more general public
view that speaking out is the appropriate response by the company. Third, companies in such situations should not act alone, but in collaboration with other
institutions. Such institutions include other companies in the same situation, which
will help them build and increase leverage, and civil society organizations, which
will help them build legitimacy for their claim. Fourth, there is no political
responsibility without public accountability. Thus, companies should be transparent
and public about their advocacy, rather than merely engage in quiet diplomacy
behind closed doors.

Conclusion

This contribution aimed at taking a first step toward bringing the two debates on
BHR and business and peace, respectively, into closer alignment. For this purpose,
we proposed to shift our attention to the foundation of the corporation in the BHR
debate and advanced an understanding of the corporation as a political institution
with political responsibilities. Such political responsibilities do not stop with doing no
harm, but include a call for businesses to engage also in the protection and realization
of human rights.

We believe joining the forces between the BHR and the business and peace
debates on these premises can be mutually reinforcing and advantageous to both
fields. Business and peace provides a view on the corporation that supports and
reinforces the political understanding outlined in this chapter. The business and
peace field has always been characterized by a balanced perspective that perceives
companies not only as a risk factor in conflicts, but equally as an institution that is
uniquely positioned to contribute in constructive ways to the elimination of conflict and the advancement of peace. BHR, on the other hand, has advanced

powerful insights on preventative and remedial tools to address corporate human rights violations, which can be of particular relevance when dealing with conflict and post-conflict contexts.

By outlining some first issues and themes of common interest and relevance, we hope that our article will prompt others to deepen and broaden the links between the two fields. Doing so, we see this chapter as a first step in working toward a valuable research agenda at the intersection of the two fields.

Bibliography

Arnold, D. G. 2010. Transnational Corporations and the Duty to Respect Basic Human Rights. *Business Ethics Quarterly* 20(3): 371–399.

Bilchitz, D. 2016. The Necessity for a Business and Human Rights Treaty. *Business and Human Rights Journal* 1(2): 203–227.

Bishop, J. D. (2008). For-profit Corporations in a Just Society: A Social Contract Argument Concerning the Rights and Responsibilities of Corporations. *Business Ethics Quarterly* 18(2): 191–212.

Bowen, Howard R. 1953. *The Social Responsibilities of the Businessman*. New York: Harper and Row.

Buhmann, K. 2013. Navigating from 'train wreck' to being 'welcomed': negotiation strategies and argumentative patterns in the development of the UN Framework. In: Deva, S. and Bilchitz, D. (Eds.), *Human Rights Obligations of Business: Beyond the Corporate Responsibility to Respect?*, 29–57. Cambridge: Cambridge University Press.

Carroll, Archie B. (ed.). 1977. *Managing Corporate Social Responsibility*. Boston, MA: Little, Brown.

Carroll, A. B. (1999). Corporate Social Responsibility: Evolution of a Definitional Construct. *Business and Society* 38(3): 268–295.

Clapham, A. 1993. *Human Rights in the Private Sphere*. Oxford: Clarendon Press.

Clapham, A. 2006. *Human Rights Obligations of Non-State Actors*. Oxford: Oxford University Press.

Clapham, A., and S. Jerbi. 2001. Categories of Corporate Complicity in Human Rights Abuses. *Hastings International and Comparative Law Review* 24: 339–350.

Cragg, W. 2000. Human Rights and Business Ethics: Fashioning a New Social Contract. *Journal of Business Ethics* 27(1, 2): 205–214.

Cragg, Wesley, Denis G. Arnold, and Peter Muchlinski. 2012. Guest Editors' Introduction: Human Rights and Business. *Business Ethics Quarterly* 22(1): 1–7.

Davis, Keith. 1960. Can Business Afford to Ignore Corporate Social Responsibilities? *California Management Review*, 2: 70–76.

De Schutter, O. 2016. Towards a New Treaty on Business and Human Rights. *Business and Human Rights Journal* 1(1): 41–67.

Deva, S. and Bilchitz, D. (Eds.). 2013. *Human Rights Obligations of Business: Beyond the Corporate Responsibility to Respect?* Cambridge: Cambridge University Press.

Deva, S. and Bilchitz, D. (Eds). 2017. *Building a Treaty on Business and Human Rights*. Cambridge: Cambridge University Press.

Donaldson, T. 1989. *The Ethics of International Business*. Oxford: Oxford University Press.

Fasterling, B. 2017. Human Rights Due Diligence as Risk Management: Social Risk Versus Human Rights Risk. *Business and Human Rights Journal* 2(2): 225–247.

Fasterling, B. and Demuijnck, G. 2013. Human Rights in the Void? Due Diligence in the UN Guiding Principles on Business and Human Rights. *Journal of Business Ethics* 116: 799–814.

Frederick, William C. 1960. The Growing Concern over Business Responsibility. *California Management Review* 2(4): 54–61.

Frey, B. A. 1997. The Legal and Ethical Responsibilities of Transnational Corporations in the Protection of International Human Rights. *Minnesota Journal of Global Trade* 6: 153–188.

Giuliani, E., and Macchi, C. 2014. Multinationals Corporations' Economic and Human Rights Impacts on Developing Countries: A Review and Research Agenda. *Cambridge Journal of Economics* 38: 479–517.

Graf, A. and Iff, A. 2017. Respecting Human Rights in Conflict Regions: How to Avoid the 'Conflict Spiral'. *Business and Human Rights Journal* 2(1): 109–133.

Hsieh, N., and Wettstein, F. 2014. Corporate Social Responsibility and Multinational Corporations. In: Moellendorf, D. and Widdows, H. (eds.), *The Routledge Handbook of Global Ethics*. Durham: Acumen.

Jägers, N. 2013. Will Transnational Private Regulation Close the Governance Gap? In: Deva, S. and Bilchitz, D. (Eds.), *Human Rights Obligations of Business: Beyond the Corporate Responsibility to Respect?*, 295–328. Cambridge: Cambridge University Press.

Joseph, S. 2004. *Corporations and Transnational Human Rights Litigation*. Portland, OR: Hart Publishing.

Karp, D. J. 2014. *Responsibility for Human Rights: Transnational Corporations in Imperfect States*. Cambridge: Cambridge University Press.

Kim, T. W. 2014. Confucian Ethics and Labor Rights. *Business Ethics Quarterly* 24(4): 565–594.

Kline, J. M. 2005. *Ethics for International Business: Decision-Making in a Global Political Economy*. London; New York: Routledge.

Kobrin, S. J. 2009. Private Political Authority and Public Responsibility: Transnational Politics, Transnational Firms and Human Rights. *Business Ethics Quarterly* 19(3): 349–374.

Londoño-Lázaro, M. C., Thoene, U. and Pereira-Villa, C. 2017. The Inter-American Court of Human Rights and Multinational Enterprises: Towards Business and Human Rights in the Americas? *The Law and Practice of International Courts and Tribunals* 16(3): 437–463.

Luke, T. 1998. The Ethics of Using Trade Policy to Evoke Change: The China–US Example. *Business Ethics: A European Review* 7(4): 231–234.

Matten, D. and Crane, A. 2005. Corporate Citizenship: Toward an Extended Theoretical Conceptualization. *Academy of Management Review* 30(1): 166–179.

McCorquodale, Robert. 2009. Corporate Social Responsibility and International Human Rights Law. *Journal of Business Ethics* 87(2): 385–400.

McCorquodale, R., L. Smit, S. Neely, and R. Brooks. 2017. Human Rights Due Diligence in Law and Practice: Good Practices and Challenges for Business Enterprises. *Business and Human Rights Journal* 2(2): 195–224.

Muchlinski, P. 2001. Human Rights And Multinationals: Is There A Problem? *International Affairs* 77(1): 31–47.

Munchus, G. 1989. Testing as a Selection Tool: Another Old and Sticky Managerial Human Rights Issue. *Journal of Business Ethics* 8(10): 817–820.

Obara, L. J. 2017. 'What Does This Mean?': How UK Companies Make Sense of Human Rights. *Business and Human Rights Journal* 2(2): 249–273.

Post, J. E. 1985. Assessing the Nestlé Boycott: Corporate Accountability and Human Rights. *California Management Review* 27(2): 113–131.

Preuss, L. and Brown, D. 2012. Business Policies on Human Rights: An Analysis of Their Content and Prevalence Among FTSE 100 Firms. *Journal of Business Ethics* 109: 289–299.

Ramasastry, A. 2015. Corporate Social Responsibility Versus Business and Human Rights: Bridging the Gap Between Responsibility and Accountability. *Journal of Human Rights* 14: 237–259.

Ratner, S. R. 2001. Corporations and Human Rights: A Theory of Legal Responsibility. *The Yale Law Journal* 111(3): 443–545.

Ruggie, J. G. 2008. *Protect Respect and Remedy. A Framework for Business and Human Rights. A/HRC/8/5.* www.reports-and-materials.org/sites/default/files/reports-and-materials/Ruggie-report-7-Apr-2008.pdf.

Ruggie, J. G. 2011. *Guiding Principles on Business and Human Rights: Implementing the United Nations "Protect, Respect and Remedy" Framework. A/HRC/17/31.* http://www.ohchr.org/Documents/Issues/Business/A-HRC-17-31_AEV.pdf.

Ruggie, J. G. 2017. Multinationals as global institution: Power, authority and relative autonomy. *Regulation and Governance.* https://doi.org/10.1111/rego.12154

Santoro, M. A. 2000. *Profits and Principles: Global Capitalism and Human Rights in China.* Ithaca, NY: Cornell University Press.

Santoro, M. A. 2009. *China 2020: How Western Business Can—and Should—Influence Social and Political Change in the Coming Decade.* Ithaca, NY: Cornell University Press.

Santoro, M. A. 2015. Business and Human Rights in Historical Perspective. *Journal of Human Rights* 14(2): 155–161.

Scherer, A. G. and Palazzo, G. 2007. Toward a Political Conception of Corporate Responsibility: Business and Society Seen from a Habermasian Perspective. *Academy of Management Review* 32(4): 1096–1120.

Schrempf-Stirling, J. 2016. State Power: Rethinking the Role of the State in Political Corporate Social Responsibility. *Journal of Business Ethics.* doi:10.1007/s10551–10016–3198–3193.

Schrempf-Stirling, J. and Van Buren, H. J. 2017. Bringing Human Rights Together with Management Studies: Themes, Opportunities, and Challenges. *Academy of Management Proceedings* 2017(1): 16791.

Schrempf-Stirling, J. and Wettstein, F. 2017. Beyond Guilty Verdicts: Human Rights Litigation and Its Impact on Corporations' Human Rights Policies. *Journal of Business Ethics* 145: 545–562.

Schrempf-Stirling, J., Palazzo, G., and Phillips, R. 2016. Historic Corporate Social Responsibility. *Academy of Management Review* 41(4): 700–719.

Thompson, B. 2017. Determining Criteria to Evaluate Outcomes of Businesses' Provision of Remedy: Applying a Human Rights-Based Approach. *Business and Human Rights Journal* 2 (1): 55–86.

Votaw, Dow. 1961. The Politics of a Changing Corporate Society. *California Management Review* 3(3): 105–118.

Waddock, S., and N. Smith. (2000). Relationships: The Real Challenge of Corporate Global Citizenship. *Business and Society Review* 105(1): 47–62.

Werhane, P. (1985). *Persons, Rights, and Corporations.* Englewood Cliffs, NJ: Prentice Hall.

Wettstein, F. 2009. *Multinational Corporations and Global Justice. Human Rights Obligations of a Quasi-Governmental Institution.* Stanford: Stanford University Press.

Wettstein, F. 2012a. CSR and the Debate on Business and Human Rights: Bridging the Great Divide. *Business Ethics Quarterly* 22(4): 739–770.

Wettstein, F. 2012b. Silence as Complicity: Elements of a Corporate Duty to Speak Out against the Violation of Human Rights. *Business Ethics Quarterly* 22(1): 37–62.

Wettstein, F. 2015. Normativity, Ethics, and the UN Guiding Principles on Business and Human Rights: A Critical Assessment. *Journal of Human Rights* 14: 162–182.

Wood, S. 2012. The Case for Leverage-Based Corporate Human Rights Responsibility. *Business Ethics Quarterly* 22(1): 63–98.

Young, I. M. 2004. Responsibility and Global Labor Justice. *Journal of Political Philosophy* 12 (4): 365–388.

Young, I. M. 2006. Responsibility and Global Justice: A Social Connection Model. *Social Philosophy and Policy* 23(1): 102–130.

Young, I. M. 2011. *Responsibility for Justice*. Oxford: Oxford University Press.

Zerk, J. A. 2006. *Multinationals and Corporate Social Responsibility. Limitations and Opportunities in International Law*. Cambridge, NY: Cambridge University Press.

3

THE MESSY BUSINESS OF PEACE AMID THE TYRANNY OF THE PROFIT MOTIVE

Complexity and culture in post-conflict contexts

Gearoid Millar

Introduction

This chapter focuses on the role businesses, and particularly multi-national corporations, might play as agents of peacebuilding in post-conflict contexts. Peacebuilding here is recognized as distinct from either peacemaking or peacekeeping. Peacemaking generally refers to efforts to bring conflicting parties together to reach agreement and end conflict, while peacekeeping refers to efforts to maintain peace between two previously conflicting parties, but primarily via their enforced separation. The focus of this chapter, peacebuilding, seeks explicitly to do more than ensure a lack of violence (negative peace) via segregation. Initially introduced by Johan Galtung, peacebuilding was conceived as the process of finding or developing "structures" to "remove the causes of war and to offer alternatives in situations in which war might occur" (1976: 111). For Galtung, peacebuilding was the means to achieve his earlier developed concept of "positive peace," a situation lacking both direct and structural violence, or one characterized by "social justice" (Galtung 1969: 183).

This approach was echoed, perhaps unintentionally, in then UN Secretary General Boutros-Ghali's *An Agenda for Peace,* published 23 years later, in which "peace-building" was defined as "efforts to identify and support structures which will tend to consolidate peace and advance a sense of confidence and well-being among people" (1992). This influential UN document – following on the heels of the Soviet collapse – augured in a period of post-Cold War "liberal internationalism" (Paris 1997), which witnessed the administration of robust peacebuilding initiatives in dozens of post-conflict settings. While such missions were initially limited in scope, relatively quickly they become "more comprehensive," tending to "have a large civilian component that focuses on forming the institutions necessary to create stable states" (Peercy 2013: 2). Such "statebuilding" programs became the go-to mechanism for promoting peace in post-conflict environments particularly, as Goetze and Guzina have described, by authors linked to policy-oriented work (2008: 320).

However, a forceful critique of such approaches had developed within a decade or so of *An Agenda for Peace*. Some critics decried what they saw as the neo-colonial impulses of such liberal internationalism (Ignatieff 2003; Chandler 2006), while others generally supported the motivations underlying such projects but worried about issues of implementation (Paris 2004). Regardless of their specific argument, these more critical works inspired substantial and ongoing efforts to reconsider both the role and the capabilities of international institutions in the process of ensuring stable peace. But scholars participating in these debates even today primarily reflect on the motivations for and operations of the supra-national organizations who dominate peacebuilding policy decisions (the UN, EU, OECD, etc.), the powerful national funders of peacebuilding operations (USAID, DfID, GTZ, etc.), or the large International Non-Governmental Organizations (INGOs) who serve as the primarily implementing agencies of the peacebuilding industry (Search for Common Ground, Accord, Carter Center, International Alert, Conciliation Resources, etc.). While they may indirectly refer to the actions of multi-national corporations, private businesses are rarely the focus of these critiques.

Indeed, private businesses have not often been directly considered as actors in their own right within the mainstream peacebuilding literature. But as it has been evident for more than two decades that private industry actors have a direct influence on dynamics related to conflict and peace, this is an omission which has become difficult to justify. This has been discussed extensively in a related field of study which will be further discussed below and which we will refer to as the "War Economies" literature (see for example, Duffield 1999; Pugh, Cooper & Goodhand 2004). This literature – largely highlighting the economic incentives for conflict as opposed to peace – has also fed into and supported the critiques of the Critical Peacebuilding literature noted above, but has generally focused on *Business* writ large as opposed to individual *businesses*, while also excluding discussions of the positive role such businesses might play as peacebuilding actors. To a great extent, therefore, discussion of any such more positive role for individual private industry actors has been excluded from both the War Economies and Critical Peacebuilding literatures.

However, the field of Business Ethics, a related literature largely unrecognized by those writing about War Economies or Peacebuilding, has developed a more positive or hopeful narrative regarding the role of private industry in peacebuilding. Instead of the often instinctively critical reaction to the motivations of private industry as witnessed in the Critical Peacebuilding literature, as will be discussed below, the "Business for Peace" literature often highlights the positive contributions private industry actors can make to peacebuilding (see Fort and Schipani 2007; Fort 2010; Oetzel et al. 2010). While the tone of this sub-field of the Business discipline is quite distinct, it also incorporates elements that can inform the debates at the core of peacebuilding theory, research, and policy. Further, it is also made clear below that many of the substantive and perhaps fundamental challenges wrestled with today in the Critical Peacebuilding literature – issues of ownership, disempowerment, friction, complexity, and unpredictability – are barely recognized within the "Business for Peace" literature; which may, as a result, be presenting an overly optimistic impression of the role Business may play.

This chapter, therefore, seeks to address the optimism of the Business for Peace literature by discussing the substantive limitations to intervention as recognized within the Critical Peacebuilding literature, informed, as it is, by the scholarship on War Economies. This will provide a more-sober assessment of how individual businesses *might* contribute to peacebuilding and the very real limitations they face. The main points will be illustrated with data from an ethnographic study of a large bio-energy project implemented in rural Sierra Leone. This bio-energy project received funding of more than €250 million from a consortium of development banks and was widely lauded for its developmental intentions and for signing up to more than a dozen international codes of good practice. As the data will exhibit, however, even with the best of intentions the difficulties of implementing a large project such as this within a social, cultural, and political environmental largely unfamiliar to those managing the project introduced many unexpected negative externalities which eventually functioned to work against the hopes often articulated within the Business for Peace agenda.

Literature review

There is today an extensive literature on peace and conflict. One can dissect it into dozens of subfields based, for example, on the 'phase' of intervention – such as the classic peacemaking, peacekeeping, peacebuilding divide (Galtung 1976) – or on the function of intervention: peace education (Harris 2004); mediation (Wall, Stark and Standifer 2001); conflict transformation (Lederach 1995); reconciliation (Bar-Siman-Tov 2004), etc. There are clearly connections between these subfields, and they often interact, complement, and feed into each other. Such interaction generates new theory and the development of new policy and practice. However, as has recently been illustrated, there are also examples of subfields which could, via more interaction, provide far more substantive contributions than either can individually (Millar and Lecy 2016). The three subfields I am primarily concerned with here – the Business for Peace, War Economies, and Critical Peacebuilding literatures – provide a glaring example of such potential, but thus far unfulfilled, complementarity.

Business for Peace

The first to be discussed is what has come to be known as the Business for Peace literature. This field has been inspired partly by the realization that peace is inherently advantageous to the majority of businesses (Nelson 2000). While some individual corporations, or even whole business sectors, may benefit from a level of instability and even outright conflict (Maher 2015), this is not true for Business writ large. As such, it is one of the starting principles of the Business for Peace literature that the vast majority of individual businesses have an interest in the maintenance of sustainable peace. Many argue, further, that the interest of business and peace are fundamentally aligned and that normal business practice should be peace promoting. As Fort and Schipani argue, "to the extent that companies stress returning value to shareholders" and "support a rule of law" … "they foster economic development and take a step toward sustainable peace" (2007: 369). In short, to some scholars in this field, Business (writ large, not every specific business), is inherently peace promoting.

Taking this a step further and unpacking why this might be so, Oetzel et al. (2010: 362) argue that by simply following good practice businesses foster peace via five mechanisms. These are:

1. Fostering economic development
2. Adopting principles of external valuation and obeying the rule of law
3. Contributing to a sense of community
4. Engaging in track-two diplomacy, and
5. Engaging in conflict sensitive practices and risk assessment

Importantly, such scholars do not argue that all business ventures will contribute to these five peace-promoting dynamics equally, nor that they will do so automatically. As Fort acknowledges, "it is not any business that fosters peace, it is an ethical business that fosters peace" (2010: 348). But, the assumption implicit within these theories is that the primary goals and activities of the majority of businesses – and therefore of Business writ large – will be consistent with and contribute to sustainable peace as long as businesses and managers act 'ethically' and with good intentions.

Recent contributions, however, have problematized this central assumption. Ganson argues, for example, that even if and when individual businesses want to act ethically, they may not have the capabilities to do so (2014). He illustrates the difficulties faced by businesses due both to the complexities of the environments in which they operate (ibid: 126), and the various competing internal structures of the corporations themselves (ibid: 127–129). As a result, and questioning the idea that all ethical businesses will have peace-promoting influence, Ganson argues that "a company's capacity for conflict prevention is a crucial explanatory variable in fragile environments" (ibid: 134). Such arguments regarding capacity and impact are echoed by others such as Katsos and Forrer (2014), and Miklian (2016), who notes – importantly – that "intent does not necessarily translate into effective action, as declarations by senior management about their CSR [Corporate Social Responsibility] programs correlate poorly to actual CSR impact" (ibid: 14). Such reservations regarding the peace-promoting influence of businesses in conflict-affected environments resonate with the more pessimistic tone of the War Economies literature.

War Economies

The War Economies literature emerged in the late 1990s in response to the various internal armed conflicts erupting in the immediate post-Cold War years. While such conflicts were initially labeled as ethnically inspired, in even classic cases such as those in Rwanda and the former Yugoslavia many scholars quickly recognized that the driving motivations for violence were as much economic as they were ethnic (Kaldor 1999; Gurr 2000; Mueller 2000). It became clear to many that the new access to international markets facilitated by the triumph of Western capitalism served as much to promote conflict as it did to promote peace. As described by Duffield, this process opened up a new "grey zone of international commercial activity" (1998: 83), which served to "promote cooperation and mutual support between private commercial interests and warlords on the global periphery" (Millar 2012: 724). In the case of Liberia, for example, Reno described the central role played by foreign corporations in supporting the National Patriotic Front of Liberia (NPFL) – Charles Taylor's violent rebel movement – by facilitating exports of hardwoods and rubber (1995: 114).

Collier and Hoeffler provided quantitative support for such assertions, providing evidence that conflict and violence were spurred more by economic greed and opportunity than they were by political or ideological grievances (1998; see also Collier 2000). This assertion led to a series of responses and more subtle analysis published in a series of volumes organized by the International Peace Academy (today the International Peace Institute) in the first years of the new century. These volumes provided extensive discussion of the economic agendas of armed actors in civil wars (Berdal and Malone 2000), deep reflection on various cases (Ballentine and Sherman 2003), an examination of the "regionalized" nature of "war economies" in Central Asia, West Africa, and Southeast Europe (Pugh, Cooper and Goodhand 2004), and – perhaps most usefully for the Business for Peace literature – substantive suggestions on how to better manage economies to support and encourage post-conflict peace (Ballentine and Nitzchke 2005).

One instructive distinction between the two literatures presented so far, however, is the level of analysis. The Business for Peace literature emphasizes the potential for individual businesses to foster peace. This is witnessed, for example, in the focus on individual business capacities in Ganson (2014), on "practices" in Katsos and Forrer (2014), or on commitment to voluntary guidelines for ethical practice such as Business for Peace in Miklian and Schouten (2017). On the other hand, the War Economies literature is more focused on Business writ large. We can see this in the critique of the "liberal peace" as a global economic order as in Pugh, Cooper and Goodhand (2004), or on war itself as a system (Keen 2006: 51) with its own "economic functions" (ibid: 66) and "vested interests" (ibid: 67). I would argue that the former is more hopeful and optimistic at least partially because the focus is on the potential influence of each individual business, while the latter is more pessimistic as a result of its focus on broader currents and patterns in global economic governance (Duffield 2007). It is this more systemic focus which also links the War Economies and Critical Peacebuilding literatures.

Critical Peacebuilding

Within this third literature peacebuilding is largely framed as a "liberal internationalist" project; as an externally driven agenda motivated by the imperative to insert democracy, rule of law, and free-markets into post-conflict states. The assumption being that those institutions are necessary for ensuring sustainable peace (Oneal and Russett 1999; Doyle 2005). It is accepted among policymakers that the implementation of free-markets and open-trade supports sustainable peace (Selby 2011: 19), and the approach has for some time dominated the policy prescriptions of major international institutions such as the World Bank and International Monetary Fund (Doyle 2000: 86). However, influential critics such as Chandler (2004), Mac Ginty (2008) Lidén (2009) and Richmond (2009) refute the benefits of such processes, and the very real "illiberal" influences of such policies have been illustrated (Pugh 2011). These broad critiques clearly question the underlying assumption of the Business for Peace literature regarding the inherent complementarity between business and peace.

In arriving at these conclusions, Critical Peacebuilding scholars have uncovered a number of problematic dynamics in the implementation of peacebuilding projects. These include the limited "local ownership" of and "buy-in" to such projects (Sending 2009; Donais 2009, 2012; Shaw, Waldorf and Hazan 2010; Richmond 2012), as well as the overly "technocratic" or "problem-solving" nature of such interventions, which excludes local actors from decision making (De Waal 2009: 100; Pugh 2011: 308; Mac Ginty 2012: 294; Autesserre 2014). Much attention has focused on the "Hybrid" results of such interactions, wherein the intentions of intervenors are redirected or restructured by local agency (Richmond 2009; Mac Ginty 2010, 2011; Laffey and Nadarajah 2012; Mac Ginty and Sanghera 2012; Millar 2014a), and more recently scholars have introduced the notion of "Friction" as an analytical lens which highlights how all interventions spur resistance and responses of various kinds in the environments to which they are applied (Björkdahl and Höglund 2013; Millar, van der Lijn and Verkoren 2013; Björkdahl et al. 2016). In this robust Critical Peacebuilding literature, it is recognized, in short, that peace interventions lead to *unpredictable* outcomes and, therefore, have the potential to foster negative effects within what are always inherently complex post-conflict contexts (Chandler 2013; Matyók, Mendoza and Schmitz 2014; Millar 2016a; De Coning 2016).

Within this literature, however, individual businesses are not given much consideration and the focus is overwhelmingly on the larger structures of "comprehensive peacebuilding interventions" and the policies and operations of the UN, EU, OECD, and major bi-lateral donors (Chandler 1999; Gizelis 2009). Further, when private industry is considered, it is largely subsumed within the larger construct of a global neoliberal agenda (Pugh 2004; Herring 2008). Few studies focus on individual businesses, and their role in fostering peace or conflict – whether real or imagined – is largely unexamined and unconfirmed. The Critical Peacebuilding literature, therefore, has not been involved in exploring whether or to what extent individual businesses can play a positive peacebuilding role as argued within the Business for Peace literature. At the same time, Business for Peace scholars have not actively assessed whether individual businesses can overcome the challenges of ownership, hybridity, friction, and complexity as recognized within the Critical Peacebuilding scholarship. The study presented in this chapter bridges that gap.

Methodology

This study focused on a single for-profit company implementing a large bio-energy project in the rural north of post-conflict Sierra Leone. The company started operating in the area in 2009 and was active constructing project infrastructure, growing sugar cane, and eventually producing initial quantities of ethanol in an on-site purpose-built factory until it was forced to abandon its operations (which have now been sold to another company) as a result of the Ebola crisis in 2014. This project was chosen as a case study by which to examine the potential peace-promoting contribution of private businesses specifically because it had received more than €250 million worth of funding from a consortium of development funders, had signed up to more than a dozen voluntary guidelines of international best practices, and explicitly claimed that it would have positive impacts on local community's income, healthcare, and education outcomes. As such, the company was identified as a "best case" to assess the influence – positive or negative – of a private industry actor on the peace and conflict dynamics within a post-conflict environment.

The purpose of the study was very explicitly to assess the local experiences of this project among residents in communities most impacted by the company's operations, and to determine if and to what extent this company was having peace or conflict-promoting influences. To achieve this task, six months of initial fieldwork were carried out between April and September 2012. This included an initial period of six weeks working within the company, participating actively in their Environmental, Economic, and Social monitoring efforts, interviewing company employees, and observing interactions between the company employees and local communities within the land-lease area. When this was completed 55 semi-structured interviews were conducted in a sample of 12 villages within the land-lease area with a wide variety of village residents: men and women; young and old; land owners and strangers (for further information regarding methodology see Millar 2014b). A further series of 60 follow-up interviews were then carried out approximately 18 months later in November/December of 2013 in the same villages and with some of the same participants, thus allowing the research to assess the changing impact of the company's operations over time.

Findings: expect the unexpected

The data collected serves to highlight the extent of the challenges facing even well-intentioned private businesses in complex post-conflict settings. I will illustrate these challenges with a number of examples from across the political, economic and social spheres, but which are each embedded fundamentally in culturally rooted misunderstandings.

Undermining local political balances

First, it is very clear that the arrival of the company in this area of Sierra Leone had significant negative impacts on the careful balance of power between local actors and within local communities. While many of the company officials and managers I interacted with hoped that the company would have the positive influences noted above, their very arrival and operational requirements led to the realignment of incentives on the ground which gave rise to new conflicts. The amount of money directly related to the operation of the project, for example, twisted incentive structures for political alignment. After being accepted by national level politicians and negotiating the level of payments required for such a project (Menzel 2015: 12), the company began negotiating directly with local Paramount Chiefs (the project area is located at the meeting point of three different Chiefdoms) and then village elders (who collectively represent the residents of individual villages) for access to the land. This only makes sense, as these are the actors empowered to make land decision in both formal and customary law, and the company required access to the land in order to carry out its work.

However, within these negotiations company officials held out promises of future reward should those actors (all elder male land owners) support its project. These promises were both directly economic and indirectly about power and influence. They included, for example, payments to local land-owning families of $3.20 per acre per year for the life of the 50-year lease. For large land-owning families, some of whom own 1,000 acres or more, that could equate to thousands of dollars per year in one of the poorest regions of one of the poorest countries on earth (see Millar 2015a: 1708–1709). Such payments are particularly attractive to elders of those families as within the local patron–client system senior family members take the lion's share of all payments and distribute only small proportions to their family members, with sums distributed decreasing depending on hierarchy and gender (Millar 2015b: 453). Thus, individual elders of land-owning families were clearly incentivized to accept the presence of and then support the operation of the company, even though, as one of my interviewees reported, many youth feel that the elders are "trying to imprison the future of those that are coming up" (Millar 2016b: 577).

The effect the company's resources had on the village elders is echoed still further in its influence on the Paramount Chiefs, each of whom gained enormously from the arrival of the project. In addition, for example, to the $3.20 per acre each received as the head of a land-owning family, each paramount chief also gained from the company's payment to the Chiefdom Councils – which the Paramount Chiefs control – to the sum of approximately $71,000 annually, and from the payment of individual "transport costs" of about $90 for attendance at community meetings related to the project (Millar 2017a: 302). It was at these meetings that the political realignment of the local elites was most evident as, in contradiction to their customary role as representatives and protectors of their clients, chiefs at these meetings consistently defended the company against critiques from the villages and praised its arrival and operations in the face of often distraught local farmers.

There are few impacts more clearly corrosive of local political stability than this disruption of political representation. In rural Sierra Leone patron–client relationships are the backbone of political life. Village residents (clients) exchange their labor and political support for the protections afforded by village elders and Paramount Chiefs (patrons) (Millar 2011: 188). But, as another interviewee described during my second round of interviews in 2013, whether intentionally or not, the company has usurped the patron role for themselves, providing resources to the local elites, in exchange for their support. As he articulated, when the company identifies anyone who is out-spoken or may have influence in the community:

> they will just bring them close to them, so that they leave them and stop dis-turbing them. They will just continue and go far with bad things. They will not even think to do good things. That is their society.

While this process of political realignment – and the associated political margin-alization of the non-elite – may not have been intended by the company, this hardly matters. The effect of negotiating access, even if that negotiation was with the appropriate actors, was nonetheless to insert previously unimaginable resources into a precariously balanced patron–client system. An injection which greatly, even if unintentionally, influenced the local political dynamics.

Amplifying existing economic grievances

Second, the operations of the company, and the decisions required regarding who and how to hire and fire within its various operational areas, had similarly unintentional and perhaps even more negative impacts. This began, again, from its earliest steps and with the initial negotiations with local Paramount Chiefs and village elders, during which the company agreed to hire the local youth from affected villages within the land-lease area. Those youth would be losing their access to some of their farmland, after all, so it was only fair in the eyes of local village elders that they should gain via employment with the company. However, there are at least two ways in which this decision had unintentional disruptive impacts.

First, what might have seemed initially like a relatively simple promise to keep, became nearly impossible as the operations of the bio-energy project matured. The initial tasks to be completed on the project were labor intensive and suited the skillsets of most youth in rural Sierra Leone, who largely lack formal education and even basic reading and math skills. Therefore, as the project began its operations in different areas of the land-lease area it did hire from among the local youth to participate in the physically laborious processes of land-clearing, irrigation works, and road and pivot construction. Across the land-lease area many women and men reported working for the company in these early stages (Millar 2015b). However, as these initial tasks were completed and more technically skilled positions had to be filled, the company hired less from within the land-lease area and more from the urban and more educated youth and those local youth who had initially been employed were "seated." This led to conflicts over income, housing, and relative status between local youth who were left both without their land and without employment and more privilege urban youth who experienced the benefits without any of the burdens (Millar 2016b: 575–756).

Second, this promise also carried with it unexpected implications for the distribution of benefits among the individuals and communities within the land-lease area. In rural Sierra Leone "local" youth are defined in a very specific way and do not include all those youth living within a given village and may, indeed, exclude all youth living within certain villages. This is due to the autochthonous system of local identification, in which the "local" label is applied only to "sons of the soil" who can claim descent from the original settlers of a village. All those who cannot claim descent are considered "strangers," and have no claim to the benefits of local status, such as ownership of land. This meant that no stranger families were eligible for land-lease payments from the company even though they lost access to land they had previously farmed, and this also excluded youth from such families from the promised employment with the company. Within the existing customary system, the same rules that gave the Paramount Chiefs and village elders the power to negotiate on behalf of the local communities also excluded "stranger" families both from participating in those discussions and from sharing in any of the benefits accruing from the agreements made.

As a result, while substantial rewards were provided to the elder males participating in these discussions, and even youth within those familial networks benefited to some extent through initial employment opportunities and the wide distribution of land-lease payments (albeit in ever decreasing amounts), the already existing inequalities between land-owning and stranger families were actually further exacerbated by the arrival and operations of the company. It is even more alarming, however, when one realizes (as the company appears not to have known) that stranger status is not simply applied to a few individuals who have recently moved to the area for work or marriage. Quite on the contrary, in rural Sierra Leone whole villages and even third or fourth generation residents can be "strangers," lacking the status of descent from the original settlers and so excluded from the benefits of the project. As one interviewee described the situation of his village:

> we are under the people of [a neighboring village], it is the people of [that village] that have this land … When they pay the ones over there, they don't give us their money … So this is what will bring the problem between we and them.

Generating new social conflicts

This brings us to the third unexpected impact of the company's presence in Sierra Leone, the generation of new conflicts within the community. It is relatively straightforward to see how both the political realignment and the exacerbation of economic inequalities discussed above foster conflict and not peace between groups. The quote from the interviewee who described the chiefs and elders as being members of the company's "society" highlights the degree of disenchantment that took hold within the project area as village residents came to feel that they had been sold out by elders trying to "imprison the future." During my initial period of fieldwork in 2012 it was not yet clear how local communities would respond. As the project rollout was not yet completed and the company claimed it was not yet profitable, the villages were still being promised that the future was bright; that once ethanol was being produced and exported the benefits to communities would be clear. However, by late 2013 the factory was complete, ethanol was being produced, and still no benefits had arrived.

In 2013 all of the tensions that had been developing between land owners and strangers, between elders and youth, between communities and their chiefs, and between unemployed local youth and employed non-local youth were becoming increasingly clear. A group of 35 land-owning families were working with a US-based legal aid NGO to sue the chiefs for misrepresenting their interests (Millar 2017a: 301), there had been a series of sit-down strikes and labor protests against the treatment of local employees by expatriate managers, and shortly after I left – in the spring of 2014 – one of the sugar cane fields was burned (Millar 2016b: 575). It is certainly not my argument that individuals working for the company (whether in Europe or on the ground in Sierra Leone) wanted to inspire these new conflict dynamics. Indeed, in all conversations with me the company leadership was quite clear, and echoed one of the central arguments of the Business for Peace literature – that private industry projects like theirs were required to help Sierra Leone to rebuild peace after the conflict. I was even warned by one manager in 2012 that to publish critical findings about the project could hinder its future and so "set back development in Sierra Leone by 50 years."

But this hubris contributed to an *ends justify the means* mindset that functioned in direct opposition to the best practices and conflict sensitive operations one would expect in such a context. The focus on process – on *how* best to foster development for peace – became subservient to the goal, and while this goal in the long-term was "Development," in the short term it was very clearly operationalized as "profitability." I was regularly informed by company staff that promises of environmental, educational, or economic progress were all dependent on achieving profitability as soon as possible. In turn, profitability demanded difficult decisions in the short-term regarding salaries, work conditions, and community engagement and services. In short, even though the company had pro-peace goals, the need to compete in a profit motivated sector meant that working towards those goals was pushed off into some unknown future. But in this case, and I would postulate in many others besides, local actor's experiences are distinctly about the present, and promises of a future that never comes to pass generate bitterness and frustrated expectations. Such experiences among individuals generate collective experiences of bitterness and frustration, which can do little but foster conflict and undermine hopes for peace.

Conclusion

This is where we return to the concerns, therefore, of the War Economies and Critical Peacebuilding literatures. First, these observations indicate that individual businesses cannot be seen as free of the constraints and incentives of Business writ large. This case highlights the difficulty of operating an *ethical* business within a profit-oriented international market. It calls into question the idea that one individual business can prioritize social relationships, gender equality, human rights, or any other pro-social, pro-peace social good in the face of demands for efficiencies and profitability. In other words, it should make us cognizant of the dangers of putting our faith in the values of individual executives or companies to the detriment of a more structural or contextual understanding of market forces and the short-term thinking they promote. Business for Peace scholars, in consultation with the Business community, must think creatively about ways to shelter projects with pro-peace goals from such short-term market directed decisions.

Such "sheltering" mechanisms could be at the international level. One can imagine economic incentives and protections which would serve to make exports from such contexts more attractive (perhaps across the board or sector specific) in order to ease the path to profitability and more smoothly pave the way for peace-promoting initiatives. They could also be at the national level, providing government support (whether funded independently or via overseas development aid) for pro-peace social initiatives in partnership with business operations that pledge their commitment to a pro-peace agenda (which is the opposite of what occurred in this case, where government and NGOs abandoned the land-lease area because they felt this was now the company's responsibility). Or such mechanisms could be implemented by the multi-national parent companies of businesses seeking to have pro-peace impacts; leveraging the resources of a larger corporate entity to shield an individual project from market demand until it is fully capable of both turning a profit and having positive pro-peace effects.

These findings also direct our attention to the significant barriers individual businesses face in overcoming the challenges of local ownership and buy-in within impoverished contexts characterized by complex and fractured political and socioeconomic communities. What is "local ownership," for example, when many different actors can claim to represent the local? In this case the company did try to engage the local via the Paramount Chiefs and village elders, but questions arise about the representation provided by such local authorities to women, to local youth, and to "strangers." These questions mirror those more commonly asked of peacebuilding interventions by supra-national, national, and INGO actors. Similarly, the three dynamics discussed above – across the political, economic, and social spheres – evidence the "frictions" that occur and the hybrid outcomes that emerge in local settings when international actors intervene in cultures about which they have little understanding (see Millar 2014a). What should we expect, other than the unexpected, if we commit to intervention via business as usual in complex cultural contexts completely different from those in which the planners and funders are socialized? How can business executives, managers, and those with their feet on the ground predict the impacts of their actions when they have no knowledge of the alternative lenses by which local actors understand the world?

As noted above, I am of the opinion that scholars from the Business for Peace, the War Economies, and the Critical Peacebuilding literatures must be encouraged to more actively share their theories, findings, and ideas for solutions. But perhaps more important is for the business community to work with those scholars to devise work-able solutions. One challenge to that is the unhelpful tendency of business communities to want broad guidelines and best practices – a trend which itself is heavily critiqued in the peacebuilding literature (Mac Ginty 2012; Millar 2017b). It should be very clear that the temptation to find such broad solutions is exactly the approach that must be avoided. It is the very diversity and complexity of local contexts of intervention (or of investment) which makes predictable implementation so difficult. It is unlikely that any recommendations and suggestions can therefore be broadly applicable. The only appropriate way to respond is with solutions that can be responsive to specific political, economic and sociocultural contexts. Designing such solutions, however, requires substantial training, skill and experience in understanding such contexts and this is a capacity largely missing from businesses in post-conflict states.

It is also a capacity missing from Ganson's model (2014: 134) of the capacities necessary for businesses to have success in fragile states. But this does not mean that such capacities cannot be folded into this model. Indeed, while Ganson makes no reference to the challenges of cross-cultural understanding, the first two "processes" within this model are to "a) recognize tensions & stress factors as experienced by stakeholders" (via "stakeholder engagement"), and for those to "b) become understood by and meaningful to company agents" (via "analytical skills"). In short, understanding local stakeholder experiences are key to the model. Businesses hoping to actually contribute to sustainable peace must, therefore, incorporate new capabilities for what we might call *cultural sensitivity for conflict sensitivity*, abilities more commonly found among social scientists than they are within businesses. Ganson's oversight was in not recognizing that such understanding across cultural divides is inordinately difficult and beyond the training and skills evident within most businesses and multi-national corporations.

Finally, and as has been evidenced elsewhere (Millar 2014b: 141), even when well-meaning businesses attempt to assess such local experiences they often rely not on those with the most appropriate skills and training, but on those already under contract for other tasks or least likely to identify any problems that might cost time or resources to remedy. After all, the profit motive overrides all other concerns and demands prioritization. The short-term thinking demanded by the *tyranny of the profit motive* incentivizes companies to deploy personnel to identify only short-term tensions and stress factors and deploy resources only to mitigate against the immediate threat those may pose. Such conflict management tactics become exercises in power and control via various avenues (see Millar 2016c, 2017a, 2018) but they cannot provide the kind of true "engagement" or "understanding" that might lead to longer-term solutions for more substantial "tensions" and "stress factors" such as those identified in the case presented above. These will remain hidden – perhaps even purposefully so – until such time down the road when they bubble up from below and undermine the security of the company as well as the sustainability of the peace. If businesses do truly want to incorporate *cultural sensitivity for conflict sensitivity*, they will need to commit more time, more effort, and more skill, to understanding the local cultures in which they intervene.

References

Autesserre, S. (2014) *Peacebuilders: An Ethnography of International Intervention.* New York, NY: Cambridge University Press.

Ballentine, Karen and Jake Sherman (2003) *The Political Economy of Armed Conflict: Beyond Greed and Grievance.* Boulder, CO: Lynne Rienner Publishers.

Ballentine, Karen and Heiko Nitzchke (2005) *Profiting from Peace: Managing the Resource Dimensions of Civil War.* Boulder, CO: Lynne Rienner Publishers.

Bar-Siman-Tov, Yaacov (2004) *From Conflict Resolution to Reconciliation.* Oxford: Oxford University Press.

Berdal, Mats and David M. Malone (2000) *Greed and Grievance: Economic Agendas in Civil War.* Boulder CO: Lynne Reinner Press Inc.

Björkdahl, Annika and Kristine Höglund (2013) Precarious Peacebuilding: Friction in Global-local Encounters. *Peacebuilding* 1(3): 289–299.

Björkdahl Annika, KristineHöglund, GearoidMillar, JairVan der Lijn and Willemijn Verkoren (2016) *Peacebuilding and Friction: Global and Local Encounters in Post Conflict Societies.* London: Routledge.

Boutros-Ghali, Boutros (1992) *An Agenda for Peace.* www.un-documents.net/a47-277.htm (accessed on 19 July 2017).

Chandler, David (1999) The Limits of Peacebuilding: International Regulation and Civil Society Development in Bosnia. *International Peacekeeping* 6(1): 109–125.

Chandler, David (2004) The Responsibility to Protect? Imposing the 'Liberal Peace'. *International Peacekeeping* 11(1): 59–81.

Chandler, David (2006) *Empire in Denial: The Politics of State-Building.* London: Pluto Press.

Chandler, David (2013) Peacebuilding and the Politics of Non-Linearity: Rethinking 'Hidden' Agency and 'Resistance'. *Peacebuilding* 1(1): 17–32.

Collier, Paul (2000) Rebellion as a Quasi-Criminal Activity. *Journal of Conflict Resolution* 44(6): 839–853.

Collier, Paul and Anke Hoeffler (1998) On the Economic Causes of Civil War. *Oxford Economic Papers* 50(4): 563–573.

De Coning, Cedric (2016) From Peacebuilding to Sustaining Peace: Implications of Complexity for Resilience and Sustainability. *Resilience* 4(3): 166–181.

De Waal, Alex (2009) Mission Without End? Peacekeeping in the African Political Marketplace. *International Affairs* 85(1): 99–113.

Donais, Timothy (2009) Empowerment or imposition? Dilemmas of local ownership in post-conflict peacebuilding processes. *Peace and Change* 34(1): 3–26.

Donais, Timothy (2012) *Peacebuilding and Local Ownership.* New York: Routledge.

Doyle, Michael W. (2000) A More Perfect Union: The Liberal Peace and the Challenge of Globalization. *Review of International Studies* 26(5): 81–94.

Doyle, Michael W. (2005) Three Pillars of the Liberal Peace. *The American Political Science Review* 99(3): 463–466.

Duffield, Mark (1998) Post-Modern Conflict: Warlords, Post-Adjustment States and Private Protection. *Civil Wars* 1(1): 65–102.

Duffield, Mark (1999) Globalization and War Economies: Promoting Order or the Return of History? *Fletcher Forum of World Affairs* 23(2): 21–38.

Duffield, Mark (2007) *Development, Security and Unending War: Governing the World of Peoples*. Cambridge: Polity Press.

Fort, Timothy L. (2010) Peace through Commerce: A Multisectoral Approach. *Journal of Business Ethics* 89: 347–350.

Fort, Timothy L. and Cindy A. Schipani (2007) An Action Plan for the Role of Business in Fostering Peace. *American Business Law Journal* 44(2): 359–377.

Galtung, Johan (1969) Violence, Peace, and Peace Research. *Journal of Peace Research* 6(3): 167–191.

Galtung, Johan (1976) Three Realistic Approaches to Peace: Peacekeeping, Peacemaking and Peacebuilding. *Impact of Science on Society* 26(1/2): 103–113.

Ganson, Brian (2014) Business in Fragile Environments: Capabilities for Conflict Prevention. *Negotiation and Conflict Management Research* 7(2): 121–139.

Gizelis, Theodora-Ismene (2009) Gender Empowerment and United Nations Peacebuilding. *Journal of Peace Research* 46(4): 505–523.

Goetze, Catherine and Dejan Guzina (2008) Peacebuilding, Statebuilding, Nationbuilding – Turtles All the Way Down? *Civil Wars* 10(4): 319–347.

Gurr, Ted Robert (2000) Ethnic Warfare on the Wane. *Foreign Affairs* 79(3): 52–64.

Harris, Ian M. (2004) Peace Education Theory. *Journal of Peace Education* 1(1): 5–20.

Herring, Eric (2008) Neoliberalism Versus Peacebuilding in Iraq. In Michael Pugh, Neil Cooper and Mandy Turner (eds.), *Whose Peace? Critical Perspectives on the Political Economy of Peacebuilding*. Basingstoke: Palgrave Macmillan, pp. 47–64.

Ignatieff, Michael (2003) *Empire Lite: Nation-Building in Bosnia, Kosovo, and Afghanistan*. London: Random House.

Kaldor, Mary (1999) *New and Old Wars: Organized Violence in a Global Era*. Cambridge: Polity Press.

Katsos, John E. and John Forrer (2014) Business Practices and Peace in Post-Conflict Zones: Lessons from Cyprus. *Business Ethics: A European Review* 23(2): 154–168.

Keen, David (2006) *Endless War? Hidden Functions of the "War on Terror"*. London: Pluto Press.

Laffey, Mark and Suthaharan Nadarajah (2012) The Hybridity of Liberal Peace: States, Diasporas and Insecurity. *Security Dialogue* 43(5): 403–420.

Lederach, John Paul (1995) *Preparing for Peace: Conflict Transformation across Cultures*. Syracuse, NY: Syracuse University Press.

Lidén, Kristoffer (2009) Building Peace Between Global and Local Politics: The Cosmopolitical Ethics of Liberal Peacebuilding. *International Peacekeeping* 16(5): 616–634.

Mac Ginty, Roger (2008) Indigenous Peace-making Versus the Liberal Peace. *Cooperation and Conflict* 43(2): 139–163.

Mac Ginty, Roger (2010) Hybrid Peace: The Interaction between Top-Down and Bottom-Up Peace. *Security Dialogue* 41(4): 391–412.

Mac Ginty, Roger (2011) *International Peacebuilding and Local Resistance: Hybrid Forms of Peace*. New York: Palgrave Macmillan.

Mac Ginty, Roger (2012) Routine Peace: Technocracy and Peacebuilding. *Cooperation and Conflict* 47(3): 287–308.

Mac Ginty, Roger and Gurchathen Sanghera (2012) Hybridity in Peacebuilding and Development: An Introduction. *Journal of Peacebuilding and Development* 7(2): 3–8.

Maher, David (2015) The Fatal Attraction of Civil War Economies: Foreign Direct Investment and Political Violence, A Case Study of Colombia. *International Studies Review* 17(2): 217–248.

Matyók, Thomas G., Hannah Rose Mendoza and Cathryne Schmitz (2014) Deep Analysis: Designing Complexity into our Understanding of Conflict. *InterAgency Journal* 5(2): 14–24.

Menzel, Anne (2015) Foreign Investment, Large-Scale Land Deals, and Uncertain 'Development' In *Sierra Leone: Impacts, Conflicts, and Security Concerns*. CCS Working Paper No. 18: www.uni-marburg.de/konfliktforschung/publikationen/wp18.pdf (accessed August 14, 2017).

Miklian, Jason (2016) Mapping Business-Peace Interactions: Five Assertions for How Businesses Create Peace. SSRN Paper: https://papers.ssrn.com/sol3/papers.cfm?abstract_id=2891391 (accessed August 8, 2017).

Miklian, Jason and Peer Schouten (2017) The Business-Peace Nexus: 'Business for Peace and the Reconfiguration of the Public/Private Divide in Global Governance. *Journal of International Relations and Development*. Online First. https://doi.org/10.1057/s41268-018-0144-2.

Millar, Gearoid (2011) Between Western Theory and Local Practice: Cultural Impediments to Truth-Telling in Sierra Leone. *Conflict Resolution Quarterly* 29(4): 177–199.

Millar, Gearoid (2012) "Our Brothers who went to the Bush": Post-Identity Conflict and the Experience of Reconciliation in Sierra Leone. *Journal of Peace Research* 49(5): 717–729.

Millar, Gearoid (2014a) Disaggregated Hybridity: Why Hybrid Institutions do not Produce Predictable Experiences of Peace. *Journal of Peace Research* 51(4): 501–514.

Millar, Gearoid (2014b) *An Ethnographic Approach to Peacebuilding: Understanding Local Experiences in Transitional States*. London: Routledge.

Millar, Gearoid (2015a) Investing in Peace? Foreign Direct Investment as Economic Justice in Sierra Leone. *Third World Quarterly* 36(9): 1700–1716.

Millar, Gearoid (2015b) 'We Have no Voice for that': Land Rights, Power, and Gender in Rural Sierra Leone. *Journal of Human Rights* 14(4): 445–462.

Millar, Gearoid (2016a) Respecting Complexity: Compound Friction and Unpredictability in Peacebuilding. In Annika Bjorkdahl, Kristine Hoglund, Gearoid Millar, Willemijn Verkoren and Jair Vanderline (eds.), *Peacebuilding and Friction: Global and Local Encounters in Post Conflict Societies*. London: Routledge, pp. 32–47.

Millar, Gearoid (2016b) Local Experiences of Liberal Peace: Marketization and Emerging Conflict Dynamics in Sierra Leone. *Journal of Peace Research* 53(4): 569–581.

Millar, Gearoid (2016c) Knowledge and Control in the Contemporary Land Rush: Marking Local Land Legible and Corporate Power Applicable in Rural Sierra Leone. *Journal of Agrarian Change* 16(2): 206–224.

Millar, Gearoid (2017a) For Whom to Local Peace Process Function? Maintaining Control through Conflict Management. *Cooperation and Conflict* 52(3): 293–308.

Millar, Gearoid (2017b) *Ethnographic Peace Research: Approaches and Tensions*. Basingstoke: Palgrave Macmillan.

Millar, Gearoid (2018) Co-opting Authority and Privatizing Force in Rural Africa: Ensuring Corporate Power over Land and People. *Rural Sociology*. Online First: https://onlinelibrary.wiley.com/doi/full/10.1111/ruso.12203.

Millar, Gearoid and Jesse Lecy (2016) Disciplinary Divides in Post-Conflict Justice and Peace: Tracking If and How we Share Ideas. *Journal of Intervention and Statebuilding* 10(3): 302–320.

Millar, Gearoid; Jair van der Lijn and Willemijn Verkoren (2013) Peacebuilding Plans and Local Reconfigurations: Frictions between Imported Processes and Indigenous Practices. *International Peacekeeping* 20(2): 137–143.

Mueller, John (2000) The Banality of "Ethnic War". *International Security* 25(1): 42–70.

Nelson, Jane (2000) The Business of Peace: Business as a Partner in Conflict Prevention and Resolution (London: Prince of Wales Business Leaders Forum): www.international-alert.org/sites/default/files/publications/The%20Business%20of%20Peace.pdf (accessed August 8, 2017).

Oetzel, Jennifer, Michelle Westermann-Behaylo, Charles Koerber, Timothy L. Fort and Jorge Rivera (2010) Business and Peace: Sketching the Terrain. *Journal of Business Ethics* 89: 351–373.

Oneal, John R. and Bruce Russett (1999) Assessing the Liberal Peace Alternative Specifications: Trade Still Reduces Conflict. *Journal of Peace Research* 36(4): 423–442.

Paris, Roland (1997) Peacebuilding and the Limits of Liberal Internationalism. *International Security* 22(2): 54–89.

Paris, Roland (2004) *At War's End: Building Peace after Civil Conflict.* Cambridge: Cambridge University Press.

Peercy, Chavanne L. (2013) *Local Leadership in Democratic Transition. Competing Paradigms in International Peacebuilding.* Basingstoke: Palgrave Macmillan.

Pugh, Michael (2004) Rubbing Salt into War Wounds: Shadow Economies and Peacebuilding in Bosnia and Kosovo. *Problems of Post-Communism* 51(3): 53–60.

Pugh, Michael (2011) Local Agency and Political Economies of Peacebuilding. *Studies in Ethnicity and Nationalism* 11(2): 308–320.

Pugh, Michael, Neil Cooper and Jonathan Goodhand (2004) *War Economies in a Regional Context: Challenges of Transformation.* Boulder, CO: Lynne Rienner Publishers.

Reno, William (1995) Reinvention of an African Patrimonial State: Charles Taylor's Liberia. *Third World Quarterly* 16(1): 109–120.

Richmond, Oliver P. (2009) Becoming Liberal, Unbecoming Liberalism: Liberal-local Hybridity via the Everyday as a Response to the Paradoxes of Liberal Peacebuilding. *Journal of Intervention and Statebuilding* 3(3): 324–344.

Richmond, Oliver P. (2012) Beyond Local Ownership in the Architecture of International Peacebuilding. *Ethnopolitics* 11(4): 354–375.

Selby, Jan (2011) The Political Economy of Peace Processes. In Michael Pugh; Neil Cooper and Mandy Turner (eds.) *Whose Peace? Critical Perspectives on the Political Economy of Peacebuilding.* New York: Palgrave Macmillan, 11–29.

Sending, Ole Jacob (2009) *Why Peacebuilders Fail to Secure Ownership and be Sensitive to Context.* NUPI Working Paper 755: https://brage.bibsys.no/xmlui/bitstream/handle/11250/277766/SIP-1-WP-755-Sending.pdf?sequence=3 (accessed July 2, 2017).

Shaw, Rosalind, Lars Waldorf and Pierre Hazan (2010) *Localizing Transitional Justice: Interventions and Priorities after Mass Violence.* Stanford, CA: Stanford University Press.

Wall, James A., John B. Stark and Rhetta L. Standifer (2001) Mediation: A Current Review and Theory Development. *Journal of Conflict Resolution* 45(3): 370–391.

PART II

Perspectives on the corporate side

4

FURTHERING BUSINESS EFFORTS TO REDUCE SOCIAL RISK AND PROMOTE PEACEBUILDING

The potential of social impact bonds (SIBs)

Jennifer Oetzel and Stone Conroy

Introduction

Businesses face a wide variety of complex political and social risks in the course of their operations. Efforts to address these challenges are often reactive and aimed at protecting the firm and its profits in the short term rather than addressing risk at its source. One reason is that governments are generally considered to be responsible for addressing political and social challenges in a country. In many cases, however, the public sector lacks the capacity, resources, or even the will to address systemic risk. The result is that the underlying conditions that create political risk and social instability in a country are left unaddressed. When the conditions that create violence and uncertainty are left to fester, the overall environment tends to become increasingly unstable and threatening to firm survival. Given that businesses and governments have an interest in reducing systemic risk, the purpose of this chapter is to discuss proactive approaches for addressing political and social risk at their source.

Political risk, as we consider it here, generally refers to the actions or inactions of government that negatively affect a firm's profitability or even survival and may affect the overall business conditions in a country (Oetzel and Getz, 2012). Risk associated with inaction can occur if a government lacks the capacity or will to address political unrest or violence within its borders (Oetzel and Miklian, 2017). Businesses are not the only ones affected by political risk. In a country where the government is unable or unwilling to address the needs of society, people must either fend for themselves or look for other avenues to solve the problems they face. Political risk may also involve purposeful actions by the government to undermine businesses' ability to operate. Governments can also create tensions among citizens by providing services or political rights to some groups but not others.

Social risk is distinct from political risk. From the business perspective, social risk can be thought of as the potential for stakeholders to challenge companies' business practices because of intended or unintended, real or perceived, actions by firms that diminish human welfare (Bekefi, Jenkins, and Kytle, 2006: 3). Companies experiencing social risk may face high costs of operation, protests, violent conflict, loss of their "social license" to operate in a community and lower profitability (Franks et al., 2014). Social risk can arise from long-simmering political problems or economic disenfranchisement. Businesses can also create social risk based on their role in the community. Mining companies that pollute the air and rivers, trample labor rights, and contribute little to the community are likely to foment social unrest (Henisz, Dorobantu, and Nartey, 2014).

While it may be in the interest of businesses and other organizations to manage political and social risk, there are at least three obstacles to getting businesses involved in making a positive social impact. These include the need to: 1) identify effective strategies for mitigating risks and promoting positive social change, 2) develop the tools to measure the effectiveness of such efforts, for the firm and for the issue in question, and 3) access financing or other resources necessary for implementing these efforts. With respect to the first point, business schools do not generally train managers to affect social change so those companies seeking to do so often rely on partnerships between firms, governments, and nongovernmental organizations (NGOs) (Dahan, Doh, Oetzel and Yaziji, 2010). NGOs are on the frontlines of addressing major social issues and often have valuable knowledge for identifying strategies and tactics for making positive change and avoiding possible pitfalls. Governments also play an important role. Given scarce resources, policy makers concerned about public welfare must prioritize the needs of society and decide what issues are most pressing. For these reasons, multi-sector partnerships are an important vehicle for leveraging the complementary skills and capabilities of each sector and organization involved. Together, each of the participating organizations can affect the type of substantial social change that none of these organizations can achieve on their own.

Regarding the second point, another factor that limits greater business involvement in multi-sector partnerships, particularly those aimed at social risk and instability, has been the lack of performance metrics available for assessing the effectiveness of firms' actions. Managers will not be eager to address social risk if there are no measures to evaluate the effectiveness of the partnership. These measures do not have to be standard performance measures. While outcomes that result in a return on investment (ROI) or contribution to the bottom line are easy to convey to stakeholders, companies are also using other metrics to assess their contributions to society. Hewlett-Packard (HP) entered a partnership with the World Wildlife Fund (WWF)-Canada to showcase their environmental (primarily) leadership in the business community and engage employees to drive sustainable practices at work. HP reportedly measured the outcome of this partnership in terms of employee engagement (e.g., sense of satisfaction with work) which has been associated with lower turnover and greater productivity. These measures do not demonstrate a direct positive impact on the bottom line, such as a positive ROI, but in a competitive market for talent, employee satisfaction and a sense of meaning at work are highly valued firm attributes (Branzei, Lin, and Chakrvarty, 2014).

One way to address businesses' need for performance metrics is to clearly define the desired outcome of a program. Businesses may engage in multi-sector partnerships to increase their legitimacy in the community, to reduce political and social risk, or to engage employees in the way that HP did in Canada. If all partners clearly define their objectives for the project in advance, it may be possible to develop performance indicators that meet each organization's needs. On the other hand, if a company is solely interested in maximizing the bottom line then the organizations involved should consider whether a partnership makes sense.

Depending upon the project, a third barrier to reducing systemic risk is access to financing. Governments often lack the resources for social initiatives and businesses have limited resources. The private sector may be willing to contribute in some cases but managers will want to be sure that government officials are committed to and supportive of their efforts. A relatively new tool for addressing complex social challenges – one that addresses many of the barriers to private sector participation – is the social impact bond (SIB). SIBs, also known as pay-for-outcome instruments, were originally developed in the United Kingdom in 2010 (Rand Europe, 2017). SIBs are financial contracts between private-sector funders, a public entity (whether local, regional or national), and typically a non-profit organization, to improve social outcomes. The parties involved enter into a contract prior to service. The organizations agree to program goals and performance metrics and the government agency (or other issuer) agrees to pay a certain ROI to the funder (usually a private-sector firm or firms) based on performance metrics (see Figure 4.1). In this way, public-sector savings associated with reducing the costs of a given social problem, are passed onto private-sector funders as ROI (Gustafsson-Wright, Gardiner, and Putcha, 2015).

Since SIBs are less than 10 years old as of this writing, there is relatively little academic research on the topic. Estimates suggest that 25 SIBs have been completed as of November 2017 and another 70 or so are currently in the implementation phase (Instiglio, 2017). Given the short period of time since SIBs have been used and the relatively slow adoption rate, it is not possible to say what the long-term prospects are (Arena, Bengo, Calderini and Chiodo, 2016; Pauly and Swanson, 2017). Recognizing these concerns, the goal of this chapter is to introduce and critique SIBs as a potential new tool that can assist managers in directly or indirectly addressing complex social problems. Businesses can consider forming SIBs to address complex problems in countries where they operate or participate in their implementation. While a SIB is not going to resolve long-standing problems in a country, it is one possible way to begin the process of positive social change. Before discussing SIBs in greater detail, we discuss the rationale and motivation for firms to engage in reducing political and social risk in a country and provide some background on PPPs.

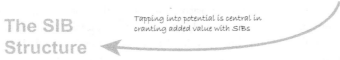

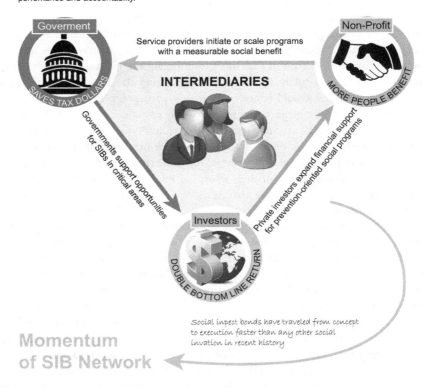

FIGURE 4.1 How a social impact bond is structured
Source Rockefeller Foundation, 2017

Rationale and motivation for engagement

So what are the motives for private-sector firms to address the challenges associated with political and social risk? Firms in the Northern Ireland Confederation of British Industry (CBI) asked themselves that very question in the early 1990s. The result of their introspection was a highly influential publication – commonly referred to as the peace dividend paper – that reportedly played a major role in reducing conflict and promoting peace in Northern Ireland (Banfield, Gündüz, and Killick, 2006). This paper focused on identifying the cost of violence to businesses and the overall economy. Since the public sector was unable to resolve the conflict or end violence, private-sector firms (and civil society more generally) had to pay substantial costs for security; costs that their competitors in more stable and peaceful countries did not have to absorb. In addition, the ongoing violence was seen as a major deterrent to foreign investment in the country and considered the reason for a dramatic decrease in tourism (Banfield, Gündüz, and Killick, 2006: 439). The impact of the violence also had serious long-term effects on North Ireland's labor force. Many of the countries' best and brightest were leaving for opportunities elsewhere. Perhaps most compelling were the estimates that if the violence ended, the $1.42 billion (in 1994) being spent on security and policing could be invested elsewhere.

After the success of the 'peace dividend paper' the CBI continued its effort to reduce risk at its sources by pushing for an end to conflict. The CBI joined with six other trade and business associations and became known as the Group of Seven (GoS). The group began to lobby government and in 1996 invited all nine political parties involved in peace talks to meet in Belfast to "urge political parties to fortify their efforts for peace" (Banfield, Gündüz, and Killick, 2006: 440). The GoS put pressure on politicians, launched media campaigns, and mobilized all companies that were represented by the GoS (as well as their employees) to demand an end to conflict. In 1998 the Good Friday Agreement was ratified which paved the way for peace.

The predictions made in the 'peace dividend paper' about post-conflict economic growth were strongly supported following the 1998 ceasefire. After the cessation of violence, tourism rose 20 percent in one year, unemployment declined to its lowest level in 14 years, and within the first 6 months $48 million in new investments flowed into the country (Banfield, Gündüz, and Killick, 2006: 439). Fast forward 20 years and there is a sense the world is 'rediscovering' the lessons learned in Northern Ireland. The Institute for Economics and Peace (IEP),[1] for example, has been leading the charge in tabulating the cost of conflict, instability, and the absence of peace around the world. IEP argues that the total economic impact of violence around the world in 2015 was $13.6 trillion in purchasing power parity; equivalent to 13.3 percent of the world GDP (IEP, 2016). If the costs to contain violence[2] were reduced by 15 percent, IEP estimated that the world would save $1.4 trillion (IEP, 2014).

Public–private partnerships

Public–private partnerships (PPPs), generally seen as cooperative arrangements between the public, private, and/or non-profit sectors, have been around for hundreds of years in various forms but over the last two decades or so they have received a great deal of renewed interest and attention. PPPs are popular because they are seen as an alternative to pure privatization and as a means to provide valuable public benefits (Hodge and Greve, 2007: 545; Rangan, Samii and Van Wassenhove, 2006). These benefits might include improving service delivery, enhancing government efficiency, reducing time-to-completion for major projects, among many others. PPPs are also a means for cash-strapped governments to develop costly projects that would otherwise be financially prohibitive (Diz, 2014; Hodge and Greve, 2007, 2017).

Despite the popularity of PPPs, they are not always as successful as many believe. Government officials do not always have an incentive to maximize public welfare (Hodge and Greve, 2007). There is no guarantee that politicians will look out for the public rather than their own short-term interests. In countries with high levels of corruption, there may be personal incentives for public officials to agree to costly but unnecessary PPPs. Another concern is that there are inconclusive findings on the performance of PPPs. In particular, more work needs to be done on strengthening accountability in these collaborations (Forrer, Kee, Newcomer and Boyer, 2010).

Although there are challenges with PPPs, there are numerous cases where they can succeed and that suggest a path forward for the use of SIBs. First, when structured properly there are clear advantages for all parties. For example, managers are generally well trained to work in teams and to facilitate projects that bring different groups of people together for a common goal. In fact, there is a record of companies working to promote positive social change, including efforts to support social stability and peace-building in post-conflict environments. In 2006, for example, five companies from the United States, including Cisco Systems, joined efforts through the Partnership for Lebanon (PFL) to help in the relief and reconstruction efforts in the country through job creation/private-sector revival and education (Jamali, 2011). These companies involved in the PFL leveraged their strengths to a further five main work streams, "namely emergency relief/response, job creation/private sector revival, developing information and communications technology (ICT) infrastructure, workforce train-ing/education and developing connected communities" (Jamali, 2011: 1). The goals of the PFL were to forge a successful public–private partnership between local and international NGOs, local and international firms, and other stakeholders to make a positive social and economic impact on Lebanon and provide long-term business-related benefits to the companies involved.

Extending the PFL example to SIBs, it is clearly important for all parties to have a common goal and to have knowledge of cross-sector partnerships and the potential pitfalls they can face. Each party must also be highly competent in their own area of expertise. When these basic conditions are met, SIBs, like other PPPs, may be valuable tools for addressing complex political, social and economic challenges.

Social impact bonds: what are they and how do they work?

SIBs are considered innovative financial mechanisms used to fund social programs through a combination of government initiation, private investment, and non-profit implementation (Rockefeller Foundation, 2017). This financing model takes place through a PPP where the private-sector intermediary is only repaid when program performance results are met. As Ernst and Young (2017) suggests, there are different types of social impact bonds including self-issued, corporate, project based, and hybrid forms. Generally speaking, an issuer – such as a government entity – enters into a contract with a service provider, often an NGO, to address a pressing social challenge. The issuer then contracts with private investors to provide the upfront costs for the initiative. In this case, the government only pays out a ROI to private-sector investors if the social initiative is successful. Project success is based on pre-established performance criteria agreed to by all parties.

At this stage in the development of SIBs, financial service and intermediary firms are the businesses most directly involved in this market. Goldman-Sachs, Bank of America, and Merrill Lynch all invest in SIBs. Ernst & Young (2017), one of the big four accounting firms, is actively working to establish itself as the go-to evaluator for SIBs performance. The firm has said that SIBs, and impact investments more generally, have attracted significant demand from private investors given the higher risk-return characteristics and clear repayment thresholds. Investors also expect that the returns from SIBs will increase with time (Ernest & Young, 2017).

As in many types of financial transactions, a neutral third-party evaluator is critical for assessing program performance. That is why firms like Ernst & Young are so important. For SIBs to be successful it is imperative that no participant is able to manipulate the program outcomes so as to underreport success (to avoid paying a ROI to investors) or overstate it (resulting in payment to investors for a program that was not successful).

Deloitte is trying to position itself as a facilitator for SIBs. It is currently offering services to Canadian organizations to help them build the capacity to participate in SIBs. Their services include: "strategy design, due diligence, workforce development, financial modelling, analysis of tax implications, readiness checks, implementation support, and independent evaluator" (Deloitte, 2017). Now that we have laid the foundation for why and how businesses might engage in social risk management through SIBs, we offer two case studies, one in Colombia and one in the early developmental stage in Chicago. At this point, the major players funding and managing these SIBs tend to be foundations, public-sector agencies, and consulting firms. As such, the scale of investment is quite low. If these efforts prove successful, private-sector investors will have a reason to scale up these projects. The benefits will be a positive reputation in the community and a contribution to lowering systemic risk. Businesses can play a variety of roles. They can provide funding to form the SIBs or, as the case of Colombia shows they can play a key role in implementing social change.

Case studies of social impact bonds

Case study 1: Colombia workforce social impact bond

After more than 50 years of war, over 200,000 deaths, and millions of people displaced, the Colombian government and the FARC rebels reached a peace agreement in November of 2016 (Felter and Renwick, 2017). According to Óscar Adolfo Naranjo Trujillo, the country's Vice-President, the peace agreement saved more than 3,000 lives in 2017 (United Nations, 2017). In fact, 2017 was reportedly the least violent year in Colombia since 1975. While there is much to celebrate, major challenges lie ahead. The most controversial aspects of the peace agreement involve the future political participation of FARC members and their reintegration into civilian life. These were reportedly the biggest factors in delaying a peace agreement (United Nations, 2017). In addition, during the conflict millions of people were displaced and many need gainful employment.

Today, the successful reintegration of former combatants is key to maintaining peace. This means that approximately 7,000 ex-combatants must find gainful employment. Without a legitimate means to supportive themselves, former FARC members may turn to criminal gangs or drug trafficking out of economic necessity. Thus, the challenge for all sectors of Colombian society is to welcome approximately 7,000 ex-FARC members – people who may have kidnapped or killed people's friends or family members – back into mainstream society.

In addition to reintegrating former FARC members, many other Colombians are also at risk for violence. Nearly 50 percent of those in extreme poverty are people who were internally displaced by years of conflict (Gustafsson-Wright and Bogglid-Jones, 2017a). As a result of the high demand for training and employment opportunities, Colombian businesses play an outsized role in maintaining peace. Most former combatants and many displaced persons do not have a formal education or marketable skills so workforce training writ large is critical.

While finding employment for individuals may be critical for national peace, for individual firms there is substantial cost and risk involved in hiring former FARC members. Companies that employ ex-combatants may become targets of those against reintegration. In addition, training is expensive and may yield uncertain results.

Recognizing these concerns, the government has committed to workforce training for ex-combatants and is providing tax incentives for businesses that hire them. In addition, The Colombian Agency for Reintegration (ACR), has formed alliances with 650 businesses to create 2,000 jobs.

Given the large number of jobs needed between ex-combatants and those at risk, PPPs are necessarily to make reintegration successful. To address issues around increasing employment, in March of 2017 several organizations got together to form the first SIB outside of the developed world. The explicit purpose of the SIB is to address unemployment among the country's most vulnerable populations (Gustafsson-Wright and Bogglid-Jones, 2017b).

The Colombian SIB is designed to address the problem of under- and unemployment that affects many at-risk populations including those displaced by conflict. More specifically, the SIB will provide workforce training for unemployed individuals in the cities of Bogotá, Cali, and Pereira. The target population is high school graduates between 18 and 40 years of age who are unemployed and below the poverty level. The total number of people in the initial program is 514. These individuals will be given job skills training and placement assistance and, where appropriate, support for reintegrating into society.

According to the Brookings Institution, the organizations that are funding the Colombian SIB include several foundations: Fundación Corona, Fundación Bolivar Davivienda, and Funadación Mario Santo Domingo. Prosperidad Social, the Colombian government's agency leading inclusion and reconciliation efforts, will provide approximately half of the outcome funds (estimated to be $765,200). The Swiss government will provide the other half. The Inter-American Development Bank and

Instiglio, a results-based financing advisory agency, are involved in managing the funds and designing the SIB (Gustafsson-Wright and Bogglid-Jones, 2017a).

The parties involved in this SIB have agreed to a set of performance metrics (see Table 4.1). The two main metrics are job placement and job retention over a three-month period. If both job placement and job retention objectives are met, all of the funds will be repaid. If only one is met, half of the funding will be returned. A 10 percent bonus payment will kick in if the targeted 6-month job retention rate is met. Table 4.1 provides more details on the payment schedules and maximum return involved. To verify outcomes, Deloitte will serve as the independent auditor (Gustafsson-Wright and Bogglid-Jones, 2017b).

TABLE 4.1 Colombia workforce SIB metrics and payments

Criteria for Evaluation	Metrics
Outcome metrics	1) Job placement 2 three-month job retention 3) six-month retention
Evaluation method	Validated administrative data from the Ministry of Health from health registry of full-time employees required to contribute to mandatory health insurance or pension program. If there is a discrepancy between administrative data and what the intermediary reports, an alternative verification method will be applied using copies of employment contracts or other official proof of employment.
Payment schedule and amounts	50 percent of outcome payment per capita: job placement (maximum of 514 individuals) 50 percent of outcome payment per capita: three months retention (maximum of 514 individuals) 10 percent bonus payment: job retention of six months retention • it is not possible to achieve >50 percent of payment with only job placement.
2017	Scenario 1: If outcome targets achieved by the end of 2017 are equal or below 1 billion Colombian pesos, the government repays investors. Scenario 2: If the outcome targets meet or exceed 1 billion Colombian pesos, the Inter-American Development Bank's (IDB) Multilateral Investment Fund (MIF) also starts paying at the end of 2017. The government will only pay for results verified in 2017.
2018	All payments to come from the IDB/MIF using Switzerland's State Secretariat for Economic Affairs (SECO's) contribution (up to 1.2 billion Colombian pesos).
Maximum nominal return	8 percent

Source: Gustafsson-Wright and Bogglid-Jones, 2017b (based on data provided by Instiglio). https://www.brookings.edu/blog/education-plus-development/2017/03/31/colombia-leads-the-developing-world-in-signing-the-first-social-impact-bond-contracts/

This SIB addresses unemployment, which can play a significant role in violence and conflict (Stewart, 2015). Unemployment among youth and those in the most conflict-affected areas of Colombia is a potential sticking point in rebuilding a resilient society in Colombia, but creating job opportunities requires private as well as public resources. The beneficiaries of this SIB are vulnerable populations that otherwise might not have access to social services; addressing their needs is critical to growing and sustaining peace, and SIBs provide a viable and scalable vehicle to do so.

One of the goals of SIBs is to create a market, in Colombia and elsewhere, for investing in social programs that shift the cost of innovation away from the government and foster novel solutions to social issues such as post-conflict reintegration. As more capital flows into post-conflict Colombia, it is critical that investment mechanisms such as SIBs are calibrated to lay the groundwork for a lasting and durable peace.

In the next case, we describe a SIB in the development stage that aims to address urban violence in Chicago. More specifically, the case study outlines a new social impact bond for gang-violence reduction in Chicago and why this is important to the business community.

Case study 2: cure for violence in Chicago

The Chicago Metropolitan Area (CMA) is home to 400 major corporate head-quarters, 31 Fortune 500 companies, and has a highly diverse economy (World Business Chicago, 2017). The CMA is an economic powerhouse, not only in the United States where it ranks 3rd in terms of economic output, but also across the world. If Chicago was a country (based on 2015 figures), it would rank 21st in terms of GDP at $641 billion; comparable in size to Saudi Arabia ($646 billion) (Beyer, 2016).

Despite its economic achievements, the city has been rocked by violent crime which spiked dramatically in 2016. The high homicide rate is not only devastating to the communities affected but also threatens long-term business prospects as the city has developed a national reputation for its high rate of violent crime. There have been numerous articles about how tragic 2016 was for shootings in Chicago. One of the most shocking was an article from September of 2016 which noted that there have been more homicides in Chicago over the past 15 years than U.S. soldiers killed in Afghanistan and Iraq during the same time period (McCarthy, 2016). In another, the *New York Times* published an article on gang violence in Chicago that focused on the Memorial Day holiday of 2016; a weekend when 64 people were shot across the city (Davey, 2016). Many more articles have compared living in parts of Chicago to living in a war zone. According to reports, children in Chicago are suffering from post-traumatic stress disorder at similar or higher levels than soldiers in conflict zones (Rosenfeld, 2016).

The economic impact of gang violence in Chicago

Since the 'peace dividend paper' in Northern Ireland, the effort to quantify the direct and indirect costs of violence has increased substantially. One estimate, based on a study by Jens Ludwig from the Crime Lab at the University of Chicago, has placed the annual cost of violence in the city at $2.5 billion a year. According to published reports, Teyonda Wertz, the head of South Shore's Chamber of Commerce has said, "violence hurts the economy, and sooner or later it permeates everything. Unless we change our crime situation, it'll kill us" (Jones and McCormick, 2013). Violence drives out people and business, reduces the tax base, and diminishes the capacity of the government to address social problems (Cullen and Levitt, 1999; Jones and McCormick, 2013; Cook and Ludwig, 2000).

Much of the violence occurs in the southern and western areas of Chicago. Despite the crime, however, there is still a significant amount of economic activity in that part of the city. Homes sell anywhere from $10,000 to $1 million (Jones and McCormick, 2013). Due to the violence, however, once thriving businesses have left the area; between 2005 and 2012 one-third of businesses left the South Shore. Putting the situation in stark terms, "If you're making $100,000 or $200,000, you're not going to want to continue to step over bodies," said Henry English, president and chief executive officer of the Black United Fund of Illinois, a South Shore-based community development group, who has seen gunshot victims lying dead outside his office and on his block at home. The violence has significant healthcare costs as well, with trauma care averaging $52,000 per shooting victim and total healthcare costs estimated in the tens of millions per year (Jones and McCormick, 2013).

Damage to the overall business environment is significant. People are less likely to venture out of their home at night if their neighborhood is plagued by violence. Estimates on the cost of violence suggest that the loss of night-time business hours – not only in Chicago but across the country – robs the U.S. GNP of as much as $7.4 billion a year (Cook and Ludwig, 2000; Jones and McCormick, 2013). In addition, high crime and homicide rates in cities, like those in Chicago, reportedly led to the departure of a substantial number of people (Cullen and Levitt, 1999). Unfortunately, the most qualified and able people – those individuals that companies would most like to employ – are the most likely to leave since they have more employment options. In contrast, those people with lower education or skill levels and thus fewer job prospects may be more likely to stay (Cullen and Levitt, 1999). These trends create a vicious circle of human capital flight and business retreat.

The gang violence reduction program

The story of violence in Chicago is a heartbreaking reality, but it is not inevitable or irreversible. A local non-profit called Cure Violence has been working successfully for years to reduce shootings and gang activity in Chicago and in other cities around the U.S. The organization also works in Kenya, Mexico, Honduras, Iraq, and other countries around the world. Cure Violence employs a method for gang-violence reduction that, reportedly, has been enormously successful. According to evaluators, Cure Violence's programs led to reductions in shootings and killings of 41 to 73 percent in the seven communities in which they operated between 1991 to 2007, and a 100 percent reduction in retaliation homicides in five of those communities (Skogan, Hartnett, Bump, and Dubois, 2009). Another set of evaluations showed that Cure Violence's interventions in targeted districts were associated with a 38 percent greater decrease in homicides, a one percent greater decrease in total violent crimes (including domestic violence), and a 15 percent greater decrease in shootings as compared to districts that did not receive an intervention (Gorman-Smith and Cosey-Gay, 2015; Henry, Knoblauch, and Sigurvinsdottir, 2014). When considering the evaluations, it is important to note that the studies did not control for the range of factors that might be correlated with changes in gang violence in Chicago (Henry, Knoblauch, and Sigurvinsdottir, 2014). Nevertheless, several independent evaluators believe that Cure Violence's work had a positive and significant effect on reducing the levels of homicides, shootings, and total violent crime in the city (Gorman-Smith and Cosey-Gay, 2015; Henry, Knoblauch, and Sigurvinsdottir, 2014; Skogan, Hartnett, Bump, and Dubois, 2009).

Cure Violence's funding issues

Despite its reported successes, Cure Violence experienced a serious loss in funding in 2016 and had to completely shut down its program in the 11th District. The vast majority of Cure Violence's funding comes from the State of Illinois, but due to a budget deficit in the state, funding for social programs has taken a big hit. The cut in funding has meant that the organization must reduce or eliminate critical programs around Chicago, including one in the 11th district which has been extremely hard hit by violence.

Impact investing and gang-violence reduction

Gang violence in Chicago is a serious problem that causes substantial suffering for the city's residents. The violence also creates a significant drain on the city's business community and overall economy. Given the substantial potential savings associated with investing in a program that reduces costs associated with gang violence, a social impact bond would allow private investors to fund Cure Violence's programming in a way that allows them to make a return on their investment and overcome the dearth of funding from the state.

In the case of Cure Violence, the focus would be on reducing healthcare costs associated with gang-related shootings and passing a percentage of those savings back to the investors. In 2015, according to a Bloomberg article, the John H. Stroger Jr. Hospital treated 846 shooting victims at a total cost of about $44 million. Seventy percent of the victims had no insurance which means those costs were passed along to the taxpayer (Jones and McCormick, 2013).

The ROI for gang-violence reduction

According to internal estimates, and extrapolating from past successes, Cure Violence estimates that if they were fully funded throughout Chicago, the city would experience a large reduction in gun violence. Using data estimating total murders at

762 in 2016, conservative estimates by the organization suggest that Cure Violence could reduce that number to somewhere between 200 and 350 murders per year (Ransford, Johnson, Decker, and Slutkin, 2016). This type of reduction would have profound impacts on the city. Costs of treating the victims, arresting the offenders, and repairing the community would be drastically cut. Schools, community organizations, and businesses would all benefit. Real estate values would rise bringing in a much-needed increase in tax revenue to the city. In all, this type of reduction would have an effect on the city that would be valued in the millions of dollars per year (Cure Violence, 2015).

Businesses around Chicago are in the perfect position to invest in what would be the first gang-violence reduction social impact bond in the world. Investors would be able to make a healthy return on an investment that does something important for the community, improving the lives of Chicagoans living in conflict and creating a more economically and socially sustainable city for all to enjoy. It will be interesting to watch whether a problem that has gained national attention can be at least partially addressed using a SIB.

The business case for supporting violence reduction

If private investors can fund Cure Violence's programs in key districts in Chicago and reduce the number of gang-related shootings and the related healthcare costs, then the government entity currently incurring the costs for uninsured shooting victims will realize significant savings. Some of those savings will be passed back to the investors, allowing them to realize a return on their investment.

The investors could be foundations, high net-worth individuals, or financial institutions, but there is a stronger case for private businesses to serve in this role. Unlike a bank or a foundation, local businesses in Chicago stand to gain twice in this arrangement if it is successful: first from the social impact bond payments, and second from the reduced gang activity in the neighborhoods where they operate. Right now, businesses and the wider community absorb the costs of violence in terms of lost economic opportunities and a reduction in the quality of life.

Given the risk of investing in social impact bonds, it makes sense for businesses to co-invest in a consortium. Some members of the Chicagoland Chamber of Commerce have already expressed interest in this particular SIB. If enough businesses band together to make an investment in reducing gang violence, each company's exposure to potential losses will be minimal, and the potential profit – both from the SIB and due to increased neighborhood security – may be well worth the investment.

Social impact bonds and socially responsible investments (SRIs)

More money may flow to those interested in SIBs if they prove effective. This is due to the rapidly increasing interest in social impact investment. In fact, if impact investing is a bell weather for the potential of SIBs, the prospects look good. It is estimated that worldwide, some $25 trillion is invested based on environment, social, or governance (ESG) factors (Knowledge@Wharton, 2017). In the U.S. alone, according to data from the U.S. Forum for Sustainable and Responsible Investment, between 2014 and 2016 SRI assets have grown 33 percent to nearly $9 trillion (Knowledge@Wharton, 2017). This number is remarkable since contemporary SRI only began in earnest in the early 1970s or so (Oh, Park, and Ghauri, 2013). Not surprisingly, UBS, Morgan Stanley, Citigroup, and other big banks are trying to stake a claim in this growing market.

There are a couple of reasons that this growth trend is only likely to continue. One reason is that millennials are eager to devote a significant portion of their investment assets to SRIs and they will have the resources to drive markets (Morgan Stanley, 2017). Over the next three decades, millennials are expected to inherit at least $16 trillion from the so-called ultra-rich (those with at least $30 million in assets); $6 trillion of that will be in the U.S. alone (CNBC, 2016). A significant portion of these funds are expected to go to SRIs.

Another reason that SRI is expected to grow is that there is increasing evidence that investors do not need to trade off doing good for doing well (Oh, Park, and Ghauri, 2013; Kotsantonis, Pinney, and Serafeim, 2016). Being a well-run company and paying attention to ESG issues may go hand-in-hand (Oh, Park, and Ghauri, 2013). Researchers have found that firms with good ratings on ESG issues that are salient (or material) to the firm outperform firms with poor ratings on salient ESG issues (Khan, Serafeim and Yoon, 2016).

Rather than being content to be passive investors, millennials and other like-minded investors may welcome the opportunity to invest in financial instruments like SIBs. In some cases, investors may even take an active role in structuring financial instruments that fit their social and financial interests. As the ability to measure ESG performance increases so too will the demand for a wider range of investment alternatives such as SIBs.

Social impact bonds: potential benefits and challenges

Social impact bonds have the potential to yield benefits well beyond the specific social issues they are designed to address. In addition, they may also provide academics a promising avenue for future research. While SIBs are still in early days, the efforts being made to assess program impact may inform how we think about social investments more broadly. If the ROI can be calculated for a wide variety of social investments, companies may be more eager to adopt strategies and programs they can defend to skeptical shareholders or board members.

Researchers have recognized the need for firms to develop non-traditional approaches for managing political and social risk (Darendeli and Hill, 2016; Oetzel, Getz and Ladek, 2007; Oetzel, and Miklian, 2017; Oh and Oetzel, 2017). By investing in programs that create positive social change, businesses may contribute toward improving the overall business environment for everyone in a given location. A formal structure like the one offered by SIBs also reduces the financial and reputational risk associated with addressing complex challenges. In addition, by forming a multi-sector partnership the firm does not need to develop all necessary capabilities in-house, they can leverage the knowledge, capabilities, and reputation of NGOs with proven track records.

Of course, there are many obstacles to overcome before SIBs become widely adopted. These financial tools are still in their infancy so their long-term viability is unknown. In addition, there is still a significant degree of risk involved in investing in SIBs. Nevertheless, some people, such as Bill Ackman, a hedge fund manager, believe that SIBs will eventually become a big asset class (Foley, 2015). To improve their odds of success, investors will need to become more knowledgeable about social issues and efforts to address them. Today, few business schools train future business leaders to affect deep social challenge. This may need to change (Fort, 2015).

An important criticism of SIBs is that, if widely adopted, they may crowd out the role of government in addressing social issues. Certainly, there are many important social issues that cannot be addressed by a SIB and that are not amenable to traditional performance metrics. These may be given lower priority (regardless of need) if other programs produce "measurable" results. In addition, if successful, SIBs may decrease the willingness of taxpayers to fund social programs. This may lead to a loss of funding for programs that are not suited to alternative financing tools. Finally, an important question is whether SIBs produce a better outcome than other forms of funding for social programs (Edmiston and Nicholls, 2017). Is there any difference in program quality? Long-term scalability? As of now, these are still open questions.

Acknowledgments

The authors would like to thank Paula Castillo for her research assistance at the early stage of this chapter. We also appreciate the comments of conference participants at the 2017 International Studies Association (ISA) Meeting in Baltimore, MD.

Notes

1 The first author is a member of the IEP Research Committee.
2 IEP defines violence containment as "economic activity that is related to the consequences or prevention of violence where the violence is directly against people or property" (IEP, 2014: 4).

References

Arena, M., Bengo, I., Calderini, M., and Chiodo, V. 2016. Social impact bonds: Blockbuster or flash in a pan? *International Journal of Public Administration*, 39(12): https://doi.org/10.1080/01900692.2015.1057852.
Banfield, J., Gündüz, C., and Killick, N. 2006. *Local Business, Local Peace: The Peacebuilding Potential of the Domestic Private Sector*. London: International Alert.

Bekefi, T., Jenkins, B., and Kytle, B. 2006. Social risk as strategic risk. Corporate Social Responsibility Initiative, Working Paper No. 30. Cambridge, MA: John F. Kennedy School of Government, Harvard University.

Beyer, S. 2016. America's 20 largest metros have higher GDPs than most foreign nations. Forbes, October 9. www.forbes.com/sites/scottbeyer/2016/10/09/americas-20-largest-metros-have-higher-gdps-than-most-foreign-nations/#6d64933d54db [Accessed May 22, 2017].

Branzei, O., Lin, H., and Chakrvarty, D. 2014. *WWF's Living @Work: Championed by HP*. Ivey Publishing. Case study number W14328.

CNBC. 2016. Preparing for the $30 trillion great wealth transfer. November 30. www.cnbc. com/2015/01/13/coming-soon-the-biggest-wealth-transfer-in-history.html [Accessed March 21, 2018].

Cook, P.J., and Ludwig, J. 2000. *Gun Violence: The Real Costs*. Oxford University Press: Oxford.

Cullen, J.B., and Levitt, S.D. 1999. Crime, urban flight, and the consequences for cities. *The Review of Economics and Statistics*, 81(2):159–169.

Cure Violence. 2015. The ROI of Cure Violence. http://cureviolence.org/wp-content/uploads/2015/08/Return-on-Investment-ROI.pdf [Accessed June 13, 2017].

Dahan, N.M., Doh, J.P., Oetzel, J., and Yaziji, M. 2010. Cooperation and Co-Creation in Cross-Sectoral Collaboration: New Business Models for Developing Markets. *Long Range Planning*, 43(2–3): 326–342.

Darendeli, I.S., and Hill, T.L. 2016. Uncovering the complex relationships between political risk and MNE firm legitimacy: Insights from Libya. *Journal of International Business Studies*, 47(1): 68–92.

Davey, M. 2016. In Chicago, bodies pile up at intersection of 'depression and rage'. *New York Times*, December 9. www.nytimes.com/2016/12/09/us/chicago-shootings-district-11.html?emc=edit_ta_20161209&nlid=70228829&ref=cta&_r=0 [Accessed June 13, 2017].

Deloitte. 2017. Paying for outcomes: Solving complex social issues through social impact bonds. https://www2.deloitte.com/content/dam/Deloitte/ca/Documents/insights-and-issues/ca-en-insights-issues-paying-for-outcomes.pdf [Accessed April 20, 2017].

Diz, H. 2014. Public-private partnership – a contribution paper. *Interdisciplinary Studies Journal*, 3(4): 111–117.

Edmiston, D., and Nicholls, A. 2017. Social impact bonds: The role of private capital in outcome-based commissioning. *Journal of Social Policy*. https://doi.org/10.1017/S0047279417000125 [Accessed June 13, 2017].

Ernst & Young. 2017. Impact bonds: What's behind the exploding growth in green and social bonds markets?www.ey.com/Publication/vwLUAssets/ey-impact-bonds/$FILE/ey-impact-bonds.pdf [Accessed April 20, 2017].

Felter, C., and Renwick, D. 2017. Colombia's Civil Conflict. Council on Foreign Relations. www.cfr.org/backgrounder/colombias-civil-conflict. [Accessed March 21, 2018].

Foley, S. 2015. Social impact bonds need to fulfil their potential. *Financial Times*, July 13. www.ft. com/content/5eee5f46-293e-11e5-8613-e7aedbb7bdb7?mhq5j=e2 [Accessed April 20, 2017].

Forrer, J., Kee, J.E., Newcomer, K.E., and Boyer, E. 2010. Public-private partnerships and the public accountability question. *Public Administration Review*, 7(3): 475–484.

Fort, T.L. 2015. *Diplomat in the Corner Office: How Business Contributes to Peace*. Palo Alto, CA: Stanford University Press.

Franks, D.M., Davis, R., Bebbington, A.J., Ali, S.H., Kemp, D., and Scurrah, M. 2014. Conflict translates environmental and social risk into business costs. *Proceedings of the National Academy of Science of the United States of America*, 111(21): 7576–7581.

Gorman-Smith, D., and Cosey-Gay, F. 2015. Residents and clients' perceptions of safety and ceasefire impact on neighborhood crime and violence. http://cureviolence.org/wp-content/uploads/2015/01/ceasefire-qualitative-evaluation-9-14.pdf [Accessed June 13, 2017].

Gustafsson-Wright, E., Gardiner, S., and Putcha, V. 2015. The potential and limitations of impact bonds: Lessons from the first five years of experience worldwide. Global Economy and Development Program, Brookings Institution: Washington, D.C. https://www.brook ings.edu/wp-content/uploads/2015/07/impact-bondsweb.pdf [Accessed June 20, 2017].

Gustafsson-Wright, E., and Bogglid-Jones, I. 2017a. Paying for social outcomes: A review of the global impact bond market in 2017. January 17. Brookings Institution: Washington, D.C.

Gustafsson-Wright, E., and Bogglid-Jones, I. 2017b. Colombia leads the developing world in signing the first social impact bond contracts. March 31. Brookings Institution: Washington, D.C.

Henry, D.B., Knoblauch, S., and Sigurvinsdottir, R. 2014. The effect of intensive ceasefire intervention on crime in four Chicago police beats: Quantitative assessment. http://cur eviolence.org/wp-content/uploads/2015/01/McCormick-CeaseFire-Evaluation-Qua ntitative.pdf [Accessed June 13, 2017].

Henisz, W.J., Dorobantu, S., and Nartey, L.J. 2014. Spinning gold: The financial returns to stakeholder engagement. *Strategic Management Journal*, 35(12): 1727–1748.

Hodge, G.A., and Greve, C. 2007. Public-private partnerships: An international performance review. *Public Administration Review*, 67(3): 545–558.

Hodge, G.A., and Greve, C. 2017. On public-private partnership performance: A contemporary review. *Public Works Management and Policy*, 22(1): 55–78.

Instiglio. 2017. SIBs and DIBs in design or implementation, or completed. www.instiglio. org/en/sibs-worldwide/ [Accessed December 5, 2017].

Institute for Economics and Peace (IEP). 2014. The economic cost of violence containment. http://visionofhumanity.org/app/uploads/2017/04/The-Economic-Cost-of-Violence-Containment.pdf [Accessed March 21, 2018].

Institute for Economics and Peace (IEP). 2016. The economic value of peace. http://vision ofhumanity.org/app/uploads/2017/02/The-Economic-Value-of-Peace-2016-WEB.pdf [Accessed March 21, 2018].

Jamali, D. 2011. Partnership for Lebanon and cisco systems: Promoting development in a post-war context, No. 9B11M050. Richard Ivey School of Business, University of Western: Ontario, Canada.

Jones, T. and McCormick, J. 2013. Chicago killings cost $2.5 billion as homicides dwarf N.Y.C.'s. *Bloomberg News*, May 23.

Khan, M., Serafeim, G., and Yoon, A. 2016. Corporate sustainability: First evidence on materiality. *The Accounting Review*, 91(6), 1697–1724.

Knowledge@Wharton. 2017. Why impact investing has reached a tipping point. May 30. http://knowledge.wharton.upenn.edu/article/social-impact-investing-interest-manp ower-and-money-pour-in/ [Accessed March 26, 2018].

Kotsantonis, S., Pinney, C., and Serafeim, G. 2016. ESG integration in investment management: Myths and realities. *Journal of Applied Corporate Finance*, 28(2), 10–16.

McCarthy, N. 2016. Homicides in Chicago eclipse U.S. death toll in Afghanistan and Iraq. *Forbes*, September 8. www.forbes.com/sites/niallmccarthy/2016/09/08/homicides-in-ch icago-eclipse-u-s-death-toll-in-afghanistan-and-iraq-infographic/#5e59652e7d75 [Accessed June 13, 2017].

Morgan Stanley. 2017. Millennials drive growth in sustainable investing. Institute for Sustainable Investing. www.morganstanley.com/ideas/sustainable-socially-responsible-investing-millen nials-drive-growth. [Accessed March 21, 2018].

Oetzel, J., and Getz, K. 2012. When and how might firms respond to violent conflict? *Journal of International Business Studies*, 43: 166–186.

Oetzel, J., Getz, K. and Ladek, S. 2007. The role of multinational enterprises in responding to violent conflict: A conceptual model and framework for research. *American Business Law Journal*, 44(2):331–358.

Oetzel, J., and Miklian, J. 2017. Multinational enterprises, risk management, and the business and economics of peace. *Multinational Business Review*, 25(4): 270–286.

Oh, C.H., and Oetzel, J. 2017. Once bitten twice shy? Experience managing violent conflict risk and MNC subsidiary-level investment and expansion. *Strategic Management Journal*, 38 (3): 714–731.

Oh, C.H., Park, J-H., and Ghauri, P. 2013. Doing right, investing right: Socially responsible investing and shareholder activism in the financial sector. *Business Horizons*, 56(6): 703–714.

Pauly, M.V., and Swanson, A.Social Impact Bonds: New Product or New Package? *The Journal of Law, Economics, and Organization*, 33(4): 718–760.

Rand Europe. 2017. *Evaluating the World's First Social Impact Bond*. https://wws.princeton. edu/sites/default/files/content/Social%20Impact%20Bonds%202014%20Final%20Report. pdf [Accessed April 10, 2017].

Rangan, S., Samii, R., and Van Wassenhove, L.N. 2006. Constructive partnerships: When alliances between private firms and public actors can enable creative strategies. *Academy of Management Review*, 31(3): 738–751.

Ransford, C., Johnson, T., Decker, B., and Slutkin, G. 2016. The relationship between the cure violence model and citywide increases and decreases in killings in Chicago (2000–2016). http://cureviolence.org/wp-content/uploads/2017/06/2016.09.22-CV-Chicago-Memo. pdf [Accessed June 20, 2017].

Rockefeller Foundation. 2017. Social impact bonds. [Accessed April 25, 2017] www.rock efellerfoundation.org/our-work/initiatives/social-impact-bonds/

Rosenfeld, L. 2016. Treating Chicago's young people traumatized by violence. *Al Jazeera America*. February 13. http://america.aljazeera.com/watch/shows/fault-lines/articles/ 2016/2/13/treating-chicagos-young-people-traumatized-by-violence.html [Accessed June 13, 2017].

Skogan, W.G., Hartnett, S.M., Bump, N. and Dubois, J. 2009. *Evaluation of CeaseFire-Chicago*. Skogan Institute for Policy Research, Northwestern University.

Stewart, F. 2015. Employment in conflict and post-conflict situations. UNDP Hum Dev Report Office. http://hdr.undp.org/sites/default/files/stewart_hdr_2015_final.pdf [Accessed March 26, 2018].

United Nations. 2017. Concerns aired over broken ceasefire, challenges to reintegrating ex-combatants, as Security Council tracks implementation of Colombia's historic peace accord. www.un.org/press/en/2018/sc13158.doc.htm. [Accessed March 21, 2018].

World Business Chicago. 2017. Strong, diversified economy. www.worldbusinesschicago. com/economy/ [Accessed June 13, 2017].

5

BEYOND RHETORIC OR REACTIVITY ON SDG 16

Towards a principled policy basis for engaging business in peacebuilding

Jolyon Ford

Introduction

Goal 16 of the 2015–2030 Sustainable Development Agenda revolves around building and maintaining peaceful and inclusive societies, and accompanying suitable institutions. It enlivens challenges that governmental actors – which are seldom the only de facto sources of governance in any society – cannot address alone. Recognition of this reality has partly driven calls, at the highest multilateral policy levels, for policymakers and others overtly to engage the private sector in achieving the SDGs. Part I of this chapter, in briefly outlining some of the institutional rhetoric on interacting with business in pursuit of development goals, reminds us that such calls and actions are relatively recent.[1] It is also less than 20 years since the emergence of incipient elements of the 'business and peace' field: the concerted study of whether, why, or how business actors might make – and be encouraged by public agencies to make – 'positive' peace-related contributions.[2]

In principle, abundant scope exists for businesspeople and commercial entities to make appropriate contributions to legitimate institution-building for 'peaceful and inclusive societies' in fragile and conflict-affected states. Exactly a decade before the SDGs' promulgation, and in one early policymaking foray into engaging with business on peacebuilding, the 2005 resolutions establishing the UN Peacebuilding Commission mandated it to consult with, among others, 'the private sector engaged in peacebuilding activities, as appropriate'.[3] Yet little to no guidance existed then on what might make any peacebuilding entity's relationship with business 'appropriate'. Some years now into the post-2015 SDGs scheme, we still largely lack conceptual frameworks for assessing not just the conditions under which such contributions might be made or be effective,[4] but also the principles that might guide public authorities on what is 'appropriate' and legitimate in collaborating with the private sector. Part IV of this chapter explores some possible building blocks of a future research agenda around addressing this gap, drawing on the insights of the preceding parts. The fact that questions of appropriateness arise at all itself raises a research question: what exactly is it about the for-profit nature of business entities (as distinct from other non-governmental actors in society) that creates possible public-policy dilemmas about engagement with private actors intended to achieve and consolidate peace, the ultimate public good?[5] Part IV reflects provisionally on how our conception of a clear public/private divide may render these dilemmas somewhat more stark and acute than is sometimes warranted by the reality of plural sources of governance in many settings.

Before such reflections, Part II critiques one prevailing policy and scholarly approach to the question of engaging business in peacebuilding and institution-building. This is the approach of what we might call 'advocates' of business *for* peace (i.e. not analysts of business *and* peace): those making the normative case for greater explicit business engagement in the peacebuilding and other goals of SDG 16. The part outlines how this body of work – caricatured in places for effect – arguably insufficiently addresses principled notions vital to questions of 'appropriate' engagement. With its aspirational, idealistic tone this work tends not to engage satisfactorily with the political, the contextual, or with sticky issues around private power, legitimacy and accountability. Part II considers two United Nations Global Compact initiatives directly relevant to the role of business in relation to SDG 16: Business for Peace or 'B4P', and Business for the Rule of Law or 'B4RoL'. Full case studies of these are beyond this chapter's scope and some aspects of these initiatives are perhaps peculiar to the UN system. Nevertheless, Part II shows how these initiatives illustrate a deeper trend,[6] including since they manifest the deficiencies of prevailing 'advocacy'-oriented policy rhetoric and scholarship around engaging business. These two initiatives highlight how the crux of debate over the Compact itself, and all models for enrolling business in peacebuilding and the SDGs, has not been on *whether these 'work'* in enhancing outcomes (whatever metric is used). Debate has instead turned on *whether these are 'right'*: the legitimacy of these 'eclectic' governance innovations.[7] It follows that to go beyond a binary 'for/against' debate on business and SDG 16, future research may need to give more contextualised, theorised accounts of appropriate or non-appropriate collaboration with business, and develop repeatable or specific conceptual frameworks for making these judgments.

Part III of this chapter swings from questioning the somewhat a-political, under-theorised and insufficiently critical deficiencies of the business for peace 'advocates', to questioning the approach of an opposing group of scholars.[8] These are 'sceptics', who arguably have taken legitimacy dilemmas around engaging business in SDG 16 activities too far. The result is twin problems of *paralysis* and *blindness*. Sceptics' paralysis features an overwhelming focus on the principled objections to closer collaboration with business without yielding much by way of practical, constructive insights and alternatives into what 'appropriate' engagement might look like or require. Sceptics are 'paralysed' because their approaches are overly attuned to the democratic legitimacy deficits of business actors in ways that artificially confine the space for virtuous cooperative cross-sector peacebuilding strategies. Such relationships might prove, in practice, to be emancipatory and empowering in ways that critical scholars might in fact appreciate. Part III argues that the sceptics' blindness occurs because these critical scholars often appear unable or unwilling to countenance the possibility of empirical accounts of 'pro-social' business activities in support of peace. They tend not to bother to advance good arguments about what is so materially different about for-profit business actors – relative to other non-state actors such as private foundations, transnational NGOs, or other civil society bodies – that so obviously (in the sceptics' eyes) disqualifies businesses as appropriate partners or stakeholders in peace, development or the rule of law.

As we approach half a decade since the SDGs' promulgation, more research is needed on what is really at stake, especially in particular contexts, sectors and scenarios, in appropriate efforts at involving business in the peaceful development agenda.[9] The aim in Part IV is to move beyond the relative naivety of the business for peace advocates (glossing as they do over the politics of 'business and peace', and the real places where that nexus happens), and the unproductive critical sceptics (with their inherent and inflexible suspicion of private and corporate power). This part explores a research agenda for a principled, politically grounded but workable basis for real-world cooperative peacebuilding, one that accounts for the valid concerns underpinning critical perspectives relating to the legitimacy of 'engagement'.[10]

I. Trends and patterns around business, peace and SDG 16

The last decade has seen greater recognition of the private sector as a developmental stakeholder, including in designing and delivering the SDGs agenda.[11] Alongside attention to the private sector's role in driving inclusive economic activity in conflict-affected areas[12] is work on engaging business in the SDGs,[13] including on SDG 16 and peacebuilding.[14] The trend of interest here is the one going beyond calling for business merely to 'do no harm', including by internalising 'conflict-sensitive business practices': it is a call for firms to make deliberate and explicit 'positive peace' contributions.[15] The corollary of the greater role envisaged for business is an imperative or opportunity for public policymaking to harness business's potential contributions to institution-building for peaceful inclusive societies, and to shape how business and investment activity might affect conflict or peace dynamics.[16] It is enough here to note that these envisaged new roles, postures and partnerships are far more infused with political power dynamics and dilemmas of principle than most prevailing policy rhetoric or practical guidance would appear prepared to acknowledge.

Efforts now to go beyond the SDGs' formal framework and give durability, meaning and substance to private sector engagement in these goals must still be seen in the context of how, until comparatively recently,[17] mainstream (Western) donors and UN-system institutions largely ignored business as a peacebuilding stakeholder.[18] Indeed, until the mid-1990s much of the UN system exhibited a deep antipathy or ideological hostility (not just ambivalence) towards big multinational business.[19]

Around 2015, donors' new-found 'discovery' of business as a potential peace and development partner saw institutional rhetoric in some respects reach the opposite extreme.[20] The UN Global Compact and others called on governments negotiating the 2015 SDGs to allow for maximum alignment where possible with corporate strategies and relationships.

The focus on private sector engagement generated some rather unrealistic expectations of businesses as peacebuilding 'institutions' – or at least to policy positions that risked overstating the interests, incentives, legitimacy and capabilities of businesses as partners and participants.[21] In any event, leading bilateral donors such as the United Kingdom have expressly put engaging with (and developing) the private sector at the centre of SDG strategy.[22] The US position is similarly overt about engagement.[23] Other OECD donors repeat this refrain.[24] For example, Australia's policy framework makes clear that the 2030 Agenda is 'not just for and about government' and privileges closer cooperation with the private sector, including by the UN system.[25] Like its peer agencies, the only reference in Australian frameworks to principles governing 'appropriate' engagement is the statement that private sector development partners must have 'demonstrated commitment to responsible business'.[26]

A gap exists since such statements focus on the qualities of business actors, not what should guide public actors engaging them. Indeed nine UN General Assembly resolutions on global partnerships have been negotiated already this century, but it is only recently that the UN system has engaged with the governance of those relationships.[27] Guidance around business and the SDGs is mainly oriented to business actors rather than policymakers who must decide how and when and with whom to engage.[28] This includes guidance for business on SDG 16.[29] In the UN system, some greater guidance on appropriate partnering relationships has been generated.[30] However, many activities around business engagement in SDG 16 will not amount to formal partnerships.

Faced with these trends, scholarship to date in the emerging 'business and peace' field has largely hung between two poles.[31] One is the *aspirational advocacy strand* (often advancing simplistic a-political 'peace-through-commerce' arguments). The other is the *determinedly critical or sceptical strand* (unwilling to accept a justifiable public role for the private sector in relation to peacebuilding, or related engagement activities). For their part, policymakers, practitioners and businesspeople faced with the imperatives, mandates or appeal of the new 'engagement' rhetoric may be mostly 'muddling through' on attempting to operationalise it despite uncertainty or misgivings about what is 'appropriate' in their relationships or endeavours. Prevailing polarised scholarship has not necessarily yielded insights of use to these groups of actors. Both the 'business drives conflict and is not a suitable partner' narrative and the 'business grounds peaceful development or is a suitable partner' narrative have an empirical basis. Ganson and Wennman have recognised that the 'corporate hero' vs. 'corporate villain' binary is inadequate in descriptive terms,[32] but recognise that this does not necessarily provide an answer to the question of how the private sector's SDGs and peacebuilding role is to be supervised in terms of principles and legitimacy by mandated authorities, or promoted by donors and policymakers.

What is the underlying principled dilemma? One can characterise external or local public authorities facilitating business activities in fragile states (including those explicitly oriented to SDG 16), as at risk of being either a 'Trojan horse' or an 'Ostrich'.[33] The Trojan horse problem describes where a peacebuilding authority engaging closely with business becomes at risk of being perceived and portrayed as helping to facilitate or legitimate commercial activities by private actors. Onlookers might then see the institution, imbued as it is with high moral authority as a public agency, as a Trojan horse for the entry of opportunist, exploitative capital into a vulnerable society. A donor engaging foreign businesses on addressing their conflict risk footprint may be open to accusations that it is simply acting as an investor 'political risk' advisor, helping firms smooth out their commercial adventures in the name of public peacebuilding objectives and with all the legitimating power of peacebuilding mandates.[34] The Ostrich problem is related. The proverbial ostrich buries its head in the sand to avoid seeing and dealing with dangers and problems around it. The risk is of public authorities acting like the proverbial ostrich and not engaging business at all on SDG 16 issues such as peacebuilding and the rule of law out of fear (among other things) of being labelled a Trojan horse.[35] Part III below explores why reassurance on appropriate engagement is necessary to reduce the peace and development 'opportunity costs' of Ostrich-like non-engagement. Part II, which now follows, helps contextualise why overly enthusiastic embrace of the new engagement mantra contributes to Trojan horse-like fears about the subversion of public values in service of private corporate ones, while legitimating the latter.

II. Problem A: proselytising advocates? Under-cooked policy and study

The 'advocacy' strand of discourse is a problematic dynamic in the imperative to move beyond rhetoric and flesh out the parameters and principles of legitimate public–private engagement on SDG 16. The strand's weakness is essentially an insufficient appreciation of the 'Trojan horse' risk. That aspirational strand is evident in many policy initiatives and products on engaging business, notably the UN Global Compact's schemes on 'Business for Peace' (B4P, 2013–) and 'Business for the Rule of Law' (B4RoL, 2015–). The strand reaches its apogee among those scholar-advocates whose work is sometimes tantamount to either championing business as a peace panacea – without question or distinctions – or in effect simply pleading for business to please 'do more' on peace. More valid, valuable contributions from this policy and scholarship strand may require far greater anticipation and explicit accommodation of contextual, principled and theoretical terrains.[36] This begins with accepting business actors as political actors (not just economic or social ones),[37] within a broader, almost axiomatic recognition of the deeply contested and complex nature of 'peacebuilding', 'statebuilding' and 'business' in higher-risk settings.

(i) 'B4P': the UN's 'Business for Peace' scheme

The B4P initiative is intended to expand and deepen private sector action in support of peace, and is expressly linked to SDG 16.[38] There is nothing necessarily problematic with initiatives (and scholarship) exploring how authorities might deliberately leverage business interest, resources and capacity so as to supplement governance, regulatory and service-delivery capacity in fragile states.[39] Instead, the issue turns on the appropriateness of encouraging or directly engaging or facilitating such actors and activity, and conceptual frameworks to assess appropriateness. The policy risk exists in pushing such a role without recognition and extensive analysis of the principled dilemmas potentially arising in such enrolment and engagement strategies. The related scholarship risk exists in an analogous a-political, a-contextual, uncritical exhortation to engage business in peace and to drive 'peace through commerce'.[40] We need to move beyond seeing the private sector as a development or peace panacea, to explore the real contours and parameters of its utility and legitimacy as a potentially useful, sometimes problematic stakeholder in the agenda.[41] Five years after B4P's conception and as we move beyond the first half-decade of SDG 16, both policy work and scholarship promoting close cooperative roles actors arguably requires a more honest account of why 'Trojan horse' fears exist at all. This entails openness to recognising the complex power relations, networks of influence and agency dynamics, and actor-overlaps that are an inevitable feature of the political economy of governance even in highly sophisticated and very peaceful democracies.

There is no paucity of critical perspectives and insights capable of enriching and rebalancing this 'advocacy' strand. At their most forceful, these perspectives display deep distrust of private commercial power, and of a state apparatus whose higher claims to moral-political authority are 'captured' in service of the interest of private power.[42] Big business and private capital, on this view, are predatory beasts interested only in exploiting vulnerable 'new' post-conflict societies on the peripheries of global society.[43] By extension, any public institution's role in engaging business risks being a Trojan horse for 'imperial'[44] motives and inappropriate facilitation of elite private interests.[45] Shrill as such perspectives sound, they at least serve to help highlight the objective risk that business actors involved in B4P-like schemes may not necessarily share peacebuilders' conceptions of and commitments to 'the public interest'. That is, business actors may cloak themselves in public authority – including through multi-stakeholder governance activities – in ways that either shield or even positively legitimise their presence and activities in fragile societies.[46] Thus, scholars such as Honke see the engagement narrative and initiatives such as B4P as simply vehicles for lending private actors an unjustifiable degree of public authority as they subvert that authority or at least pursue essentially self-interested ends.[47] Miklian and Schouten argue that even if drawing big business into globalised value frameworks such as the Global Compact may help to ensure a greater reach of public governance norms over private sector behaviour, things like the B4P framework might create risks at other levels.[48] By legitimising businesses as peace actors with all the authority that the UN system imports, such schemes risk 'institutionalising asymmetrical encounters' between companies and those affected by their operations.[49] Most scholarship on B4P's subject-matter does not really engage with these sorts of risks, reflecting a broader weakness in corporate responsibility scholarship generally.[50]

Miklian and Schouten observe that initiatives such as B4P – and the phenomenon they represent – are partly about framing who is a legitimate actor in global governance.[51] Yet the 'advocacy' strand and the B4P narrative in their sunny promotion of engagement and shared governance have not really confronted that reality and its philosophical and practical implications for *principled* engagement. The policy risks on which critical scholars are fixated are non-negligible and real risks. Even the pragmatic author of the 2011 *UN Guiding Principles on Business and Human Rights* was careful to emphasise that companies are not 'public interest democratic institutions' such that we need to be cautious in ascribing or extending to them peacebuilding, statebuilding and co-governance roles.[52] The policy risk in schemes within the B4P mould is that public peacebuilding agencies become (or become perceived as) mere 'consultants' or handmaidens to big businesses,[53] smoothing out their uncomfortable edges in tricky places, and facilitating their political risk, reputational and social impact footprints while legitimating their activities – and without necessarily advancing the (localised) public interest. At very least, as SDG 16 oriented international peacebuilding and statebuilding efforts are shared among multiple public and private actors, including under the B4P motif, a distinctive risk emerges. This is that with the diffusion of authority and role-sharing, the possibility of allocating identifiable and discrete responsibility might diminish proportionately. Eventually, it becomes unclear who is accountable for what exercises of power. Everyone is co-responsible, yet no one is.[54]

Critical scholars' insights do address the principal weakness of the proponents – scholars and policymakers – of the prevailing engagement paradigm. The latter 'advocacy' group's tendency, which finds institutionalised reflection in the assumptions underpinning schemes such as B4P, is to proceed largely as if business activity is solely an economic phenomenon with potential upsides for peace, social cohesion and institutional strengthening. By extension, this approach portrays business actors as unproblematic, neutral, a-political well-meaning but under-used peace agents. There is insufficient institutionalised anxiety (among pro-engagement policymakers) or critical reflection (among scholar-advocates) on that agency. The assumption is often that we can always identify neatly distinct spheres of 'business' and 'politics', comprising distinct people. The assumption becomes that SDG 16 would be enhanced if only we could bring the public and private together in cooperative ways. This belies the reality of power relations and multiple identities. Sometimes business and government are too close, whereas B4P can assume they are not close enough and need to 'engage'. In fact in many fragile states the problem is not insufficient engagement with business, but that 'business' and 'government' are headed by people from the same elite circles, and sometimes (as in Angola) the same handful of families.

As we move beyond mere rhetoric on engaging business in SDG 16, greater openness to the deeply political, context-specific and contested nature of business (let alone of business for peace initiatives) will hold significance for what might be 'appropriate' levels of cooperative peacebuilding strategies. B4P is expressly framed by reference to SDG 16. Yet its proponents and scholars have not necessarily taken seriously the evident 'buzz'[55] in civil society (and certainly among critical scholars) which, around and since the SDGs' design and adoption, has taken the corporate capture concept (private capture of public development policymaking and governance) as a major concern.[56] One alliance statement accordingly calls for reclaiming public policy space and 'weakening the grip of corporate power' on the SDGs agenda.[57] The B4P initiative arguably reflects a wider narrative within which an essentially uncritical business role in the SDGs has been promoted.[58] This wider policy voice (and its academic equivalent) has not advanced any overt institutional acknowledgement of undue influence, legitimation and authority-appropriation risks, nor involved sufficient honest reflection on the fact that there is not always an alignment between the corporate and policy agendas.[59]

That the 'advocacy' strand of scholarship (and its reflected tone in B4P and other policy manifestations) has not sought to problematise concepts such as 'peace' or 'statebuilding' or confronted the politics of business for peace has consequences. It leaves us ill-equipped to assess the appropriateness of 'engagement' or of business uptake of governance roles. B4P and the like are accordingly short on what 'peace positive' contributions or outcomes involving business or attributed to business might mean, in any claimed case or generally.[60] A revealing exemplar is Westermann-Behaylo and others' 2015 aspirational account of the potential role of business in building more peaceful societies.[61] This leaves the most significant concepts entirely undeveloped. It makes no particular effort to unpack assertions about firms 'creating value for society', 'having a positive impact on international relations' and 'improving governance gaps'. Yet what counts as 'value', 'positive impact' or 'improve[ment]', and who decides this? Despite the warnings of critical scholars, such scholarship displays little interest in or even acknowledgement of the deeply political, difficult, dilemma-filled, potentially crowding-out nature of such interventions and contributions. Scholars in this class do sometimes advert to legitimacy issues,[62] but without necessarily engaging them as such. There is typically no sense of recognition, let alone of being troubled, around the possibility that business actors might lack the real or perceived legitimacy (as well as the skills, incentives, etc.) to take on these roles in any sustained or systematic and appropriate manner. Such scholarship, like B4P in some ways, can amount more to an appeal to business to shoulder more of the development and governance burden than an analysis of why or how firms would, could or should do so, and with what policy risks. What motivates firms to explicitly expand their social and governance footprint? How are such firms' motives potentially relevant to assessing appropriateness around engagement or facilitation or validation, by public authorities, of this expansion?

Where does 'the state' fit in, and how do such accounts justify glossing over or ignoring the agency of local actors to whom these things are (on such accounts) simply 'done' by Western firms? B4P scholarship such as Westermann-Behaylo and others focuses on large Western listed firms yet do not seem to explore those with whom these entities must perforce interact in multiple, complex and often contradictory ways. This creates the impression that foreign big businesses are or can be instrumental and decisive actors in peacebuilding and conflict prevention (if only they would try). The approach is blind to various factors and forces that might shape peace (for better or worse), irrespective anything even an influential investor might do. The approach ignores or ascribes a puzzling passivity to state and civic actors whose agendas and interests will invariably affect any B4P-driven initiatives. Such approaches lead to risks of overstating the significance of business actors in the political dynamics of peace and conflict, as if such actors are 'the most important institution' in determining generally whether countries remain peaceful or descend into conflict.[63] To be fair, some scholarship in this strand has begun to engage with the need to factor in plural sources of governance in fragile and conflict-affected states.[64] Yet most scholars outside the 'business and peace' core would find entirely unremarkable insights about the hybrid nature of many political orders.

In terms of Part IV's ideas for future research and policymaking, these will arguably benefit from greater self-awareness and reflection on the embedded preferences and assumptions that underpin the engagement narrative. For instance, Westermann-Behaylo and others have argued that corporations have 'equal footing' with government and civil society actors to determine whether, which, and how activities are undertaken for the public interest.[65] But bold statements of such equivalency in legitimacy or authority terms are deeply contested and contestable. Future work would need greater grounding in accounts of the politics of statebuilding and governance in fragile states, or at least recognition of what we know about the legitimacy (and efficacy) shortcomings of externally driven peace and development initiatives in conflict-affected societies.[66] Haufler describes the advocacy strand of business for peace scholarship as comprising 'optimistic' scholars, who 'want it to be true' that business can build peaceful, inclusive societies.[67] She notes that this is not the same as showing that it *is* true (generally or in some settings), nor does such an approach explain how it is appropriate for public policy to foster and facilitate such activities given the policy risks. Haufler is right in observing that despite the abundance of available insights from various disciplines, the advocacy stream have generally not attempted to ground their approaches in any meaningful account of the legitimacy concerns around nature and effect of private power when it is wielded in the context of peacebuilding and statebuilding initiatives and partnerships.[68] For Iff, too, a far richer and nuanced discussion is needed given the limited engagement (outside the critical scholarship 'bubble') with the legitimacy issues that arise within the new 'engagement' paradigm.

(ii) 'B4RoL': the UN's Global Compact's 'Business for Peace' scheme

Invoking SDG 16 directly and as something of a lower-profile twin sister to B4P, in 2015 the Compact launched the 'Business for the Rule of Law Framework' (B4RoL).[69] The Framework is intended to 'engage responsible business to support the building and strengthening of legal frameworks and accountable institutions'.[70] The Framework defines 'rule of law' (RoL),[71] explaining B4RoL's rationale by reference to the RoL being key to the 'enabling environment for responsible business to play an optimal role' in helping to drive sustainable development.[72] Explaining 'strong' RoL as an essential foundation for development, it delineates this as 'including the protection of investments, property rights, contractual rights, and legal identity'.[73]

The B4RoL idea mimics the B4P debate in terms of envisaging minimalist ('do no harm') and more maximalist ('do some good') spectrum. The Framework explicitly divides business B4RoL activities into 'respect' and 'support' ones, such that any business taking proactive deliberate measures to *support* RoL programming must themselves *respect* the RoL. Much as the B4P project assumes that participant entities are 'doing no harm' before they might be partnered or encouraged to 'do some good', the Framework talks of engagement with *responsible* business, and provides that 'support' is a complement to, not substitute for, 'respect' for the RoL: 'respect is the 'must do' and support is the 'optimal'.[74] It defines 'support' as voluntary action taken by businesses that goes beyond the responsibility to respect by making a positive contribution to help strengthen legal frameworks and promote more accountable institutions.[75] It contemplates three kinds of activity. First is 'core business': acting to strengthen the RoL through general business activities in ways that 'help close RoL gaps, including those that assist with the process of law-making and implementation, access to information, and the administration of and access to justice'.[76] It is not obvious what sort of activities are envisaged here.

Second, 'funding and assistance' support contemplates financial and in-kind assistance to governments and others including 'specialized expertise, volunteering, thought-leadership, training or mentoring, or ... contributions of products or services to help address gaps in the legal framework and institutions'.[77] The Framework gives as an example supporting judicial training 'in jurisdictions with overburdened judicial systems' and loaning staff, especially lawyers, to government or civil society 'to help support the drafting and implementation of laws, and law reform proposals'.[78] Third, the Framework envisages 'business advocacy': inviting business to take public positions on RoL issues such as corruption, taking action 'independently or collectively, through advocacy and/or public policy engagement', because 'collective action from the responsible business community can be a powerful agent of change'.[79] B4RoL is one manifestation of a broader prevailing narrative calling on business and investors to 'look beyond the factory doors' and consider how to partner with or support host state governments in 'developing and improving the Rule of Law'.[80] This directly informs some US government development policy products in this area.[81]

The Framework makes clear that the activities it promotes are intended as a complement to, but not substitute for, government action. Yet it otherwise spends no time reflecting on questions of legitimacy or appropriateness around business interventions in legal or justice systems. Nor have scholars done so. The RoL's significance as a public good goes well beyond property and contractual rights, notwithstanding the Framework's narrow articulation of a RoL rationale. But there is more fundamental concern. Nothing in and around the Framework and its promotion contains any real overt acknowledgement of (let alone principled guidance or safeguards for) how truly deeply contested and politically charged things are that relate to 'RoL', law, and legal institutions in peacebuilding and development contexts.[82] These are highly contested arenas even without injecting the private sector as a partner, or ideas such as investing businesses (for example) seconding experts into the developing country governments that partner and regulate them. The Framework is unduly 'light' not only on these realities, but on basic organisational strategic risk perspectives. The Framework does briefly acknowledge that some governments may be sensitive to direct engagement by businesses on RoL issues,[83] and that correspondingly businesses may be averse to taking action in support of the RoL 'due to concerns that a government may not view their actions positively and for fear of retaliation against the business'.[84] Business activities are properly framed as 'support' ones implying that they are not displacing primary state responsibility or authority. The Framework does talk of strengthening the RoL *in line with international standards,* [85] but it is not obvious what this means. There is otherwise no sense among UN system or business engagement scholars that this initiative (like B4P) raises potentially troubling issues around the appropriation of governance authority, the blurring of responsibilities, or the risk of undue influence over public bodies through supposedly innocuous business interventions into the RoL.

Initiatives to build state institutional capacity do not necessarily build peace, inclusivity, social cohesion or respect for human rights.[86] Strengthening the capacity of some institutions in some contexts is consistent with enhancing the RoL in only its 'thin', domination-legitimating conception. These sorts of issues have gone unremarked upon around the B4RoL initiative and Framework. Hansen is an exception, observing rightly that the viability (and suitability) of methods to promote the RoL remains contested enough as it is: 'the entry of business into this swirling mix must be approached with caution'. He continues:

> The ability of corporations to assist the struggling legal infrastructure of countries that are short on both cash and expertise should not be dismissed out of hand .... [but] business involvement in *building* legal frameworks could easily be blurred with business involvement in *designing* legal frameworks. This intermingling of actors and functions is sufficiently alarming to give pause. The potential for abuse demands that stringent precautions be taken by host governments and businesses themselves.[87]

A deep critical perspective would observe that niche token interventions in justice systems or law reform by corporate actors obscure structural frameworks by which extraction and production benefits such actors, and which they have no real incentive to amend. Seen this way, any 'support' activities are merely therapeutic, cosmetic and disingenuous exercises in public relations. One does not need such a deep critique to feel troubled by the premises and implications of an uncritical enthusiasm around ideas such as B4RoL in fragile settings. There is something alarmingly superficial about a UN agency promoting direct support activities (such as staff loans to governments: the regulatee loaning capacity to the regulator) in settings with weak institutional safeguards or deep power imbalances relating to corporate actors and investors. This sort of flexibility can be justified for example during exceptional periods of post-conflict recovery.[88] Yet the Framework's promotion of such practices and the lack of critical reflection or reception of it creates the impression of a 'policy innovation' that has not necessarily been thought through. Warning bells should sound when UN-sponsored business engagement initiatives speak of 'doing some good'. Whose good, defined and judged by whom?[89]

Along with the open-ended content of 'RoL', the institutional authority it intrinsically conveys makes the RoL concept and discourse highly susceptible to being appropriated. It is available as an unarguable, inevitable ordering force that can be deployed by those with power over its use so as to privilege some preferences over others. The danger of blending the RoL with particular conceptions of substantive laws for the ideal society, and then lending them the institutional imprimatur of the United Nations, is that substantive value agendas might be promoted as neutral, everyone-needs-this RoL initiatives that are neutral as to ideological cause. Now on one view, it is entirely appropriate to view business as an important stakeholder in ensuring that governments adhere to the RoL: a constituency-of-demand, a source of oversight, and possibly a source of capacity. Yet scholars have not yet appeared troubled by some of the assumptions and implications of this initiative, nor provided any theorised account of the rationale underpinning it. On one level, flaws in the Framework are of little consequence since the initiative has not received significant uptake. It may also be unsurprising that a 'marketing-style' call-to-action document – intended to engage business in practical activities in support of SDG16 – does not dwell on policy risks and principled dilemmas. Yet academic networks around and on the UN system should still be asking questions about the assumptions underpinning the Framework, the scope for inappropriate use of such legitimating structures, and models for assessing what is 'appropriate' and 'legitimate' in public–private RoL and statebuilding engagement.

III. Problem B: paralysed sceptics? Over-reach among critical scholars

Critical perspectives add much-needed colour and context to this field. Most 'business-for-peace' advocate-scholars' inputs could be greatly enriched by more, not less, attention to notions of power, agency, context and legitimacy, and perceptions thereof. Real policy risks and principled dilemmas do arise, generally and in specific settings, in closely engaging private-sector actors in publicly grounded schemes to promote peace, development and the RoL. Yet the critical perspective is handicapped, too. It typically overdoes its case. Its scholars arguably reveal a general reluctance to explore whether there is as much scope for corporate virtue in peacebuilding engagement (including in specific settings) as there is for the social vice that some critical scholars seem to see as inherent in the corporation as a thing. Vigilance about abuse of power in the name of peacebuilding and the SDGs is important, but excessive preoccupation with legitimacy is paralysing and even counter-productive.[90] Future critical scholarship might increase its own legitimacy (and reach) by displaying greater openness *a priori* to exploring whether, where and when the promise of principled engagement might in fact have been fulfilled, at least partially. Especially where investment and re-investment in conflict-affected or post-conflict areas is inevitable, Ostrich-like non-engagement by public actors with private business may be a more difficult posture to justify by the very standards that critical scholars of peace and development invoke. Critical scholars profess a monopoly of concern over empowerment and emancipation of 'local people' (often without differentiating for local elites), yet would need to be open to investigating where business-linked RoL or peacebuilding initiatives might in fact have advanced these values in ways that critical scholars might relish.

Consider Bougainville, a relatively rare 'classic case' for business and peace scholarship in the sense of the high degree of direct relationship between investor conduct and peace or conflict trajectory.[91] Braithwaite has argued that one factor in Bougainville's unnecessary descent into conflict was the role of some influential Australian public figures who engaged in self-righteous and ideological vilification of multinational mining firms there. Such critics appeared uninterested, at key points, in asking what possible means existed to avoid or resolve the mining-related civil war, and what role the relevant firms might play as potential partners or at least participants in conflict prevention or peacebuilding.[92] Likewise, the ideological posturing of many critical scholars and their in-built knee-jerk condemnation or suspicion of business actors at some level disqualifies them (as indeed it does the positive 'advocates') as objective analysts of issues at the nexus of business and peace. Ironically (since they seek transformative peace outcomes), this approach might also ultimately deprive critical scholars' work of the scope for generating an audience of policymakers and others who must navigate these complex activities and arenas, and who could most benefit from critical insights. Some critical and cosmopolitan peacebuilding theorists accept that their work has yet to offer alternatives, counter-factuals of non-engagement, or 'substantial operational modes' for constructive engagement in conflict prevention or peacebuilding.[93] There is more to do.

Engaging with businesspeople and entities to explore and enrol their contributions to SDG 16 may, and should, be approached with a critical eye. Yet in general and in some settings, blanket non-engagement may be more irresponsible, and more inimical to the protective and emancipatory values that critical scholars purport to speak for. Such scholars have generally not made out their case. They would surely need to show how dialogue and partnership with business on peacebuilding issues (again, generally and in specific settings) of itself poses any greater policy risks or any more complex principled dilemmas than the very familiar donor activity of working with civil society.[94] Both 'business' and 'civil society' anywhere are comprised of myriad, multi-motivated players with no uniform, inherent attributes of legitimacy or appropriateness. Public authorities (whose own legitimacy varies, including depending on whose view one seeks) routinely engage with non-state non-profit entities in conversations and actions to enhance peace. What is so materially different about for-profit actors? For those serious about peacebuilding mandates, the relevant question is not really whether an actor or partner is public or private, business or civic, but *whether they might help build peace*. Going beyond SDG 16 rhetorical criticism will require a new approach. Critics and sceptics cannot deify civil society and damn (or ignore) business without considering what peacebuilding merits and legitimacy claims each actor has. Both civil society and business engagement matter. Both are very politicised. But both involve manageable policy risks.[95]

Whatever the macro-level structural forces that shape poverty, corruption, under-development and conflict, at the operational level the risk of peacebuilding institutions acting as 'moles' or 'Trojan horses' for business interests seems slightly overstated. Again, a far more problematic posture would be an Ostrich-like refusal to engage in outreach, dialogue and partnership with business actors capable of influencing peace dynamics simply because of officials' ambivalence towards the private sector or concern about undue influence, capture and avoiding accusations of enabling 'empire'.[96] While the 'advocates' adopt a rather naïve world-view of virtuous Western corporations helping to 'fill governance gaps' in the public interest, sceptics resistant to any engagement display an indefensibly rigid and pre-determined mindset in which 'the private sector' automatically comprises corrupt, self-interested, predatory elites only interested in using peacebuilding schemes to promote their own narrow interests in illegitimate ways. Such approaches contradict the very traditions of critical peacebuilding scholarship, which prize empirical and nuanced accounts of these spaces, places and activities.

Undue influence by business is a policy risk of promoting collaborative and business-led initiatives under SDG 16. Yet businesspeople (whether local, foreign, diaspora etc.) would seek to exercise political influence on external or local political authorities (which we tend to cast as inherently 'more legitimate') regardless of whether those authorities adopted an official engaged or non-engaged posture. A posture of non-engagement may reflect uncertainty about what might render relationships more 'appropriate', putting a premium now on offering greater assurance and advice. But non-engagement will not immunise institutions from influence, and only ensure it remains shadowy. An accountable policy of dialogue and outreach and cooperation might be preferable. Risks such as corporate 'capture' do generate serious concerns, but are not alone a reason for non-engagement by public authorities with an SDG 16 mandate.[97] Instead, they put a premium on defining – generally and for specific contexts – workable principles to guide responsible policy engagement with responsible business actors.[98]

The case for close cooperative relationships with business actors in peacebuilding contexts is perhaps not as difficult to make as 'sceptics' would suggest.[99] Honke seems to accept that there is merit in the idea that schemes for collaboration and co-governance have a socialisation dimension that holds some potential for 'civilising' business's peace footprint (rather than just legitimating profit-making).[100] Whatever the risk of schemes such as B4P and B4RoL being used as a subterfuge to legitimise corporate adventures in fragile societies, such schemes also carry the promise of situating these actors in 'the realm of accountable political action'.[101] Firms may have less space to enjoy being simultaneously politically influential actors that can then choose to be answerable only on economic and commercial impacts. Ambiguity remains (among policymakers, civic actors, and business itself) around the private sector's role in the peacebuilding and development agendas. Some of this is healthy scepticism and caution, and so something to cultivate institutionally in the interests of ensuring 'appropriate' relationships. However, unlike the outright hostility towards business evident in earlier decades (at least within the UN system), a 'more measured appreciation' of both the potential and limits of private sector roles is emerging.[102] This provides the context for exploring, in the final part, ways to move beyond binary debates on business and the SDGs.

IV. Beyond the beginning: a research agenda for business and peace

Like SDG 16 itself, the multi-disciplinary 'business and peace' field is a relatively new and emerging one, such that a whole agenda exists just to map and 'typologize' the field.[103] Yet the field traverses disciplines, from international relations to corporate criminology, with a somewhat stronger and longer pedigree than many 'business and peace' scholars might acknowledge, or draw upon.[104] Haufler has also called for greater convergence, by 'business and peace' scholars, with international relations and global governance theory,[105] to which one might add political science and area studies, management theory, development economics, the political economy of peace and conflict, and so on. Part II above made clear how 'advocates' might enrich their insights in this way, but critical scholars too might consider descending from sceptical generalities about the nature and effects of private power (etc.). This would help generate empirical and case-specific insights into the ways in which private-sector activity may have affected (or not) peace and conflict dynamics in particular settings or 'types' of settings.[106] In one example of 'business and peace' studies maturing, Miklian and Schouten have observed how efforts to engage business in co-governance activities might contribute to reshaping the balance between public and private authority in global governance,[107] although such schemes may of course also be a product of those extant shifts.

Any work into the 2020s exploring what might comprise 'appropriate' (or not) engagement with business around SDG 16's agenda will take as a backdrop the emerging ecosystem of regulatory schemes and normative standards on responsible business conduct, such as the 2011 *UN Guiding Principles on Business and Human Rights.*[108] However, giving content to actionable principles to guide and shape 'principled engagement' is not just about reciting the standards that we might use to judge whether particular commercial entities are sufficiently socially responsible for partnering purposes. As this chapter has explored, the task involved is rather more comprehensive. It arises in parallel to other related important lines of enquiry, such as understanding better the structural, operational, policy or commercial incentives and conditions that shape whether and how businesses come to be involved, with public agencies or of their own accord, in explicit efforts towards building more 'inclusive and peaceful societies'.[109]

The challenge of giving substance to appropriate and legitimate engagement has various elements.[110] It is *partly normative* in the sense outlined above: what are the principles and standards against which the governance of and engagement with business by public agencies (not just the standards of corporate responsibility itself) should be judged in fragile and conflict-affected contexts? How and with what and whose regulatory impulses are these standards evolving? The research agenda challenge is *partly conceptual*, even if one seeks practical insights, since among other things we need to unpack what theories of agency or power relations inform ideas about public–private 'engagement' on peacebuilding, social cohesion and related institutional strengthening. The challenge is *partly typological*: about ordering and organising streams of activity depending, for instance, on what they purport to achieve.[111] This can include a greater attentiveness to dynamics that might be peculiar to particular industry sectors, given how greatly these vary in exposure, interest or incentive, capacity and other factors relevant to explicit commitments to SDG 16 outcomes. The task is *partly operational*: fleshing out exactly what activities we mean by/and what constitutes 'engagement',[112] so as to know where to look for issues of appropriateness or inappropriateness. It is *partly empirical*: the need for more contextualised, place-specific studies of business impact and involvement in/on peacebuilding and institutional strengthening.[113] The task is also *partly institutional*: which actors do or should bear the authority or responsibility for influencing conflict-sensitive or peace-enhancing business conduct, or for assessing the legitimacy of public–private collaboration on the SDGs? There are also *temporal* and *generic* dimensions to this: at what point(s) in time, around a business 'intervention' around SDG 16, can we make claims about the principled or unprincipled nature of the engagement concerned? How do generic research challenges about measuring and attributing success on such vague criteria as 'strengthening institutions' affect any assessment of how legitimate or appropriate a purported engagement was?[114]

Finally, any research agenda calculated to give greater meaning to 'appropriate' and 'legitimate' principled public–private engagement on SDG 16 themes may need to reappraise some fundamental premises. A viable avenue of exploration is whether the dilemmas around closer development relationships with business, and around greater involvement and 'authority' of business actors in shaping and delivering the SDGs agenda, might only arise in the stark ways described in this chapter if one tries to maintain a particularly rigid conception of the public/private divide. On one view, it is only important to police that divide (i.e. ensuring attempted cooperation or drift across it) if the divide is viable and valuable. It is a viable distinction if one can readily distinguish public from private actors, activity, authority and agency. It conceivably is a valuable distinction (for SDG 16 purposes, which are not the totality of what is at stake) if it helps in achieving peaceful, inclusive societies under an institutionalised RoL. On the viability question, there are good reasons to suppose that public officials in peacebuilding and RoL contexts may often or sometimes be acting for essentially 'private' purposes (or a mix of purposes, with mixed implications). Those nominally classed as private-sector actors may act in ways that are best described as 'public' in nature, intent, effect or significance.

There is nothing new in the insight that it is not only governments that govern, and not only formal regulators who influence behaviour in society. The net governance effect in most societies in fact is typically a function of the inputs of a range of 'public' and 'private' actors.[115] Legal pluralism in post-conflict governance settings – norms made and administered by multiple social sources not necessarily neatly public or private – is increasingly seen as a resource for inclusive governance, not just a hitherto under-appreciated fact.[116] Our perception of dilemmas existing around principled and appropriate engagement with business, and on business drifting or being drafted into co-governance roles and institutions, may change if we see peacebuilding as a nominally 'public domain'[117] but not one that is (or perhaps ought to be) exclusively the preserve of public authorities.[118] That is, peacebuilding may be seen as typically comprising an arena of purposive, purportedly pro-social political activities in which a whole multiplicity of actors and stakeholders operate and sometimes cooperate.[119] These actors may have varying degrees of de facto popular, democratic or political legitimacy irrespective of their ostensible 'public' or 'private' labels. Not only are many of these contexts best understood as 'hybrid' political orders,[120] in many places non-state governance providers (from firms to cooperatives to militia groups) are far from being empirically illegitimate. In reflecting on peacebuilding in the DRC, Iff observes that if one accepts a hybrid understanding of statebuilding, it is normatively neither good nor bad that a company engages in service delivery; it is simply a fact.[121] The conventional approach to SDG 16 involves encouraging public actors to engage and enrol private sector ones, in the shadow of concerns about illegitimate gains in influence by less accountable non-state actors. An alternative approach would explore beyond the notional public / private distinction, without necessarily devaluing that divide or its rationale. This approach sees the public sphere of institutionally supported peacebuilding – generally and in any one setting – as typically comprising a whole collection of socio-political activities and practices of common concern.[122]

This approach may not be very neat, and may trouble critical scholars even further, but is hardly one disinterested in ensuring 'appropriateness' in development and democratisation. Rather it accepts complexity but calls – as we move beyond 2020 into the full final decade of the SDGs – for highly contextualised and open-minded analyses and accounts of what is 'appropriate' collaboration and cooperation, rather than generalised notions of principled approaches. Such analyses might raise the question of whether a principled dilemma exists at all, in some specific spaces and places, on engaging business or on observing business taking on governance roles. For one thing, any dilemmas that do exist may not be different in kind from the dilemmas that arise for peacebuilding and development institutions when interacting with various non-business actors (host governments, civic groups, political parties, and so on). Some of the anxiety around private-sector engagement in or encroachment on the 'public' processes of peacebuilding might ease if one accepts this as a mixed domain or space, criss-crossed with various governance contributions from plural sources in ways that a conventional 'public vs. private' lens might not recognise, or would likely be wont to reject automatically on legitimacy grounds.[123]

Conclusion

As the years progress since the SDG's 2015 promulgation, so does the need to move beyond either rhetoric or reactivity about involving business in the peaceful development agenda. In particular, both policymakers and businesspeople will need or expect greater clarity generally and in precise circumstances on what makes collaboration with the other 'appropriate' or not. Of course, as the 2017 'Better Business – Better World' report noted, business can use its obvious potential influence on policymaking and implementation in a more responsible, transparent and accountable way.[124] Yet more guidance to business will generally be needed than, for example, a general call not to lobby for policies that undermine the SDGs.[125] Avoiding undue influence of business actors on the SDG agenda will require greater attention to norm-setting and principled frameworks capable of generating public confidence that business participation is transparent and accountable.[126] Much of the available guidance is oriented to business actors, whereas on questions of 'engaging business' it is policymakers – donors and their partner governments, and multilateral institutions – who may need more granular guidance than is currently provided by a general exhortation to avoid advancing the interests of anti-societal commercial actors. As it is, in the Compact's B4P and B4RoL schemes even that basic exhortation has not been overtly articulated.

There is a strong basis for Ganson and Wennmann's call for greater pragmatism in engaging business in peacebuilding and the activities intended by SDG 16.[127] Yet donors and peacebuilding institutions are to feel safe enough to explore being more pragmatic about business-SDG engagement they will likely need a greater sense of the practical dimensions of the principled basis and parameters around such engagement. In public-policy terms, somewhere between the sceptics' paralysis and the advocates' proselytising is a defensible, increasingly mainstream 'principled yet pragmatic' approach to the private sector's role in peacebuilding. It is an approach open to engaging responsible business actors in those institution-building, RoL, peacebuilding and other activities that, under SDG 16, might ground more peaceful, inclusive societies. It is open to exploring unusually close and dialogic public–private, donor–business and other relationships in pursuit of these goals. Yet is also an approach that is not a-contextual and a-political, but clear-eyed about the complexity and context-specificity of development activities and relationships, and the contingency and precariousness of claims valorising these. It is also an approach that is not normatively neutral nor open-ended. Instead, it is framed by an increasingly dense and proliferated normative and regulatory ecosystem around responsible business conduct. It is an approach that institutionalises a healthy but not excessive or paralysing level of systemic anxiety about private corporate influence. It is primed to be alive always to the risks that such cross-sector collaborative activities might be, become, or be seen as inappropriate, illegitimate, or non-transparent. The B4P and B4RoL initiatives are interesting as examples of the wider effort to engage business in issues within the scope of the SDG 16 agenda.[128] Their influence has not been significant; B4RoL in particular has not attracted significant attention. This tempers the risks and problems that they exhibit (Part II above). Nevertheless, they reveal how far we still are from approaches to 'engagement' that are more attuned to the complexity, context-specificity and contestation invariably involved in these relationships.

Beyond the mere promulgation and then promotion of the SDGs framework, there are now increasingly authoritative calls for efforts to translate high-level rhetoric and ambitions about business engagement into detailed operational plans.[129] Likewise, a viable and indeed necessary research agenda exists beyond merely the more nuanced recognition of the risks/benefits dynamic to such engagement. That is, as the 'business and peace' field matures, we see movement beyond both mere rhetoric about policies on engaging business in peacebuilding (on the one hand) and knee-jerk critical reactivity against the notion (on the other).[130] Indeed the section above reflects the pattern of contributions evident now in the literature: 'engaging business in peacebuilding and around SDG 16 carrier policies risks, but these are manageable and worth taking'. Attaining this phase of evolution as a field suggests that much of the more useful 'business and peace' scholarship (and practical guidance products) will move well beyond identifying generic risks and rewards around engagement.[131] It will be scholarship, and indeed policymaking, that explores the 'multiple and contradictory implications'[132] of business and peace, beyond binary depictions of positive and negative impacts. It will include empirical insights and encounters, rather than just conceptual or normative propositions. It will seek insights generated within specific geographies and contexts, so as to immerse and examine 'business for peace' ideas in the political economy of particular locales. It will feature firm-specific and sector-specific insights, rather than statements about 'business' as a whole. It will display awareness of temporal factors highly relevant to claims made that even particular interventions had peace-positive, social cohesion or institution-building effects. It will be work that is truly cross-disciplinary, living up to the claims of cross-disciplinarity that the 'business and peace' field has to date made. Finally, it will be work capable of offering contextually relevant responses to the important questions that remain around what 'engagement' of business in and around SDG 16's agenda actually means and entails, and when it might be appropriate or otherwise.

Notes

1 2004 marked the first time that our peak global peace and security body discussed how business actors and activity can affect dynamics of conflict and peace: 'The Role of Business in Conflict Prevention, Peacekeeping, Post-Conflict Peace-Building' 4943rd Meeting of the UN Security Council, S/PV/4943 (15 April 2004).
2 Nelson, 'Business of Peace', 2000; Gerson, 'Peacebuilding and the Private Sector', 2001. Of course, before 2000 there was a rich literature already on the negative impact of business activity on conflict dynamics: see for example Ford, *Regulating Business for Peace*, 2015, 56–57.
3 S/Res/1645 (20 December 2005), [21] (UN Security Council); A/RES/60/180, 30 December 2005, [21] (UN General Assembly).
4 See Ganson and Wennmann, 'Business and institutional reform in hybrid orders', 2017.

5 This chapter does not address definitional issues relating to 'the private sector': scholars generally do not make enough of what the huge diversity of actors falling within these labels might mean, including for questions about the 'appropriateness' of engagement; see Ford, 'Perspectives on the evolving 'business and peace' debate', 2015, 453–454.
6 Thérien and Pouliot. 'The Global Compact', 2006, 69. See more recently Miklian and Schouten, 'Business–peace nexus', 2018, who likewise see B4P as the 'most visible public symbol' of efforts to include business in the challenges of peacebuilding and development.
7 Thérien and Pouliot. 'The Global Compact', 2006, 63.
8 See Ford, 'Engaging Business in Peacebuilding', 2016. Likewise Miklian, 'Mapping Business-Peace', 2016, 6–8 describes these two thrusts in recent 'business and peace' scholarship. I use 'advocates' to describe the business-*for*-peace scholars that Miklian would call 'potentialists'. See Thérien and Pouliot, 'The Global Compact', 2006, 63–69 contrasting the 'enthusiasm of the advocates' and 'mistrust of the critics' (of the UN Global Compact).
9 This chapter focuses on 'private sector engagement' (involving foreign or local business in the SDGs agenda) from conventional 'private sector development' (support to and enabling environment for free enterprise).
10 This chapter does not attempt to map the spectrum of 'hard' and 'soft' norms and standards, nor the myriad relevant frameworks and mechanisms, by reference to which one might assess responsible business conduct, for example, in the context of cross-sector peacebuilding collaboration. For one mapping, see Ford, *Regulating Business for Peace*, 2015, Ch. 5.
11 UNGC, *Architects of a Better World*, 2013; Kindornay and Fraser-King, *Investing in the Business of Development*, 2013; see analysis of this trend in Ford, 'Engaging the Private Sector', 2014; Bailey *et al., Investing in Stability*, 2015.
12 See among others Avis, *Private Sector Engagement in Fragile States*, 2016; Vernon, 'Peace through Prosperity', 2015; and Peschka and Emery, *The Role of the Private Sector*, 2010.
13 Nelson *et al., Business and the SDGs*, 2015. See too the sources in n. 28 and n. 29 below.
14 Ernstorfer *et al., Advancing the SDGs*, 2015. 'Inclusivity' in peacebuilding now encompasses involving the private sector: Ford, 'Inclusive Peacebuilding', 2015.
15 See for example Bailey *et al.*, 'Investing in Stability'.
16 Business & Sustainable Development Commission. *Better Business Better World*, 2017.
17 See the 2004/5 treatment in n. 1 above; see too *Peacebuilding in the aftermath of conflict: Report by the Secretary-General of the United Nations*, New York, 8 October 2012, UN Doc. A/67/499–S/2012/746, [39].
18 This institutional 'blind-spot' for business is a theme throughout Ford, *Regulating Business for Peace*, 2015.
19 Ibid, 48–49. See too Thérien and Pouliot. 'The Global Compact', 2006, esp. 57–60 ('from hostility to partnership').
20 It is possible to over-state the new embrace of the private sector, since the contested nature of this (resistance or uncertainty in the 'deep state' of donor and development institutions over the business engagement agenda) is not necessarily apparent from a reading of the upbeat official policy positions: see Ford, *Regulating Business for Peace*, 2015, Ch. 8.
21 Ford, 'Inclusive peacebuilding'.
22 House of Commons International Development Committee, 'UK Implementation of the SDGs', 2016, [58]–[65]. See too DFID, *Agenda 2030*, 2017, and DFID, *Engine of Development*, 2011.
23 USAID, *Global Development Alliance*, 2016; *Partnering for Impact*, 2017; and *A Guide to Economic Growth*, 2009.
24 For an authoritative repository, see www.enterprise-development.org/agency-strategies-and-coordination/.
25 DFAT, *2017 Foreign Policy White Paper*, 2017, 88, 108–109 and Ch. 6. For other resources see too http://dfat.gov.au/aid/topics/development-issues/2030-agenda/Pages/engaging-business.aspx, and DFAT, 'Investments in private sector development', 2015.

26 DFAT, *Creating Shared Value*, 2015, 10.
27 Adams, 'United Nations and business community', 2016.
28 See for example UNGC, *Making Global Goals Local Business*, 2017; GRI, UNGC and WBCSD, *SDG Compass*, 2015; SDG Fund, Harvard Kennedy School CSR Initiative and Inspiris Ltd, *Business and the United Nations*, 2015. See also the multi-stakeholder 'Business Call to Action': www.businesscalltoaction.org/recent-resources and the business platform 'Global Business Alliance for 2030' www.gbafor2030.org/position-papers.html.
29 https://sdgcompass.org/sdgs/sdg-16/ and https://sdgcompass.org/business-tools/.
30 Guidelines do now exist in terms of a principles-based approach to cooperation between UN entities and the private (business) sector. See 'Towards global partnerships: a principle-based approach to enhanced cooperation between the United Nations and all relevant partners', A/RES/70/224, UN General Assembly, 23 February 2016; See too Resolution A/RES/68/234, 7 February 2014; and related UN Global Compact Guidelines www.unglobalcompact.org/docs/issues_doc/un_business_partnerships/guidelines_principle_based_approach_between_un_business_sector.pdf.
31 See n. 8 above.
32 Ganson and Wennmann, *Business and Conflict in Fragile States*, 2016.
33 Ford, *Regulating Business for Peace*, 2015, Ch. 6.
34 For instance, in 2013, a UN secretariat official helping coordinate with the private sector on peacebuilding described sometimes feeling treated by public service colleagues as if he were a 'mole' for big business simply because he encouraged greater engagement with business: interview with author, described in Ford, *Regulating Business for Peace*, 2015, 263.
35 Early 'business and peace' scholarship referred to the concept of a 'fig leaf' (as something intended to conceal a difficulty or embarrassment) in ways that advert to the same risk: Killick *et al.*, *Role of Local Business*, 2005.
36 Ford, 'Perspectives on the evolving "business and peace" ', 2015; see Part IV below.
37 The political identity of business actors is central to the analysis in Ford, *Regulating Business for Peace*, 2015.
38 See www.unglobalcompact.org/library/381. Assessing the literature on the broader Compact concept is beyond this chapter's scope. For an early analysis whose insights remain relevant, see Thérien and Pouliot, 'The Global Compact', 2006.
39 Ford, *Regulating Business for Peace*, 2015; also Borzel and Risse, 'Governance without a state', 2010.
40 See for example Fort and Schipani, *The Role of Business*, 2004; Fort and Gabel, 'Peace through Commerce', 2007; Williams, *Peace through Commerce*, 2008; Sweetman, *Business, Conflict Resolution and Peacebuilding*, 2010.
41 See Ford, 'Inclusive Peacebuilding', 2015, and see too in this regard Miklian, 'Mapping business-peace', 2016, 7.
42 See for example Coleman, *The Asymmetric Society*, 1982; Korten, *When Corporations Rule the World*, 1995; Hertz, *The Silent Takeover*, 2001.
43 See Klein, *The Shock Doctrine*, 2007.
44 Chandler, *Empire in Denial*, 2006.
45 See for example Pugh, 'The political economy of peacebuilding', 2005.
46 See for example Whitman, 'Global governance as the friendly face', 2002; Turner, 'Taming Mamon', 2006; Fransen and Kolk, 'Global rule-setting', 2007; Lim and Tsutsui, 'The globalisation of CSR', 2010. See too some of the critical scholarship discussed by Miklian and Schouten, 'The business-peace nexus', 2018, 8–9, 12.
47 Honke, 'Business for Peace?', 2014, discussed in Ford, 'Towards a principles basis'. See too more broadly Banerjee, 'Corporate social responsibility', 2008.
48 Miklian and Schouten, 'The business-peace nexus', 2018, 5, 15–20.
49 Ibid.
50 See Banerjee, 'Corporate social responsibility'.
51 Miklian and Schouten, 'The business-peace nexus', 2018, 3.

52 John Ruggie, 'Interim report of the Special Representative of the Secretary-General on the issue of human rights and transnational corporations and other business enterprises' New York, 22 February 2006, UN Doc. E/CN.4/2006/97, [68].

53 See for example, in the context of regulating corporate crime, Pearce and Tombs, 'Policing "skid rows"', 1991 (the influential tip of a large iceberg of critical literature in this regard).

54 Some time ago, Le Billon, 'Getting it done', 2003 adverted to this risk in relation to cooperative multi-stakeholder business-government schemes for regulating 'conflict economies'.

55 Lopez, 'Regulating Corporate Responsibility', 2016, 88.

56 See for example European Coalition for Corporate Justice. *EU Action Plan on SDGs overlooks human rights risks of corporate activity*. (Press release). Brussels, 23 November 2016. http://corporatejustice.org/eu-action-plan-on-sdgs-overlooks-risks-of-corpora te-activity-eccj-press-release-.pdf.

57 Civil Society Reflection Group, 'Spotlight on SDGs', 2017, 128.

58 Pingeot, 'Corporate Influence in the Post-2015 Process', 2014, esp. Chapter 4, 20–26, 29. See too, in relation to business engagement in the 2030 Agenda, Martens, Jens. 'Corporate capture becomes a snag'. *The New Age*, 17 July 2017.

59 Pingeot, 'Corporate Influence in the Post-2015 Process'.

60 See our discussion of this in Bailey *et al., Investing in Stability*.

61 Westermann-Behaylo *et al.*, 'Enhancing the concept of corporate diplomacy', 2015.

62 For one encounter with legitimacy concerns, see Fort, *The Diplomat in the Corner Office*, 2015, for example at 8–12.

63 Forrer and Katsos 'Business and peace in the buffer state', 2015.

64 Forrer and Katsos, 'Business and peace in the buffer state', 2015; Ganson and Wennmann, 'Business and institutional reform in hybrid political orders', 2017.

65 Westermann-Behaylo *et al.*, 'Enhancing the concept of corporate diplomacy'.

66 See for example Duffield, *Global Governance and the New Wars*, 2001; Cooper, 'Picking out the pieces of the liberal peaces', 2005; Chandler, *Empire in Denial*, 2006.

67 Ford, *Regulating Business for Peace*, 2015, 461–462.

68 Haufler, 'Symposium', 2015, 463–464; Ford, 'Perspectives on the evolving "business and peace" ', 456–457, 459–460.

69 www.unglobalcompact.org/library/1341; and www.unglobalcompact.org/take-a ction/action/business-rule-of-law (hereafter 'Framework').

70 Ibid.

71 Framework, 7; it otherwise incorporates a 2004 UN policy definition on the rule of law and transitional justice in conflict and post-conflict societies: UN Doc. S/2004/ 616, 3 August 2004, [6] (UN Security Council).

72 Framework, 6.

73 Framework, 6. The Framework provides at least two other 'business case' rationales of this sort (at 14): first, that strengthening the rule of law is a matter of 'pre-competitive common interest' for all businesses and 'addresses the root causes of systemic challenges that all responsible businesses face'; and second, that 'taking action in support of the rule of law can help prevent or address situations of uncertainty and inconsistency.

74 The Framework's conception of 'respect' is that businesses 'respect the letter and spirit of applicable laws, and do not take action that undermines or interferes with the administration of justice, or the effectiveness and accountability of institutions': 9.

75 Framework 8, 10–12.

76 Framework, 10.

77 Framework, 11. The Framework document is accompanied by another listing summaries of examples of these sorts of RoL interventions, directly and in partnership with governments, NGOs and others: www.unglobalcompact.org/docs/issues_doc/ rule_of_law/B4ROL_Framework_Business_Examples.pdf

78 Framework, 11–12. The Framework gives the example of Vale (the Brazilian mining firm) which ahead of its big investment in an African country (presumably,

Mozambique's coal sector) worked with the World Bank Group to support various projects to improve governance and help reform the legal sector. This included bringing judges from Brazil for judicial training.

79   Framework, 12. More generally in this vein, see for example Li, 'Corporations have a role' 2015; Smith, 'Strange bedfellows', 2015.
80   Hogan Lovells *et al.*, 'Risk and Return', 2015, 60.
81   USAID, *Building Alliances*, 2009.
82   Presumably, a UN or other public organisation would feel compelled to decline any offer of support from a business that does not itself respect the RoL (howsoever and by whomsoever that might be judged). This sort of scenario is not discussed.
83   Framework, 12.
84   Framework, 14.
85   Framework, 14.
86   See in particular Call and Wyeth (eds.), *Building States to Build Peace*, 2008.
87   Hansen 'How should businesses interact with the Rule of Law' (undated).
88   This is one recurring theme of Ford, *Regulating Business for Peace*, 2015.
89   Hence too the title question in Adams and Martens, 'Fit for whose purpose?' 2015.
90   See Ford, *Regulating Business for Peace*, 2015, Ch. 6.
91   See Braithwaite *et al.*, *Reconciliating and Architectures for Peace*, 2010; McKenna, *Corporate Responsibility and Natural Resources Conflict*, 2016.
92   Braithwaite *et al.*, *Reconciliating and Architectures for Peace*, 2010.
93   Notably Woodhouse and Ramsbotham, 'Cosmopolitan peacekeeping', 2005, 150–152.
94   See in this regard Ford, *Regulating Business for Peace*, 2015, 264–269.
95   Ibid.
96   Ibid, 263.
97   See Scheyvens *et al.*, 'The private sector and the SDGs', 2016. Pingeot also argues that the risk can be mitigated and is one worth taking: 'Corporate Influence in the Post-2015 Process'. See too the gist of Adams and Martens, *Partnerships and the 2030 Agenda*, 2016. See in this vein too and earlier Abramov, 'Building Peace in Fragile States', 2009.
98   In the UN institutions context, Adams and Martens have suggested that systematic assessment include the 'added value' of the relationship to UN goals; the dynamic between the risks, costs and side-effects and the potential benefits; human rights impacts; the existence of safeguards on the use of public resources; and the possible alternatives to the planned activities: 'Fit for Whose Purpose'.
99   Haufler, 'Symposium', 464 argues that one factor that might enhance the legitimacy of engagement is for institutional actors and agencies to deal with business collectives (such as chambers of commerce) rather than individual firms. However, such umbrella groups vary in their composition and coverage and may mask complex power relationships.
100 Honke, 'Business for peace?'.
101 See too Miklian and Schouten, 'The business-peace nexus', 14.
102 Black and O'Bright, 'International development and the private sector', 2016, 165.
103 See for example Miklian, 'Mapping business-peace'.
104 See generally Ford, 'Perspectives on the evolving "business and peace" '; Haufler, 'Symposium'.
105 Haufler, 'Symposium'. Likewise Miklian and Schouten, 'The business-peace nexus', 3–4, note how 'business and peace' must engage 'core' international relations studies debates on the public/private governance mix.
106 A recent mini case-study is the Congo-Kinshasa (DRC) example in Miklian and Schouten, 'The business-peace nexus'.
107 Ibid. Thérien and Pouliot, 'The Global Compact' engaged with the ways in which schemes like the Compact might be seen to shift (and/or reflect) patterns in global governance.
108 See n. 10 above: this chapter does not purport to map this framework.

109 See Ganson and Wennmann, *Business and Conflict in Fragile States*.
110 Ford, 'Towards a principled basis'. See too Bailey *et al.*, *Investing in Stability*; Miklian 'Mapping business-peace'.
111 For one basic typology aimed at promoting more coherent discussion of the various ways that business might impact on or engage in peacebuilding (directly/indirectly, jointly or individually, locally or nationally or regionally, etc.), see Ford, 'Inclusive peacebuilding'; See too Bailey *et al.*, *Investing in Stability*; Miklian 'Mapping business-peace'.
112 See too on this point Miklian, 'Mapping business-peace', 6.
113 See also Miklian and Schouten, 'The business-peace nexus', 20 (calling for a 'grounded' approach).
114 On questions of 'success' in this field, including measurement, attribution and causation concerning claims of positive business impacts on peace, see the final section in Bailey *et al.*, *Investing in Stability*.
115 See for example, in a very large literature now, Avant *et al.*, *Who Governs the Globe*, 2010.
116 See Ford, *Regulating Business for Peace*, 2015, Ch. 2.
117 Ruggie, 'Global Public Domain', 2004.
118 Ford, 'Towards a principled basis', 15–16.
119 Ibid.
120 Forrer and Katsos, 'Business and peace in the buffer state'; Ganson and Wennmann, 'Business and institutional reform'.
121 Iff, 'Timber companies and statebuilding', 2016.
122 See in this regard the editors' intent in Best and Gheciu, *Return of the Public*, 2014.
123 Ford, 'Towards a principled basis', 16. See more recently the discussion in Miklian and Schouten, 'the business-peace nexus', 15, 20–21.
124 See Business & Sustainable Development Commission. *Better Business Better World*, 2017.
125 Ibid, 94.
126 Pingeot, 'Scrutinizing the corporate role', 2014.
127 Ganson and Wennmann, *Business and Conflict in Fragile States*.
128 See discussion at n. 6 above.
129 Independent Commission for Aid Impact, 'Business in Development', 2015, 1. For one call for more meaningful engagement beyond rhetoric, see Agarwal *et al.*, 'Raising the bar', 2017.
130 See too Miklian and Schouten, 'The business-peace nexus', 11, decrying the 'zero-sum' debate typical in this field.
131 See generally Ford, 'Perspectives on the evolving "business and peace"'.
132 Miklian and Schouten, 'The business-peace nexus', 20.

Bibliography

Abramov, Igor. 2009. 'Building peace in fragile states: building trust is essential for effective public-private partnerships'. *Journal of Business Ethics* 89(4): 481–494.
Adams, Barbara. 2016. 'United Nations and business community: out-sourcing or crowding in?'. *Development* 59(1–2): 21–28.
Adams, Barbara and Jens Martens. 'Fit for whose purpose? Private funding and corporate influence in the United Nations'. New York: Global Policy Forum. September 2015. https://sustainabledevelopment.un.org/content/documents/2101Fit_for_whose_purpose_online.pdf.
Adams, Barbara and Jens Martens. *Partnerships and the 2030 Agenda: Time to Reconsider their Role in Implementation*. New York: Friedrich-Ebert-Stiftung and Global Policy Watch. May2016.
Agarwal, Namit, Uwe Gneilting and Ruth Mhlanga. 'Raising the bar: Rethinking the role of business in the sustainable development goals'. Oxfam Discussion Papers. Oxford, February 2017; www.oxfam.org/sites/www.oxfam.org/files/dp-raising-the-bar-business-sdgs-130217-en_0.pdf

Avant, Deborah D., Martha Finnemore and Susan K. Sell, eds. 2010. *Who Governs the Globe?* New York: Cambridge University Press.

Avis, W. *Private Sector Engagement in Fragile and Conflict-affected Settings* (GSDRC Helpdesk Research Report 1331). Birmingham, UK: GSDRC, University of Birmingham, 2016.

Bailey, Rob, Siân Bradley, Oli Brown, and Jolyon Ford. 2015. *Investing in Stability: Can Extractive-Sector Development Help Build Peace?*London: Chatham House.

Ballentine, Karen, and Virginia Haufler. 2005–2009. *Enabling Economies of Peace: Public Policy for Conflict-Sensitive Business.* New York: UN Global Compact.

Banerjee, Subhabrata. 'Corporate social responsibility: The good, the bad and the ugly', *Critical Sociology* 34(1) (2008): 51–79.

Best, Jacqueline and Alexandra Gheciu, eds. 2014. *The Return of the Public in Global Governance.* Cambridge: Cambridge University Press.

Black, David and Ben O'Bright. 'International development and the private sector: the ambiguities of "partnership" ', *International Journal* 71(1)(2016): 144–166.

Borzel, Tanja, and Thomas Risse. 2010. 'Governance without a state: can it work?', *Regulation and Governance* 4(2): 113–134. doi:10.1111/j.1748-5991.2010.01076.x.

Braithwaite, John, Hilary Charlesworth, Peter Reddy, and Leah Dunn. 2010. *Reconciliation and Architectures of Commitment: Sequencing Peace in Bougainville.* Canberra: ANU E-Press.

Business & Sustainable Development Commission. *Better Business Better World.* London, 2017; http://report.businesscommission.org/uploads/BetterBiz-BetterWorld_170215_012417.pdf.

Call, Charles and Vanessa Wyeth. *Building States to Build Peace.* Boulder: Lynne Reinner. 2008.

Chandler, David. 2006. *Empire in Denial: The Politics of Statebuilding.* London: Pluto.

Civil Society Reflection Group on the 2030 Agenda for Sustainable Development. 2017. 'Spotlight on Sustainable Development 2017: Reclaiming policies for the public: privatization, partnerships, corporate capture, and their impact on sustainability and inequality – assessments and alternatives'. Global Policy Forum et al. July; www.2030spotlight.org/sites/default/files/download/spotlight_170626_final_web.pdf.

Coleman, James S. 1982. *The Asymmetric Society.* Syracuse, NY: Syracuse University Press.

Cooper, Neil. 2005. 'Picking out the pieces of the liberal peaces', *Security Dialogue* 36(4): 463–478. doi:10.1177/0967010605060451.

Department for International Development (DFAT). 2011. *The Engine of Development: The Private Sector and Prosperity for Poor People.* London: Department for International Development.

Department of Foreign Affairs and Trade (DFAT). 2015. *Creating Shared Value through Partnership: Ministerial Statement on Engaging the Private Sector in Aid and Development.* Canberra: Australian Government, August; http://dfat.gov.au/about-us/publications/aid/Documents/creating-shared-value-through-partnership.pdf.

Department of Foreign Affairs and Trade (DFAT). 2015. *Strategy for Australia's aid investments in private sector development.* Canberra: Australian Government. October; http://dfat.gov.au/about-us/publications/Documents/strategy-for-australias-investments-in-private-sector-development.pdf.

Department for International Development (DFAT). 2017. *Agenda 2030 The UK Government's approach to delivering the Global Goals for Sustainable Development - at home and around the world.* London/Glasgow: United Kingdom Government, 28 March; www.gov.uk/government/uploads/system/uploads/attachment_data/file/603500/Agenda-2030-Report4.pdf.

Department of Foreign Affairs and Trade (DFAT). 2017. *2017 Foreign Policy White Paper.* Canberra: Australian Government. November; www.fpwhitepaper.gov.au/foreign-policy-white-paper.

Duffield, Mark. 2001. *Global Governance and the New Wars: the Merging of Development and Security.* London: Zed Books.

Ernstorfer, Anita, Adrienne Gardaz Cuendet, Diana Chigas, and Lemer Tejeda. 2015. *Advancing the SDGs by Supporting Peace: How Business Can Contribute*. New York: UN Global Compact.

Ford, Jolyon. 2014. *Engaging the Private Sector in Africa's Peaceful Development*. Pretoria: Institute for Security Studies.

Ford, Jolyon. 2015. *Regulating Business for Peace*. New York: Cambridge University Press.

Ford, Jolyon. 2015. 'Inclusive peacebuilding: the private sector as a stakeholder in peacebuilding'. *Development Dialogues* 63(3): 138–151.

Ford, Jolyon. 2015. 'Perspectives on the evolving "business and peace" debate'. *Academy of Management Perspectives* 29(4): 451–460.

Ford, Jolyon. 2016. 'Promoting conflict-sensitive business activity during peacebuilding.' *Working Paper Series*, Paper 1/2016. Bern: Swisspeace.

Ford, Jolyon. 2016. 'Towards a principled basis for engaging business in peacebuilding', Conference Paper, Business and Peace Panel, International Studies Association AGM, Atlanta GA, February.

Forrer, John, and John Katsos. 2015. 'Business and peace in the buffer state'. *Academy of Management Perspectives* 29(4): 438–450. doi:10.1080/10246029.2016.1264439.

Fort, Timothy and Cindy Schipani. 2004. *The Role of Business in Fostering Peaceful Societies*. New York: Cambridge University Press.

Fort, Timothy and Joan Gabel, eds. 2007. 'Peace through commerce' (Special Issue) *American Business Law Journal* 44(2): 207–415.

Fort, Timothy. 2015. *The Diplomat in the Corner Office: Corporate Foreign Policy*. Stanford: Stanford University Press.

Fransen, Luc and Ans Kolk. 2007. 'Global rule-setting for business: a critical analysis of multi-stakeholder standards' *Organisation* 14(5): 667–684. doi:10.1177/1350508407080305@@@

Ganson, Brian and Achim Wennman. 2016. *Business and Conflict in Fragile States: The Case For Pragmatic Solutions*. London: Routledge, 2016.

Ganson, Brian and Achim Wennmann. 2017. 'Business and institutional reform in hybrid political orders' in *Institutional Reforms and Peacebuilding: Change, Path-Dependency and Societal Divisions in Post-War Communities*, edited by Nadine Ansorg and Sabine Kurtenbach, 137–160. Abingdon/New York: Routledge.

Gerson, Allan. 2001. 'Peacebuilding: the private sector's role'. *American Journal of International Law* 95(102): 102–119. doi:10.2307/2642040.

Graff, Andreas, and Andrea Iff. 2014. *Conflict-Sensitive Business Practices: Review of Instruments and Guidelines*. Bern: Swisspeace.

GRI, UNGC and WBCSD. *SDG Compass: The Guide for Business Action on the SDGs*. 2015; www.unglobalcompact.org/docs/issues_doc/development/SDGCompass.pdf.@@@

Hansen, T. (online, undated). 'How should businesses interact with the Rule of Law' http s://business-humanrights.org/en/how-should-businesses-interact-with-the-rule-of-law.

Haufler, Virginia. 2015. "Symposium on conflict, management and peace: comments from an IR scholar" *Academy of Management Perspectives* 29(4): 461–468. doi:10.5465/amp.2015.0158.

Hertz, Noreena. 2001. *The Silent Takeover: Global Capitalism and the Death of Democracy*. London: Heinemann.

Hogan Lovells, Bingham Centre for the Rule of Law, British Institute of International Comparative Law, The Economist Intelligence Unit. (2015) *Risk and Return: Foreign Direct Investment and the Rule of Law*. London, 3 June. www.biicl.org/documents/625_d4_fdi_main_report.pdf?showdocument=1

Honke, Jana. 2014. 'Business for peace? The ambiguous role of "ethical" mining companies'. *Peacebuilding* 2(2): 172–187. doi:10.1080/21647259.2014.910383.

House of Commons International Development Committee. 2016. *UK Implementation of the Sustainable Development Goals*. First Report of Session 2016–2017. London: United

Kingdom Government, 18 May; https://publications.parliament.uk/pa/cm201617/cm select/cmintdev/103/103.pdf.

Iff, Andrea. 2016. 'Timber companies and statebuilding in the Congo Basin.' In *Corporate Responsibility and Sustainable Development: Exploring the Nexus of Private and Public Interests*, edited by Rayman-Bacchus, Lez and Phillip R. Walsh, 197–220. London: Routledge.

Independent Commission for Aid Impact. 2015. *Business in Development*. Report 43. London: United Kingdom, May, 1. https://icai.independent.gov.uk/wp-content/uploa ds/ICAI-Business-in-Development-FINAL.pdf.

Killick, Nick, VS Srikantha, and Canan Gündüz. 2005. *The Role of Local Business in Peace-building*. Berlin: Berghof Research Centre for Constructive Conflict Management.

Kindornay, Shannon, and Fraser Reilly-King. 2013. *Investing in the Business of Development*. Ottawa: North-South Institute / NSI.

Klein, Naomi. 2007. *The Shock Doctrine: The Rise of Disaster Capitalism*. Penguin: London.

Korten, David C. 1995. *When Corporations Rule the World*. Hartford, CT: Kumarian Press.

Le Billon, Philippe. 2003. 'Getting it done: instruments of enforcement'. In *Natural Resources and Violent Conflict: Options and Actions*, edited by Ian Bannon and Paul Collier, 215–286. Washington, DC: World Bank.

Li, Victor. 2015. 'Corporations have a role in promoting the rule of law', *ABA Journal* 101(8): 67.

Lim, Alwyn, and Kiyoteru Tsutsui. 2010. 'The globalisation of CSR: cross-national analyses on global CSR framework commitment'. Working Paper. Department of Sociology, University of Michigan.

Lopez, Carlos. 'Regulating corporate responsibility and finance for development'. *Development* 59(1–2)(2016): 88–93.

McKenna, Kylie. 2016. *Corporate Responsibility and Natural Resources Conflict*. Abingdon: Routledge.

Miklian, Jason. 2016. 'Mapping business-peace interactions: five assertions for how businesses create peace'. Paper presented at International Studies Association Conference, Atlanta, March.

Miklian, Jason, and Peer Schouten. 'The business–peace nexus: "business for peace" and the reconfiguration of the public/private divide in global governance', *Journal of International Relations and Development* 21(2018): 1–22.

Nelson, Jane. 2000. *The Business of Peace: The private sector as a partner in conflict prevention and resolution*. London: International Alert.

Nelson, Jane, Beth Jenkins and Richard Gilbert. 2015. *Business and the SDGs: Building Blocks for Success at Scale*. Cambridge, MA: Business Fights Poverty / Harvard Kennedy School.

Pearce, Frank, and Tombs, Steve. 1991. 'Policing "skid rows": a reply to Keith Hawkins'. *British Journal of Criminology* 31: 415–426.

Peschka, Mary, and James Emery. 2010. *The Role of the Private Sector in Fragile and Conflict-Affected States*. World Development Report 2011 Background Papers; Washington, DC: World Bank.

Pingeot, Lou. 2014. 'Scrutinizing the corporate role in the post-2015 Development Agenda' in *State of the World 2014: Governing for Sustainability*, edited by The Worldwatch Institute, 165–173. Washington, DC: Island Press.

Pingeot, Lou. 2014. 'Corporate influence in the post-2015 Process'. Aachen/Berlin/Bonn/ New York: Bischöfliches Hilfswerk MISEREOR e.V et al. January. www.globalpolicy. org/images/pdfs/GPFEurope/Corporate_influence_in_the_Post-2015_process_web.pdf.

Pugh, Michael. 2005. 'The political economy of peacebuilding: a Critical Theory perspective', *International Journal of Peace Studies* 10(2): 23–42.

Ruggie, John Gerard. 2004. 'Reconstituting the global public domain: issues, actors and practices', *European Journal of International Relations* 10: 499–531. doi:10.1177/1354066104047847.

Ruggie, John. 2006. '*Interim report of the Special Representative of the Secretary-General on the issue of human rights and transnational corporations and other business enterprises*' New York, 22 February, UN Doc. E/CN.4/2006/97.

Scheyvens, Regina, Glenn Banks, and Emma Hughes. 2016. 'The Private Sector and the SDGs: The Need to Move Beyond "Business as Usual" ', *Sustainable Development* 24(6): 371–382.

SDG Fund, Harvard Kennedy School CSR Initiative and Inspiris Ltd. 2015. *Business and the United Nations: Working together Towards the Sustainable Development Goals: A framework for Action*; www.sdgfund.org/sites/default/files/business-and-un/SDGF_BFP_HKSCSRI_Business_and_SDGs-Web_Version.pdf.

Smith, David. 'Strange bedfellows or old friends? Business courts the global rule of law'. Centre for International Governance Innovation, 11 June2015.

Sweetman, Derek. 2010. *Business, Conflict Resolution and Peacebuilding*. Abingdon: Routledge.

Thérien, Jean-Pierre, and Vincent Pouliot. 2006. 'The Global Compact: shifting the politics of international development?'. *Global Governance* 12: 55–75.

Turner, Mandy. 2006. 'Taming Mammon: corporate social responsibility and the global regulation of conflict trade'. *Conflict, Security and Development* 6(3): 365–387. doi:10.1080/14678800600933530.

United Nations. 2006. *Interim report of the Special Representative of the Secretary-General on the issue of human rights and transnational corporations and other business enterprises*. New York, 22 February, UN Doc. E/CN.4/2006/97.

United Nations. 2012. *Peacebuilding in the aftermath of conflict: Report by the Secretary-General of the United Nations*, New York, 8 October, UN Doc. A/67/499–S/2012/746.

United Nations Global Compact (UNGC). 2013. *Architects of a Better World: Building the Post-2015 Business Engagement Architecture*. New York: UN Global Compact Office.

United Nations Global Compact (UNGC). 2017. *Making Global Goals Local Business: A New Era for Responsible Business*. New York: United Nations; www.unglobalcompact.org/docs/publications/MGGLB-2017-UNGA.pdf.

United States Agency for International Development (USAID). 2009. *A Guide To Economic Growth In Post-Conflict Countries*. Washington, DC: United States Government. January. http://pdf.usaid.gov/pdf_docs/PNADO408.pdf.

United States Agency for International Development (USAID). 2009. *Building Alliances Series: Democracy and Governance*. Washington, DC: United States Government. October. www.usaid.gov/sites/default/files/documents/1880/Democracy_Guide.pdf

United States Agency for International Development (USAID). 2016. *Global Development Alliance: Achieving Goals by Working*. Washington, DC: United States Government, 29 November; www.usaid.gov/sites/default/files/documents/15396/2016-10-11%20GDA%20Private%20Sector_Branded_final.pdf.

United States Agency for International Development (USAID). 2017. *Partnering For Impact Report: USAID And The Private Sector*, Washington. DC: United States Government, 13 January. www.usaid.gov/sites/default/files/documents/15396/usaid_partnership%20report_17_web_0.pdf.

Vernon, Phil. 2015. *Peace through Prosperity: Integrating Peace-building into Economic Development*. London: International Alert.

Wenger, Andreas, and Daniel Möckli. 2003. *Conflict Prevention: The Untapped Potential of the Business Sector*. Boulder: Lynne Rienner.

Westermann-Behaylo, Michelle K., Kathleen Rehbein, and Timothy Fort. 2015. 'Enhancing the concept of corporate diplomacy'. *Academy of Management Perspectives* 29(4) 387–404. doi:10.5465/amp.2013.0133.

Whitman, Jim. 2002. 'Global governance as the friendly face of unaccountable power'. *Security Dialogue* 33(1): 45–57.

Williams, Oliver F., ed. 2008. *Peace through Commerce: Responsible Corporate Citizenship and the Ideals of the UN Global Compact*. Notre Dame, IN: University of Notre Dame Press.

Woodhouse, Tom and Oliver Ramsbotham. 2005. 'Cosmopolitan peacekeeping and the globalisation of security', *International Peacekeeping* 12(2): 139–156. doi:10.1080/01439680500066400.

6

FROM WAR-TORN TO PEACE-TORN?

Mapping business strategies in transition from conflict to peace in Colombia

Jason Miklian and Angelika Rettberg[1]

1. Introduction and main proposition

In a 1998 survey conducted by Colombian business magazine *Dinero*, the majority of respondents—executives and owners of the country′s largest firms—expressed their concern that insecurity and the lack of public order was a leading problem (Dinero 1998). The investment climate was unfavorable, they complained, and a third of respondents said they would leave the country and relocate operations if they could. They were skeptical about expanding production or hiring new staff. Negotiating peace with the main leftist guerrilla groups was considered a priority. To accomplish that goal, respondents claimed to be willing to spend up to 20 percent of their companies' earnings and 15 percent of their own assets (Dinero 1998). While not to be taken as a forecast of actual intentions, the survey reflected what management as well as business and peace scholars prescribe happens in contexts of conflict-related crisis: Risk-averse firms shy away from innovation, new investments, production and job creation.

More than fifteen years later, Colombia is enjoying the consequences of significant security gains and steady economic growth. In December 2016, a peace agreement was signed between the national government and the *Fuerzas Armadas Revolucionarias de Colombia* (FARC), formally ending the longest armed conflict of the Western Hemisphere. As will be shown, Colombian companies' reactions to this milestone ranged from indifference, to fear that the agreement may affect market rules, to positive expectations for business opportunity. Businesses have become involved in formal and informal post-conflict peacebuilding and reconstruction ventures, even if simply by lending their names to public peace events. While a referendum in October rejected the peace deal by a razor-thin majority, a revised deal was approved overwhelmingly by Congress and has unleashed a legislative and executive frenzy to implement the agreement. The process elicits interest by the international community, with then-United Nations Secretary-General Ban Ki-moon describing it as a "bright flare of hope that illuminates the world" (UN 2016). Domestic opinion is generally less optimistic as 'peace' and the judicial and political concessions it implies are divisive topics in society after more than fifty years of civil war, and other rebel groups have yet to be integrated into the peace process.

In contrast to the 1990s, contemporary strategies that firms adopt to prepare for and help build peace are less clear. While the "logic of the firm" is well documented for crisis during conflict and the resultant increased political risk (Chambers and Jacob 2007; Gao 2009), we know little about how firms respond and adapt their strategies in conflict-to-peace transitions. Just as crisis does not spell overall downturn but hits firms differently—even serving some with opportunities for growth (Branzei and Abdelnour 2010; Jallat and Shultz 2011)—business strategies for peace are likely to present similar variation and will not simply amount to the opposite of strategies during conflict and crisis. So how do firms prepare for peace?

This chapter intends to provide a framework that builds theory on business strategies during transition from conflict to peace. Our main proposition is that business strategy[2] has unique yet heretofore under-researched characteristics during vital transition periods from armed conflict to peace. Here we define strategy as a set of coordinated actions to achieve goals such as competitive advantage or sustainability. Independent variables include perceived costs and benefits for operations, reputation, and profit, and relations with the state or government. Our first hypothesis is that desperation is the mother of change in corporate behavior, so that the higher the perceived cost and uncertainty of the transition, the more likely it is that key business actors will innovate and explore alternative routes of action. Conversely, the lower the perceived costs of transition, the more cautious companies will be to explore change and innovation that is not clearly linked to their bottom line. Our second hypothesis is that the greater access business actors have to public decision-making (from peace negotiations to agreement implementation), the more likely it will be for business actors to adhere to peace policy and to respond to state incentives in the course of implementation. We study these hypotheses in the context of Colombia.

To turn these hypotheses into a roadmap for testable research, we make several assumptions about the key drivers for a business to navigate a conflict to the peace transition period. First is that the transition calculations are integrated into existing firm operational and political risk strategies for growth (there is unlikely to be a 'peace-specific' agenda), and that firms support peace over conflict in the assumption that peace is more profitable for society and by extension themselves (the 'rising tide lifts all boats' argument).[3] Second is that a firm assigns value to building the perception of 'making a positive difference' to society by attempting to contribute to peace in a manner either substantial or superficial in nature. Third, acting more aggressively during a transition period can help a firm gain a head start on competitors, growing market share and penetration into previously off-limit sectors or regions. Fourth, national firms use these periods to prepare for the increased competition that will come when a peace deal is finalized and international firms recalibrate their own risk calculations, which may be more or less risk-adverse than their local counterparts, depending on the sector of the economy (the extractive sector has historically been known for its greater resilience, while other sectors, such as commerce and finance are more reluctant to risk). Fifth, we assume that firms place an outsize value on building and maintaining close ties to government as they are gatekeepers of lucrative contracts and regulatory opportunities after peace is inked as the country rebuilds from conflict.

We note that none of these factors are universally applied, but all are commonly enough seen from previous research that we can confidently use these as a baseline for our purposes (Miklian and Bickel 2016; Miklian 2017; Rettberg 2001, 2003, 2005, 2007, 2016). Moving beyond 'common sense' assumptions allows us to build new theory and create a more testable platform for our hypotheses. For background, we have reviewed open-ended interviews conducted over the past fifteen years with Colombian business leaders across major sectors in an effort to consider the above assumptions as solid and create a base to map a theoretical framework that carries a potentially broad level of generalizability. Further, we also have reviewed a series of primary sources (such as Planning Department and Finance Ministry strategic and forecast papers, association guidelines for investments, business leader speeches, and company webpages) and secondary sources (such as academic papers on business strategy, especially in contexts of uncertainty) to seek out alternative explanations as a robustness check. The purpose of this background 'scraping' was to cast a wide conceptual net and seek out commonalities intended to enrich our propositions.

This chapter proceeds as follows. First, we offer a brief literature review on business strategies and peacebuilding in Colombia, paying particular attention to risk calculations and divergences between strategies taken during conflict and peace. We explore two existing knowledge gaps: how do businesses strategize operations in the oftentimes messy and unpredictable periods of transition from conflict to peace; and what is the importance, relevance and impact of these strategies on peace and peacebuilding?

We then propose that peace transition strategies are operationalized in four distinct forms: operational strategies, philanthropic strategies, external/political strategies, and public relations strategies. Finally, we build theory through discussion of our two hypotheses, showing where this mapping can help us better understand business strategies in transition from conflict to peace, suggesting five specific research streams that we feel are worthy of forward study.

2. Peace, conflict and business strategy in Colombia: a review

Although still an emerging relationship, scholars and practitioners have expanded our general understandings of the potential and practical value in encouraging business participation in sustainable peacebuilding (e.g. Bond 2014; Carroll 2016; Ford 2015a; Forrer and Fort 2016; Kolk and Lenfant 2015; Oetzel and Breslauer 2015; Rettberg 2016). These overviews have been coupled with calls for the business community to be more involved in post-conflict peacebuilding processes and peace mediation (Alleblas 2015; Ford 2015b; Iff and Alluri 2016; UNGC 2016), especially through international frameworks like the Responsibility To Protect, the UN Sustainable Development Goals, the Business and Human Rights Framework, the UN Global Compact, and similar. Colombia has been a prominent locale for business activity in peacebuilding, and national firms have often attempted to positively influence the peace process (Rettberg and Rivas 2012). In the 1990s, some business leaders supported peace negotiations in the hopes of bringing a 'peace dividend' to the country (Rettberg 2004), while others actively undermined negotiations for personal gain or from their allegiance to paramilitaries (Beittel 2015).

There is also a rich scholarship on the political economy of conflict in Colombia, often through the lens of the drug trade or other informal economies (e.g. Angrist and Kugler 2008; Richani 2013; Thoumi 2002), or via extractives such as the oil and gold sectors (Idrobo et al. 2014; Masse and Munevar 2016; Rettberg and Ortiz-Riomalo 2016). Business openings for conflict reduction and peacebuilding action have emerged, including the peacebuilding potentials in the gas and mining sectors (Rettberg 2015). Firms have begun to employ internationalized conflict-sensitive business practices that attempt to merge peacebuilding and development (Guáqueta 2013; UNDP 2015; UNSC 2009), implementing multi-faceted strategies that assign value to stability, philanthropy and profit (Rettberg 2016). These trends complement internal desires for firms to increase their ethical footprint in operational areas, but also reflect the realities of weak state institutions, which are incapable of providing the basic services that firms seek to develop a stable environment for their operations. We situate business within state-of-the-art literature in the Colombian context to illustrate business strategies in conflict, and transition strategies.

Business strategies in conflict: framing risk, peace, politics and the state

Strategies for working within conflict include how conflict recalibrates the relationship between social risk and costs of doing business (Franks et al. 2014); specific investment strategies and calculations taken by multinational firms and states in conflict zones (Driffield et al. 2013); how cultural variations of conflict can influence business environments and vice-versa (Trompenaars 1996; Davis and Franks 2014); and how a more moral or 'humanistic' approach can positively influence business decision-making in challenging environments (Pirson and Lawrence 2010). Others study business and investment strategies specifically in the post-conflict period (e.g. Mills and Fan 2006; Nielsen and Riddle 2009), and the motivations, value and variation of firm responses to violent conflict (Oetzel and Getz 2012). Notably, much of this literature sees the business-conflict relationship as *reactive*, or one where firms respond to political developments in myriad ways. Like their counterparts in many of the cases studied in this literature, Colombian firms are traditionally more responsive to issues when framed as conflict reduction and risk mitigation measures as opposed to peace-positive ventures.

Peacebuilding and development scholars tend to be more systems and process oriented, exploring the relationships between business and society in attempts to develop understandings of firm action in conflict. Notable analyses include Ganson (2011, 2014) on corporate frameworks and strategies of conflict resolution; Jamali and Mirshak (2010) on the complexity and diversity of business–conflict linkages; Deitelhoff and Wolf (2010) on how corporate security is a function of corporate governance; Kolk and van Tulder (2010) on Corporate Social Responsibility (CSR) and sustainable development linkages in international firms; and Meyer et al. (2011) on how multinational corporations navigate local conflict through development strategies. Others explore the complex decision-making that firms calculate as they become more deeply ingrained 'social actors' with increasing responsibilities as they push the boundaries of global governance action (Mikler 2013; May 2015). For example, while scandals associated with the destructive behavior of large multinational companies attracted global attention to the role of corporations in unstable contexts (such as with Shell in Nigeria), it was also these companies that pioneered conflict awareness and do-no-harm best practice, many times in more ambitious terms than domestic companies in conflict countries. Colombia is a useful case in point, as the extractive sector has pioneered CSR since the 1990s (Rettberg and Rivas 2012).

Existing findings on the business–politics relationship also illustrate the importance of the political context of conflict to business strategy. An extensive literature has underscored the extent to which business interests are embedded in and shaped by specific political environments. The type and strength of state–business relations can explain variation in aspects ranging from economic development to democratic stability and policy quality, underscoring the importance of institutions in shaping the business environment (Maxfield and Schneider 1996; Steinmo et al. 1992). According to Schneider (2004), business–politics relations in Latin America range from collaboration, even collusion, to different forms of contestation, suggesting variation in access and leverage over policymaking at different points in time. In part, the difference between a virtuous and a vicious model of business and government relations can be attributed to the existence of formal or informal routes of access to government, to the existence and strength of business organizations, and to mechanisms of domestic and external accountability.

The relationship between business and the state in Colombia has historically been close (Rettberg 2003), shaped by formal and informal venues of consultation, collaboration, and overall policy alignment. In regard to contexts of armed conflict and transitions to peace, private-sector factions have had privileged access to peace policy, either directly, through participation in the policymaking process or by being appointed to negotiator roles, or indirectly by frequent consultation with government officials. Rarely have recalcitrant business factions interfered in the shape and results of peacebuilding activities. To the contrary, the Colombian government has made it a point to systematically involve the private sector in peace-related tasks such as reintegration of former fighters, victims' social inclusion, and training (Rettberg 2009). Thus, contemporary business-state closeness and the awareness that business' privileged position will not fundamentally be questioned suggests that the stakes are lower than could be expected and that the impact of context on transition strategy may be tilted more towards seeking and benefiting from opportunity than towards escaping from obvious harm.

The essential lessons for our purposes from the above studies are threefold: that firms are reactive – but adaptive – to conflict and peacemakers; that conflict and peace strategy is a function of risk; and that the political-institutional context has significant influence on strategy. We return to this discussion in our analysis, contextualizing these expectations through our strategic framework.

Business strategies in transition from conflict to peace: commonalities and divergences

Any discussion of 'business strategies' must first reflect on the sheer diversity of what such strategies entail in practice. The existence of diverse production profiles or sectors of the economy (e.g. Gourevitch 2007; Shafer 1996) can explain business political preferences based on, for example, labor or capital intensity. In addition to sector, factors such as company size and the nationality of capital matter. The larger a company or conglomerate, the stronger its economic veto power and access to politics (Rettberg 2001). In contrast, the smaller a company, the more it will rely on the strength of numbers and be vulnerable to the dilemmas of collective action (Olson 1965). The literature on multinational companies has been keen on high-lighting the distortions that foreign investment can produce in the political and economic development of host countries (Bucheli 2005). Following, the nationality of capital has implications for business strategy in terms of corporate set-ups, recruitment strategies, investment decisions, and depth and breadth of CSR activities. Moreover, multinational companies are not lone top-down actors, but typically engage in alliances with both government and domestic business, shaping their preferences.

Several other contextual transition factors are of interest, including cultural and historic backgrounds (e.g. Fisman and Khanna's (2004) discussion of emerging markets' business groups as opposed to Western corporate milestones); economic and political crises (e.g. Kingstone's (1999) and Özel's (2015) work on why neoliberal reform—despite the costs it imposed on large social sectors was smoother and more diverse than expected at the time of its implementation); and sub-sector differences in corporate culture and practices, as in the extractives sector (Rettberg et al. 2011).

Coming closest to our questions on business transition is the emerging literature on business in situations of crisis and political stalemate or 'frozen conflict'. Moving beyond classic understandings of economic openings as a bridge from conflict to peace, Naidoo (2010) and Roemer-Mahler (2012) explore this issue within internal crisis and firm–firm disputes, respectively, but each sidestep the question of if their findings hold for political conflict in particular. Recognizing that conflicts them-selves rarely follow a linear pattern, firms can also be encouraged to be conflict transformation actors in their own right (Ghimire and Upreti 2012), as no 'perfect peace' may ever be on the horizon. This desire is a bookend goal of actors like the UN in conflict settings as they promote deeper peace engagement by business.

These works imply a more proactive role for business in conflict, exploring how firms can re-define and re-shape fragile environments in areas of crisis or stalemate by recognizing their own local agency. Smith et al. (2010) see these decisions as emblematic of 'strategic paradoxes,' wherein firms must tackle seemingly contradictory, yet integrated challenges—in this case rapidly fluctuating political environments of conflict transition and the maintenance of business operations. Business strategies assign varied importance to risk mitigation, public relations, making a positive contribution to society, improving corporate responsibility, and improving the immediate and future bottom line. However, many of these strategies are viewed through different lenses during times of transition, when cautious optimism about future opportunities—combined with a growing fear that competitors may pass them by—can reduce existing negative perceptions of uncertainty and lead to a re-weighting of classical 'risk versus opportunity' calculations. The following sections develops these multiple simultaneous stimuli into a map of business in transition.

3. Mapping 'business in transition'

Despite the rich scholarship outlined in the previous sections, three key questions remain: in what ways do businesses strategize operations during the oftentimes messy and unpredictable periods of transition from conflict to peace; how do they implement these strategies; and what is the importance, relevance and impact of these strategies on peace and peacebuilding? We propose that business strategies in transition periods are worthy of study in their own right, and can be analyzed in a structured, replicable manner. This section presents a brief framework for analysis of these gaps, augmented with findings from Colombia.

For most Colombian firms the calculation of a 'peace contribution' is less about absorbing or shouldering the costs of peace-writ-large, and more about firm-specific issues like tax reform, US-Colombian trade, contract stability and the rule of law, the future of commodity markets, and the prospects of expansion into unexplored markets of the country. To some extent, this "dividend" approach to peace reflects steady improvements in security and growth over the past fifteen years, causing conflict to wane from private-sector concerns.

Still, many are developing or redefining their business strategies in reaction to the end of political conflict. These strategies, we find, are of four types, presented here to complement existing theoretical discussions of business-peace activity (Miklian 2017):

1. **Operational strategies**. Firms will seek to expand or contract their investments, production, location, or staff in response to opportunities provided by the end of armed confrontation. Examples include some of the following. First, the Colombian government has sought to draw the private sector to remote and underdeveloped areas in order to develop infrastructure, invest in

rural businesses, and train and provide jobs for local communities (El Espectador 2015; Dinero 2016a; Dinero 2016b). Summed up under the name of "Public Works for Taxes" (Obras por Impuestos, Law 1819 of 2016), this government strategy is targeted at companies operating or willing to operate in regions listed as particularly affected by armed conflict (Zonas más Afectadas por el Conflicto Armado – ZOMACs), generally considered as complex investment environments. In exchange for their investments, companies will be entitled to swap part of their taxes for developing public works. However, these incentives are contingent on a certain type of companies: It will be harder to convince smaller companies in the service, consumer goods, and industrial sectors that rely heavily on the kind of investment conditions (skilled labor force, infrastructure) provided only by more advanced urban areas. It will also require significant leverage by national and sub-national state institutions in terms of complementing and stimulating local job and consumer markets. *Alquería*, a dairy company, is a case in point. The company was used to source its primary resource—milk—from farms around the capital, Bogotá. However, a combination of factors—competition by other companies over limited dairy resources, a motivated manager, and proper incentives designed by USAID and Colombian national and local state offices in terms of security and distribution infrastructure—provided the company with the necessary impulse to venture into the Macarena region, formerly a FARC stronghold, where it has been developing supply and distribution networks with local communities. *Telefónica*, a telecommunications giant, is an additional example. With the support of the national government and USAID it developed a contact call center in Quibdó, one of the poorest cities in the country, providing formal jobs to over 100 employees. Finally, CEMEX, a global leader of Mexican origin in the building materials industry, decided on building a new plant in Antioquia, one of the regions with the highest levels of political violence in Colombia. It, too, reached the decision in response to government incentives.

2. **Philanthropic strategies**. Firms will attempt to provide public goods beyond yielding returns to shareholders on their investments. A case in point is Colombian companies' support of demobilization schemes for former fighters, which included business support to the Agencia de Reincorporación Nacional (ARN), the Colombian agency in charge of regulating the demobilization and reintegration of over 56,000 former combatants. The strategy is designed to bring renewed impetus to involving larger numbers of companies in economic and social reintegration efforts. While the Colombian private sector has a long-standing record of pursuing social value and philanthropic activity in areas such as the environment, health, education, and supporting victims of the armed conflict (Rettberg and Rivas 2012), engagement with demobilization programs was not high on its list of priorities. Firms feared alienating customers and increasing their vulnerability in the face of potential links between former combatants and crime. However, the successful signature of a peace agreement has brought increased corporate interest towards

involving companies in reintegration efforts and in doing so more openly (Suárez 2017). Other philanthropic projects using business-peace framing have included biodiversity and conservation programs (Castro and Stork 2015), and the Motor Route skills training by General Motors subsidiary Colmotores. The peace agreement itself is also reshaping Colombian companies' forward philanthropic agendas, with broadened attention to more 'global' issues such as the environment, anti-corruption efforts, youth, health, and education, and less attention to the needs of conflict-related populations.

3.   **Political strategies**. Firms will seek to gain or protect access to state decision-making via funding of electoral or media campaigns, strategic lobbies, or the organization of interest groups or associations to pursue special sectoral interests. Colombia's private sector has historically had a close relationship of mutual benefit with the state (Rettberg 2003; Thorp and Durand 1997). At times collusive, this relationship has nevertheless been credited for Colombia's superior macroeconomic performance in an otherwise more erratic Latin American context. Peace policy has been no exception, and the private sector has supported funding of mediators, advice on design, and actual participation in negotiations and corporate stakeholder engagement as a form of local corporate peacemaking. However, collaboration with government was much stronger and more visible in the 1990s than in recent peace negotiations. Today, several business factions tied to rural as well as urban interests voice their disagreement with having achieved less than military victory over the insurgents and with the trade-off between peace and justice in the coming to terms with past Human Rights violations. Industrial interests were also found to fund the "no" campaign of October 2016 against the peace agreement (Dinero 2016c). In addition, the purpose to have a truth commission investigate the responsibilities of third actors (in addition to guerrillas and state actors) in human rights violations has been eyed warily by business people. Lobbying on these aspects was significant during the period between the 'no' vote and the new agreement, and businesses were successful in reducing emphasis on investigation of businesses for payments to insurgent actors, among other changes. While calls that Colombia would turn into another Venezuela were frequent in the past years, few in the business community believe the Colombian liberal market model is seriously at risk, as illustrated by surveys as well as the ongoing creation of new companies and low levels of capital flight (Confecámaras 2017). Growing numbers of companies are also becoming engaged in conversations about the "Public Works for Taxes" discussion, which is viewed favorably albeit cautiously.

4.   **Public relations strategies**. Public relations (PR) strategies are those that are designed primarily to promote a positive impression of the firm and, consequently, greater consumer demand. Here, the linguistics and discourse of business and peace are derived from the importance of the projection of altruism in business, the importance of morality in peace action, and the importance of projecting legitimacy upon inviting business into such

activities. Thus, PR activities promote positive action, and most are designed in an effort to be mediated and broadly disseminated for mass consumption shortly thereafter. Examples include press releases promoting peace and celebrating positive peace momentum, membership and/or association in peace forums, and creating 'partnerships' with peace and development agencies and non-governmental organizations. PR examples in Colombia include the Business For Peace award for tech entrepreneur and local peace promoter Juan Andrés Cano (Katsos and Fort 2016), the Bogotá Chamber of Commerce's collaboration with the UN Global Compact and support/branding of peace conferences and public events, and the Soy Capaz peace campaign of 100 national private-sector firms and the Colombia National Industry Association, which sought to show how peace can be produced in any realm of social (and commercial) interaction, but ended up being questioned for its emphasis on boosting sales. Another example is Masglo, a Colombian beauty products company, developed a line of nail polish products under the guideline of reconciliation, including "tolerant blue," "inclusive pink," "glitter/shine of trust." The company, which intends to "make a tribute to Colombian women and their efforts towards reconciliation," has vowed to donate part of the proceeds to women's projects in regions marked by the legacies of conflict (Fucsia Magazine 2017). However, PR strategies can also be some of the most contentious in practice. Gardner (2016) explores how the use of 'partnership' has allowed firms to institute CSR and PR programs that imply mutual engagement but are often just as top-down and unresponsive to local needs as the projects that came before them, especially when the language of sustainable development and peace is used by PR arms of corporations to pitch operational expansion to local communities.

These different strategies illustrate the complexity of choice businesses face in transitional contexts. Outlining the purpose and goals of respective strategies can thus help build a framework for more rigorous study of such particulars. In defining these strategies, we assume that firms understand that leveraging self-interest measures can also create a value-added for peace, although it may require reframing standard conceptions of 'risk' and 'opportunity'. For example, if firms are encouraged to pursue their self-interest by expanding to previously abandoned regions, jobs and institutions are thus bolstered as a peace-related by-product. Such activities can be positive for local communities, and diminish the interests and opportunities of companies or informal economic actors that may have profited from conflict. Notably, all of these strategies are mediated by company size, sector of the economy, and the firm's necessity of its relationship to local communities.

How corporate peace actions are made

Returning to our two hypotheses: first, that the higher the perceived cost and uncertainty, the more likely it is that key business actors will innovate and explore alternative routes of action. Here, the role of the leadership likely is a more significant explanatory factor for business-peace activity than the structure of the company or sector of operation, specifically because corporate political risk frameworks prioritize reducing harm over positive action. Generally, the CEO or owner provides the 'inspirational spark' for strategic peace action in nearly all cases in Colombia, particularly given the hierarchical line-of-command of most Colombian firms.[4] While the existence of 'enlightened firms' that holistically operationalize peace strategy as entities may indeed exist, we argue instead that the role and desire of the CEO is determinant and paramount. We further argue that this structure holds not only for issues of peace, but also for sustainable development and other societal engagements by business.

The actions and motivations of the CEO tend to be of critical importance for peace action. Companies during transition constantly face pressure to act in some way, encouraging decisive action to fold these inputs into an opportunistic strategy and guiding which specific strategies to follow. For firms with more active peacebuilding portfolios, the change agent is nearly always the CEO, typically a founder with an activist mindset (Fort 2016). Or put more provocatively, a CEO with a narcissistic need for praise (Petrenko et al. 2016). CEO-led peacebuilding initiatives are often presented through individual ethics or 'moral leadership' (Skubinn and Herzog 2016; Liu and Baker 2016). Preliminary evidence shows that firms who pay CEOs for CSR activities have more robust CSR mandates (Hong et al. 2016), and it is plausible that the same holds for incentivizing peacebuilding if business leaders also see themselves as transformed into 'peace leaders' in conflict settings of operation (Ledbetter 2016; Miller 2016). Following, Golan-Nadir and Cohen (2016) explore the notion of businesspersons as 'policy entrepreneurs' for peace in the Israel-Palestine conflict, highlighting the incremental successes of such initiatives at a time of political deadlock.

Beyond compartmentalizing the CSR sphere or allowing for an activist CEO to see peacebuilding as a pet project, institutional change is harder to implement—especially if the firm has a vigilant board of directors. While most firms that engage in conflict areas recognize the need to engage in 'peace,' few see their role as integral to peacebuilding, and most see peacebuilding as the primary responsibility of the state. Rettberg (2016) defines the multiple strategic goals of security, social change philosophy, and profit-making that business leaders confront as tripartite elements of "need, creed, and greed" that can institutionalize deeper corporate peace involvement. But CEO buy-in is essential to generate a sense of corporate ownership for peace among staff and facilitate resources for strategic peace actions under any of the four categories above. That said, it is rare for CEOs themselves to involve themselves in local-level managing of peace operations, and the bigger the company, the less likely that the CEO has the capability to act upon peace interest beyond broad strokes.[5]

We represent our understandings visually, showing through a flowchart model how pro-peace business strategy calculations are conceived and operationalized in a 'typical' firm:

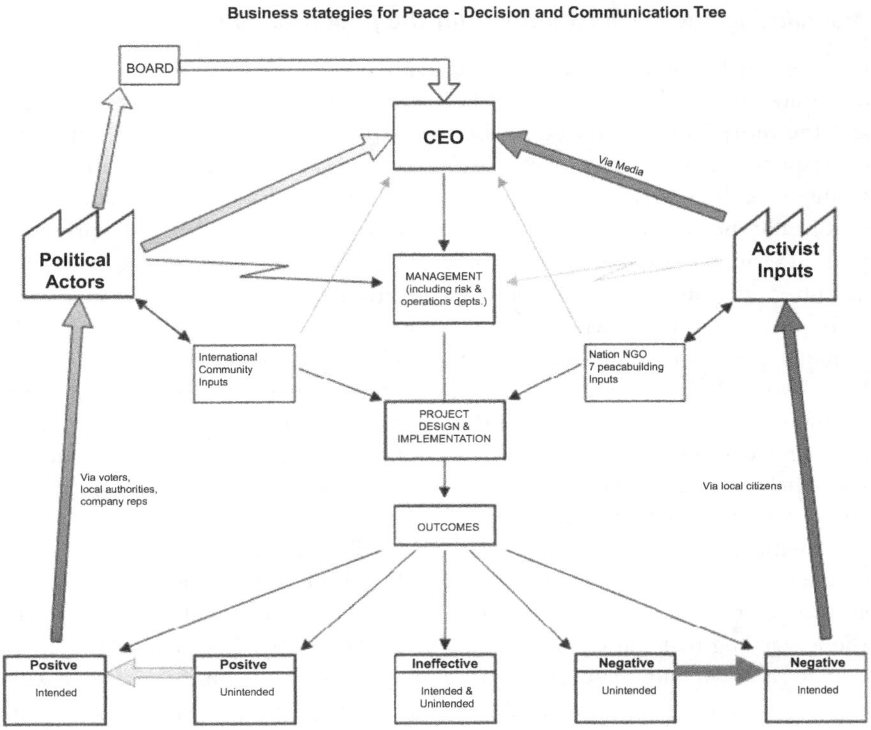

Business stategies for Peace - Decision and Communication Tree

FIGURE 6.1 Business strategies for peace

Shading and thickness represent approximate importance and strength of communication, respectively. This model is not designed to show everyday business strategy, but specifically the generation and application of peacebuilding actions by business. For example, 'management' is a much more complicated entity than illustrated here, and any one peace action might only incorporate a sliver of such. Notably, even strongly positive peace initiatives are hard to import back to political actors, and harder yet to import from politicians or government actors back to business leaders. In contrast, negative actions tend to carry more weight and may be amplified through the media and activist networks. Ineffective peace actions are typically quickly forgotten, with few lessons learned applied elsewhere. Additional arrows could be drawn (for example between the international community and activist actors, or from management or shareholders up to the CEO/Board), but we have prioritized those interactions that most significantly influence peace strategy by business. We add a caveat that many multinational firms have management divisions dedicated to these issues at the topical or country levels where the CEO is less integrated into peace strategy (for example to implement conflict-sensitive business practice), but such models are less common in Colombia.

Assimilating the corporation within the peacebuilding state

Our second hypothesis is that the greater access business actors have to public decision-making, the easier it will be for officials to involve the private sector and the more likely it will be for business actors to adhere to peace policy and to respond to state incentives. As mentioned above, and in contrast with countries such as Mexico or Argentina, where the business-state relationship has historically been more contentious, Colombian business has had privileged access to public decision-making processes. As one business leader poignantly described it: "Business people are pro-government (*gobiernistas*). It's insane not to be pro-government when you are a businessman" (Nicanor Restrepo 2012, former leader of the Antioquia Group of Companies, interview by the author, Medellín).[6] This closeness is both of an informal kind—stemming from common social and economic elite networks developed through family, social class, and educational ties—as well as formal in nature, as many state agencies and offices, from the extractive to the state vocational training agencies, include business leaders in their boards, which facilitates the flow of information, the development of mutual trust, and effective collaboration.

As a reflection of this close relationship, Colombian businesses have served key roles in advising, supporting, or even leading peace negotiations for decades, complementing a long-standing tradition of philanthropic and CSR work. "If you want peace, you need to sit down with those barbarians" as one business leader in the extractive sector explained (Ramón de la Torre 2002, former president of an oil company, interview by the author, Bogotá). The leader of the Federación Nacional de Comerciantes (Fenalco) put it more simply: "Peace is better business" (Sabas Pretelt de la Vega 2002, former president of the Trade Association, interview by the author, Bogotá). In the 1980s, two of the largest Colombian companies, *Suramericana de Seguros S.A.*, the country's largest insurance company, and *Bavaria S.A.*, the largest beer company paid for a USD20,000 satellite telephone, labeled the "red phone" (*teléfono rojo*) in reference to its purpose to keep the negotiating sides in contact (Nicanor Restrepo 2012, former leader of the Antioquia Group of Companies, interview by the author, Medellín). In a time before internet and cell phones, the red phone served to solve emergencies in the negotiation process and to maintain communication and open channels between the sides.

This support has been compensated by privileged business access to peace policy design. In the most recent peace process between the government and FARC, business leaders paid for foreign mediators to support secret preliminary talks. In return, the government consulted candidly and frequently with the representatives of the largest companies and sectors. When the public debate about rural land reform escalated in 2015 amid rumors that the government was making too many concessions, a group of eight prominent business leaders traveled to Havana to discuss the issue first-hand with both negotiating teams. This served as a poignant reminder to both sides of the business community's veto power over the content of the peace agreements. In addition, government has the power of appointment, putting visible business leaders in leading roles in the peace process. This was the case of Gonzalo Restrepo, the CEO of Éxito, the country's largest consumer goods company, and most recently Juan Sebastián Betancur, the former leader of business think tank Proantioquia, who serve(d) as members of the negotiating teams with FARC. Luis Carlos Villegas, former president of the National Association of Business Leaders, was a member of the negotiation team in peace talks with FARC, and the Fundación Ideas para la Paz, a key point of reference for producing conflict insights and in staffing key peace-related Colombian government positions, was founded in 2002 by prominent business leaders. In this way, the government achieved three goals: buy-in by crucial factions of the business community, legitimacy by the opposite side (which saw the presence of their "class enemy" as a guarantee of commitment), and support by the general population, which trusts the business community more than it does politicians or the guerrillas.

4. Conclusions

Business is a complex social actor. In contexts of transition from conflict to peace it faces multiple choices and needs. In this chapter, we have proposed a framework for analyzing business strategies during such unique moments. Some of these strategies are path-dependent and reflect previous corporate practice in managing risk and change. Others result from specific organizational forms or context-specificities. We suggest that each strategy choice or combination of strategies is contingent on depth of crisis, perception of opportunity, and access to policymaking. The description of these strategies as well as tracing when and why they are actually chosen by different companies or groups of companies is important for scholars and policymakers alike, as it puts to the test theories about the impact of conflict on corporate activity as well as the centrality of the private sector in peacebuilding. In order to develop this framework, we have based ourselves on the recent Colombian experience of private-sector participation in peacebuilding. Further research is needed to test the validity of our framework beyond the Colombian case.

Notes

1 Jason Miklian is a senior researcher at PRIO. Angelika Rettberg is an associate professor at the Political Science Department at Universidad de los Andes (Bogotá – Colombia) and a PRIO Global Fellow. The authors thank Juan Pablo Medina Bickel, Daniel Medina Jaime, and Liset Pimienta for their valuable research assistance.
2 This chapter does not intend to challenge the rich literature on business strategy *per se*, as it is more interested specifically in business reactions and strategies within peace and conflict dynamics. For further reading on the former, see Grant (2013) and Spender (2014) on general business strategy; Porter and Cramer (2006) on responsible business strategy; Spieth et al. (2016) on strategy innovation; Lee and Klassen (2016) on strategy during times of uncertainty (using the case of climate response); and Winkler et al. (2014) and Song (2016) on local market uncertainty and strategic decision-making.
3 There of course exist firms that explicitly intend to profit from conflict and/or crisis, but, as they are the minority of businesses in such settings we exclude them from consideration here.

4 It may be the case that this inspirational spark is more concentrated in sectors that are outward-looking and innovative before peace 'hits,' but more research would be needed to make this claim more definitively. Also see Katsos and Fort (2016).
5 Thanks to Ben Miller for this point.
6 The exact phrase in Spanish was: "Los empresarios de todo el mundo son gobiernistas. Es una locura no ser gobiernista si se es empresario."

Bibliography

Alleblas, Tessa, 2015. "The Responsibility to Protect and the Private Sector: Making the Business Case for Private Sector Involvement in Mass Atrocity Prevention." Hague Institute for Global Justice Working Paper 5. The Hague: Hague Institute.

Angrist, J.D. and A.D. Kugler. 2008. "Rural Windfall or a New Resource Curse? Coca, Income, and Civil Conflict in Columbia." *Review of Economics and Statistics* 90(2): 191–215. https://doi.org/10.1162/rest.90.2.191.

Beittel, June, 2015. "Peace Talks in Colombia." CRS Report 7–5700. Washington DC: Congressional Research Service.

Bond, Carol, 2014. "Positive Peace and Sustainability in the Mining Context: Beyond the Triple Bottom Line." *Journal of Cleaner Production* 84: 164–173.

Branzei, O. and S. Abdelnour. 2010. "Another Day, Another Dollar: Enterprise Resilience Under Terrorism in Developing Countries," *Journal of International Business Studies* 41(5): 804–825.

Bucheli, Marcelo, 2005. *Bananas and Business: The United Fruit Company in Columbia, 1899–2000.* New York and London: New York University Press.

Carroll, Archie, 2016. "Global Codes of Conduct," in Robert W. Kolb (Ed.) *Encyclopedia of Business Ethics and Society.* London: Sage.

Casadesus-Masanell, R. and J. Ricart, 2010. "From Strategy to Business Models and onto Tactics." *Long Range Planning*2010: 195–215.

Castro, Lorena Jaramillo and Adrienne Stork, 2015. "Linking to Peace: Using BioTrade for Biodiversity Conservation and Peacebuilding in Colombia," in Helen Young and Lisa Goldman (Eds.), *Livelihoods, Natural Resources, and Post-Conflict Peacebuilding.* London: Routledge.

Chambers, R. and Rachel Jacobs, 2007. "Assessing political risk," *The Internal Auditor*, August: 58–64.

Confecámaras, 2017. *Informe de Dinámica Empresarial 2016.* www.ccpalmira.org.co/portal/images/Docs/Informe%20de%20Dinamica%20Empresarial%202016.pdf.

Davis, R. and D. Franks, 2014. "Costs of Company-Community Conflict in the Extractive Sector." Corporate Social Responsibility Initiative Report No. 66. Cambridge, MA: Harvard Kennedy School.

Deitelhoff, N. and K.D. Wolf (Eds.), 2010. *Corporate Security Responsibility?*London: Palgrave Macmillan.

Dinero, 1998. "El país que piden los empresarios," March 16, www.dinero.com/caratula/edicion-impresa/articulo/el-pais-piden-empresarios/16224

Dinero, 2016a. "Las inquietudes del sector privado de cara al postconflicto," September 15, www.dinero.com/pais/articulo/rol-del-sector-privado-en-la-construccion-de-paz-despues-del-plebiscito/231980. Accessed February 9, 2017.

Dinero, 2016b. "Los beneficios de la paz por los que Colombia tendría que esperar," March 30, www.dinero.com/economia/articulo/los-beneficios-del-postconflicto-y-el-papel-del-sector-privado/221841. Accessed February 9, 2017.

Dinero, 2016c. "Aquí el listado de donantes a campaña del No… y no está Ardila Lülle," October 6, www.dinero.com/pais/articulo/empresario-que-aportaron-a-la-campana-del-no-en-el-plebiscito/234634. Accessed February 9, 2017.

Driffield, N., C. Jones and J. Crotty, 2013. "International Business Research and Risky Investments, an Analysis of FDI in Conflict Zones." *International Business Review* 22(1): 140–155.

El Espectador, 2015. "Gobierno busca que empresarios y sector privado aporten recursos al posconflicto," March 25, www.elespectador.com/noticias/politica/gobierno-busca-emp resarios-y-sector-privado-aporten-rec-articulo-551345.

Fisman, Raymond and Tarun Khanna, 2004. "Facilitating Development: The Role of Business Groups." *World Development*April32(4): 609–628.

Ford, Jolyon, 2015a. "Perspectives on the Evolving 'Business and Peace Debate." *Academy of Management Perspectives* 4(1):1–10.

Ford, Jolyon, 2015b. "The Private Sector as a Stakeholder in Inclusive Peacebuilding." *Development Dialogue* 1(3): 138–151.

Forrer, John and Timothy Fort, 2016. "The PACO Index." *Business Horizons*.

Fort, T., 2016. *The Diplomat in the Corner Office*. Stanford, CA: Stanford University Press.

Fucsia Magazine. 2017. "Reconciliación Colombia y Masglo se unen en una campaña a todo color por un país en paz," www.fucsia.co/estilo-de-vida/articulo/esmaltes-ma sglo-y-reconciliacion-colombia-campana-por-la-paz/75894.

Franks, D., R. Davis, A. Bebbington, S. Ali, D. Kemp and M. Scurrah, 2014. "Conflict Translates Environmental and Social Risk into Business Costs." *PNAS* 111(21): 7576–7581.

Ganson, B., 2011. "Business and Conflict Prevention: Towards a Framework for Action." Geneva: Geneva Peacebuilding Platform Report #2.

Ganson, B., 2014. "Business in Fragile Environments: Capabilities for Conflict Prevention." *Negotiation and Conflict Management Journal* 7(2): 1–18.

Ganson, B. and A. Wennmann, 2015. "Business and Conflict in Fragile States." *Adelphi Series* 55(457–458): 11–34.

Gao, Y. 2009. "Managing Political Risk in Cross-National Investment: A Stakeholder View," in *Singapore Management Review*, 31(1): 99–114.

Gardner, Katy, 2016. "Disconnect Development: Imagining Partnership and Eperiencing Detachment in Chevron's Borderlands," in Catherine Dolan and Dinah Rajak (Eds.), *The Anthropology of Corporate Social Responsibility*. New York: Berghan.

Ghimire, S. and B. Upreti, 2012. "Corporate Engagement for Conflict Transformation: Conceptualising the Business-Peace Interface." *Journal of Conflict Transformation and Security* 2(1): 77–100.

Golan-Nadir, Niva and Nissim Cohen, 2016. "The Role of Individual Agents in Promoting Peace Processes: Business People and Policy Entrepreneurship in the Israeli-Palestinian Conflict." *Policy Studies* 2016: 1–18.

Gourevitch, Peter. 2007. "The Political Drivers of Corporate Governance," in Stephen Haber, Douglass C. North and Barry R. Weingast (Eds.), *Political Institutions and Financial Development*. Stanford, CA: Stanford University Press.

Grant, Robert, 2013. *Contemporary Strategy Analysis: Concepts, Techniques, Applications*. 8th Edition. London: Wiley.

Guáqueta, Alexandra, 2013. "Harnessing Corporations: Lessons from the Voluntary Principles on Security and Human Rights in Colombia and Indonesia." *Journal of Asian Public Policy* 6(2): 129–146.

Hong, Bryan, Frank Li and Dylan Minor, 2016. "Corporate Governance and Executive Compensation for Corporate Responsibility." *Journal of Business Ethics* 136(1): 199–213.

Idrobo, N., D. Mejia, A. Tribin. 2014. "Illegal Gold Mining and Violence in Colombia." *Peace Economics, Peace Science and Public Policy* 20(1): 83–111.

Iff, A. and R. Alluri, 2016. "Business Actors in Peace Mediation Processes." *Business and Society Review* 121(2): 187–215.

Jallat, F. and C.J. Shultz, 2011. "Lebanon: From Cataclysm to Opportunity—Crisis Management Lessons for MNCs in the Tourism Sector of the Middle East," *Journal of World Business* 46(4): 476–486.

Jamali, D. and R. Mirshak, 2010. "Business-conflict Linkages: Revisiting MNCs, CSR, and Conflict." *Journal of Business Ethics* 93(3): 443–464.

Katsos, John and Timothy Fort, 2016. "Leadership in the promotion of peace: Interviews with the 2015 Business for Peace honorees." *Business Horizons*, 463–470.

Kingston, Peter, 1999. *Crafting Coalitions for Reform: Business Preferences, Political Institutions, and Neoliberal Reform in Brazil.* University Park, PA: Pennsylvania State University Press.

Klettner, Alice, Thomas Clarke and Martijn Boersma, 2014. "The Governance of Corporate Sustainability: Empirical Insights into the Development, Leadership and Implementation of Responsible Business Strategy." *Journal of Business Ethics* 122(1): 145–165.

Kolk, A. and F. Lenfant, 2015. "Partnerships for Peace and Development in Fragile States: Identifying Missing Links." *Academy of Management Perspectives* 29(4): 422–437.

Kolk, A. and R. van Tulder, 2010. "International Business, Corporate Social Responsibility and Sustainable Development." *International Business Review* 19(2): 119–125.

Ledbetter, Bernice, 2016. "Business Leadership for Peace." *International Journal of Public Leadership* 12(3): 239–251.

Lee, Su-Yol and Robert Klassen, 2016. "Firms' Response to Climate Change: The Interplay of Business Uncertainty and Organizational Capabilities." *Business Strategy and the Environment* 25(8): 577–592.

Liu, Helena and Christopher Baker, 2016. "Ordinary Aristocrats: The Discursive Construction of Philanthropists as Ethical Leaders." *Journal of Business Ethics* 133(2): 149–160.

Massé, F. and J. Munevar. 2016. *Due Diligence in Columbia's Gold Supply Chain.* Paris: Organisation for Economic Co-operation.

Maxfield, Sylvia and Ben Ross Schneider (Eds.). 1996. *Business and the State in Developing Countries.* Ithaca, NY: Cornell University Press.

May, Christopher, 2015. "Who's in Charge? Corporations as Institutions of Global Governance." *Communications* 15042(1):2015.

Meyer, K., R. Mudambi and R. Narula, 2011. "Multinational Enterprises and Local Contexts: The Opportunities and Challenges of Multiple Embeddedness." *Journal of Management Studies* 48(2): 235–252.

Mikler, John (Ed.). 2013. *The Handbook of Global Companies.* Hoboken, NJ: Wiley and Sons.

Miklian, J., 2017. "Mapping Business-Peace Interactions: Five Assertions for How Businesses Create Peace." *Business, Peace & Sustainable Development* 10(1): 3–27.

Miklian, Jason and Juan Pablo Medina Bickel, 2018. "Theorizing Business and Local Peacebuilding Through the 'Footprints of Peace' Coffee Project in Rural Columbia." *Business and Society*, doi:10.1177/0007650317749441: 1–40.

Miller, Whitney, 2016. "Toward a Scholarship of Peace Leadership." *International Journal of Public Leadership* 12(3): 216–226.

Mills, R. and Q. Fan, 2006. "The Investment Climate in Post-conflict Situations." Policy Research Working Paper 4055. Washington DC: World Bank.

Naidoo, Vikash, 2010. "Firm Survival Through a Crisis: The Influence of Market Orientation, Marketing Innovation and Business Strategy." *Industrial Marketing Management* 39(8): 1311–1320.

Nielsen, T. and L. Riddle, 2009. "Investing in Peace: The Motivational Dynamics of Diaspora Investment in Post-conflict Economies." *Journal of Business Ethics* 89(4): 435–448.

Novick, Rebecca, 2012. "Private Sector Peacebuilding in Colombia and Ciudad Juárez." Master of Arts Thesis. Washington DC: American University.

Oetzel, J. and M. Breslauer, 2015. "The Business and Economics of Peace: Moving the Agenda Forward." *Business, Peace and Sustainable Development* 2015(6): 3–8.

Oetzel, J., and K. Getz, 2012. "Why and How Might Firms Respond Strategically to Violent Conflict?" *Journal of International Business Studies* 43: 166–186.

Olson, Mancur, 1965. *The Logic of Collective Action.* Cambridge, MA and London: Harvard University Press.

Özel, Işik, 2014. *State-business Alliances and Economic Development: Turkey, Mexico and North Africa.* London: Routledge.

Petrenko, O., F. Aime, J. Ridge and A. Hill, 2014. "Corporate Social Responsibility or CEO Narcissism? CSR Motivations and Organizational Performance." *Strategic Management Journal* 37(2): 262–279.

Pirson, M. and P. Lawrence, 2010. "Humanism in Business-Towards a Paradigm Shift?" *Journal of Business Ethics* 93(4): 553–565.

Porter, M. and M.R. Kramer, 2006. "Strategy and Society: The link between Competitive Advantage and Corporate Social Responsibility." *Harvard Business Review*, December.

Rettberg, A. 2016. "Need, Creed, and Greed: Understanding How and Why Business Leaders Focus on Issues of Peace," *Business Horizons*, 59(5): 481–492.

Rettberg, A., 2015. "Gold, Oil and the Lure of Violence: The Private Sector and Post-Conflict Risks in Colombia," the Norwegian Peacebuilding Resource Centre, www. clingendael.nl/publication/oil-and-gold-private-sector-and-post-conflict-risks-colombia

Rettberg, A. 2009. "Business and Peace in Colombia: Responses, Challenges, and Achievements," in V. Bouvier (Ed.), *Colombia: Building Peace in a Time of War*, Washington DC: USIP Press, pp. 191–204.

Rettberg, A. 2007. "Business and Peace in El Salvador, Guatemala, and Colombia." *Journal of Latin American Studies* 39(3) (August): 463–494.

Rettberg, A. 2005. "Business versus Business? Economic Groups and Business Associations in Colombia." *Latin American Politics and Society* 47(1): 31–54.

Rettberg, A., 2004. "Business-Led Peacebuilding in Colombia: Future or Fad for a Country in Crisis," Working Paper No.56, Crisis States Progamme, December, www.crisisstates. com/download/wp/wp56.pdf

Rettberg, A., 2003. *Cacaos y tigres de papel: El gobierno de Samper y los empresarios colombianos.* Bogotá: Ediciones Uniandes (Facultad de Administración y Departamento de Ciencia Política) – Centro de Estudios Socioculturales (CESO), Universidad de los Andes.

Rettberg, A., 2001. "The Political Preferences of Diversified Business Groups: Lessons from Colombia (1994–1998)." *Business and Politics*, 3(1): 47–63.

Rettberg, A. and Rivas, A., 2012. "Sector privado y construcción de paz en Colombia: Entre el optimismo y el desencanto," in Angelika Rettberg (Ed.), *Construcción de paz en Colombia.* Bogotá: Ediciones Uniandes, pp. 305–347.

Rettberg, A. and Ortiz-Riomalo, J.F., 2016. "Golden Opportunity, or a New Twist on the Resource-Conflict Relationship: Links Between the Drug Trade and Illegal Gold Mining in Colombia." *World Development*, 84: 82–96.

Rettberg, Angelika, Ralf Leiteritz y Carlo Nasi, 2011. "Entrepreneurial Activity in the Context of Violent Conflict: Business and Organized Violence in Colombia." *Journal of Small Business and Entrepreneurship* 24(2): 179–196.

Richani, Nazih, 2013. *Systems of Violence, Second Edition: The Political Economy of War and Peace in Columbia.* New York: State University of New York Press.

Roemer-Mahler, A., 2012. "Business Conflict and Global Politics: The Pharmaceutical Industry and the Global Protection of Intellectual Property Rights." *Review of International Political Economy* 20(1): 121–152.

Scherer, A. and G. Palazzo, 2011. "The New Political Role of Business in a Globalized World." *Journal of Management Studies* 48(4): 899–931.

Schneider, Ben., 2004. *Business Politics and the State in Twentieth-Century Latin America.* Cambridge: Cambridge University Press.

Shafer, Michael. 1996. "The Political Economy of Sector and Sectoral Change," in Ben Ross Schneider and Sylvia Maxfield (Eds.), *Business and the State in Developing Countries*, Ithaca, NY: Cornell University Press.

Skubinn, Rebekka and Lisa Herzog, 2016. "Internalized Moral Identity in Ethical Leadership." *Journal of Business Ethics* 133(2): 149–160.

Smith, W., A. Binns and M. Tushman, 2010. "Complex Business Models: Managing Strategic Paradoxes Simultaneously." *Long Range Planning* 43(2): 448–461.

Song, Sangcheol. 2016. "Host Market Uncertainty, Subsidiary Characteristics, and Growth Option Exercise." *Long Range Planning* online first.

Spender, J.C., 2014. *Business Strategy.* Oxford: Oxford University Press.

Spieth, Patrick, Dirk Schneckenberg, and Kurt Matzler, 2016. "Exploring the Linkage Between Business Model (&) Innovation and the Strategy of the Firm." *R&D Management* 46(3): 403–413.

Steinmo, Sven, Kathleen Thelen, and Fred Longstreth (Eds.), 1992. *Structuring Politics: Historical Institutionalism in Comparative Analysis.* New York: Cambridge University Press.

Suárez, M., 2017. Interview by Authors. January 13, Bogotá, Colombia.

Thorp, R. and Durand, F., 1997. "A Historical View of Business – State Relations: Colombia, Peru, and Venezuela Compared," in Schneider, B. and Maxfield, S. (Eds), *Business and the State in Developing Countries*, Ithaca, NY: Cornell University Press, pp. 216–236.

Thoumi, Francisco E., 2002. "Illegal Drugs in Columbia: From Illegal Economic Boom to Social." *The Annals of the American Academy of Political and Social Science* 582(1), https://doi.org/10.1177/000271620258200108

Trompenaars, F., 1996. "Resolving International Conflict: Culture and Business Strategy." *Business Strategy Review* 7(3): 51–68.

United Nations Development Programme (UNDP), 2015. "Sustainable Development Goals: Introducing the 2030 Agenda for Sustainable Development." New York: UN.

United Nations Global Compact (UNGC), 2016. "Business For Peace Indicators Project," www.unglobalcompact.org/what-is-gc/our-work/governance/peace/sdg-indicators. Accessed January 10, 2017.

United Nations Global Compact (UNGC), 2013. "Responsible Business, Advancing Peace: Examples from Companies, Investors and Global Compact Networks." New York: UNGC.

United Nations News Centre. 2016. "As Colombians Bid Farewell to 'Decades of Flames,' Ban Pledges UN Support to Historic Peace Deal," September 26, http://www.un.org/apps/news/story.asp?NewsID=55127

United Nations Security Council (UNSC), 2009. "Statement by the President of the Security Council." S/PRST/2009/23.

United Nations News Centre, 2016. "As Colombians bid farewell to 'decades of flames,' Ban pledges UN support to historic peace deal," September 26, www.un.org/apps/news/story.asp?NewsID=55127#.WJYrnvnhCUk. Accessed January 20, 2017.

Winkler, Jens, Christian Kuklinski and Roger Moser, 2015. "Decision Making in Emerging Markets: The Delphi Approach's Contribution to Coping with Uncertainty and Equivocality." *Journal of Business Research* 68: 1118–1126.

PART III

Empirical reflections

7

"THE ONLY HOPE LEFT"

Differences between multinational and local company peacebuilding activities in Syria and Iraq

John E. Katsos

Introduction

This chapter examines the conflict impacts of businesses operating in Iraq and Syria in the period during the Syrian Civil War and its associated violent conflicts. The current state of the business and peace literature, as noted by other chapters in this, routinely note the disconnect between the positive impacts on peace that companies *can* have and the negative impacts on peace that companies have *actually* had. Academic and practitioner research and advice often sidesteps the difficult issues associated with doing business in active violent conflict zones, ones that theorists and practitioners in business and human rights have been all too willing to address.

From 2015 to 2018, the author conducted over 150 interviews with individuals representing 73 for-profit organizations operating in Iraq and/or Syria. The individuals had each self-identified as doing business in areas directly impacted by the violent conflicts in these countries at some point since the onset of the Syrian Civil War in 2011.

The chapter proceeds as follows. First, we detail the existing literature in the business for peace field. The second section of this chapter discusses the relevant conflict context in Syria and Iraq during the time of our study. After highlighting the relevant conflict context, we detail our methodology. We then detail our findings on company activities. The findings were split between those impacts that multinational companies (MNCs) had and can have and those impacts that local companies had and can have. MNCs were viewed as peace promoting when they enhanced the rule of law, invested in local capacity building, and provided funding for initiatives aimed at social cohesion. MNCs were viewed as contributing to violence when they worked with non-state armed groups, made corrupt payments of any kind to government officials, hired local private security firms, and did not have conflict-party aware practices in hiring employees and contractors. Local firms were viewed as peace promoting when they continued to operate their businesses through paying employees and providing necessary goods and services. Importantly, local businesses perceived that peace-promotion must include cooperation with all parties to the conflict including non-state armed groups. Our findings support portions of the existing business and peace categories related to multinationals, but undermines the theory with respect to local companies. We conclude by noting the limitations of the research, principally the limited ability to generalize the findings to other active conflict settings without further research.

The current theory of business and its contribution to peace and conflict

Various disciplines address the concepts of peace and conflict. It is a vast and contested field. We discuss below, concepts and definitions of peace and conflict to set out a basic understanding of the terms, how they are used, and their implications for business and peace research.

The philosophy, political science, sociology, psychology, economics, and management disciplines have all attempted to define peace (Azam and Mesnard, 2003; Bannon and Collier, 2003; Coser, 1967; Fogarty, 2000; Fort and Schipani, 2004; Galtung, 1969; Galtung, 1996a; Rummel, 1979; Spreitzer, 2007; Wani, 2015). There is, however, no consensus on its definition (Anderson, 2004). One dimension common among definitions of peace is the recognition of the absence of violence, also referred to as "negative peace" (Galtung, 1969). When defining peace in specific terms—that is, "positive peace"—the definitions often become confusing, ill-defined, or impractical (Anderson, 2004; Rapoport, 1999).

Johan Galtung, founder of the Peace Research Institute and considered one of the founders of the peace studies field (Buhaug, Levy, and Urdal, 2014), noted that the term *peace* should always be considered problematic. It should be constantly evolving, much like the medical profession's approach to the term *health* (Galtung, 1996). "Structural violence" also receives considerable attention from researchers defining peace. Societies experiencing structural violence typically have poor human rights records, affecting large segments of the population. In addition to fostering political and economic problems, persistent structural violence can result in a weakened government capacity to provide basic government services, such as health services (Farmer, Nizeye, Stulac, and Keshavjee, 2006).

Studies exploring comparative peace (Barometer, 2015; Institute for Economics and Peace [IEP], 2014)—that is, the relative peacefulness of different countries—have relied on the premise that structural violence is a hindrance to positive peace in the same way actual violence is. These studies presume that peaceful societies experience both negative peace and a general lack of structural violence. In the economics literature, positive peace does have quantifiable measures, critiques of the concept notwithstanding. For example, countries that have high levels of structural violence (though low levels of actual casualties) are classified as being not as peaceful as those countries with low levels of both structural and actual violence (Barometer, 2015).

Conflict is also a contested concept. The Heidelberg Institute's definition of conflict is both practical and quantifiable: conflict is any:

> positional difference, regarding values relevant to a society, between at least two decisive and directly involved actors, which is being carried out using observable and interrelated conflict measures that lie outside established regulatory procedures and threaten core state functions, the international order or hold out the prospect to do so.
>
> *(Barometer, 2015)*

Despite the unique characteristics of specific conflicts, scholars note some similarities among them. First, since the end of the Cold War, most conflicts have been intrastate—that is, civil wars (Azam and Mesnard, 2003; Elbadawi and Sambanis, 2002; Barometer, 2015; Institute for Economics and Peace [IEP], 2014; Sandler et al., 2000; Wani, 2015). Second, approximately half of all conflicts involve countries returning to a state of conflict within 10 years of the end of a previous conflict (Collier and Hoeffler, 2002).

One unresolved issue is how to incorporate a concept like structural violence into a definition of conflict. When a country is experiencing structural violence, the expression of conflict will often be in forms other than casualties. This unresolved conceptual ambiguity presents a challenge to the most widely accepted conflict metrics. An example is the Uppsala Conflict Database, which measures conflict only in terms of casualties over time: Minor conflicts are between 25 and 1,000 battlefield deaths per year, whereas war is more than 1,000 battlefield deaths (Collier, 2009; Elbadawi, Kaltani, and Schmidt-Hebbel, 2007).

The general agreement around the ideas, but not the precise definitions, of peace and conflict is important for management scholars to note. Peace is not just the absence of violence, and conflict is not always overtly violent. Understanding the full complement of definitions for peace and conflict support richer and more robust conceptualizations addressing business and peace.

Business and peace theory

Oetzel et al.'s (2009) review of the business and peace literature remains the primary expression of how businesses can positively promote peace. Oetzel et al. highlight four ways that business can achieve peace promotion: through promoting economic development, engaging in track-two diplomacy, enhancing rule of law through adoption of international codes of conduct and risk assessment, and promoting a sense of community.

First, business promotes economic development. This is the most basic form of violence reduction a business can engage in, yet it is also one of the most powerful. Firms generate economic benefits for the societies in which they operate by design. Economic development in this context is simply business doing what it does naturally: creating value for shareholders (Friedman, 2009), employing local workers (Milliken et al., 2015), transferring valuable technology (Spencer, 2008), and making foreign direct investment (Buckley, 2014; Getz and Oetzel, 2009). By providing these basic inputs in conflict-sensitive regions, business helps advance economic development and reduce prospects for violent conflicts.

Multinational companies also regularly look to developing economies as a source of greater global growth gains (Borensztein, De Gregorio, and Lee, 1998; Haufler, 1997; Obstfeld, 1994) and conflict zones are regarded as one of the two "base of the pyramid" markets, the other being the global poor (Anderson, Markides, and Kupp, 2010). Although there can be tremendous growth opportunities in developing countries, the risk of conflict re-emerging in post-conflict countries often scares away substantial business activities. Developing countries have a 40 percent risk of returning to violence whereas all others have only a 9 percent risk (Collier, Hoeffler, and Soderbom, 2008). This troubling condition is counterbalanced by recognizing that even modest increases in economic growth greatly reduce the likelihood that those countries will revert to conflict (Collier, 2009). There are great opportunities and risks for business to achieve substantial growth rates and, at the same time, reduce the risk of violence in communities throughout the world. Business operations themselves could enhance peace by adopting specific management practices such as enhancing employee voice within the company (Milliken et al., 2015).

Second, business can engage in track-two diplomacy. Track-two diplomacy is usually defined as informal, nonbinding negotiations that are explicitly intended to reduce conflict through face-to-face meetings (Diamond and McDonald, 1996; Westermann-Behaylo, Rehbein and Fort, 2015), but it also refers to any time corporations act as brokers between sides in a conflict (Galtung, 1996; Montville, 1991; Oetzel et al., 2007; Ramsbotham, Woodhouse, and Miall, 2011). Of the four factors, this is the highest level of explicit engagement that business has in the political process (Montville, 1991; Oetzel et al., 2009; Westermann-Behaylo, Rehbein and Fort, 2015). Within track-two diplomacy, however, there are multiple levels of engagement. Business can engage in conflict resolution through NGO partnerships that help to alleviate the causes of conflict (Kolk and Lenfant, 2015; Oetzel and Doh, 2009; Westley and Vredenburg, 1991), participation in global multilateral agreements (Oetzel et al., 2007), and direct informal negotiations between the two sides engaged in active conflict (Lieberfeld, 2002). Westermann-Behaylo, Rehbein and Fort (2015) have further suggested that multinationals could have greater influence on peace through the pursuit of corporate diplomacy.

Third, business can contribute to a sense of community and enhance social cohesion (Dworkin and Schipani, 2007; Fort and Schipani, 2004; Spreitzer, 2007). Management theorists are perhaps most familiar with the notion of contributing to a sense of community as it is embedded within the literature on corporate social responsibility (CSR) (Aguilera and Rupp, 2005; Davies et al., 2003; Freeman and McVea, 2001). By taking all stakeholders into account, rather than just owners of the firm (Freeman, 1984), businesses can obtain their "social license" to operate in a foreign country (Gunningham, Kagan, and Thornton, 2003). This is especially important for reducing operational risks in conflict-sensitive regions (Oetzel and Getz, 2012). Milliken et al. (2015) also note the importance of incorporating employee voice into management of companies in conflict-affected regions as an important way to enhance the sense of community.

Fourth, business can promote rule of law by adopting third-party standards such as international codes of conduct (Emmelhainz and Adams, 1999; Kolk and Tuldere, 2002; Steelman and Rivera, 2006) and engaging in conflict risk assessment before entering and while operating within conflict countries (Anderson, Markides, and Kupp, 2010; Guáqueta, 2008; O'Neill, 2008). By adopting what the literature terms "principles of external valuation," companies can advance the rule of law within countries by binding themselves to more stable international norms. This is often called "hard trust," indicating the need for stakeholders to know that companies are bound by legally enforceable mechanisms that compel them to follow rules of operations (Bies et al., 2007). Examples of external valuations include International Organization for Standardization (ISO) 26000, the UN Global Compact, the UN Guiding Principles on Business and Human Rights (sometimes referred to as the Ruggie Principles), and the International Labor Organization's labor standards. Principles of external valuation not only set a model of behavior that engenders social and economic justice but also are a way for business to contribute to peace (by setting examples of good citizenship). Often, business unintentionally generates more conflict in a region through missteps that could be avoided by better understanding the consequences of its policies and practices. Guidance documents such as Conflict-Sensitive Business Practice (Banfield et al., 2005) and the Guidance on Responsible Business in Conflict-Affected and High-Risk Areas (Compact, 2010) are just two examples of resources available to firms to assess and manage risk in conflict countries.

In recent years, scholars have highlighted some exceptions to the four methods proposed in Oetzel et al. (2009), but without challenging the core of the theory (Forrer and Katsos, 2015; Westermann-Behaylo et al., 2015). For instance, Oetzel et al. (2009) acknowledged the realities of persistent structural violence and argued that basic peacebuilding practices by the private sector will be effective only when conflicts are in the lowest three levels of intensity on the Heidelberg Institute's Conflict Barometer and not in its highest two levels of intensity, termed "War" and "Limited War" (Barometer, 2015). This means that the recommendations are tailored to areas with limited violence. Forrer and Katsos (2015) noted that it was precisely in these three areas that businesses could have their greatest impact on peace and further noted a triadic construct that presents countries as existing in three basic conditions—war, buffer condition, and peace—that has several advantages for businesses to understand how they can best promote peace. They convincingly assert that the buffer condition is the most effective time for business to enhance peace.

The buffer condition also allows businesses to better integrate addressing structural violence (Farmer et al., 2006; Galtung, 2006) in their peacebuilding operations. The buffer condition has six research-backed characteristics: less than a decade since war or limited war (Collier, 2006, 2009; Elbadawi, Kaltani and Schmidt-Hebbel, 2007), political and economic uncertainty (Mills and Fan, 2006), disrespect for rule of law (Mills and Fan, 2006; Santos, 2003), depleted physical and human capital (Santos, 2003), a damaged financial system (Mills and Fan, 2006; Santos, 2003), and heavy reliance on foreign aid (Elbadawi, Kaltani and Schmidt-Hebbel 2007). The buffer condition retains many of the traits of violence and the war economy even after war or limited war has ceased (Ballentine et al., 2005). Major differences among war, buffer, and peace economies can be captured by the levels of informal and black-market activity. Buffer economies, for instance, often have high levels of black economic output because the government monopolizes the formal economy, forcing anti-government groups to use the informal and black economies to fund their activities (Fearon, 2004; Winer and Roule, 2003). Sometimes black markets have been found to provide benefits for certain types of legal activities (Andreas, 2009; Baumol, 1996), but generally black-market activity is viewed as a hindrance to transitioning toward peace (Bannon and Collier, 2003; Farmer et al., 2006; Reade and Lee, 2012). These elements of the buffer economy do not simply vanish when the intensity level of the conflict declines from war to buffer condition. In buffer economies, consumption and investment decline and there is mass movement of people as either refugees or internally displaced persons (The Institute for Economics and Peace, 2013). Social, political, and economic processes are hindered, and prospects for sustainable growth and development are reduced. All of these factors prevent business from operating efficiently (Compact, 2010).

The context of Iraq and Syria during the period of study

We conducted our study over a roughly two-year period from 2016 to early 2018. Iraq has been in a state of war every year but two since 2003. Syria has been in a state of war since 2011. Since 2012, essentially three wars have taken place concurrently in Syria—one between the Syrian government and opposition groups, one among the opposition groups, and one between the self-proclaimed "Islamic State" ("IS") and the government, opposition groups, and an international coalition led by the US. During the time of the study, IS – an ultraorthodox, Sunni Muslim militant group – was at war with the government of Iraq (HIIK, 2017a) which was the only conflict classified as a war in Iraqi territory. During the time of the study period, approximately 100,000 people were killed in Syria due violence from the three wars (SOHR, 2016, 2017; Watch, 1991) and in Iraq approximately 15,000 people have been killed (HIIK, 2017a, 2017b; UCDP Conflict Encyclopedia, 2013). During the study, the forces of the government of Iraq and its allies were able to largely re-take IS territory within the Iraqi border, with only small pockets of resistance remaining (HIIK, 2017a). Within Syria during the time of the study the Syrian government forces and their allies made substantial territorial gains against all other non-state armed groups in the country (HIIK, 2017a).

Iraqi and Syrian business environments

Businesses in both countries face the dual challenges of operating under both conflict and poverty. The vast majority of the populations of Iraq and Syria are at the "base of the pyramid" (Kolk et al., 2013; Anderson, Markides and Kupp, 2010). Iraq and Syria are consistently ranked as one of the most difficult countries to conduct business in the world (World Bank, 2017). Challenges facing companies in both countries include poor infrastructure (World Bank, 2017), shortage of electricity (World Bank, 2017), lack of physical security (World Bank, 2017), and corruption (Transparency International, 2016).

The economy of Iraq has long been dominated by oil (Makiya, 1998; World Bank, 2016), while the economy of Syria before 2011 was substantially more diverse (Haddad, 2011; World Bank Group, 2017). In 2011, Iraq produced 2.6 million barrels per day of oil (good for 12th most in the world) while Syria produced only 369,000, good for 33rd in the world and less than 1 percent of global oil production (EIA, 2015). By 2017, Iraq had nearly doubled its output to become the world's 7th largest oil producer, while Syria's oil output had plummeted to 18,000 barrels per day, or 77th in the world. Though Syria was not a major oil producer before 2011, oil revenues for the state represented more than 25 percent of the government's annual revenue (International Monetary Fund, 2010).

Prevailing theory predicts the absence of legitimate private enterprise and the prevalence of violence in such an environment (Bannon and Collier, 2003). While that has been the case in Syria, the Iraqi business environment has been substantially stronger. Many businesses are resilient and accustomed to do business in Iraq in the worst of situations, whereas Syrian business owners and managers were taken substantially by surprise by the years of conflict since 2011. Many Iraqi companies are optimistic about the future of Iraq, whereas their Syrian counterparts are not (Mace, 2014). Iraqi businesses also believe that they can positively influence government policies and build trust through business associations and chambers of commerce (Mace, 2014). More than half of the business activities in Iraq are within the informal or gray market (Mace, 2014). In government-controlled territories in Syria, the number and amount of legitimate business activities seemed higher according to those interviewees who had done business in both countries, but data is not available to confirm these impressions.

Doing business in non-state armed group territory in Iraq and Syria

There were three main non-state armed groups that our participants noted engaging with. By far the largest number did business in territories controlled by the so-called IS and a grouping of Salafist jihadist organizations, the largest being what was then called the Al Nusra Front, and that mid-way through our study period merged into one organization called Tahrir al-Sham.[1] Both organizations have been designated as terrorist organizations by the United States and its allies (Walt, 2017). By the end of the study period, IS had been almost entirely routed in all parts of Iraq and Syria

(Walt, 2017). Tahrir al-Sham, which operates only in Syria, has at the time of this writing been confined to relatively small areas of the country.

The brutalities of IS are well-established (McCoy, 2014; Gerth and Warrick, 2016). The organization was mostly built on the ruin of al-Qaeda in Iraq. The core group who formed the organization are mostly former Saddam Ba'athist lieutenants (Al-Hashimi, 2014). Our participants often compared the brutality of IS to Saddam Hussein's regime. Like Saddam's regime, the use of brutality was to intimidate the population into submission. IS allied with enough locals to know the situation on the ground immediately—some of them even allied with IS before they took over making the taking over of cities easier, especially Mosul. According to our partici-pants, non-Sunni Muslims bore the brunt of violence perpetrated by IS in Mosul. But the remaining people—largely Sunnis—could count on safety if they obeyed. The interviewees made it clear that IS-controlled territories are substantially safer in an everyday sense than many parts of government-controlled Iraq. Iraqis had learned obedience in the face of terror under Saddam and now are doing it again under IS, as stated by our interviewees.

IS's acts are barbaric by any standard, yet they are comprised of highly sophis-ticated and intelligent actors many of whom believe in their cause (Wood, 2015; Al-Hashimi, 2014). They control in part through fear and in part through better administration (Al-Hashimi, 2014). All of our Iraqi interviewees made it clear that the failure of the Iraqi government to provide a meaningful governance alternative to IS is the strongest component of IS's continued control over Iraqi territory.

Unlike al-Qaeda which relied on outside donations and functioned more as a militia, IS has many of the capabilities of a state. IS raises revenues through taxation and from various sources including oil, agriculture, kidnapping, and stolen-antique selling (Giovanni, Sharkov, and Goodman, 2014). IS relies on a complex system to manage its far-reaching networks by dealing with cash, crude and contraband which allows it to operate outside the legitimate banking channels (Giovanni, Sharkov, and Goodman, 2014). IS uses more than 1,600 currency exchange offices throughout Iraq, Jordan, Syria and Turkey to transfer millions of dollars across borders (Coker, 2016). IS even has an immigration office where it stamps passports when individuals leave or enter its territories (Engel, 2015).

Methodology

Our data is derived from in-depth, semi-structured interviews, conducted on con-dition of anonymity, with 156 individuals from 73 companies who were either owners or senior managers in companies that had active business operations in Iraq and/or Syria since the onset of the Syrian Civil War and its associated violent conflicts in 2011. The interviews were part of a multi-year project to examine the impact of the ongoing Syrian Civil War and its related violent conflicts on private sector activity. Interview questions were broadly focused on the impact of the conflict on the private sector and on the impact of the private sector on the con-flict. Interviews were semi-structured and each interview lasted 40–60 minutes if done in person, via video chat, or over email. Email participants were sent the questions and returned typed responses. All interviews were conducted in English.

The interviews were conducted in person, over video chat, by telephone, and by email between 2016 and 2018. Video chat, email, and telephone interviewees were all located in Iraq or Syria at the time of the interview. In-person interviews were conducted in Iraq, Turkey, the United Arab Emirates, and the United States. The participants were selected for interviews based on recommendations from educational institutions, non-governmental organizations, and international organizations that operate in Iraq and/or Syria. The authors looked to these organizations for recommendations because of their central role in peacebuilding and because of the relative lack of government responsiveness and control over the private sector in both countries. These organizations acted as insiders to assist in finding appropriate participants for the current research. The research participants were recommended by these organizations as leaders in the private sector who were also greatly concerned with peacebuilding issues. The environment in Iraq and Syria is not a "normal" or recurring case and thus participant selection was done as applied for "extreme/deviant cases" (Flyvbjerg, 2006; Seawright, 2016). The data is thus not representative of all private sector actors in Iraq and Syria nor even of all of the private sector actors who might be promoting peace.

Of the interviewees, all were at the senior executive level and higher. Nine industry sectors were represented among the 73 companies: construction/engineering, energy, financial services, food and beverage retail, other retail, manufacturing, medical, security, telecom and IT, and transportation/logistics. Approximately two-thirds of the participant companies were local companies with most (though not all) being family-owned firms. An attempt was made to get a broad cross-section of participants of major sects in both Iraq (Sunni, Kurd, Shi'a) and in Syria (Sunni, Shi'a, Druze, Kurd, Alawite, Christian).

Data analysis methodology

All interviews were digitally recorded, transcribed, and coded. Codes were created at the same time as the study of the data (Bryant and Charmaz, 2007; Charmaz, 2006). Interviews were first coded for any information related to potential peace-building strategies by businesses. Portions of the interviews were tagged with one or more codes to organize the data. After the first round of coding-related codes were grouped or sharpened into more descriptive codes. Codes were combined, added, and refined as different or new themes emerged. The final set of codes were settled upon and are the basis for the discussion below.

Research findings

The findings were different for those impacts that multinational companies (MNCs) had and can have and those impacts that local companies had and can have. MNCs were viewed as peace promoting when they enhanced the rule of law, invested in local capacity building, and provided funding for initiatives aimed at social cohesion. MNCs were viewed as contributing to violence when they worked with non-state armed groups, made corrupt payments of any kind to government officials, hired local private security firms, and did not have conflict-party aware practices in hiring employees and contractors. Local firms were viewed as peace promoting when they continued to operate their businesses through paying employees and providing necessary goods and services. Importantly, local businesses perceived that peace-promotion must include cooperation with all parties to the conflict including non-state armed groups. Our findings support portions of the existing business and peace categories related to multinationals, but undermines the theory with respect to local companies. We conclude by noting the limitations of the research, principally the limited ability to generalize the findings to other active conflict settings without further research.

Perceived positive and negative impacts by multinational companies

Both within multinationals and among local companies, a perception of peace promotion through following international standards exists. All of the multinational managers noted international due diligence requirements as one of if not *the* most important way in which the company helped to promote peace in Iraq and Syria. While some country managers noted that their jobs were often on the line for not following these rules, most noted that international regulations, especially with those from multinationals home countries, provided the MNCs with political cover to avoid paying bribes or enmeshing themselves in situations that might exacerbate the conflict. One energy company executive noted that, without home country due diligence requirements against corrupt payments to government officials, "[the company] would never make money of our own or even pay our workers" in their operations in Iraq.

For all participants—MNC and local managers—corruption was the top challenge repeatedly mentioned as a hindrance to any type of peacebuilding. Closely linked with corruption were non-merit-based hiring and procurement decisions, which took the form of sectarianism, cronyism, nepotism, or combinations of these. One of our interviewees noted in detail that:

> some politicians have set up private companies and hired their brothers or their relatives, have created fictitious businesses, and suddenly [these new companies are] taking contracts, taking the money, delivering maybe 10% of the quality and service, and then expatriating money.

MNC country managers saw capacity building as another of the core ways in which they can reduce violence and enhance peace. Internal company training programs that focused on diversity, teambuilding, negotiations, and conflict resolution in particular were noted by some MNC country managers as having a large impact on the behavior of their workers. One senior manager from a multi-national company with operations in Syria noted that they inserted interpersonal conflict resolution into the regular training of company employees after they "noticed that our employees were bringing their home issues to the workplace much more after [2013]" causing increases in disputes that occasionally turned violent in the workplace. The manager attributed this violence to the violence that the workers were experiencing as part of the violent political conflict. The man-ager viewed the conflict resolution program as a key means of equipping workers with conflict resolution skills that would extend beyond the company offices to the workers' communities. Some managers also noted the importance of such trainings for contractors as well.

Efforts by MNCs to build social cohesion were also viewed as having impacts on peace. These largely took the form of charitable spending by the local branch of the MNC, often under the banner of "corporate social responsibility." In all cases where charitable spending on social cohesion was mentioned, an NGO partner was actively managing the program. Interestingly, there seemed to be a particular focus on children and refugee camps for those MNCs noting their charitable spending as a contribution to peace. In each case, interviewees from MNCs with CSR programs that they viewed as peace-enhancing provided additional material such as printouts and website informa-tion detailing the initiatives. All of the initiatives reviewed addressed the eco-nomic hardships of local communities as opposed to other conflict sources. It was unclear how the company viewed these as contributing to social cohesion in spite of it being the aim of the programs.

For MNC managers, working with non-state armed groups was cited as an impossibility. Five managers working in the Kurdistan region of Iraq noted that they were obliged to work with Kurdistan Regional Government's security forces as no alternatives existed. This was cited as common practice given the lack of presence of Iraqi government security (or other) services in the area.

The largest risk to peace that MNCs executives and managers themselves noted were those related to hiring employees and contractors, in particular those employees and contractors engaged in security and protection of company assets and employees in Iraq and Syria. Interviewees from MNCs consistently reported that they were particular sensitive in hiring employees from diverse backgrounds, but that this was especially challenging in portions of both countries that were highly segregated. In particular, those companies that operated in Iraq found it very difficult to recruit fairly in ways that did not discriminate based on sect. One executive, whose responsibilities did not directly include human resources, found himself spending "more than half my time ensuring that we are hiring the right people for the right reasons [in Iraq]." In Syria, the problem centered more around being able to do proper due diligence for contractors than around hiring new employees.

Perceived positive and negative impacts by local companies

Local managers especially in Syria saw their greatest contribution to peace in continuing to employ workers and continuing to supply necessary goods and services. The owner of a food services chain in government-controlled Syria noted that the private sector is "the only hope left as there is no hope or support from the government...without [the private sector] I don't see my country surviving." The hope that he and others described came mainly from the provision—for free or at cost—of necessary items such as food and clothing and the decision by many businesses not to fire anyone. One garment factory owner cited the latter as the core way that he tries to enhance peace he "always treat[s] them like family and brothers ... they know [he] will never fire them so they are less likely to join a rebel group." The threat of employees leaving to join a rebel group was a real one for many interviewees in Syria and one confirmed by other researchers (Alexander, 2015; Lister, 2015; Ohl, Holger, and Koehler, 2015). The economic incentives ranged by rebel groups included not only base pay, but also opportunities for income from kidnappings, smuggling, and corruption.

The corruption was described as endemic to almost every ministry and federal government department in Iraq and Syria. Participants who were conducting business in Iraq often noted the dramatic difference between corruption under the Saddam Hussein regime and the current democratic government. Corruption under the Hussein regime was unanimously viewed as less than under the current democratic system. In Syria, businesses dealing with the government of Bashar al-Assad noted that corruption was approximately the same both before the Syrian Civil War and at the time of the interview. Some of the businesses noted that corruption at borders is what had specifically increased, raising the costs of transportation substantially for those goods that had to cross land borders. Most companies referred to this process as an import problem, but one manager specifically mentioned the incessant corruption in shipping goods out of Syria.

Local company managers routinely mentioned that they refused to do direct contracts with the government. One CEO of a health company noted,

> the Ministry of Health [of Iraq] sent me some people to ... do new projects, I told them 'Sorry, I have faced an issue related to corruption, there are some [in your Ministry] who are looking for their personal benefit' so I refused to engage with them again.

Stories like this were quite common among our local company participants. Most MNC managers, however, noted their heavy reliance on government contracts to support the business in Iraq, without which their business would not be profitable in country. This was especially true of companies in the energy sector.

Some of our participants saw themselves as examples to the community and so believed they were promoting peace by refusing to pay bribes and refusing to do business directly with the government at all. The local companies' senior managers expressed their desire to make their community better and promote peace by refusing to "line the pockets" of corrupt officials and thereby in their view reduce the chaos and violence. This was notably different from the reasons given by MNC executives for not paying bribes which was part peacebuilding and worry about potential liability exposure for corruption in their home country.

Though some local participants mentioned their own refusal to pay bribes in a company context, almost all openly admitted to paying bribes in their personal lives and approximately half admitted to doing so on behalf of their business. The most typical reason provided for bribing in the professional context was to reduce the burden on the company. Iraqi managers routinely noted that bribing the tax inspectors meant avoiding tax liabilities that would bankrupt the business. A small bribe to the tax authorities and the business would have its tax re-assessed until the following year (when another bribe would be requested, often of a larger amount).

An additional rule of law problem that was noted by the majority of our participants was the lack of clear regulations in almost every area. Another participant noted that his and many other businesses had taken to setting up one licensed company and numerous unlicensed companies simply to avoid this problem. The final rule-of-law challenge noted by participants in certain industries dominated by the government—especially energy and health—was that government officials talked about developing the private sector even though the government itself acted more like a "loan shark" in doing so.

Discussion and conclusion

The interviews revealed a major split in the approach to peacebuilding by multinational and local companies. The findings were split between those impacts that MNCs had and can have and those impacts that local companies had and can have. MNCs mostly promote peace through rule-of-law enhancements, investments in local capacity building, and funding for initiatives aimed at social cohesion. MNCs saw themselves as contributing to violence when they worked with non-state armed groups, made corrupt payments of any kind to government officials, and hired employees and contractors without conflict-aware due diligence. Local firms felt they were promoting peace when they continued to operate their businesses. Paying (and not firing) employees, providing necessary goods and services at cost or for free, and continuing operations in spite of the conflict were viewed as the most important elements in local company peace promotion.

Rule of law and social cohesion support are standard advice within the business for peace literature on how companies can enhance peace (Oetzel et al., 2009; Bies et al., 2007; Fort, 2015; Fort and Schipani, 2002; Fort, 2009). The theoretical assumption with regards to rule of law throughout the literature was that it could promote peace in a war environment (in addition to the other four less violent HIIK (2017b) categories of conflict) and our study provides additional supporting evidence for that claim.

In addition, two categories often mentioned in the prevailing literature—risk assessment and track-two diplomacy—were unmentioned and viewed as negative impacts on peace respectively. In particular when raised by interviewers, many local interviewees specifically noted the risk of any interference by businesses in the political process to settle the dispute as forcing business to lose its trusted status. It may be that track-two diplomacy in high-violence contexts is not possible because of the volatility but that, at lower levels of conflict, track-two diplomacy may be highly effective.

Risk assessment, viewed as one of the two peace-promoting activities that business could engage in during conflict, was not mentioned at all by our participants. Our interviewees were all companies that had a business presence in Iraq and/or Syria before 2011. Risk assessment as described in the literature seems to apply more to those companies that are contemplating entering a conflict zone, not those who are already there. A similar issue that was repeatedly mentioned by our MNC participants was the need for stringent due diligence processes, especially in hiring employee and contractors.

Although social cohesion (or "community building") was mentioned in the literature (Oetzel et al., 2009) it is not generally viewed in the literature as a viable peacebuilding strategy in a war or limited war environment. Some studies have challenged that assertion (Katsos and AlKafaji, 2017) and this chapter provides additional evidence that social cohesion efforts may work in war and limited war settings. Interestingly, MNCs and local companies viewed social cohesion efforts differently. For MNCs, social cohesion efforts largely took the form of traditional CSR initiatives. This may reflect a base-of-the-pyramid and resource-based view toward the firm and its role in conflict alleviation noted by some scholars (Tashman and Marano, 2009; Kolk et al., 2013). In particular, it appears that this may be further evidence of what Kolk and Lenfant (2016) describe as a "hybrid business model for peace and reconciliation."

Almost all of our participants noted that business is a core actor in society. Their descriptions further provided evidence of business as a "mediating institution" (Fort, 1999), a concept that underpins much of B4P theory. Based on our study, this assumption seems entirely justified. Fort (2015) describes businesses that use this operational, intentional approach as "peace entrepreneurs." Though Fort (2015) allows that "peace entrepreneurs" may also be multinationals, our study indicates that local companies are much more likely to be peace entrepreneurs than MNCs. Our participants from multinationals almost all described their companies in ways that meet Fort's (2015) description of "unconscious peacebuilders," where those companies that act ethically in a conflict zone which then has unintended peacebuilding impacts. Our local participants seemed not to view "unconscious peacebuilding" as peacebuilding at all. Rather, the intentionality of companies in peacebuilding was seen as having the strongest impact, as opposed to economic development alone. As one interviewee put it, "jobs are great, but they are not enough."

Note

1 Throughout the interviews, managers and executives referred to each of these groups by their original names, not by "Tahrir al-Sham." For the convenience of the reader, we have chosen to refer to these groups as "Tahrir al-Sham," even if the interviews took place before the merger.

References

Aguilera, R. V., and Rupp, D. E. (2005). Putting the S Back in Corporate Social Responsibility : A Multi-Level Theory of Social Change in Organizations. *Academy of Management Review*, 32(3), 836–863.

Al-Hashimi, H. (2014) Revealed: The Islamic State 'Cabinet', from Finance Minister to Suicide Bomb Deployer, *The Telegraph*. Retrieved from www.telegraph.co.uk/news/worldnews/middleeast/iraq/10956193/Revealed-the-Islamic-State-cabinet-from-finance-minister-to-suicide-bomb-deployer.html

Alexander, D. (2015). U.S. military pays Syrian rebels up to $400 per month: Pentagon, *Reuters*. Retrieved June 3, 2018, from www.reuters.com/article/us-mideast-crisis-syria-usa/u-s-military-pays-syrian-rebels-up-to-400-per-month-pentagon-idUSKBN0P22BX20150622

Anderson, R. (2004). A Definition of Peace. *Peace and Conflict: Journal of Peace Psychology*, 10(2).

Anderson, J., Markides, C., and Kupp, M. (2010). The Last Frontier: market creation in conflict zones, deep rural areas, and urban slums. *California Management Review*, 52(4), 6–28. https://doi.org/10.1525/cmr.2010.52.4.6

Andreas, P. (2009). Symbiosis Between Peace Operations and Illicit Business in Bosnia. *International Peacekeeping*, 16(1), 33–46. https://doi.org/10.1080/13533310802485518

Azam, J., and Mesnard, A. (2003). Civil war and the social contract. *Public Choice*, (April 2001), 455–475.

Ballentine, K., Ballentine, K., Nitzschke, H., and Nitzschke, H. (2005). The Political Economy of Civil War and Conflict Transformation. *Berghof Research Center for Constructive Conflict Management*.

Banfield, J., Barbolet, A., Goldwyn, R., and Killick, N. (2005). *Conflict-Sensitive Business Practice: Guidance for Extractive Industries*. London. International Alert.

Bannon, I., and Collier, P. (2003). *Natural Resources and Violent Conflict: Options and Actions*. The World Bank. https://doi.org/10.1596/0-8213-5503-1

Baumol, W. (1996). Entrepreneurship: Productive, Unproductive, and Destructive. *Journal of Business Venturing*, 11(1), 3–22.

Bies, R. J., Bartunek, J. M., Fort, T. L., and Zald, M. N. (2007, July 1). Corporations as Social Change Agents: Individual, Interpersonal Institutional, and Environmental Dynamics. *Academy of Management Review*. https://doi.org/10.5465/AMR.2007.25275515

Borensztein, E., De Gregorio, J., and Lee, J. (1998). How does Foreign Direct Investment Affect Economic Growth. *Journal of International Economics*, 45(1), 115–135. https://doi.org/10.1016/S0022-1996(97)00033-0

Bryant, A. and Charmaz, K. (2007) The SAGE The Development of Categories: Different Approaches in Grounded Theory, In *The SAGE Handbook of Grounded Theory*, pp. 191–214. doi:10.4135/9781848607941.n9

Buckley, P. (2014). Twenty Years of the World Investment Report: Retrospect and Prospects. *The Multinational Enterprise and the Emergence of the Global Factory*, 363–385.

Buhaug, H., Levy, J., and Urdal, H. (2014). 50 Years of Peace Research. *Journal of Peace Research*. https://doi.org/10.1177%2F0022343314521649

Charmaz, K. (2006) *Constructing Grounded Theory, Constructing Theory in Grounded Theory*. London: Sage Publications.

Coker, M. (2016) How Islamic State's Secret Banking Network Prospers, *Wall Street Journal*.

Collier, P. (2006). Post-Conflict Economic Recovery. *ReCALL*, 49(6), 929–929. https://doi.org/10.1016/j.neuron.2006.02.007

Collier, P. (2009). Post-conflict Recovery: How Should Strategies be Distinctive? *Journal of African Economies*, 18(Suppl 1). https://doi.org/10.1093/jae/ejp006

Collier, P., and Hoeffler, A. (2002). AID, Policy and Peace: Reducing the risks of civil conflict. *Defence and Peace Economics*, 13(6), 435–450. https://doi.org/10.1080/10242690214335

Collier, P., Hoeffler, A., and Soderbom, M. (2008). Post-Conflict Risks. *Journal of Peace Research*, 45(4), 461–478. https://doi.org/10.1177/0022343308091356

Compact, U. G. N. G. (2010). Guidance on Responsible Business in Conflict-affected and High-risk Areas : A Resource for Companies and Investors. *UN Global Compact Reports*, 48.

Coser, L. (1967). *Continuities in the Study of Social Conflict*. New York: Free Press.

Davies, G., Chun, R., Vinhas da Silva, R., and Roper, S. (2003). Corporate reputation and competitiveness. *Corporate Reputation Review*, 5. https://doi.org/10.1057/palgrave.crr.1540185

Diamond, L., and McDonald, J. W. (1996). *Multi-track Diplomacy: A Systems Approach to Peace*. Westhartford, CT: Kumarian Press.

Dworkin, T., and Schipani, C. (2007). Linking Gender Equity to Peaceful Societies. *American Business Law Journal*, 44(2), 391–415.

EIA. (2015). *International Energy Statistics. Independent Statistics and Analysis, U.S. Energy Information Administration*.

Elbadawi, I., and Sambanis, N. (2002). How Much War Will We See? Explaining the Prevalence of Civil War. *The Journal of Conflict Resolution*, 46(3), 307–334. https://doi.org/10.1177/0022002702046003001

Elbadawi, I., Kaltani, L., and Schmidt-Hebbel, K. (2007). Post-conflict Aid, Real Exchange Rate Adjustment, and Catch-up Growth. *World Bank Policy Research Working*.

Emmelhainz, M., and Adams, R. J. (1999). The Apparel Industry Response to "Sweatshop" Concerns: A Review and Analysis of Codes of Conduct. *Journal of Supply Chain Management*, 35, 51–57. https://doi.org/10.1111/j.1745-493X.1999.tb00062.x

Engel, P. (2015) ISIS is Revolutionizing International Terrorism, *Business Insider, Military and Defense*.

Farmer, P. E., Nizeye, B., Stulac, S., and Keshavjee, S. (2006). Structural Violence and Clinical Medicine. *PLoS Medicine*, 3(10), 1686–1691.

Fearon, J. D. (2004). Why Do Some Civil Wars Last So Much Longer than Others? *Journal of Peace Research*, 41(3), 275–301. https://doi.org/10.1177/0022343304043770

Flyvbjerg, B. (2006). Five Misunderstandings About Case-Study Research. *Qualitative Inquiry*, 12(2), 219–245. https://doi.org/10.1177/1077800405284363

Fogarty, B. (2000). *War, Peace, and the Social Order*. Boulder, CO: Westview Press.

Forrer, J. J., and Katsos, J. E. (2015). Business and Peace in the Buffer Condition. *Academy of Management Perspectives*, 29(4), 438–450. https://doi.org/10.5465/amp.2013.0130

Fort, T. L. (1999). Business as Mediating Institutions. *American Business Law Journal*, 36(3), 391–435. https://doi.org/10.2307/3857620

Fort, T. L. (2009). Peace Through Commerce: A Multisectoral Approach. *Journal of Business Ethics*, 89(Supple 4), 347–350. https://doi.org/10.1007/s10551-010-0413-5

Fort, T. L. (2015). *Diplomat in the Corner Office: How Business Contributes to Peace*. Stanford, CA: Stanford University Press.

Fort, T. L., and Schipani, C. A. (2002). The Role of the Corporation in Fostering Sustainable Peace. *Vand. J. Transnat'l L.*, 35, 389–435.

Fort, T. L., and Schipani, C. A. (2004). *The Role of Business in Fostering Peaceful Societies*, 1–232. https://doi.org/10.1017/CBO9780511488634

Freeman. (1984). *Strategic Management: A Stakeholder Approach*. Cambridge: Cambridge University Press.

Freeman, R., and McVea, J. (2001). A Stakeholder Approach to Strategic Management. *SSRN Electronic Journal*, (January). https://doi.org/10.2139/ssrn.263511

Friedman, M. (2009). *Capitalism and Freedom*. Chicago, IL and London: University of Chicago Press.

Galtung, J. (1969). Violence, Peace, and Peace Research. *Journal of Peace Research*, 6(3), 167–191.

Galtung, J. (1996a). On the Social Costs of Modernization. Social Disintegration, Atomie/Anomie and Social Development. *Development and Change*, 27(1).

Galtung, J. (1996b). *Peace by Peaceful Means: Peace and Conflict, Development and Civilization* (Google eBook), 280. https://doi.org/10.2307/2623565

Galtung, J. (2006). Twenty-Five Years of Peace Research: Ten Challenges and Some Responses. *Theories of International Relations*, 2, 22(2), 38–61.

Getz, K. A., and Oetzel, J. (2009). MNE Strategic Intervention in Violent Conflict: Variations Based on Conflict Characteristics. *Journal of Business Ethics*, 89(Suppl 4), 375–386. https://doi.org/10.1007/s10551-010-0412-6

Giovanni, J., Sharkov, L. M. and Goodman, D. (2014) How Does ISIS Fund Its Reign of Terror?. *Newsweek*.

Guáqueta, A. (2008). Occidental Petroleum, Cerrejón, and NGO Partnership in Colombia: Lessons Learned. *Peace Through Commerce: Responsible Corporate Citizenship and the Ideals of the United Nations Global Compact*. Notre Dame, IN: University of Notre Dame Press.

Gunningham, N., Kagan, R., and Thornton, D. (2003). *Shades of Green: Business, Regulation, and Environment*. Stanford, CA: Stanford University Press.

Haddad, B. (2011). The Political Economy of Syria: Realities and Challenges. *Middle East Policy*, 18(2), 46–61. https://doi.org/10.1111/j.1475-4967.2011.00484.x

Haufler, V. (1997). *Dangerous Commerce: Insurance and the Management of International Risk*. Ithaca, NY: Cornell University Press.

Barometer, C. (2014). Disputes, Non-violent Crises, Violent Crises, Limited wars (2015). *Heidelberg Institute for International Conflict Research. Heidelberg*, 23.

HIIK. (2017a). *2017 HIIK Conflict Barometer*, 202.

HIIK. (2017b). *Conflict Barometer 2016. Disputes, Non-Violent Crises, Violent Crises, Limited Wars*, 25, 208.

Institute for Economics and Peace (IEP). (2014). *A Global Statistical Analysis on the Empirical Link Between Peace and Religion*, 1–38.

International Monetary Fund. (2010). *Syrian Arab Republic: 2009 Article IV Consultation*, (10).

Katsos, J. E., and AlKafaji, Y. (2017). Business in War Zones: How Companies Promote Peace in Iraq. *Journal of Business Ethics*, 1–16. https://doi.org/10.1007/s10551-017-3513-7

Kolk, A., and Van Tuldere, R. (2002). Child Labor and Multinational Conduct: A Comparison of International Business and Stakeholder Codes. *Journal of Business Ethics*, 291–301.

Kolk, A., and Lenfant, F. (2015). Cross-Sector Collaboration, Institutional Gaps, and Fragility: The Role of Social Innovation Partnerships in a Conflict-Affected Region. *Journal of Public Policy and Marketing*, 34(2), 287–303. https://doi.org/10.1509/jppm.14.157

Kolk, A., and Lenfant, F. (2016). Hybrid Business Models for Peace and Reconciliation. *Business Horizons*, 59(5), 503–524.

Kolk, A., Rivera-Santos, M., Rufin, C., and Rufin, C. (2013). Reviewing a Decade of Research on the "Base/Bottom of the Pyramid" (BOP) Concept. *Business and Society*, 20 (10), 1–40. https://doi.org/10.1177/0007650312474928

Lieberfeld, D. (2002). Evaluating the Contributions of Track-two Diplomacy to Conflict Termination in South Africa, 1984–1990. *Journal of Peace Research*, 39(3), 355–372. http s://doi.org/10.1177/0022343302039003006

Lister, C. (2015). *The Syrian Jihad*. London: Hurst Publishers.

Mace, J. (2014). *Finding the Private Sector's Voice in Iraq. Economic Reform*. Washington, DC: Center for International Private Enterprise.

Makiya, K. (1998). *Republic of Fear: The Politics of Modern Iraq*. California: University of California Press.

Milliken, F. J., Schipani, C. A., Bishara, N. D., and Prado, A. M. (2015). Linking Workplace Practices to Community Engagement: The Case for Encouraging Employee Voice. *Academy of Management Perspectives*, 29(4), 405–421. https://doi.org/10.5465/amp.2013.0121

Mills, R., and Fan, Q. (2006). *The Investment Climate in Post-Conflict Situations*. World Bank Institute.

Montville, J. (1991). Transnationalism and the Role of Track-two Diplomacy. *Approaches to Peace: An Intellectual Map*, pp. 259–269.

O'Neill, D. A. (2008). Impact Assessment, Transparency and Accountability – Three Keys to Building Sustainable Partnerships between Business and Its Stakeholders. In *Peace Through Commerce: Responsible Corporate Citizenship and the Ideals of the United Nations Global Compact*, 157, p. 198.

Obstfeld, M. (1994). Risk-taking, Global Diversification, and Growth. *American Economic Review*, 84(5), 1310–1329. https://doi.org/10.2307/2117774

Oetzel, J., and Doh, J. P. (2009). MNEs and Development: A Review and Reconceptualization. *Journal of World Business*, 44(2), 108–120. https://doi.org/10.1016/j.jwb.2008.05.001

Oetzel, J., and Getz, K. (2012). Why and How Might Firms Respond Strategically to Violent Conflict? *Journal of International Business Studies*, 43(2), 166–186. https://doi.org/10. 1057/jibs.2011.50

Oetzel, J., Getz, K. A., Ladek, S., and Ntroduction, I. I. (2007). The Role of Multinational Enterprises in Responding to Violent Conflict: A Conceptual Model and Framework for Research. *American Business Law Journal*, 44(2), 331–358.

Oetzel, J., Westermann-Behaylo, M., Koerber, C., Fort, T. L., and Rivera, J. (2009). Business and Peace: Sketching the Terrain. *Journal of Business Ethics*, 89(Suppl 4), 351–373. https://doi.org/10.1007/s10551-010-0411-7

Ohl, D., Holger, A., and Koehler, K. (2015). *For Money or Liberty? The Political Economy of Military Desertion and Rebel Recruitment in the Syrian Civil War*. Carnegie Middle East Center.

Ramsbotham, O., Woodhouse, T., and Miall, H. (2011). Contemporary Conflict Resolution. In *Contemporary Conflict Resolution*. Cambridge and Malden, MA: Polity, pp. 35–62.

Rapoport, A. (1999). Peace, Definitions and Concepts of. L. Kurtz (Editor-in-Chief), *Encyclopedia of Violence*.

Reade, C., and Lee, H. H. J. (2012). Organizational Commitment in Time of War: Assessing the Impact and Attenuation of Employee Sensitivity to Ethnopolitical Conflict. *Journal of International Management*, 18(1), 85–101. https://doi.org/10.1016/j.intman.2011.09.002

Rummel, R. (1979). *Understanding Conflict and War: Vol. 4: War, Power, Peace*. Beverly Hills, CA: Sage.

Sandler, T., Boulding, K., Hirshleifer, J., Grossman, H., Mcguire, M., Olson, M., … Collier, P. (2000). Economic Analysis of Conflict, *Journal of Conflict Resolution*, 44(6), 723–729. http s://doi.org/10.1177/0022002700044006001

Santos, N. (2003). Financing Small, Medium and Micro Enterprises in Post-conflict Situations. *Development*, (March).

Seawright, J. (2016). The Case for Selecting Cases That Are Deviant or Extreme on the Independent Variable. *Sociological Methods and Research*, 45(3). https://doi.org/10.1177/0049124116643556

SOHR. (2016). About 60 Thousand were Killed in 2016 and We Still Wait for an International Trial for the Criminals: The Syrian Observatory for Human Rights. Retrieved May 9, 2018 from www.syriahr.com/en/?p=58114

SOHR. (2017). 2017…the Year of the Military Change and the Rise of the Regime and Its Allies to Head the List of Military Powers and Influences Followed by the SDF…and the Loss of the Opposition and the Organization to Large Spaces of their Controlled Areas ● The Syria. Retrieved May 9, 2018 from www.syriahr.com/en/?p=81564

Spencer, J. W. (2008). Spillovers and Crowding out in Developing Countries: The Impact Enterprise of Multinational Strategy on Indigenous enterprises. *Academy of Management Review*, 33(2), 341–361. https://doi.org/10.5465/amr.2008.31193230

Spreitzer, G. (2007). Giving Peace a Chance: Organizational Leadership, Empowerment, and Peace. *Journal of Organizational Behavior*, 28(8), 1077–1095. https://doi.org/10.1002/job.487

Steelman, T., and Rivera, J. (2006). Voluntary Environmental Programs in the United States: Whose Interests are Served? *Organization and Environment*, 19(4), 505–526. https://doi.org/10.1177/1086026606296393

Tashman, P., and Marano, V. (2009). Dynamic Capabilities and Base of the Pyramid Business Strategies. *Journal of Business Ethics*, 89(S4), 495–514. https://doi.org/10.1007/s10551-010-0403-7

The Institute for Economics and Peace. (2013). *Pillars of Peace*, 63.

UCDP Conflict Encyclopedia. (2013). Uppsala Conflict Data Program. Retrieved May 9, 2018 from www.ucdp.uu.se/gpdatabase

Walt, S. M. (2017). What the End of ISIS Means. Retrieved June 1, 2018, from http://foreignpolicy.com/2017/10/23/what-the-end-of-isis-means/

Wani, H. A. (2015). Understanding conflict resolution. *Centre for Promoting Ideas*, 104–111.

Watch, H. R. (1991). *Human Rights Watch World Report*.

Westermann-Behaylo, M. K., Rehbein, K., and Fort, T. L. (2015). Enhancing the Concept of Corporate Diplomacy: Encompassing Political Corporate Social Responsibility, International Relations, and Peace Through Commerce. *Academy of Management Perspectives*, 29(4), 387–404. https://doi.org/10.5465/amp.2013.0133

Westley, F. R., and Vredenburg, H. (1991). Strategic Bridging: The Collaboration Between Environmentalists and Business in the Marketing of Green Products. *Journal of Applied Behavioral Science*, 27(1), 65–90. https://doi.org/10.1177/07399863870092005

Winer, J., and Roule, T. (2003). Follow the Money: The Finance of Illicit Resource Extraction. *Natural Resources and Violent Conflict. Options and Actions*, pp. 161–214.

Wood, G. (2015). What ISIS Really Wants. *The Atlantic* 21(2), 26.

World Bank. (2016). Doing Business 2017: Equal Opportunity for All. https://doi.org/10.1596/978-1-4648-0948-4

World Bank Group. (2017). *The Toll of War: The Economic and Social Consequences of the Conflict in Syria*, 1–148.

8

THE CONTESTED ROLE OF LOCAL BUSINESS IN PEACEBUILDING

Reflections from Sri Lanka and El Salvador

Andrea Iff and Rina M. Alluri[1]

1 Introduction

Significant research in the field of business and peacebuilding has focused on how multinational corporations navigate, engage and have an impact on local conflict contexts. However, considerably less research has been done on the role that local businesses play in peacebuilding within their *own* contexts (some exceptions include Nelson 2000; Killick et al. 2005; Banfield et al. 2006). The perspective of local businesses offers insights into how the integration into their own economic, political and conflict context provides them with particular opportunities and limitations to engaging in peacebuilding that their multinational counterparts experience differently. Local companies are likely to: "operate alone, beyond the direct influence of foreign shareholders western consumers, global media coverage and international operating standards in areas such as human rights and the environment" (Nelson 2000, 60). While this provides them with some independence and important access to engage in political activities on the ground, it is also likely to limit the ability and scope of international human rights watchdogs to hold them accountable to potential violations. Local businesses are likely to have historical relationships to political actors that may grant them particular access, while also inhibiting their capacity and ability to engage in political issues for fear of repercussions. Mobility can also be a factor of engagement. While foreign companies may be able to react to a conflict outbreak by withdrawing or relocating their offices, local companies are more likely to search for options which enable them to remain in the country. This also makes them more susceptible to the impacts of violent conflict and their ability to compete in local and international markets. Identity should also not be underestimated as a major determinant of local businesses to engage in peacebuilding, particularly when the conflict is linked to issues of nationalism, ethnic identity or religious politics (Joras 2009).

The main factor that contributes to the role that business can play after a peace process is linked to their relationships with political actors and the impact that the political economy has on their core business (see, for example, Bull 2004). Cohen and Ben-Porat (2008) explain the lack of significant involvement of businesses in the Israeli-Palestinian peace process through business' limited commitment to peace, their lack of significance in the political process, the inability to organize collective action, and the fear of economic losses vis-à-vis a powerful Israeli government. As others have confirmed for further peace processes (Iff 2013; Iff et al. 2010) they argue that if there is cooperation of businesses in peace processes, it is 'quiet' (Cohen and Ben-Porat 2008, 426). This chapter focuses on two peace processes in Sri Lanka and El Salvador and analyses what role *local businesses* have played in their 'home' conflict contexts.

2 Methodology

The chapter has been developed within research in a larger international research project 'Private sector in peace promotion' that was conducted within the Swiss National Science Foundation-funded NCCR North-South Program from 2009–2014.[2] This chapter focuses on the results of two of the cases of that project, namely El Salvador and Sri Lanka. The primary and secondary data on Sri Lanka and El Salvador was collected through qualitative research methods from a PhD project from 2009–2014 (Sri Lanka) and a smaller case study in 2012 (El Salvador). The Sri Lanka data is based on 112 in-depth expert interviews carried out in Europe (Switzerland, United Kingdom, Germany) and Sri Lanka (Colombo, Jaffna and Batticaloa), while the smaller case study is based on 14 interviews and one focus group discussion in El Salvador (San Salvador) and 3 interviews in Switzerland. The kinds of actors interviewed included: business, business associations, universities, local NGOs and research institutes, international NGOs, organizations and donors, government, religious and other actors (i.e. media, independent consultants, lawyers).

The political economy of business involvement in peace processes will be scrutinized through three different elements: (1) Role of businesses in conflict; (2) role of businesses during peace processes, and; (3) interconnection of this role with party politics. The analysis of these three roles and relationships help to assess the long-term effects of the business involvement in peacebuilding. In the conclusions, caveats are formulated for the tendency of bilateral and multilateral actors to 'automatically' include businesses in peace processes and peacebuilding activities.

3 Rising up and simmering down: The changing role of local business in peace in Sri Lanka

The Sri Lankan civil war broke out in 1983 between the Government of Sri Lanka (GoSL) and the Liberated Tigers of Tamil Eelam (LTTE). While the civil war has often been described as being polarized along ethno-political lines (Ropers 2008), economic root causes have also played a significant role (Abeyratne 2004). After four failed attempts at peace (1985; 1987; 1989–1990; 1994–1995), the peace process in 2002 between Ranil Wickremasinghe's United National Front (UNF) and the LTTE appeared to present hope for the end of the protracted conflict. The peace process was mediated by Norway, and appeared to come at a time where both the GoSL and the LTTE were willing to negotiate terms. It was within this peace process that local businesses also saw a role in supporting peacebuilding in the country.

3.1 The impact of conflict on the economy and role of businesses

The post-colonial economic liberalization policies in the 1970s and 1980s contributed to several economic and political divisions and impacts on the local private sector. Firstly, the emergence of a competitive political and economic crisis between the two main opposing political parties, the United National Party (UNP) and the Sri Lanka Freedom Party (SLFP). While the UNP made efforts to establish an open market economy that encouraged foreign direct investment and the privatization of state-owned enterprises, the opposing SLFP continued to focus on the state as the main 'entrepreneur' in the country that was founded on patronage, corruption and increased bureaucracy (Abeyratne 2004, 1305). Secondly, the civil war led to internal economic shocks such as a quadrupling of external debt (Dunham and Kelegama 1997, 180) and the emergence of the private sector as the 'engine of growth' in the Southern capital of Colombo as part of the second wave of liberalization reforms in the early 1990s that focused on the industrial and agricultural sectors. This contributed to a shift in the national economy from one that was predominantly reliant on plantation agriculture to one that was increasingly based on industries and services such as garment exports and tourism. However, while the majority of these industries emerged in the West and South of the country, government efforts were made to impose a regional development program in the LTTE stronghold in the North and East. This only further angered the LTTE and led to an intensity of the violence and eventually a drop in economic growth from 6.9 per cent in 1993 to 5.6 per cent in 1994. Thirdly, as the majority of the fighting took place in the North and East, these businesses faced distinct impacts depending on their location, sector and access to trade routes and markets. Only the international airport bombing in 2001 led to some negative impacts on businesses in the South.

3.2 Role of Sri Lanka First during the peace process

A number of business-led peace initiatives emerged from the late 1990s to the early 2000s; each playing different roles in different periods or under changing political conditions (for example, the National Committee for Peace and Economic Development, SOLO-U, Sri Lanka First (SLF) and the Business for Peace Alliance (BPA) and the Business for Peace Initiative (BPI)). In addition, the Ceylon Chamber of Commerce (CCC) supported several of these initiatives.

Led by the CCC, a group of trade associations from the garment, tea, tourism and freight sectors came together to form SLF in 2001 as a coordinated attempt to establish a lobbying campaign for peace (Killick et al. 2005, 11; Mayer and Salih 2006, 570). It emerged as a direct reaction to the 2001 attack on the international airport. Its activities included: direct endorsement of the pro-peace UNF Alliance party in the 2001 election; a targeted media campaign that focused on promoting the benefits of the 'peace dividend', and; working with other non-governmental organizations to lead demonstrations and events that raised awareness on the negative impacts of the war (Killick et al. 2005, 11.12). With the election of the pro-peace government of the UNF and the signing of the ceasefire agreement (CFA) in 2002, there was a renewed hope for a peaceful resolution to the conflict (Stokke in Stokke and Uyangoda 2011, 17–18). While SLF saw itself as having a role in the face of an economic and political crisis, once a certain level of stability emerged with the election of the UNF and the signing of the CFA, it no longer saw a role for itself. While they would continue to participate in events and meetings organized by others such as International Alert, their engagement would slowly dissipate. However, in 2004, they would renew their engagement in the wake of renewed fear that the peace process was failing. In 2005, the election of a new SLFP government that advocated for a military solution, the failure of the ceasefire agreement and subsequent resumption of violent conflict led to renewed fears that peace was not possible. This had direct impacts on SLF with many of its members having an 'about-face', while others returned to 'business as usual'.

3.3 Interconnection of Sri Lanka First with party politics

SLF has been spearheaded as an exemplary case of 'local business for peace' in academic and civil society literature (Killick et al. 2005; Marikkar 2005; Mayer and Salih 2005) with only a few critically highlighting the challenges they faced (Tripathi and Gündüz 2008; Venugopal 2010). SLF was composed of export-dependent, big businesses who predominantly resided in the Colombo metropolitan area (Mayer and Salih 2006, 570). In terms of their historical role and linkages to political actors, SLF was closely aligned to the platform and campaign of the UNP – a pro-business party who also ran on a pro-peace agenda in the 2001 elections. However, the UNP was not always considered to be pro-peace. They have been accused of implementing policies that exacerbated minority grievances and were known to have taken violent measures in the 1970s and 1980s when face-to-face with uprisings from the Janatha Vimukthi Peramuna / People's Liberation Front (JVP) (then a militant Sinhala youth group) and Tamil militants. Thus, their pro-peace campaign was not always seen as legitimate or sincere by opposition groups nor by the LTTE who questioned their emphasis on the 'economic peace dividend' over their political grievances. Similarly, as a representative of the economic and business elite of the country and a close ally of the then elected UNP alliance, the UNF, SLF was also treated with suspicion by actors who questioned whether they were using a 'veil of peace' to hide their true *homo economicus* or self-interest. When the SLF began to receive some support and financing from the same international donors as the local civil society, non-governmental organizations working on peacebuilding and human rights felt that they had "failed to put their money where their mouth is" and diminished their contributions to the peace process as minimal (Author Interview, NGO, 7.4.10). Despite acquiring international support and praise, SLF failed to obtain significant backing of representatives from Sri Lankan opposition political parties, the LTTE and non-governmental organizations. This prevented them from being able to go beyond their awareness campaigns and significantly penetrate the political and peacebuilding sphere.

Despite their political engagement in the peace process in Sri Lanka, there has not been evidence that the local companies involved in SLF and other business-led peace initiatives implemented coherent corporate social responsibility (CSR) strategies that took their *political responsibility* into account.

3.4 Long-term effects of the involvement of Sri Lanka First in peacebuilding.

The example of SLF provides scholars and practitioners with an important empirical case that shows both the opportunities and limitations of businesses to engage in peacebuilding. SLF was engaged in specific activities such as lobbying efforts, awareness campaigns, support of pro-peace political parties, multi-stakeholder dialogues and international exchanges for knowledge building. However, despite these activities, the SLF was unable to have a long-term impact on peacebuilding in Sri Lanka. This is linked to four key factors.

Firstly, the over-emphasis of the 'economic peace dividend' by the ruling UNF and SLF placed the LTTE's ethno-political grievances on the backbench; demonstrating that they were not able to fully comprehend the politics involved in order to achieve the peace that they were advocating for.

Secondly, while the access to local parties such as the UNF may have provided them with some political clout and access to certain actors, it is likely that this 'partisan approach' did not help them in gaining political credibility and trust of other political parties and the LTTE. Further, when the UNF failed to achieve a successful peace agreement, the SLF was seen as accompanying the party's shortcomings.

Thirdly, while the SLF saw that it possessed a certain ability to raise awareness and promote peace in periods of economic and political crisis, its non-engagement during times of political stability did not take full advantage of the peace momentum and were thus not long-term or sustainable. Their lack of engagement and 'about-face' in the face of a new SLFP government and the resumption of hostilities in 2006 demonstrated that they no longer saw a role for themselves to advocate for a peace which did not appear to be likely. Moreover, the lack of implementation of their political campaigns into concrete CSR policies within the companies themselves demonstrates a short-term vision and unwillingness to establish internal practices that promote social and political change.

Finally, a more political economy approach to the Sri Lanka case demonstrates the historical and long-term factors that were likely to contribute to both SLF's access and opportunities to engage in peacebuilding as well as their constraints and limitations. There is a need for both scholarly and practitioner literature to take a political economy approach into account when researching the role of local business in peacebuilding. Focusing merely on the period or phase (such as the peace process) where the business-supported peacebuilding fails to take the complex role of companies into account. The impact of the conflict on their business activities, their role during the peace process, their historical relationship to political parties and the long-term impacts (if any) of their activities need to be analysed in order to fully understand the different aspects that contributed to their engagement and dis-engagement. In the case of Sri Lanka, it is clear that while SLF did accomplish significant peacebuilding achievements during the peace process, they failed to have a long-term effect on peacebuilding in the country.

4 Business for peace vs. socio-economic peace in El Salvador?

El Salvador is the smallest but most populated country in Central America. Its peace agreement was one of the first that has been brokered by the UN and ended a civil war that lasted from 1979 until 1992. After a series of pre-agreements, a peace agreement was signed in 1992 in Mexico between the main conflict parties, the government of El Salvador and the FMLN, the *Frente Farabundo Marti para la Liberacion Nacional*. The civil war cost the lives of approximately 75,000 civilians (Seligson and McElhinny 1996, 212). Between 85 and 95 per cent of these deaths have been attributed to the military and so-called death squads of the rightist governments during the civil war (Pineda Depaz 2014, 17). Today, El Salvador is one of the countries with the highest homicide rates and is suffering strongly from the different economic crises that have shattered the overall Central American region.

4.1 Role of business during conflict

During the civil war period in the 1980s, the economy collapsed. Most of the economic activity during that time was based on agriculture, and the conflict took place in those rural areas. Economic activity, mainly the cultivation of maize, sugar cane and some of the coffee plantations came to a halt. Extortion and some murders of businesspeople led to a bad investment climate and overall economic insecurity. The majority of the wealthy business class of the 'cafetalera' at the time fled to Miami and left their companies in the hands of their most trusted managers. Unemployment increased and some experts suggest that in 1988, the economy was at a level that the economy was in the year 1960 (Author Interview Business, 6.11.2012). Even though the government would nationalize the international trade of the coffee sector as well as the banks, this did not lead to an economic 'turnaround' rather, it led to a brutal campaign by the wealthy business class. The cost of human capital was enormous.

Apart from the 75,000 civilian deaths, there were innumerable disappearances based on the death squads that were controlled by the same politico-economic elite that ran the country. Those that suffered most were the poor, as they could not leave: "Fue una guerra entre pobres" – "This was a war between poor people" (Author Interview, University, 8.11.2012).

After an initial arrest for the killing of Oscar Romero in 1980, an outspoken cleric that condemned the torture and killings of the death squads, Roberto d'Abuisson was set free and founded the business-oriented party ARENA in 1981. The party won the elections against the Democratic Action Party and the Christian Democratic Party in 1983 with its new president Alfredo Christiani taking power. Christiani is himself a businessman representing one of the wealthy Salvadoran elite families. Together with a large economic think tank, FUSASES, the party changed its previous discourse on the business elite from being the victims of the civil war to being the 'true Salvadorans' (Author Interview, University, 10.11.2012). It was during this time also that the connections between the business elite and the military have been subsequently weakened, which opened up the opportunity for peace negotiations.

4.2 Role of business during peace agreement

The Farabundo Martí National Liberation Front (FLMN) and President Christiani reached a final peace agreement in January 1992 (after several negotiations). The agreement included several areas: armed forces, national civilian police, judicial system, electoral system, economic and social questions, political participation by FMLN, and cessation of armed hostilities. Around Christiani, and with financial and technical help of the United States, the business elite in the country changed. It was not the 'old' elite of the 'cafetalera' that influenced the negotiations, but a 'new' elite that was regionally integrated in Central America, with an interest in services and industry. It was the first time that a majority of businesspeople supported the government's peace talks.

One of the areas in the peace agreement were economic and social questions (Chapter 5: tema economico y social). Already in the preamble of the chapter, it is argued that this is a minimal compromise (Chapultepec Agreement 1992, 34).[3] The chapter includes the following issue: the agricultural problem, land in conflict zones, agreement of 1991 on occupied land, credit for agriculture and small and medium enterprises, means to alleviate structural adjustments, modalities of support for economic development, political and economic consultation forum (tripartite forum with private sector, labour unions and government) and national reconstruction plan. It was argued at the time that the workers and unions as well as the managers were an important part of the peace process and gave the negotiations a certain kind of sustainability (Author Interview, business association, 9.11.2012). However, in terms of urgency and follow up, it was later agreed that first there needed to be a solution to the security issues of the conflict (reintegration of former combatants, establishment of a national police force) and the implementation of economic and social issues, like land, will follow later.

One of the interviewees who today works in the ministry of Labor and Social Welfare (MTPS) argued that there were two main reasons for the lack of continuation on the social and economic agreement discussions. First, some of these issues were non-negotiable from an ideological standpoint (different understandings of what property means). Second, FLMN did not understand that the country had profoundly changed economically. The interviewee from the ministry also cited a former colleague from the FLMN who said: 'If we had known that the economy had changed, we would have asked for banks, not land' (Author Interview, Government, 10.11.2012). Further, it was mainly in these social and economic negotiations where the dilemmas that the structural adjustment programs posed for the overall peace process (aiming towards social and economic peace) came to the fore (Boyce and O'Donnell 2007; Del Castillo 2001). Economically, the peace agreement coincided with the Washington Consensus of 1989. There was no majority for the main elements of the Washington Consensus amongst the Salvadoran society in the earlier years before 1992. However, the newly formed banking and industries business elites supported the peace agreement because they thought it could help with the implementation of the consensus (Author Interview, NGO, 8.11.2012). As a result, institutionalized negotiation on social and economic issues as foreseen in the peace agreement has been subsequently dismantled.

Some analysts portray a very positive interpretation of the business involvement in the peace agreement phase and the subsequent involvement of business in economic development (see, for example, Rettberg 2007). Interestingly, the interviewees of this study have not supported such a discourse. Some were even cautious to say that the 'private sector' as such was influential in the agreement, as they wanted to make a distinction of the private sector that was close to Christiani and the private sector close to FLMN. One interviewee argued for a similar pattern analysis like amongst the church leaders: some of them were closer to one or the other party. Others establish a clear distinction between the Christiani government and the overall private sector and see no involvement of the private sector as such (Author Interview, NGO, 11.11.2012). Rather, they argue, it was other factors that coincided with the peace agreement that made it happen like the final offensive '*hasta el tope*' (to the top) of the FLMN that came very close to the heart of San Salvador, the murder of the Jesuit priests of the UCA following on this offensive and the end of the cold war.

4.3 Political parties and business related interests

ARENA was the political party that signed the peace agreement from the side of the government. While its economic base changed from the traditional 'cafetalera' families to the new regionally integrated and globalized business elite, the right wing political rhetoric stayed the same until today (Author Interview NGO, 7.11.2012). Most of the political party members of ARENA are business people and when they were in the government, most of the functionaries had a business background. This business dominated party has a strong backing from the civil society sector that is active in supporting business interests through associations.

There are mainly two business associations that are dominant: Associacion National de la Empresa Privada (ANEP) and La Fundación Salvadoreña para el Desarrollo Económico y Social (FUSADES). Since the civil war, the influence of those two associations changed and they were close to different political parties throughout these years. ANEP, the Associacion National de la Empresa Privada, is an organization founded in 1966 with the purpose of defending free enterprise. ANEP was traditionally the most important business association in the country. However, in the year 1975, the military-backed government wanted to promote agrarian transformation particularly in the East of El Salvador and this led to a clash between the military and ANEP. After this, the business elite was looking for another vehicle to gain more political influence. With strong support from Reagan administration-backed USAID, a new economic think tank was founded in 1989: FUSADES. For almost 15 years, ANEP was less influential than FUSADES. It was only with Tony Sacca (elected president in 2004) and his party Gran Aliance por la Unidad (GANA) that the ANEP grew stronger again. GANA was formed not from the 'old' families but representatives from medium to larger business like restaurants or private security companies. Tony Saca, the successful presidential candidate of GANA was president of ANEP. It was with GANA the first time that a conservative party went into coalition with the FLMN. The strengthening of GANA made visible what some interviewee of an NGO said: 'Historically, when we talk about the private sector in El Salvador, we talk about a small elite, however, there are many more business-people that do not have anything to say' ('ni voz ni voto'). The think tank FUSADES played a very important role in supporting the first ARENA government and imple-menting the Washington Consensus leading to the privatization of the banks. The second presidency under ARENA comes with a focus on services, ports and the transformation of the airport into a giant warehouse (to compete with Panama). Until today, a lot of funds for development purposes were channelled through FUSADES or through other organizations founded by the same people (Wolf 2009).

Finally, what was the role of the left party, FLMN with regards to economic reconstruction? Most of the interviewees that were closer to FLMN did not have many good words for the economic policies of FLMN. The very same interviewee that was critical of FUSADES was critical with the FLMN. He argued that in his view the 'frente' (short for FLMN) has fallen prey to empty globalization promises with a focus on the attraction of private investments. As one of the first in history, the former rebel group FLMN turned into a successful political party. However, most of the party representatives are politicians, some are social entrepreneurs (leading an NGO) but none of them are in the productive sector.

4.4 Long-term effects of the involvement of companies in peacebuilding

ARENA's structural adjustment program had negative effects on the peacebuilding efforts (Boyce and O'Donnell 2007; Del Castillo 2001). While effective in con-trolling inflation and stabilizing the economy, the fiscally restrictive policies imposed heavy limitations on state spending which jeopardized the implementation of many key programs. As indicated above, the key personnel in the ARENA party were representatives from the private sector. As such, the long-term effect of the policies that they pushed had an overall negative effect on broader social and economic peace in El Salvador. While the economic situation changed to the better for a restricted circle of economic elites, the situation of the overall population worsened.

Looking at the overall discourse on business and peacebuilding that is often located in business governance issues (Fort 2009; Oetzel et al. 2009), it is interesting that generally, in El Salvador, businesses are not viewed as 'good guys'. They are often viewed as polluters of the environment or as violators of labour laws. If there are companies that are engaging in CSR, it is large multinational companies like CALVO, Coca Cola or Microsoft. CSR and human rights are not part of a general awareness; there is also no customer awareness to ask for this. Most of the companies are involved in exploitation, there is a strong ideological burden and the society is very polarized. There seems to be a political apathy of the young generations; it is the old ones that have been politicized earlier that are interested. The young ones are oriented towards the US and interested in large shopping malls. A specific company called CALVO tried to reintegrate former members of the 'pandillas', however did not prove very successful. The economic think tanks are not interested in helping the companies cope with the current violence. As one of the interviewees of an economic think tank said that such kind of help is not in their mandate (Focus group discussion, 5.11.2012). Like one interviewee said (Author Interview, University, 9.11.2012), there is no economic vision for the country and it is not clear what kind of economic system the society favours.

Thus, while there is a renewed emphasis on the role of the private sector in development in general and in peacebuilding in particular, the case of El Salvador shows a political economy analysis of a possible role.

5 The economic dimensions of political conflict: Comparing Sri Lanka and El Salvador

The Sri Lanka and El Salvador cases provide some important comparative factors for the deeper understanding of the role of business in peacebuilding. These can be summarized through four main factors of engagement.

Firstly, the coupling of a national economic liberalization process and a long-term civil war. Both countries were undergoing economic liberalization reforms that were transforming their economies from one heavily reliant on agriculture to one that focused more on the development of industries. In both cases, the processes were often led by rightist nationalist political parties that were also investing in high-defence expenditures and who were known to use violent tactics against opposition groups and critics.

This led to frustration amongst classes and groups in both countries who did not feel that they were able to profit from these reforms and processes and who felt that it was only an opportunity for the 'haves' to get richer and the 'have-nots' to become more marginalized. This contributed to also political ideologies that pitted neo-liberals against Marxists (particularly in the case of El Salvador and to a lesser extent in Sri Lanka). Further, it contributed to the development of land areas in which some were able to highly profit and others were completely isolated and not able to compete in the same markets. This also contributed to different groups of 'business' – some who were historically part of the political and economic elite and who were geographically located in the economic 'centres' of the country and those who were more remote and more negatively affected by government-imposed regional development programs etc. These grievances significantly contributed to both the outbreak of violent conflict and eventually civil war in both countries, but also their long-term inability to find a solution.

This has several implications such as: the historical relationship between the military, the conflict parties and political parties and the business elite; the root causes of civil war as related to politico-economic grievances; the motivation of business to engage in peacebuilding being linked to an 'economic peace dividend', and; the way in which economic issues are tackled during the peace process as well as afterwards (either through implementation or lack thereof). The interaction between the economic liberalization process and the protracted civil wars contributed to economic and political crises that also supported particular opportunities. For example, an opening of space for power changes in the economic and political elite as well as a change of discourse that saw the prospect of peace as a solution. It represented a moment in time where oftentimes new or modernized business elites (industry, services) also saw a role for themselves within political processes.

Secondly, the role that international donors play in contributing to aid and peacebuilding in the realm of business for peace. This is particularly linked to issues such as high levels of indebtedness (i.e. IMF), neo-liberal development processes such as trade liberalization policies and the creation of 'donor darlings'. While this provides opportunities for civil society, business and government to engage in (funded) peacebuilding activities, it also raises liberal peacebuilding critiques on whether or not peace is then internally motivated or externally enforced. That is, that peace becomes a condition for donor aid; making actors more likely to promote it. However, the long-term 'buy-in' may remain lacking.

As businesses are increasingly seen as important interlocutors of peace agreements as well as long-term peacebuilding, there are opportunities for aid to be targeted to the private sector in conflict-affected countries. While there are studies that focus on the 'negative' influence of international aid in El Salvador (Wade 2008) and Sri Lanka (McGregor 2006) peace processes, a focus on the impacts of donor funding for economic growth and business-led peace initiatives would require further research.

Thirdly, a mediated peace process that appears to offer an opening for business engagement. A peace process offers business persons with the opportunity to engage in particular roles and activities which may be limited under extended violent warfare. For example, the opportunity to take a more direct role as part of the mediation team or a seat at the negotiating table. Further, there are many indirect activities that businesses can engage in such as lobbying the government for a peaceful resolution to the conflict or for the implementation of policies and peace agreement terms that include economic dimensions, providing good offices, supporting or in some cases mediating dialogue processes between the conflict parties or other relevant actors etc. (Tripathi and Gündüz 2008; Iff et al. 2010; Iff and Alluri 2016).

Having said this, while the business and peace literature tends to 'glorify' the role that businesses played in both Sri Lanka and El Salvador during the peace processes, empirical interviews in both countries demonstrate that the perception of the role of business was not always seen as 'positive' or even 'noteworthy' amongst the larger scale of the peace process. Thus, the question of the relevance of business in the peace-*making* process is still in the room and should not be overestimated.

Fourthly, the way in which economic dimensions were addressed during the peace process and thereafter. While there are several elements where the developments in Sri Lanka and El Salvador were similar, there are also significant differences. While in El Salvador, the peace agreement has been negotiated with a peaceful end, in the case of Sri Lanka, the ceasefire agreement broke and the peace process collapsed, leading to a resumption of violent conflict in 2006. One of the factors that have been seen to have contributed to this was the way in which the economic peace dividend was over-emphasized by the UNF, failing to take political grievances into account. The failure of the peace process also led to Sri Lanka First no longer seeing a role for itself, ceasing the majority of its activities and in the case of some representatives, changing their discourse in relation to the war to support a military approach.

In El Salvador, however, the acceptance of a peace agreement in 1992 signified the end of the decade-long civil war and a movement towards peace. Following the peace process, ARENA and eventually a new economic elite emerged that would finally enter into dialogue with FLMN. When the FLMN would be elected 17 years after the signing of the peace agreement, it signified a major transformation in the country. At the same time, the FLMN's over-emphasis on political issues and reluctance to address and promote economic development has also contributed to a national crisis wherein the former combatants and victims of the civil war remain marginalized, unable to access economic opportunities and excluded from market access. They have been criticized by some for then falling into the old neo-liberal discourses that they used to advocate against because they never took the opportunity to reform the economy in a sustainable, inclusive manner.

Finally, both country cases demonstrate that despite business engagement in political processes and peacebuilding, companies failed to integrate such positions into their own company policies and practices. The lack of CSR policies within the companies that actively promoted peacebuilding is rather striking. This illustrates a disjuncture with how the 'political' role of businesses during peace agreements corresponds or translates to CSR approaches. It also supports the perspectives of interviewees that businesses themselves did not necessarily see a long-term role and responsibility for themselves to support peacebuilding and an unwillingness to 'talk the talk'. This appears to confirm the hypothesis that the involvement of businesses in these cases has rather been 'externally' induced and motivated by long-term market strategies rather than because of a more general shift in the functioning and forms of engagement of businesses in those societies.

6 Conclusions: Companies respond to 'openings' but are not in it for the long haul

The qualitative empirical field research carried out in El Salvador and Sri Lanka demonstrates that although the private sectors played important roles in peace-building during both mediated peace processes, the inter-relationships between businesses and political actors had not previously been adequately taken into account. Further, in the aftermath of the peace processes in both contexts, the private sector did not necessarily play a positive role. In the case of El Salvador, the integration of business actors *into* the new government very likely had negative impacts on the economic conflict factors, socio-economic development and the implementation of the peace agreements. Moreover, it has been argued that the ongoing violence in the country continues to be linked to socio-economic inequalities that were not addressed in the implementation of the peace agreement by the new government. Further, this demonstrates how socio-economic inequalities are likely to have never been a high priority for the private sector despite having advocated for them during the peace negotiations.

In the case of Sri Lanka, the collapse of the peace process and the return to civil war in 2006 caused many once peace-promoting business actors to have an 'about-face' and begin to support a military solution. While the El Salvador example shows how historically strong the private sector remains, in Sri Lanka, it is the lack of political muscle as well as political awareness of the private sector which is important to understand. While the peace process provided an 'opening' for the private sector to promote peace, once that window of opportunity closed with the collapse of the peace process, so did the clout, influence and muscle of the private sector. This needs to be understood in relation to the strong militarized Sri Lankan state vis-à-vis the local business sector that remains reliant on government tenders, handouts, policy initiatives, security guidelines and sector-specific development.

Both of these case studies have brought to light the lack of nuance in many academic studies on the role of the private sector in peacebuilding until now. They argue that in order to better understand the role of business in peace promotion, one needs to take a political economy approach that not only looks at a particular time period or phase (such as a peace process) but takes into consideration both the historical role that business has played in the country in terms of politics and rela-tionships with political actors but also a long-term analysis of what occurs once a peace process has been concluded or collapsed. It is important to explore what role business can indeed play in a post-peace process period or post-conflict period as well in order to fully understand their potentials and limitations.

Notes

1 Andrea Iff is currently Governance Advisor at the Swiss Development Agency and Cooperation. Rina M. Alluri is Senior Fellow at the University of Zurich, Human Geography Department and an Independent Consultant.
2 NCCR (National Center of Competence in Research) North South financed by the Swiss National Science Foundation.
3 The agreement is available on the UN Platform Peacemaker: http://peacemaker.un.org/ elsalvador-chapultepec92 (accessed, 12 October 2014).

Bibliography

Abeyratne, S. 2004. *Economic Roots of Political Conflict: The Case of Sri Lanka*. Oxford: Blackwell Publishing Ltd.

Amnesty International. 2000. Sudan: The Human Price of Oil. *Amnesty International*. www. amnesty.org/ailib/aipub/2000/AFR/15400100.htm; accessed on 29 October 2013.

Anderson, MB. 2002. Developing Best Practice For Corporate Engagement In Conflict Zones: Lessons Learned From Experience. Proceedings of Public Bads - Economic Dimension of Conflict organized by Inwent and BMZ in Bonn, Germany on 26 November 2002. Collaborative for Development Action (CDA).

Banfield, J, Lilly, D, Haufler, V. 2003. *Transnational Corporations in Conflict-Prone Zones: Public Policy Responses and a Framework for Action*. London: International Alert.

Banfield, J, Gündüz, C, Killick, N, editors. 2006. *Local Business, Local Peace: The Peacebuilding Potential of the Domestic Private Sector*. London: International Alert.

Bennett, J. 2001. *Business in Zones of Conflict: The Role of the Multinational in Promoting Regional Stability*. IPF [International Peace Forum] Prepared for the UN Global Policy Dialogues. New York: International Peace Forum.

Blowfield, M, Murray, A. 2008. *Corporate Responsibility: A Critical Introduction*. Oxford: Oxford University Press.

Boyce, James K, O'Donnell, Madeline. 2007. *Peace and the Public Purse: Economic Policies for Postwar Statebuilding*. Lynne Rienner Publishers, Inc.

Bull, Benedicte. 2004. Responsabilidad Social de Las Empresas: Una Solucion Para El Desarollo En America Latina? *Revista Venezolana de Generica Universidad de Zulia* 9(028): 1–24.

Carroll, AB. 1999. Corporate Social Responsibility: Evolution Of A Definitional Construct. *Business and Society* 38(3): 268–295.

Cohen, N and Ben-Porat, G. 2008. Business Communities and Peace: The Cost-Benefit Calculations of Political Involvement. *Peace and Change* 33(3): 426–446.

Colburn, Forrest D. 2009. The Turnover in El Salvador. *Journal of Democracy* 20(3): 143.152.

Crane, A, Matten, D, Moon, J. 2008. The Emergence of Corporate Citizenship: Historical Development and Alternative Perspectives. In: Scherer, AG, Palazzo, G, editors. *Handbook of Research on Corporate Citizenship*. Cheltenham: Edward Elgar Publishers, pp 25–49.

De Bremond, Ariane. 2007. The Politics of Peace and Resettlement through El Salvador's Land Transfer Programme: Caught between the State and the Market. *Third World Quarterly* 28(8): 1537–1556.

Del Castillo, G. 2001. Post-Conflict Reconstruction and the Challenge to International Organizations: The Case of El Salvador. *World Development* 29(12): 1967–1985.

Doane, D. 2005. Beyond Corporate Social Responsibility: Minnows, Mammoths and Markets. *Futures* 37 :215–229.

Dunham, D, Kelegama, S. 1997. Does Leadership Matter in the Economic Reform Process? Liberalization and Governance in Sri Lanka, 1989–1993. *World Development* 25(2): 179–190.

Federation of Chambers of Commerce and Industry of Sri Lanka (FCCISL). 2008. Business for Peace Initiative: Components. *FCCISL*. www.bpi.fccisl.lk/Components.php; accessed on 10 March 2010.

Foley, Michael W. 1996. "Laying the Groundwork: The Struggle for Civil Society in El Salvador". *Journal of Interamerican Studies and World Affairs* 38(1): 67–104.

Fort, TL. 2009. "Peace Through Commerce: A Multisectoral Approach". *Journal of Business Ethics* 89: 347–350. doi:10.1007/s10551-010-0413-5.

Global Witness. 1998. *The Logs of War. The Timber Trade and Armed Conflict.* Oslo, Norway: Fafo Institute of Applied International Studies. Also available at: www.fafo.no/pub/rapp/379/; accessed on 6 November 2013.

Global Witness. 1999. *A Crude Awakening: The Role of Oil and Banking Industries in Angola's Civil War and the Plunder of State Assets.* London: Global Witness Ltd.

Grim, Ryan, and Stangler, Cole. 2012. Mitt Romney Started Bain Capital With Money From Families Tied To Death Squads. *The Huffington Post*, 24 October.

Goodhand, J. 2001. *Aid, Conflict and Peacebuilding in Sri Lanka.* London: Centre for Defence Studies, Kings College.

Goodhand, J and Walton, O. 2009. The Limits of Liberal Peacebuilding? International Engagement in the Sri Lankan Peace Process. *Journal of Intervention and Statebuilding* 3(3): 303–323.

Harker, J. 2000. *Human Security in Sudan: The Report of a Canadian Assessment Mission.* Ottawa, Canada: Ministry of Foreign Affairs and International Trade. Also available at: www.ecosonline.org/reports/2000/Human%20Security%20in%20Sudan.pdf; accessed on 5 July 2012.

Haufler, V, editor. 2002. *Case Studies of Multistakeholder Partnership: Policy Dialogue on Business in Zones of Conflict.* United Nations Global Compact (UNGC). www.unglobalcompact.org/docs/issues_doc/Peace_and_Business/MultistakeholderInitiativeinZonesofConflict.pdf; accessed on 4 November 2013.

Human Rights Watch. 1999. *The Price of Oil: Corporate Responsibility and Human Rights Violations in Nigeria's Oil Producing Communities.* New York: Human Rights Watch.

Humphreys, M. 2003. *Economics and Violent Conflict.* Cambridge, MA: Harvard University. www.unicef.org/socialpolicy/files/Economics_and_Violent_Conflict.pdf; accessed on 6 November 2013.

Iff, A. 2013. "What Guides Businesses in Transformations from War to Peace?" In *Companies in Conflict Situations*, edited by Antoni Pigrau and Maria Prandi, 153–178. International Catalan Institute for Peace.

Iff, A, Alluri, RM. 2016. "Business Actors in Peace Mediation Processes". *Business and Society Review* 121(2): 187–215.

Iff, A, Sguaitamatti, D, Alluri, RM, Kohler, D. 2010. Money Makers as Peace Makers: Business Actors in Mediation Processes. swisspeace Working Paper 2.

Jamali, D, Mirshak, R. 2007. Corporate Social Responsibility (CSR): Theory and Practice in a Developing Country Context. *Journal of Business Ethics* 72: 243–262.

Joras, Ulrike. 2009. "Motivating and Impeding Factors for Corporate Engagement in Peacebuilding". Swisspeace Working Paper 1.

Killick, N, Srikantha, VS, Gündüz, C. 2005. *The Role of Local Business in Peacebuilding.* London: Berghof Research Centre for Constructive Conflict Management.

Le Billon, P. 2001. The Political Ecology of War: Natural Resources and Armed Conflicts. *Political Geography* 10(5): 561–584.

Marrikar, N. 2005. Sri Lanka First: The Business of Peace. In: Durham, H, Gurd, T, editors. *Listening to the Silences: Women and War.* Leiden, The Netherlands: Koninklikje Brill BV, pp 37–42.

Mayer, M, Salih, M. 2006. Sri Lanka: Business as an Agent for Peace. In: Banfield, J, Gunduz, C, Killick, N, editors. *Local Business, Local Peace: The Peacebuilding Potential of the Domestic Private Sector.* London, UK: International Alert, pp 551–582.

McGregor, L. 2006. Beyond the Time and Space of Peace Talks: Re-appropriating the Peace Process in Sri Lanka. *International Journal of Peace Studies* 11(1) Spring/Summer.

Nathan, L, Lamb, G. 2000. *A Literature Review on the Current Relationship Between War and Economic Agendas in Africa.* Cape Town: Centre for Conflict Resolution.

Nelson, J. 2000. *The Business of Peace: The Private Sector as a Partner in Conflict Prevention and Resolution.* London: Prince of Wales Business Leaders Forum, International Alert, Council on Economic Priorities.

Oetzel, J, Westermann-Behaylo, M, Koerber, C, Fort, TL, Rivera, J. 2009. Business and Peace: Sketching the Terrain. *Journal of Business Ethics* 89: 351–373.

Pineda Depaz, Salvador Ernesto. 2014. Transitional Justice in El Salvador: A Case Study. *Democracy and Society Georgetown University* 11(2): 17–22.

Power Rodrigo, S. Hungry Egocentric Business People. *Lanka Monthly Digest.* http://lmd. lk/archives/2006/December/public.htm; accessed on 30 March 2013.

Renner, M. 2002. *The Anatomy of Resource Wars.* World Watch Paper 162. Washington, DC: Worldwatch Institute.

Rettberg, Angelika. 2007. The Private Sector and Peace in El Salvador, Guatemala, and Colombia. *Journal of Latin American Studies* 39(3): 463–494.

Ropers, N. 2008. *Systemic Conflict Transformation Reflections on the Conflict And Peace Process in Sri Lanka.* Berghof Handbook Dialogue No. 4. Berlin, Germany: Berghof Research Center for Constructive Conflict Management.

Ruggie, J. 2011. *Guiding Principles on Business and Human Rights: Implementing the United Nations "Protect, Respect and Remedy" Framework.* Report of the Special Representative of the Secretary-General on the issue of human rights and transnational corporations and other business enterprises, John Ruggie. United Nations Human Rights Council.

Samarasinghe, SWR de, A. 2003. Political Economy of Internal Conflict in Sri Lanka. Working Paper 16. The Hague: Netherlands Institute of International Relations 'Clingendael'. Conflict Research Unit.

Samath, F. 2001. Politics-Sri Lanka: String of Woes Makes a Worried People. *IPS News.* Also available at: www.ipsnews.net/2001/08/politics-sri-lanka-string-of-woes-makes-a -worried-people/; accessed on 30 March 2013.

Perera, R and MacSwiney, M. 2002. EC Conflict Assessment Mission. *Special Report.*

Seligson, Mitchell A, McElhinny, Vincent. 1996. Low-Intensity Warfare, High-Intensity Death: The Demographic Impact of the Wars in El Salvador and Nicaragua. *Canadian Journal of Latin American and Caribbean Studies* 21(42): 211–241.

Stokke, K. 2006. Building the Tamil Eelam State: Emerging state institutions and forms of governance in LTTE-controlled areas in Sri Lanka. *Third World Quarterly* 27(6): 1021–1040.

Stokke, K, Uyangoda, J, editors. 2011. *Liberal Peace in Question: Politics of State and Market Reform in Sri Lanka.* London: Anthem Press.

Sunday Observer. 2002. SOLO-U Bids to Release LTTE detainees. *Sunday Observer.* www. sundayobserver.lk/2002/02/17/sec01.html; accessed on 17 February 2012.

Garriga, E, Melé, D. 2004. Corporate Social Responsibility Theories: Mapping the Territory. *Journal of Business Ethics* 53(1–2): 51–71.

Tripathi, S, Gündüz, C. 2008. *A Role for the Private Sector in Peace Processes? Examples, and Implications for Third-Party Mediation.* Oslo Forum 2008. Center for Humanitarian Dialogue. www. hdcentre.org/uploads/tx_news/2SalilTripathiMediationBusinessWEB.pdf; accessed on 4 November 2013.

United Nations Industrial Development Organization and (UNIDO) and United Nations Global Compact. 2015. Series of Dialogues on Means of Implementation of the Post-2015 Development Agenda: Engaging with the Private Sector. Consolidated report on 2014 consultations.

United Nations News Centre. 2015. UN Forum Highlights 'Fundamental' Role of Private Sector in Advancing New Global Goals. 26 September. Available at: www.un.org/apps/news/story.asp?NewsID=51981#.VsiMJccdDdk; accessed on 20 February 2016.

Uyangoda, J. 2007. Ethnic Conflict in Sri Lanka: Changing Dynamics. East-West Center. Washington. *Policy Studies* 32.

Venugopal, R. 2010. Business for Peace, or Peace for Business?: The Role of Corporate Peace Activism in the Rise and Fall of Sri Lanka's Peace Process. In: Raman, RK, Lipschutz, R, editors. *Corporate Social Responsibility: Comparative Critiques.* New York: Macmillan. pp. 148–164

Wade, CJ. 2008. El Salvador: Contradictions of Neoliberalism and Building Sustainable Peace. *International Journal of Peace Studies* 13(2): 15–32.

Wenger, A, Möckli, D. 2003. *Conflict Prevention: The Untapped Potential of the Business Sector.* Boulder: Lynne Rienner Publishers.

Wolf, Sonja. 2009. Subverting Democracy: Elite Rule and the Limits to Political Participation in Post-War El Salvador. *Journal of Latin American Studies* 41(3): 429–465.

9

PRACTICING BUSINESS AND PEACE?

Considerations overheard in the field

Ben Miller and Sarah Cechvala

Introduction

During the course of our work with companies in and out of the field, it has been striking to observe how little their concerns, needs, and challenges correspond to the preoccupations of the discourses about the role of business in peace and in achieving the Sustainable Development Goals (SDGs). The gulf between these two sets of concerns appears in even starker relief when one considers that discussions about business and peace purport, at least in some instances, to describe the impacts and outcomes of the work of those very companies. Field-level company staff are concerned with the bewildering array and complexity of issues, dilemmas, and setbacks that threaten to draw them into conflicts of one sort or another. We suspect that the corporate practitioners we work with would be quite surprised by the proposition that their work contributes to peace, or to SDG 16: "the promotion of peaceful and inclusive societies for sustainable development, the provision of access to justice for all, and building effective, accountable institutions at all levels" (United Nations Sustainable Development, 2018).

This gap between perspectives came to our attention during the course of a consultation convened among companies and industry associations by CDA Collaborative Learning Projects (CDA)[1] in 2014.[2] Among the participants was a senior executive of a multinational oil and gas company. Some years previously, there was a sustained period of violent conflict among communities at one of the company's operations sites in Africa. The company's response to this conflict was a highly regarded initiative to engage communities and a range of other stakeholders in a comprehensive effort to rework the basis of the company's engagement with communities, improve economic conditions and the quality of life in the wider region of the company's operations, and to develop capacities to mediate and resolve conflicts at the grassroots level over a wide geographical area. Following the executive's discussion of the initiative, another participant referred in an offhand way to the company's "peacebuilding work". Surprised, the executive rejoined, "Peacebuilding? No, we're definitely not doing peacebuilding. Peacebuilding is outside of our scope."

From the perspective of field-level corporate operations, so to speak, it seems clear that current debates about the business role in peace are uninformed by the experiences of corporate practitioners, and that, possibly for this reason, those debates do not speak in any obvious way to the dilemmas and challenges that 'frontline' company staff experience in their day-to-day activities. Reflection on the experiences of corporate practitioners in contexts of fragility and conflict reminds us that, despite substantial investments of time and energy to ameliorate conditions in the vicinity of their operations, and despite ever-more sophisticated understandings of corporate social impacts and best practices in managing those, companies find it very difficult indeed to avoid getting entangled in conflict dynamics. It is this practical concern, rather than the prospect of contributing to peace, that vexes and animates company staff at site-level.

In this chapter, we explore the experiences of companies operating in contexts of fragility and conflict to argue that the conceptual underpinnings and assumptions that are pervasive in contemporary discussions of business and peace would benefit from re-examination in light of the experiences and perspectives of corporate field staff. In particular, reflection on the practical realities of companies in conflict-affected and fragile states suggests that some of the basic propositions of current thinking about the role of the private sector in peace are made possible by setting to one side learning relating to the role of business in conflict. Experience from the field suggests that the inclusion of considerations of corporate impacts on conflict will make discourses about business and peace more practically useful to companies at the operational level. We would suggest that this is an avenue by which this discourse can take on fresh relevance to companies as well as greater internal analytical coherence.

Whereof we speak

The experiences discussed throughout this chapter derive from CDA's engagements with private-sector companies. Since 2000, CDA has performed more than 40 site assessments with more than 60 companies in over 25 countries. The bulk of this work has been performed with companies in the extractive industries, though other industries are also represented. Many of these site assessments have been part of two distinct learning projects. The first of these, conducted between 2000 and 2009, identified causes of conflict between companies and the communities affected by their operations.[3] This evidence base underpins a framework for examining corporate social impacts and ways to mitigate negative effects on the operating environment stemming from the company's presence and activities (Zandvliet and Anderson 2009).

The second of these learning projects ran from 2016–2018 and was a case-study-based enquiry into approaches to corporate operations that are effective in building peace in conflict-affected contexts. Over the course of the project,

CDA and its partner organizations, the Africa Centre for Dispute Settlement at the University of Stellenbosch Business School[4] and the Peace Research Institute Oslo,[5] undertook eleven case studies[6] that sought to document the intentional efforts by private-sector actors to affect the dynamics of conflict and peace, to trace those efforts to discernible outcomes, and to analyze patterns across those experiences. The aim of the project was to better understand why, how, and when companies engage effectively in peace-related activities.[7]

In our engagements with corporates we have made commitments to varying degrees of confidentiality and circumspection.[8] Throughout what follows, we endeavor to honor those commitments, and thus will not in all cases specify the companies and countries under discussion. We are also cognizant of the fact that the majority of the concrete examples presented in this chapter come from the extractive industries. We believe that examples from the extractive sector have a wider relevance, but we concede that some of our contentions may not apply completely, or particularly well, to other industries, and that some may apply to other industries in ways that diverge significantly from the assertions that we make herein.

Business and peace, business and conflict

Recent years have witnessed a striking renaissance of the timeworn notion that the private sector will, can, or should contribute to peace. A range of policy and peacebuilding actors have joined in calls for business to take on a role in building peace in fragile and conflict-affected states. United Nations agencies, defense actors, and international non-governmental organizations have all begun to stress the importance and urgency of mobilizing private-sector actors as peacebuilders (Ganson 2017a). Multi-actor initiatives such as the SDGs,[9] United Nations Global Compact Business and Peace Platform,[10] and the New Deal,[11] for example, all call for a robust and dynamic role for the private sector in the international agenda for fragile and conflict-affected states. Then UN Secretary General Ban Ki-Moon recently launched the United Nations Global Compact Business For Peace Platform with a call to "mobilize high-level corporate leadership to advance peaceful development through actions at the global and local levels," mentioning expressly the need for the private sector to assist the UN in fulfilling the Millennium Development Goals and the SDGs (Miklian 2018).

A notable and puzzling aspect of this emergent discourse on business and peace is its apparently wilful omission of issues relating to business' role in conflict, as well as a rich and historically deep vein of literature on that topic. To our reading of the literature on business and peace, there are two aspects of this omission. First, the discourse about business and peace leaves to one side any consideration of business operations and investments that demonstrably create, sustain, or intensify conflict; these are often treated as irrelevant to the analysis and implications of positive cases. Second, the literature purposefully focuses on the positive aspects of particular investments or business operations to the exclusion of aspects of those same operations that also, simultaneously, create, sustain, or intensify conflict.

The first of these omissions is consistent with, and may contribute to, a certain misplaced exuberance in policy and international development circles about the potential of foreign direct investment and expansion of the private sector in fragile states. The World Bank Group's and International Finance Corporation's (IFC) approaches to fragile states in some cases appear to encourage or facilitate any and all private-sector investment in states affected by conflict and fragility. The IFC's Conflict-Affected States in Africa Initiative, for example, measures its success by the number of laws that have been amended, the number of dollars invested, the number of loans provided, and so on, treating these outputs as proxies for the amelioration of conditions of fragility and conflict.[12]

The second of these omissions results in an inventory of what may very well be legitimate examples of "business contributions to peace" in which the business operations under consideration are decontextualized. Such efforts to catalogue typically present no treatment of the conditions under which the efforts took place, why they were effective in a particular context of conflict, or the specific impacts on violence, conflicts, or sources of instability that the efforts yielded. In effect, this strips away all of the details that enable an understanding of the applicability and replicability of these approaches in different contexts, and of the ways in which those efforts might be predicted to achieve particular outcomes. Oetzel has rightly observed that, in such instances, the range of ways in which businesses might contribute to peace are presented as a "menu of options" (Oetzel et al. 2010) from which a company might freely pick and choose according to its tastes, while offering little, if any, basis for discriminating between those options. This approach is of little value for specific businesses that are trying to manage conflicts in the vicinity of their operations.

The reality of business operations is that they are always undertaken by specific firms in specific contexts, and that, almost invariably, these firms have some good and some bad impacts. Analysis that omits consideration of some part of those impacts is no longer analysis of a specific firm in a specific situation. By way of illustration, a colleague once argued that a certain group of companies contributed to peace in a situation of violent conflict by working with their staff to help them manage the effects of conflict on their own lives. These same firms, however, were regularly paying a cash "tax" to an armed terrorist organization as a condition of staying in business inside of insurgent-held territory. The discrete practice of working with staff may have had meaningful effects, but the firms themselves contributed to sustaining, and possibly even incentivizing, conflict. To focus exclusively on an individual practice and its benefits is to lose sight of the firms' actual impacts on peace in the context of their operations, as well as the challenges – in this case extortion and a high risk of violence – that the conflict imposed on those firms.

Corporate practitioners in the field face a slew of such concerns, dilemmas, and risks (most of them less dramatic, but no less concrete) that can encumber their basic operational activities. We posit that the inclusion of a corporate field-level perspective that acknowledges these challenges and difficulties will significantly enhance contemporary discourses and add an element of realism to current, hopeful calls for private-sector engagement in peace efforts.

Overheard in the field

This section presents experiences of corporate practitioners operating in fragile environments and elicits some of their most exigent challenges. Examples presented here can point out some of the gaps between rhetoric and reality, and illuminate sources of fresh thinking that might strengthen the existing conceptualization of business and peace.

Managing conflict impacts is a full-time job

Our evidence indicates that the

> introduction of new resources into a resource-scarce society that is also in conflict rarely (if ever) leads to people sharing these resources and living happily together. Rather, resources brought into a conflict environment always become a part of the conflict.
>
> *(Anderson 2008 pp. 124–125)*

The resources that people fight over include much that is intrinsic to corporate operations – jobs, contracts, and influence with the company, as well as everything about corporate social responsibility practices or social investment, from what projects the company undertakes to who benefits from those projects. This is to say nothing of the harms flowing from business activity, which also fall unevenly across populations affected by corporate operations. These often drive a sense of injustice or unfairness among people affected by business activity. Some people's crops get covered in dust from heavy vehicle traffic, and other people's do not. Some people's wells get contaminated, and other people's do not. Opportunists and spoilers – individuals who manipulate their neighbors or local government offices in order to generate pressure on the company as a means to pursuing their own ends – are also often key actors in these conflicts.

Managing corporate impacts, and the ways people outside of the company respond to them, requires the incessant effort of company staff. Corporate practitioners often describe it as a non-stop job, where as soon as one emergent issue is resolved, another crops up. Field-level practitioners are charged with obtaining and sustaining the company's "social license to operate" – the collective approval of communities for the company's presence, resulting from a balance between good impacts and bad in which the good tips the scales for most people. When impacts on affected populations are left unmanaged or inadequately managed, particularly in contexts of fragility, they predictably enflame existing conflicts or spark new ones.

Our own experience in the field demonstrates this amply. Take for instance the town of Añelo, in the Province of Neuquén, Argentina. While oil and gas operators have been present in the region for over 40 years, the discovery of Vaca Muerta has led to a sudden and dramatic increase in the number of oil and gas operators and contractors using local towns as a base of operations. Because of the road network and geography, Añelo and a handful of towns like it are key points of access to the Vaca Muerta shale formation.

The rapid expansion of the sector has led to rising local expectations of production, revenue, and the economic benefits that may follow. Migration into villages and towns (such as Añelo) in the operational areas has spiked. Añelo itself grew in population by over 70 percent between 2007 and 2015. The large influx of people into the small town in a resource-poor area has had predictably negative impacts on the local population. The town is experiencing ongoing problems with its local water system and electrical grid that cannot meet growing demand. Prostitution, drug and alcohol addiction, and gambling have all become pervasive. Localized inflation has made housing unaffordable for many local residents of Añelo. One teacher explained to us that she and her colleagues do not earn enough money to rent property in Añelo anymore, and now their commute to work from the nearest affordable area is between one and two hours in each direction (Bardouille and Cechvala 2015).

At the time of CDA's visit to the region, operators were experiencing challenges due to road blocks and protests responding to the sector's impact on the local communities. Representatives of one oil and gas operator explained that managing their impacts in Vaca Muerta is an onerous task for which the company is not appropriately staffed. Lack of capacity and staffing has increased the risks to the company's social license to operate as corporate practitioners struggle to continuously manage a broad range of impacts in a constantly evolving context. As one oil and gas representative noted, "I have so much responsibility. I have all the responsibility for all the communities. But to build trust you need a lot of time. I do not have enough time" (Bardouille and Cechvala 2015).

In the Niger Delta, local benefit captors – individuals who advance their personal interests by exerting control over the distribution of corporate benefits that are intended for communities – have found ways to keep one oil company under nearly constant pressure. Committees representing local communities are able to incite local youth to engage in violent protests against the company and its staff. Kidnappings are common. Fear of violent community action keeps the company from engaging the community broadly, or in open, public fora. As a consequence, most members of local communities are unaware of the company's efforts to improve the local economy and the infrastructure in nearby villages. Lack of transparent two-way communication and engagement with communities has enabled the community committee to misappropriate significant resources that have been allocated to community development and to manipulate popular opinion of the company. The end result is an environment where the company continually faces thinly veiled threats from influential individuals, periodic demonstrations, sporadic acts of violence, and a stream of constant requests, demands, suggestions, and business cards from putative local enterprises, all focusing on ways to gain from the company presence (Bardouille and Miller, 2013).

These examples offer evidence about the difficulty of managing social impacts and the challenges unmanaged or inadequately managed social impacts create for companies. Even the most experienced corporate practitioners with ample budgets and sophisticated social engagement and investment strategies can quickly and easily find themselves entangled in conflict despite substantial efforts to avoid exactly that. Corporate practitioners' primary focus in these environments does not center on how they can contribute to peace, but rather on how they can avoid contributing to conflict.

Local development is a problem, not a solution

One of the most commonplace assertions about businesses as peace actors is that businesses influence peace by "encouraging local development and facilitating local capacities for peace" (Miklian 2018 p. 8).[13] But the question that is at the top of corporations' minds with respect to issues of local development, is not whether or not they should support such efforts. In the extractive industries, at least, it is established best practice to contribute to local development through social investment, hiring policies, and contracting local small and medium enterprises, and there are widely recognized guidance and industry associations that are dedicated to this purpose.[14] The question that is top-of-mind for corporate practitioners is how to support local development in ways that do not drive competition for resources between local actors, fragment local communities, finance conflict and conflict actors, sustain corrupt officials, or motivate benefit captors. In other words, how to support local development in ways that do not generate, sustain, or finance conflict.

A significant area of concern to many corporate practitioners is social investment – direct support by the company to the development of local communities. Partly this is a strategic concern because if such initiatives succeed in improving the quality of life of affected populations and creating new local economic opportunities, they may reduce the pressure and local attention to which the company is exposed. But the concern also relates partly to conflict. Corporate social investment projects frequently become bones of contention between the company and local populations, and between local communities themselves. For many corporate practitioners, they are, in practice, more often problems than solutions.

In some cases, companies' efforts to foster local development have the perverse effect of intensifying conflict. Chevron Nigeria Limited (CNL) is perhaps the best-known example of this phenomenon, thanks to several published studies. CNL went to some lengths to benefit the communities affected by its operations. It developed large-scale infrastructure projects designed to benefit the region as a whole, established scholarship programs for local students, and went out of its way to maximize its contracting and recruitment from local communities. None of these measures succeeded in securing Chevron's social license to operate, and in 2003, tensions among communities, and between communities and the company, reached a crisis point. Violent and destructive conflict broke out between communities and against the company. The conflict resulted in multiple fatalities, the destruction of villages, and losses estimated by Chevron to be in excess of 1 billion dollars. Tellingly, during the violence, conflict actors targeted the very infrastructure projects that were ostensibly undertaken for their benefit. CNL's assessment, as well as those of third-party analysts, partially attribute the period of violence that started in 2003 to CNL's efforts to enhance local development (Hoben et al. 2012).

We have seen similar, if less dramatic, phenomena in our own work with corporations. For instance, we worked in a South American country with an oil company that went to considerable lengths to foster social and economic development among its local stakeholders, including a number of indigenous groups. These efforts stalled when an aspiring benefit captor moved into one of the local villages, bringing with him a number of associates from outside of the local area, and managed to get himself elected head of the village. One of his first acts as the village head was to attempt to establish his village as an officially recognized indigenous group separate from the encompassing group. Due to the nature of host-state law, success in this endeavor would have given this individual a great deal of leverage to pressure the company, as well as near complete, personal control of any resources he managed to secure in the name of his community. His efforts led to a protracted dispute between him and his allies, on the one hand, and the larger indigenous group to which the village belonged, on the other hand. One consequence of the dispute was a request by the head of the indigenous group that the company halt development efforts in the affected village, until such time as the dispute was resolved. In this instance, the efforts of the company to push local development forward led to intra-communal tensions driven by efforts to capture the benefits of company-sponsored development.

Colombia provides numerous examples that illustrate how difficult it is, in conflict settings, for companies to operate in ways that enhance local development and local capacities for peace. Much of the difficulty relates to the tactics of Colombia's armed groups. The latter were largely predatory with respect to businesses and populations in the countryside. Extortion or "taxation" of communities and companies was a common means by which armed groups financed their activities. In many parts of the country, overtly sympathizing with any of the parties in conflict carried substantial personal risks – targeted assassinations of enemy partisans was a tactic employed by all of the conflict parties. The armed groups also infiltrated institutions at all levels, giving them substantial intelligence-gathering capacities. Consequently, a culture of secrecy, circumspection, and at times deception developed in relation to disclosure of personal political sympathies, affiliations, and connections to politically active individuals.

Most responsible companies operating in Colombia adopted anti-extortion and anti-bribery policies of one sort or another, in an effort to prevent money from passing directly from the company to one or the other of the armed groups. Among the challenges that those companies faced in this connection, however, was ensuring that contractors also adhered to those same policies. One oil company operating in Colombia reported to us that "everyone knows that all contractors in the oil supply chain mark up their rates by 10%" to cover the cost of anticipated extortion payments to armed groups. Under such circumstances, it would appear to be almost impossible to work with contractors in a manner that avoided financing Colombia's armed conflict.

Parallel challenges existed for companies in Colombia in the area of local hiring and social investment. Infiltration of companies by armed groups was often accomplished through companies' local recruitment processes, a risk of which companies themselves were well aware. Given the importance of concealing one's political affiliations as a matter of personal safety, however, it was nearly impossible to effectively check the backgrounds of job applicants. Most companies operated under the assumption that insurgent groups had placed operatives within the company. This could have major potential consequences for companies' day-to-day operational safety and security. For example, if a company were to hire a partisan of an armed non-state actor, the company would have no way to ensure that its salary payments to that individual would not be used to support the armed group. The possibility that an employee affiliated with an armed group might pass on information that would allow the group to extort, kidnap, or murder staff of the company or its contractors was also a concrete risk.

The most basic operational activities frequently imposed difficult decisions upon companies to which there were no clear, good answers, either practically or ethically. In one instance, a company was approached by the state security agency, which requested the company's permission to place intelligence agents within the company as a counter-insurgency measure. The company declined, saying that it did not want Colombia's conflicts within its own "four walls." The state security agency pushed back against the company's refusal, replying that the company had already been infiltrated by an illegal armed groups.

With respect to social investment in Colombia, most companies recognized that funds handed over to local organizations could easily be extorted by the armed groups. In view of the intelligence gathering capacities of those groups, companies could never assume that transfers could be made without the armed groups learning of them, and local organizations rarely had adequate security to protect themselves from concerted extortion attempts. In addition, it was often impossible for companies to know for certain the political affiliations of their local partners – companies went ahead with social investment activities assuming that there was always a risk that funds allocated to community development might be embezzled and diverted to the armed groups by their partisans within local community organizations.

Colombia's conflict is obviously unique in many respects, but we see broadly similar issues in other fragile and conflict-affected states. It is commonplace that companies find formal institutions and administrative processes to be unreliable because government agencies are absent from the location, exhibit substantial deficits in their capacity to fulfill their own mandates, or are themselves involved in conflict as a conflict actor. We have seen many instances in which individuals in positions of influence outside of the company pursue self-interested agendas that they are intent on concealing or at least denying plausibly. And few companies have not learned from experience that monies allocated to external actors for purposes of development or other community benefit may be stolen, diverted to the relatives and associates of those actors, or used for illicit purposes.

Our own argument is not to gainsay the potential of local development to contribute to peace, but to point out that many company staff charged with implementing development activities – to say nothing of company stakeholders – find those activities to be difficult, technical, and fraught with tension and risk. To argue that community development activities have the potential to contribute to peace may be accurate, but from the standpoint of how business operations unfold in practice, it is quite clearly incomplete. The concerns and experiences of corporate practitioners indicate that community development activities also have the potential to contribute to conflict and violence, and that they require careful strategy and substantial management and oversight if they are to achieve positive outcomes.

Working with, and without, external institutions

A good number of the difficulties that practitioners face in their day-to-day work arise from the external environment, and host governments are particularly conspicuous in this regard. Fragile states are characterized by formal governance institutions that are unable to fulfill their mandates or contain social conflicts effectively; they may be under-resourced, incompetent, corrupt, working in the interest of a narrow segment of the population, or they may themselves be conflict actors – particularly in the case of state security agencies.[15] It is hardly surprising, then, that in fragile and conflict-affected states, host-state governance and regulatory actors create significant dilemmas for corporate practitioners.

With few exceptions, foreign and domestic companies[16] alike operate in these jurisdictions with the consent of the host-state, and on its terms. Most multinationals commit to complete adherence to host-state law as a matter of respect for state sovereignty, and because the alternative exposes them to unacceptable legal and financial risks. In some cases, this requires companies to adjust their operational practices to meet local norms and operating requirements. To mention but two examples, in some countries, local law prohibits companies from reporting publicly on payments to the government, in contravention of the principles of the Extractive Industries Transparency Initiative (EITI). In one African country, companies in the oil and gas sector were obliged to use a particular private security company that had a human rights track record that made companies very concerned about their commitments to the Voluntary Principles on Security and Human Rights. The private security company was rumored to be owned by the president's brother, which underscores the realities of state fragility.

Some countries structure operational licenses in ways that make foreign companies dependent upon the state. In some South American countries, for example, foreign mining and oil and gas companies operate as contractors of a state enterprise.[17] This in effect makes the host state the client of the company. In these situations, it is relatively common for decisions about social issues – e.g. compensation for land, social investment, stakeholder engagement, and so on – to be shaped fundamentally by the host-state enterprise. Corporate practitioners working in these environments explain that they often find themselves in weak negotiating positions in relation to the government and its regulatory agencies. Foreign companies operating in these environments have little choice but to adapt to the requirements of the state, irrespective of the ways those practices might impact peace and conflict.

In an oil producing region of a South American country, for example, land laws are such that few people own the land on which they reside. Instead, much of the land is controlled and managed by the provincial government. This redounds to the advantage of elite local families that have historically participated in and influenced provincial governments – they have managed to establish control over huge acreages of oil-bearing land on which small-scale ranchers and cattle herders reside. Oil and gas companies operating in this context are obliged to use the land laws as a basis for compensating local populations for use of or impacts on their land. Benefits accrue to the owners, however, and not to the residents, who are themselves impacted by oil operations far more than the landowners.

The lack of equitable compensation for impacts on local residents has generated tensions between local residents and the oil operators in the region. Many local residents explained to us that they benefit very little from the companies, even as more and more operators and contractors move into their communities and use their ranchlands. The nature of the relationships between companies and locals strains efforts at meaningful engagement and social investment by corporations; residents do not trust the companies and are suspicious of their motives. Effective means for companies to resolve these issues are hard to find. Lobbying the federal and provincial governments for reform of land and compensation laws would put the companies at odds with powerful elites with close ties to government at the local and national levels. In the worst case scenario for the companies, this course of action could lead to revocations of contracts or licenses.

In another South American country with a populist government, where the same contractual arrangement applies to foreign oil companies, it is relatively common for state institutions to allow blame for unpopular events or regulations to fall on the shoulders of foreign oil companies, even where state institutions are themselves directly responsible for them. In one instance, the state oil company organized an event launching a major oil installation. It invited locals from the project's "zone of influence" and politicians, but not communities from outside the zone. Local dignitaries from several communities located just outside the zone tried to attend anyway, but were turned away by police providing security for the event. The dignitaries were infuriated by the slight, and by their treatment by police, and blamed the foreign company for the sequence of events. When the foreign company explained the situation to the state company and asked permission to inform the slighted community leaders, their request was denied. More than a year after these events, the community leaders continued to seethe with resentment of the company and threatened to close down the operation.

State absence can be as difficult as state intransigence. At an oil operation in a remote region of East Africa characterized by recurring, low-intensity armed clashes between ethnic groups, a multinational company recognized the almost complete absence of formal governance institutions as an underlying driver of risks to its operation. In the company's analysis, basic operational activities, such as local recruitment and land acquisition, would generate significant risks of conflict because of the absence of land titles and the absence of a credible body to establish and manage a recruitment protocol that is acceptable to a broad range of company stakeholders. The fragmentary nature of informal governance institutions – elders' councils, in this instance – meant that relying on those institutions would pose unmanageable logistical challenges. Without unified, legitimate, or competent governance institutions, corporate practitioners are left with little external support for managing their impacts in ways in which will not fuel localized violence.

While we have seen cases in which a company has been able to influence government in ways that substantially improved local conditions, such examples are few and far between, and improvement has come at the cost of an enormous investment of time and energy by company staff. One example is an oil and gas company operating in Myanmar (then Burma) while it was governed by the military junta. Forced labor was a common practice employed by the military in remote areas. In this case, the company determined that human rights violations by the state were bad both for business and for the local community in its area of operations. In a calculated effort to eliminate forced labor in its operational area, the company consistently and carefully lobbied the national government to alter its practices. As the only Western company operating in the country during the period of international sanctions, the company had a degree of leverage with the government. Over time, the effort proved to be effective, reducing forced labor to zero within the company's area of operation, and local people indicated unambiguously that the company's presence protected them from abuses by the military. But the course of action taken by the company was by no means easy or obvious from the start. International advocacy groups campaigned against the company over its willingness to do business with the military regime, and this had ramifications for the company at the international level. One can imagine a much different outcome for the company if the military junta had been less willing to negotiate its authority in the region (Bardouille and Cechvala 2014).

The proposition that business contributes to peace by influencing local institutions to be more accountable and effective does not ring true to the companies we work with. Many day-to-day challenges and dilemmas experienced by company field staff stem from their inability to exert influence over the institutions and requirements of the host state, the need to adapt their own operations to those institutions and requirements of the host state, or to negotiate acceptable compromises with those requirements. A number of adverse impacts, often with a significant potential to create or worsen conflict, flows from these.

Revitalizing the discourse

For company field staff seeking ways out of the kinds of difficulties we have enumerated, options for contributing to peace are only concretely useful if they respond to
the realities of the context. Those realities include the dynamics of conflict, the
nature of the other actors in the context, and the company itself – its capacities, its
business activities, its position vis-à-vis the host state, its negative and positive
impacts. To illustrate concretely, it would be helpful for companies to know how to
foster local development without driving community fragmentation in Papua New
Guinea, attracting predatory armed groups in Colombia, or getting entangled with
benefit captors in Nigeria. Company field staff need to understand how a given
practice or approach will interact with the context in which they are operating, how
they might be able to implement the practice given the particular constraints that
they face, and what outcomes they can reasonably expect as a result. Practitioners'
needs and experiences, in short, return the focus of the discussion to practical
implementation and the specificities of the contexts in which it unfolds.

If a focus on the practical aspects of implementation in context constitutes a
challenge to certain branches of the literature on business and peace, then we
contend that it is a healthy one. Addressing the challenge directly may yield
insights that are both conceptually fresh and more relevant to practice. While the
literature points to a number of means through which companies can foster peace,
the experience of practitioners as presented here suggests that many, if not all of
those means can also drive conflict. Responding to the challenge posed by the
experience of company field staff requires understanding of why and how an
approach can support peace in one context and drive conflict in another. To return
to the example adduced above, it would be very useful indeed for corporate
practitioners to have an analysis, tool, or set of principles that might help them to
implement processes of local development in ways that effectively manage benefit
captors, armed groups, or intracommunal tensions in their operational context. The
outcomes in the field, whether for better or for worse, are determined as much by
how the practices are implemented in relation to the dynamics of the context as by
the intrinsic nature of those practices themselves.

Conclusion

The experiences of company field staff in fragile and conflict-affected states are
inconsistent with several key elements of the discourse on business and peace. In
several of the critical areas where the discourse about business and peace suggests
that companies can contribute to peace, companies experience significant struggles
staying out of conflict. This gap between rhetoric and practice suggests a failure
within the literature to learn from the experiences of 'frontline' company staff in
real-world operational contexts. Some of what the literature puts forward as means
by which companies can contribute to peace is, in fact, exceptionally difficult to
achieve in practice.

One way to address this gap is a far more comprehensive treatment of the interaction between company and operational context. This would point discussions of business in fragile and conflict-affected states towards issues that are presently underrepresented in the business and peace literature, namely how – through what steps and processes, working with which partners, and leveraging which resources – companies can surmount challenges of the sort that we have described herein. Such an approach would eschew typologies or "menus of options" and focus instead on the contexts in which companies operate, the challenges that these contexts pose to companies, and the options available to companies to surmount those challenges.

Notes

1 For more see: http://cdacollaborative.org/what-we-do/responsible-business/
2 See the Consultation Report: www.cdacollaborative.org/publication/report-of-the-sixth-consultation-of-the-corporate-engagement-program/
3 All case studies can be found online at www.cdacollaborative.org
4 For more see: www.usb.ac.za/disputesettlement
5 For more see: www.prio.org/
6 All case studies can be found online at http://cdacollaborative.org/cdaproject/business-and-peace/
7 For the final report see: www.cdacollaborative.org/publication/a-seat-at-the-table-capacities-and-limitations-of-private-sector-peacebuilding-2/
8 Our experience working with companies has taken place under a range of circumstances. Some of our engagements have been confidential. Some parts of the evidence referenced here derive from dialogues that were convened under the Chatham House Rule, which allows for the reproduction of comments, but not for the attribution of those comments to any particular individual.
9 For more see: www.un.org/sustainabledevelopment/sustainable-development-goals/
10 For more see: www.unglobalcompact.org/engage-locally/manage/engagement/business-for-peace
11 For more see: www.pbsbdialogue.org/en/new-deal/about-new-deal/
12 For more see: www.ifc.org/wps/wcm/connect/REGION__EXT_Content/IFC_External_Corporate_Site/Sub-Saharan+Africa/Priorities/Fragile+and+Conflict+Affected+Situations/
13 cf. Oetzel et al. 2010.
14 For more see: www.icmm.com/en-gb/about-us
15 Ganson provides a useful discussion of fragility in the introduction section of Ganson, B., and Näringslivets internationella råd. (2013). *Management in complex environments: Questions for leaders*. Stockholm: NIR Näringslivets internationella råd.
16 We are aware of exceptions among small enterprises, as well as larger enterprises in operating in states that are particularly predatory.
17 It should be noted, that such investment structures are not unique to South American countries and can be seen throughout the world.

Bibliography

Anderson, M. B. (2008). False Promises and Premises? The Challenge of Peace Building for Corporations. In *Peace through commerce : Responsible corporate citizenship and the ideals of the United Nations global compact* (p. 124). Notre Dame, IN:University of Notre Dame Press.
Bardouille, D., and Cechvala, S. (2014). *Total E&P Myanmar Field Visit* (Rep.).
Bardouille, D., and Cechvala, S. (2015). *Total E&P Austral Argentina Field Visit* (Rep.).

Bardouille, D., and Miller, B. (2013). *Total E&P Nigeria Field Visit* (Rep.).

Ganson, B. (2017a). *Business and Peace: A Need for New Questions and Systems Perspectives* (Working paper). Cambridge, MA: CDA Collaborative Learning.

Ganson, B. (2017b). The Risky Business of De-Risking in Fragile and Conflict Affected States [Web blog post]. Retrieved from http://cdacollaborative.org/blog/risky-busi ness-de-risking-fragile-conflict-affected-states/

Ganson, B., and Näringslivets internationella råd. (2013). *Management in Complex Environments: Questions for Leaders*. Stockholm: NIR Näringslivets internationella råd.

Hoben, M., Kovick, D., Plumb, D., and Wright, J. (2012). *Corporate and Community Engagement in the Niger Delta: Lessons Learned from Chevron Nigeria Limited's GMOU Process* (Rep.). Consensus Building Institute.

Kim, J. Y. (2017, April 11). *Rethinking Development Finance*. Speech presented in UK, London. Retrieved from www.worldbank.org/en/news/speech/2017/04/11/speech-by-world-bank-group-president-jim-yong-kim-rethinking-development-finance

Miklian, Jason (2018) Mapping Business-Peace Interactions: Five Assertions for How Businesses Create Peace, *Business, Peace and Sustainable Development* 10(1): 1–19.

OECD. (2016). *OECD States of Fragility 2016 report* (Issue brief No. 11).

Oetzel, J., Westermann-Behaylo, M., Koerber, C., Fort, T. L., and Rivera, J. (2010). Business and Peace: Sketching the Terrain. *Peace Through Commerce*, 5–27.

United Nations Sustainable Development. (2018). *Peace, Justice and Strong Institutions - United Nations Sustainable Development*. Retrieved from www.un.org/sustainabledevelopment/pea ce-justice/ [Accessed June 1, 2018].

Zandvliet, L., and Anderson, M. B. (2009). *Getting it Right: Making Corporate-community Relations Work*. Sheffield: Greenleaf Publishing in association with GSE Research.

10

LARGE-SCALE INVESTMENT MANAGEMENT

The peace potential of a sovereign wealth fund

Gregory M. Reichberg and Henrik Syse

Introduction[1]

The literature on business and peace that has emerged over the last decade has focused on the role exercised by corporations – most especially multinationals – in fragile and conflict-affected settings. By their presence and operations, do these corporations exacerbate conflict? If so, what steps can they take to eliminate or at least minimize such an outcome? Beyond this avoidance of harm, can firms become positive contributors to conflict prevention and peacebuilding? It has been rightly emphasized that firms will follow up on these questions only when top management and corporate boards understand that their fiduciary responsibility demands this of them. But often left out of the equation is the role of corporate *owners*. Management and boards ultimately view themselves as being at the service of a company's owners. If the owners remain uncommitted to a business and peace agenda, or only passively support it, how likely is it that decisive action will be taken on a company level?

It is in this respect that a fundamental challenge arises. Most multinational companies have many individual owners. Each owns a small fraction of the whole. Occasionally a very wealthy individual owns a large share of a single company (as in the case of Bill Gates and Microsoft). Nowadays, however, such large ownership positions are typically held by institutional entities that pool and manage the holdings of many thousands of investors. While individually most small investors have little say in how the firm is run, what goals it should pursue and by what means, the large-scale institutional investors can be agenda setters. Whether such investors take seriously the linkage between business and peace will often impact on (or has the potential to impact on) the commitment shown by corporate boards and top management to adopt conflict-sensitive practices in fragile, conflict-affected settings.

Some institutional investors are for-profit entities that manage the individual holdings for a fee. The largest of these pool financial resources in excess of a trillion dollars, as with the firm BlackRock, whose CEO, in a letter addressed to the companies in its portfolio, has advocated for an increased attention to the social impact of business.[2] Other institutional investors are public entities that have responsibility for the management of government pension funds or the accumulated wealth of a state, as in what are nowadays referred to as "sovereign wealth funds."

In what follows, we examine Norway's sovereign wealth fund – currently the largest in the world – to understand what role it could play within the business and peace arena. The reason for this choice is threefold. First of all, the fund has ethical guidelines covering both active ownership and exclusion of companies, and is often seen as a leading exponent of responsible investments. Secondly, it serves as a good example of a *global investor*, with a large and diversified portfolio, and for this reason provides a useful window on the challenges of finding oneself, directly or indirectly, as an owner of companies in all kinds of environments, including conflict zones. And thirdly, although adherence to ethical norms is integral to its stated mandate, it does not frame itself as a specialized SRI (Socially Responsible Investment) fund. Hence, it avoids the bias of analyzing a fund that fills a special niche and thus hardly would be representative of the broader investment culture and universe.

The Norwegian sovereign wealth fund, formally called the "Norwegian Pension Fund Global," is managed by a separate unit – Norges Bank Investment Management (NBIM) – within the Norwegian Central Bank.[3] To the extent that NBIM engages with individual companies, some of which operate in conflict settings, it is possible (at least in theory) to track how NBIM, through such engagements, can have an impact on peace. In this respect it should be emphasized that NBIM impacts on peace only indirectly, in the measure that it modifies the behavior of its companies (i.e. those in which it has an ownership stake) that operate in conflict zones. Compared to these companies, NBIM is one step removed, so to speak, from involvement in actual conflict. In other words NBIM acts in conflict settings *mediately*, through the immediate action of its investee companies. And as a fractional owner of such firms, its influence will be partial only, and is consequently often difficult to trace out in actual fact. Because NBIM has on average a 2 percent ownership stake in so many individual firms worldwide, the *depth* of its influence on any single firm will be limited. Inversely, because NBIM's reach is so wide, extending to thousands of firms worldwide, the *breadth* of its influence is potentially enormous. The same could be said of other large investment funds, whether public or private.

In addition to the reasons already given above, our interest in studying NBIM stems first of all from the recognition that the already extensive literature on business and peace has had an "overwhelming focus on business corporations (firms) rather than the hugely influential banking, financial, and insurance sectors (funds),"[4] and, consequently, there is a need to rectify this imbalance. And secondly, because of their financial clout, the largest of these investment vehicles – whether holding companies such as Berkshire Hathaway, pension funds such as CALPERS, or sovereign wealth funds such as Norway's – have the potential to impact on peace, both peace writ little and peace writ large, by virtue of the distribution of its investments, and by virtue of the policies that they set (or fail to set) for the thousands of companies under their ownership.

NBIM does not expressly cite the promotion of "conflict-sensitive" business practice as an express aim of these procedures, but we would argue that they *de facto* approximate this result. This chapter attempts to render this linkage to peace more explicit, and thereby to show how the "responsible investment" procedures that have been implemented by NBIM have relevance to the research agenda of business and peace.

Because NBIM has yet to recognize the fostering of conflict-sensitive business practice is implicit in its mandate, it is difficult to identify how its past actions may have impacted on peace. The approach elucidated in this chapter is, by contrast, forward-looking, insofar as our aim is to determine whether the fund *could* impact on peace. Does the mandate of the fund allow for the adoption of conflict-sensitive business practice in its investment decisions and the management of its assets? The supposition behind this case study is that the Fund *could* have such an impact. Consequently, we examine how the various structures, processes, and mechanisms within NBIM can be marshaled to such an end.

Context overview

NBIM has increasingly emphasized over the past 15 years a commitment to fostering sustainable business practices on the part of the companies in its portfolio. The avoidance of negative social impacts by companies that NBIM invests in – particularly with respect to human rights violations – forms a core aspect of NBIM's stated mandate as a "universal investor." By NBIM's definition, a "universal investor" has a long-term horizon with investments in diversified industries and regions. Such an investor is vulnerable to market failures across sectors and over time, such as disruptions caused by violent conflict, trade wars, or climate change, due to its widely diversified investments.[5] Other more narrowly invested funds may designate such risks as "externalities" over which companies and funds have limited sway or control. The "universal investor" instead views these risks as core issues affecting the long-term stability and profitability of its holdings.

NBIM emphasizes that its management principles are:

> based on ... considerations of good corporate governance [as well as] environmental and social conditions ... in accordance with internationally recognized principles and standards such as the UN Global Compact, the OECD's Principles of Corporate Governance and the OECD's Guidelines for Multinational Enterprises.[6]

In NBIM's mandate document it is said, moreover, that NBIM "shall actively contribute to the development of relevant international standards in the area of responsible management."[7]

As NBIM frequently reviews its own priorities and updates the expectations it communicates to the firms in its portfolio, it is conceivable that in the future it will establish a closer and more explicit linkage between beneficial social impacts and peace. In thereby taking steps to discourage firms in its portfolio from causing harmful social impacts, NBIM could underscore the special care that must be taken when firms operate in conflict-prone and other fragile settings. Issuing guidelines for such conflict-sensitive business practice, and perhaps even divesting from firms that fail to observe acceptable practice in this domain, could eventually become part of NBIM's mandate. The current case study explores the possibilities of such an approach within NBIM's current institutional framework.

This case study was conducted on a fourfold basis. (i) First, it involved review of documents on NBIM's website www.nbim.no and pertaining to the Council on Ethics for the Norwegian Pension Fund Global (http://etikkradet.no/en/counci l-on-ethics). (ii) Second, two interviews of 1–2 hours each, were conducted with key personnel from NBIM. The first was with an employee who has worked at the bank on active-ownership issues for well over ten years. Another interview was with a member of the bank's five-member divestment committee ("Council on Ethics"). (iii) Third, information was gathered from a one-hour closed seminar ("The Government Pension Fund Global in a Foreign Policy Context Constraints and Opportunities for the Norwegian Sovereign Wealth Fund") at PRIO (February 9, 2017), with Yngve Slyngstad, CEO of NBIM. (iv) Fourth, this study benefited from Henrik Syse's experience as head of the NBIM's Corporate Governance unit, from 2005 to 2007, and his subsequent work as an advisor to the Corporate Governance unit from 2008 to 2009, where he contributed toward developing principles and practices for the active ownership of the Fund.

Basic facts about the Fund

Despite its name, the Government Pension Fund Global is not actually a pension fund.[8] The Fund's capital is derived not from the contributions of future pensioners (nor is it earmarked for their benefit, see note 4), but is derived from a share in the royalties that are collected by the government from offshore oil and gas concessions (hence it was previously called the "Petroleum Fund of Norway").[9] Close behind Norway's fund in size are the sovereign wealth funds of Abu Dhabi and China, with Kuwait's fund in fourth place.[10]

The Fund is owned by the Norwegian Finance Ministry "on behalf of the Norwegian people." The Fund's investment strategy is set by the Ministry. Management of the Fund is delegated to NBIM, which functions as an autonomous unit within the Norwegian Central Bank.[11] In addition to selecting investments for purchase (or sale), NBIM is tasked, *inter alia*, with establishing "ethical guidelines"[12] for "responsible management" of the Fund's assets, based on guidelines set by the Finance Ministry, based on decisions in Parliament. In this connection, NBIM is not merely a passive recipient of instructions from the Finance Ministry; it has been given the authority to advise the Ministry on all relevant aspects of its investment policy for the Fund, and to specify and execute the enactment of several more general guidelines from the Norwegian government.[13]

All of the fund's holdings are located abroad, "to avoid overheating the Norwegian economy and to shield it from the effects of oil price fluctuations."[14] Its mandate requires that NBIM should emphasize "the long-term horizon for the management of the investment portfolio" and that "the investment portfolio shall be broadly diversified across the markets included in the investment universe."[15] In what follows, we consider, as already mentioned, only the equity investments of the Fund; the responsible investment principles that NBIM identifies are for the most part directed at this part of its portfolio.[16] Equity investments currently represent approximately two-thirds of the fund's total value.

The average equity stake per company is 2 percent, although in some instances the fund's holding amounts to 10 percent of the total publicly traded shares. The fund owns 1.3 percent of all companies listed worldwide, and 2.3 percent of companies listed in Europe. Many of its stock holdings are in large multinational firms that operate far afield from the countries in which they are based. Current top holdings include Alphabet, Apple, Microsoft, Nestle, ExxonMobil, Royal Dutch Shell, Johnson & Johnson, Novartis, and BlackRock. The Fund has equity positions in emerging markets, including Nigeria, Uganda, Tanzania, Peru, Sri Lanka, and Indonesia. A total of 77 countries are represented in the Fund's equity investments. Indirectly through the multinational companies it is invested in, many more countries are represented.

How NBIM defines "responsible investment"

"Responsible management" is the heading used for Chapter 2 of NBIM's mandate document. Another document employs the alternative terminology of "responsible investment."[17] As employed by NBIM, these terms are together intended to convey two different functions, namely:

- Safeguarding the economic value of the assets under NBIM's control, i.e. exercising financial probity in the selection of stocks, assuming moderate risk while at the same time seeking to maximize return on investments. Selection of stocks is done both actively (in-house and sub-contracted to outside firms) and through indexing, the emphasis being on the latter.[18]
- Being an "active owner," namely voting in shareholder meetings, holding meetings with corporate management, exercising due diligence and generally holding corporate boards accountable for the management of negative externalities that arise in the course of these business activities. This includes tracking the risk profile of companies within its portfolio, and taking remedial action when necessary, including divestment.

Both functions are integral to NBIM's conception of "responsible investment," but linkage between them is, on our view, less clear. The two are joined, for instance, in its assessment of "long-term risk and return," which takes into account market and capital risks, but also risks associated with environmental, social, and governance (ESG) factors.[19] A firm could be removed from the Fund's portfolio because of what is perceived to be excessive risk with regard to one or several of these factors. In so doing, the stated goal is to preserve the Fund's capital in the long term. NBIM thus "views risk-based divestment as a tool to reduce our exposure to risks that we believe could have a negative impact on the portfolio over time."[20] Further elucidating this point, NBIM affirms that "failure to manage risks related to social and governance issues could result in operational disruptions, financial penalties, loss of contracts, and reputational damage to companies."[21] Working from the assumption that the profitability of the fund's investments will depend, over time, on "well-functioning, legitimate, and efficient markets," NBIM perceives an inherent linkage between a "good long-term return" and "sustainable development in economic, environmental and social terms."[22]

In 2016, "[s]ector assessments and company analysis resulted in risk-based divestment from 23 companies." In addition, a number of other companies were placed under observation for possible divestment on these grounds. In contrast to purely ethical exclusions (discussed below on p. 000), NBIM does not publish a list of the companies that are included in the category of "risk-based divestment."[23] Management appears to express a preference for this approach, stating that "as an integrated part of our investment management" it is "more flexible than formal decisions by Norges Banks's Executive Board to exclude companies from the investment universe."[24]

On the other hand, the two functions mentioned above (safeguarding the Fund's economic value and exercising active ownership) sometimes diverge. This can happen when companies in the portfolio are thought to be engaged in wrongdoing (direct or indirect) or are otherwise deemed to have fallen short of important norms. Such violations are treated under the heading of "ethical exclusions."[25] In these cases, the decision to divest (or exclude from prospective investment) is made on grounds wholly apart from the financial impact on the Fund's returns. If a firm is suspected to be in violation of the stated rules ("Guidelines for observation set by the Ministry of Finance"), irrespective of its expected profitability or size, it will be placed "under observation" or excluded from the Fund. NBIM calculates that the Fund missed out on an additional 1.1 percent gain on its equity portfolio over the past 11 years through excluding stocks on ethical grounds.[26]

Two tracks toward divestment

NBIM thus recognizes two tracks toward divestment based on ESG failures. One track is focused on risks that can adversely impact on a firm's expected profitability. The larger the firm (and the size of the position held by the fund) the more likely it is that NBIM will scrutinize its performance along these parameters. Similarly, for "substantial investments," dialogue with management with the aim of applying pressure on the firm to change will often be preferred over exclusion.[27] Analysis and decisions about "risk-based divestment" on ESG grounds are carried out under the supervision of NBIM's "Investment Ownership Committee" (in contrast to market, credit, and counterparty risks, that are handled within NBIM's "Investment Risk Committee").

By contrast, the other divestment track is premised on violations of the ethical norms recognized by the Finance Ministry based on several Acts of Parliament. As this does not account for considerations of profitability and value to the Fund, the size of the holding is, in principle, less relevant than in the previous case. Analysis of potential ethical exclusions is handled by an independent Council on Ethics (five sitting members and a secretariat). The Council issues recommendations that the Executive Board of NBIM is, in theory, at liberty to follow (or not). The fact that these recommendations are based expressly on Finance Ministry guidelines (issued from Acts of Parliament) makes it likely that recommendations put forward by the Council on Ethics will be followed or at least that these recommendations will lead to active intervention vis-à-vis the companies in question. When it becomes clear that an ethical breach is likely to persist for systemic reasons – such as when a firm manufactures products blacklisted in the ethical guidelines of the fund – the divestment recommendation will occur more or less automatically. In cases, however, where NBIM sees a likelihood that engagement can induce the firm to change its behavior, it will be placed ("under observation") on a watch-list. Usually this is combined will often be combined with a process of active engagement whereby NBIM dialogues with the firm through correspondence and meetings.

The Ministry of Finance's criteria in its "Guidelines for Observation and Exclusion"[28] (based, as already noted, on Acts of Parliament) from the Fund are of two kinds: product-based and conduct-based. The product-based exclusions ban from the Fund's portfolio firms that (i) manufacture tobacco products, (ii) produce or sell prohibited weapons (weapons, e.g. cluster munitions that through normal use violate fundamental humanitarian principles), or (iii) sell military materials to specified countries. The product-based criteria result in exclusion regardless of the amount this production (or sale) represents within the firm's overall business.[29] In other words, should a large proportion of a firm's business be devoted to acceptable activities, engagement in a proportionately small amount of prohibited arms trade (and even if lawful according to the applicable domestic jurisdiction) will nonetheless result in exclusion. Moreover, if a violation is documented, there will be no provision for placing the firm under observation. It will automatically be excluded from the fund, although if later it sheds the said activity, re-admission will be possible.

Conduct-based exclusions are of considerably broader scope. On this set of criteria, companies can be excluded (or placed under observation) where there is "an unacceptable risk of grossly unethical corporate conduct" that contributes "to serious or systematic human rights violations, serious violations of the rights of individuals in situations of war or conflict, severe environmental damage, gross corruption or other serious violations of fundamental ethical norms."[30] An example of exclusion on these grounds would be the Fund's divestment of its holdings in Kosmos Energy in 2016 on the rationale that the company was engaged by Moroccan authorities to explore for oil deposits offshore the disputed territory of Western Sahara.[31] According to our discussion with a member of the Council on Ethics, Kosmos was excluded, rather than being placed on observation, because it was unable to meet the basic condition that would be needed to avoid exclusion: public dialogue with the Polisario, which the UN takes to be the authorized representative of the people of Western Sahara, a dialogue that the Moroccan authorities refused to allow.[32] Going back a decade, the first firm to be excluded on social, conduct-related grounds (after a recommendation from the Council) was Walmart, which was removed from NBIM's portfolio in 2006 due to concerns over human rights, and more specifically workers' rights, in several of its third-world operations.[33]

Avoidance of negative social impacts versus promotion of good

NBIM does not engage in positive-impact investing, with the exception of its special allocation for businesses in the environmental technology field.[34] In other words, this one exception aside, the Fund's investments are not steered toward industries or regions that are thought to be especially beneficial from a social point of view. No allocation of financial resources is set aside, for instance, to support private-sector growth in impoverished settings. The rationale for not engaging in social impact investing is that financial resources have been set aside for this purpose within other Norwegian government programs, most prominently Norfund.[35] In this respect NBIM deems that its mandate does not allow the Fund to be placed at the service of "political objectives" as formulated, say, by the Norwegian Ministry of Foreign Affairs. The Fund's capital is not directed to (or diverted from) specific investments in order to achieve determinate policy goals.

Managing social risks

The Fund is expected to concentrate exclusively on its mandate of accumulating wealth for "future generations."[36] In measuring the broader societal impact of its investments, NBIM as the Fund's manager is concerned primarily with the avoidance of harm, not with any broader, positive societal agenda, although several of the bank's ESG initiatives are clearly related to broader societal agendas.

The bank's main mechanism in the ESG area is its active engagement (also termed "active ownership") mechanism, by which NBIM works with the companies under its ownership to steer them away from activities that harm social well-being, insofar as these activities endanger the long-term accumulation of wealth for future generations. In addition, comes the exclusionary mechanism by which the Fund divests itself of companies that are deemed to be engaged in norm violations. The latter mechanism, however, is not geared toward safeguarding the accumulation of wealth, but is grounded directly in the fund's ethical guidelines. As was discussed above, both mechanisms are managed by NBIM, the first by its Investment Ownership Committee, and the second by the Council on Ethics, which operates as an autonomous unit within NBIM.[37] These two units were established by an Act of Parliament in 2004. At that time, the occurrence of large-scale corporate fraud – Enron and World Com were the most visible cases – led to calls for enhanced governance procedures within corporations, and for tightened shareholder oversight.

We now examine the bank's active-engagement policy, since this is of the most immediate relevance to our task here, namely, to understand what role NBIM could play as shareholder vis-à-vis questions of social conflict and peace.

Active engagement with corporate troublemakers

Under the supervision of its Investment Ownership Committee, NBIM tracks non-financial data – or what we can broadly call ESG data – on the firms within its equity portfolio. This includes "qualitative and quantitative information on material governance and sustainability topics"[38] According to a list provided by NBIM, this includes, *inter alia*, the following topics: biodiversity, carbon, climate change, water, child labor, corruption, health and safety, and human capital.[39] The data itself is gathered from a variety of sources. External data providers, academic institutions, and NGOs are mentioned, with NBIM's additional comment that stakeholders are encouraged "to provide non-financial information they believe may be of relevance to our investments." Based on the information gathered from these sources, NBIM carries out "focus area assessments" across different markets (in selected countries or regions) and business sectors. The process begins with an examination of corporate disclosure in one or more of the five focus areas selected by NBIM as special areas of its competence and concern: children's rights, water management, climate change, and human rights and tax transparency (although the fund is also free to engage companies on other ESG issues).[40] Within these four focus areas, "Expectation documents" that outline NBIM's expectations and principles have been published and distributed. Companies are more generally urged to include ESG factors in their reporting. Although it is said that NBIM adopts a "systematic approach to risk monitoring,"[41] it is nonetheless made clear that attention is especially directed to those "sectors and markets" that "particularly exposed to [ESG] risks."[42] NBIM's risk monitoring also includes the drafting of reports and briefs on specific companies. Sixty-four such assessments were produced in 2016, distributed across the three overarching thematic areas of ESG risks. Reports are of two kinds: *Material ownership reports* elaborate on the risks (both short- and long-term) faced by firms in which the Fund has a "significant ownership share,"[43] while *company reports* provide a more detailed look at these "business drivers and risk factors." *Briefs* typically focus on particular "incidents" at the company level, e.g. allegations of corruption, fraud, or violations of human rights.[44] These company reports and briefs are not made available to the public.

As indicative of the approach taken, NBIM notes[45] that in 2016 it carried out 2,392 company assessments under the focus areas (representing 36 percent of the equity portfolio's value at the end of the year). Most of these assessments concerned climate change (1,238), water management (600) and children's rights (554).[46] In the 2017 report on responsible investments, which was made available shortly before the finalization of this article, 2,902 assessments were carried out, of which 1,701 concerned climate change, 600 water management, and 601 children's rights.[47]

In 2016 "human rights" was added as a fourth focus area, and in 2017, a fifth was added, namely tax and transparency. Specific engagement figures for the two latter (human rights and tax and transparency) are not listed in the 2017 report, although it is clear that the "expectation documents" on these issues have been shared with a number of relevant companies, and furthermore, many of the children's rights engagements directly pertain to human rights more broadly.

The company assessments provide a springboard for NBIM's dialogue with corporate management and boards. Problematic issues ("red flags") that have been identified in the assessments will be addressed in these meetings. This engagement with corporations is not, however, limited to discussion of findings from the focus area assessments. Also taken up in these meetings are issues that have come to NBIM's attention by other means, for instance through media reports of corporate activities in or around setting of armed conflict (the treatment of Syrian refugees in apparel supply chains in Turkey is one such example).[48] In sum, of a total of 3,790 meetings held in 2016 (with 1,589 companies), nearly half involved ESG issues.[49]

In selecting companies for "governance and sustainability" dialogues, NBIM prioritizes on "the basis of portfolio holding value and ownership share." It does so with the goal of "maximizing" its "influence as a shareholder." NBIM does not, however, view itself as an "activist investor," meaning an investor that builds a stake in a company so as "to directly influence the board of directors and management to bring about a particular corporate goal."[50]

Of the examples given of corporate dialogue (which may involve only one or more single meetings or numerous meetings over several years) two might be cited here, as they are of immediate interest to conflict-related aspects of investment. First, NBIM recounts how it has had discussions over a prolonged period with ENI and Royal Dutch Shell regarding oil spills from their facilities in the Niger Delta. These discussions include the setting of goals, monitoring of progress, and company commitment to make reduction of spills, including those due to sabotage, theft and operational failures, a priority. Another dialogue has been pursued with AngloGold Ashanti about environmental damage caused by mining activities (now suspended due to technical problems) at its Obuasi mine in Ghana. NBIM's monitoring efforts focus exclusively, we have been told, on staunching the environmental harm that results from past mining. Although it is acknowledged that riots and other negative social impacts (widespread unemployment in a nearby city consequent upon company layoffs) are also part of the wider picture, these are not taken up in the company dialogue, which, as noted, is restricted to the environmental issues.[51] As was explained to us in an interview, when NBIM takes up a case, it is nearly always in response to a specific complaint. In the subsequent dialogue, the company is given clear instructions about what it must do in order to avoid divestment (the three companies in question had in effect been placed on a divestment watch-list). Even though wider problems might very well come to light in the course of the ensuing investigation, in the absence of a framework with a wider mandate, NBIM is reluctant to take up these additional issues, on grounds that, without such a framework, demands placed on the company would be hard to operationalize. In every company dialogue, "company specific ownership goals are set;" progress is measured "over the duration of a company engagement."[52] This also makes it easier for the company and its board to know with more accuracy what the investor expects of it. Formulating instead broader societal goals and wishes, for instance related to peaceful development, could easily be seen as too fuzzy or overwhelming, whereas engagement around a tightly defined agenda is in principle much easier to manage.

It should also be noted that NBIM takes special care not to be viewed as a political actor that functions on behalf of the Norwegian Government, a point emphasized by our interviewees. Going very far in addressing social ills and politically controversial states of affairs without a clear "business case" or a very concrete complaint would entail the risk of being seen *not* as a financial investor and a concerned owner of companies, but rather as an activist arm of Norwegian foreign policy. Arguably, the Fund's legitimacy and standing within the community of financial institutions depend on it not being thus understood and interpreted.

Expectation documents

Beyond communicating with companies through individualized meetings, NBIM also seeks to exercise wider influence by producing the "Expectation documents" that were briefly mentioned above. These are communicated to "the chairpersons of [NBIM's] 500 largest company investments."[53] (It is unclear why these documents are not sent to all of the companies represented in the Fund's portfolio, but this presumably pertains to relevance.) These documents are "aimed primarily at company boards." In communicating these expectations, the goal is to emphasize how for NBIM, precisely insofar as it is a "financial investor" it is important that "boards assume responsibility for corporate strategy concerning sustainability issues." Some of these documents have been written at NBIM's own initiative and at least one at the instigation of the Norwegian parliament.[54]

As indicated above, five expectation documents have thus far been produced: on water management, climate change strategy, children's rights, human rights, and tax and transparency.[55] The two last-mentioned are the most recent to appear in the series (2016 and 2017).[56] In what is perhaps the most explicit mention in NBIM's publications of the special situation faced by companies operating in conflict-prone and fragile environments, it is stated in the human rights document that these expectations "are especially relevant for companies with direct operations, supply chains or other business relationships in high-risk sectors, high-risk geographical areas, or otherwise high-risk operational environments."[57] The document urges that human rights considerations be integrated into (i) business strategy and planning, (ii) risk management, (iii) disclosure and reporting, and (iv), engagement with stakeholders and grievance reporting.

In our interview with a member of the Council on Ethics, we asked about the procedures that are used to identify targets for exclusion (or observation) on human rights grounds. It was explained that these are very similar to NBIM's procedures outlined above: sector and market analysis, with a focus on industries or places where the risk of ethical violations is heightened. In addition to research conducted by the Council's secretariat (often using outside consultants), information is regularly received from external organizations, including NGOs and media. It was admitted that some sectors receive considerably more attention than others. Financial companies are hardly ever investigated for possible violations. In this connection, we were told that providing financing to producers of prohibited items or of activities in prohibited places (say of settlement construction in the West Bank, or of oil exploration in the Western Sahara) was not itself deemed a violation of the ethical guidelines. A violation would arise only if a further condition were added, for instance if the lender to a settlement builder were to receive government subsidies with the express intent of facilitating population growth of one group over another in the specified area.

Regarding the very limited oversight of financial companies vis-à-vis potential social risks (the same does not hold for governance and corruption risks, which are more attended to), we asked whether the Council tracks the holdings of large conglomerates such as Berkshire Hathaway (in which the Fund does have a significant position). Should such a conglomerate include in its portfolio firms engaged in prohibited activities, would it too be excluded from the Fund? The response was that this sort of case was not currently being examined by the Council, both because such financial intermediaries are several steps removed from potential wrongdoing, and for reasons of economy and practicality, as the Council lacks the resources to examine all the relevant possibilities, hence it must prioritize. Although the number of companies included in the Fund's portfolio has increased threefold since the Council was established in 2004, the size of its secretariat has remained more or less the same.

Social risk and conflict

As noted above, in exercising "responsible investment," NBIM identifies three sorts of risks that fall within its mandate to manage: governance risks (including corruption), environmental risks, and social risks, often abbreviated, ESG. All three can have possible linkages to conflict, although the third has in this connection the greatest salience. In its public documentation the fund does not specifically highlight risks associated with armed conflict or social unrest. Our interviews indicate that when NBIM engages with firms on, say, the environmental risks associated with their operations, it will typically exclude from consideration the social conflicts that might arise from these environmental harms (as in the example of the Obuasi mine given above). This being the case, it would seem then that the category of "social risk" affords the most plausible opening for NBIM to include conflict-sensitive business practice among the expectations that it communicates to corporate boards.

At present, however, "social risk" is the least developed of the three categories of risk that NBIM has attempted to operationalize in its responsible investment mandate.

From our experience and analysis, there are no publicly disclosed cases in which NBIM has explicitly included social conflict and peaceful development as points of engagement, apart from the Kosmos exclusion, mentioned above, which does refer to the risk of increased conflict in West Sahara. In other cases, for instance, in the engagement process from 2007 onwards with a number of major cotton-seed manufacturers active in India, most prominently Monsanto and Bayer,[58] NBIM stuck to a children's-rights agenda. Wider social goals of reducing tension in society, addressing poverty-related unrest and the risk of increased instability and civil conflict, were not addressed as part of the engagement process. The reasoning, which seems to be echoed by the way in which NBIM still operationalizes company engagement today, is that narrower and more concise agendas help ensure more tangible results and more constructive dialogue. However, if the impact of companies on civil conflict were to be more explicitly addressed as a social risk in, for instance, one of NBIM's Expectation Documents, NBIM would also be obliged to formulate more specific agenda points that could be raised vis-à-vis companies operating in conflict zones or having a direct influence on conflict dynamics. These authors have earlier explicated how that could be done, using the ethical framework of "double effect," namely an analysis focused on the moral (and often legal) responsibility that agents have for the side-effects that flow from their actions.[59]

There are, in our view, several ways in which NBIM could incorporate questions of social and armed conflict in its engagement processes as an active investor. Among these could be the following:

1. NBIM could engage in dialogue with companies about how they can reduce the risk of conflict by making sound decisions about hiring and the localization of installations. In several countries and regions where multinational companies operate – Sri Lanka, India, Nigeria, and Ethiopia could be cited – relations between ethnic and religious groups are often tense in some areas, and frequently erupt into shorter or longer periods of conflict. Businesses can play a role in reducing such tensions by, for instance, placing their operations in some areas rather than others in order to forestall perceptions of injustice, by hiring across ethnic divides, and not least importantly by engaging with research environments and NGOs in making such decisions, ensuring that exigencies societal peace are duly taken into consideration.
2. Closely related to this first point, NBIM could make a more concerted effort to understand drivers of conflict as well as conflict trends in countries and regions where their companies operate and ensure that such knowledge informs company dialogues.
3. NBIM is already committed to fighting corruption. How corrupt practices fuel conflict and lead to illicit financial flows that benefit conflict entrepreneurs and actors could explicitly be incorporated into its dialogue with companies, industry standard setters, and political authorities.

4.   And finally, NBIM could do more to track how companies in its portfolio directly or indirectly support parties to conflict, either through material or political support, and express expectations toward how such support should be transparent and should not contribute to human rights abuse resulting from prolonged conflict.

Such engagement would have to be balanced against the need for NBIM not to be seen as a political actor engaged in executing Norwegian foreign policy. However, all of the concerns listed above pertain to managing financial risk for a universal investor whose long-term interests, financial as well as ethical, are strongly influenced by the presence of social conflict. We believe that NBIM could help formulate expectations related to these questions in the form of an expectations document that explicitly addresses social conflict and peaceful development.

This leads to some important quandaries and challenges, many of them related to mechanisms already in place at NBIM.

Firstly, the Kosmos case could serve as an example of conflict-related and human rights-related concerns coming together to form the basis of engagement with a company or its exclusions from the Fund's portfolio. Firms whose conduct is fueling or exacerbating conflict in ways that are empirically verifiable over time, in any of the four ways outlined above (or in other ways), should be singled out. Some would fall directly under categories already present in the current ethical guidelines and expectation documents, such as human rights and children's rights, while others would be more closely and exclusively related to armed (and social) conflict *per se*. In these cases, it will be hard to know exactly where to draw the line between active and continued engagement on the one hand and actual exclusion on the other, but that is the case for most such issues, not just this within this thematic area. The point is that conflict-related and human rights-related (and others) concerns are often closely interrelated, and that such issues will have to be approached through a range of mechanisms, including active engagement and in some cases exclusion.

Secondly, the sensitive politics of taking sides in conflict must be addressed and tackled, not least for a government-owned fund. In settings such as the Israeli-Palestinian conflict, opting for some policies over others – for instance, labeling corporate actions, such as building factories in a certain areas, as creating more conflict, and thus engaging with or withdrawing from companies that do this – will almost unavoidably be seen by one of the two (or more) sides as unfair. The status of large parts of the West Bank and Gaza as occupied or not, the placement of Israeli settlements, and the call among some parties for boycotts (not least of Israel) are cases in point and illustrate how difficult it is for an investor to address such issues, even if only quietly, without becoming *de facto* a political player. Adhering and referring to the broadest and least controversial interpretations of international law in such engagements will be a good rule of thumb, but in some cases, one would have to be more concrete and specific in order constructively to sort out the relevant issues. When companies operate legally in an area that is rife with conflict, and where they have hiring policies that verifiably or very likely contribute to social unrest because some groups are always excluded or discriminated against, special care must be taken not to exacerbate the situation further. Large-scale investors who seek to address such issues fairly and clearly, but who understandably wish to avoid alienating segments of the community, or the fanning of political controversy will recognize what a daunting task this is likely to be. But often it is one well worth undertaking, and indeed sometimes required by a basic concern for justice.

Thirdly, an investor needs to look beyond its immediate holdings to the complex supply chains that underlie and interact with them and that may have a substantial influence on a conflict environment. Businesses can, after all, fuel and sustain conflict by contributing financially and politically to key conflict entrepreneurs – from traffickers and smugglers to governments – often with the aim of greater and more inexpensive market access. The companies whose shares are owned by large international investors will often have explicit policies prohibiting such collaboration with corrupt, conflict-fueling actors, yet they will, not least through their supply chain, often contribute materially to the activities of such actors.[60] An investor approach to business and peace would have to take such a broader view at the interactions and networks of its company holdings.

Finally, conflict settings are often complex, with local perceptions and culturally based expectations influencing what creates tension and violence.[61] If investors are to ask the right and relevant questions of its companies about whether their operations are conflict-sensitive or not, such local perceptions and expectations must be taken into account. Large-scale investors are arguably well-placed to ask such questions, since they will customarily have holdings in several, competing companies within such settings, and may use its ability to maintain dialogue with all of them also to address such common, complex concerns, and pressure whole sectors (and, as noted above, supply chains) to become more aware of them and to tackle them prudently and sensitively.

We have now listed some salient points where investors in general, and large-scale investors such as pension funds, and sovereign wealth funds in particular, can play a role in addressing violent disruptions and conflicts that could materially influence the operations of the companies in their portfolios – in the short as well as long run – as well as create major legal and ethical problems. The list is not meant to be exhaustive, but to indicate how an active owner could contribute to raising more awareness and encouraging or even demanding more conflict-sensitive business practices. NBIM is clearly a case in point, with its broad reach and its exclusionary as well as active-engagement policies in place, yet it is faced with the dilemma of tackling such issues without becoming a *de facto* political actor, thereby risking its independence and its standing as an investor.

Conclusion

NBIM has at its disposal advanced mechanisms for addressing social risk, not least through its work on active ownership. Given that fact, NBIM could clearly address several conflict-related questions vis-à-vis the relevant companies in its portfolio.

Examples would be a company's political or moral support for warring regimes, its employment (or non-employment) of individuals or groups involved in conflict, its profiteering off armed conflict, or its material support for or dependence on a particular side in an armed conflict.

Currently, as is clear from the above, NBIM does not thus engage companies directly on questions of peace and conflict, unless such engagement can be subsumed under another, more limited goal of corporate engagement, for instance, the maintenance of human rights standards. However, given our findings above, it is by no means impossible that the fund *could* have a separate policy – for instance in the form of a new Expectation Document – dealing with contributions to societal peace and the peaceful resolution of conflict. In fact, we would argue that such a course of action could be highly beneficial, as it would highlight the importance that a major financial actor places on conflict-sensitive business practice.

This could admittedly be complicated by the seemingly political nature of such engagement, and the accompanying difficulty of arguing that such engagement would fall squarely within NBIM's mandate to promote the accumulation of wealth for the sake of future generations. Yet, given the high social and often also environmental and governance-related costs of armed conflict, it could surely be argued that "NBIM Expectations" toward companies in its portfolio dealing with contributions to peaceful conflict resolution, or at least insisting on avoiding active contributions to armed conflict, would dovetail well and logically with the Expectation Documents and more generally the ESG engagement already enacted and carried out by NBIM. (Whether one could also envisage further *exclusion criteria* related to armed conflict and peace is a question we will not take a stand on here, given our emphasis on NBIM and its active-ownership policy.) Should NBIM issue an expectation document on conflict-sensitive business practice, this would become the basis for dialogue with companies that stand in need of improvement in this domain, and it could serve as an important standard or example for other large funds to follow.

Notes

1 This chapter builds on a case study that was developed as part of a project called "Engaging the Business Community as a New Peace Building Actor" undertaken by CDA Collaborative learning Projects (CDA), Peace Research Institute Oslo (PRIO), and the Africa Centre for Dispute Settlement (ACDS) at Stellenbosch University. Each case study tells the story of an intentional effort by a business actor (or a set of actors) to affect the dynamics of conflict and peace in a specific locale (whether a city, country, or region) with discernible outcomes in relation to these dynamics. Most of the case studies examine actions undertaken by single companies, although also taken into consideration within the project are some collective initiatives, for instance the Colombian Coffee Growers Association, insofar as a unified process of decision-making and agency is traceable to them. In the present case study, this order is inverted, because NBIM is not a company, but a part-owner of companies through its stock portfolio.
2 www.nytimes.com/2018/01/15/business/dealbook/blackrock-laurence-fink-letter.html.
3 Of late there has been a debate whether NBIM should be moved outside of the Central Bank, and established as an independent organization with its own board and culture that would be directly answerable to the Finance Ministry. www.aftenposten.no/

okonomi/i/m7VPl/Norges-Bank-svarer-tja-til-a-flytte-ut-Oljefondet. It is difficult to say at present whether such a change would impact on the fund's positioning vis-à-vis conflict sensitive business practice.

4 Jolyon Ford, "Perspectives on the Evolving 'Business and Peace' Debate," *Academy of Management Perspectives* 29.4 (2015): 451–460, at 253.

5 See, for instance, United Nations Finance Initiative (UNEP) & United Nations Principles of Responsible Investment (UN-PRI), 2011, *Universal Ownership: Why Environmental Externalities Matter to Institutional Investors* (available at www.unepfi.org/fileadmin/documents/universal_ownership_full.pdf), and Roger Urwin, 2011, "Pension Funds as Universal Owners," *Rotman International Journal of Pension Management*, vol. 4, no. 1 (available at www.calpers.ca.gov/docs/board-agendas/201507/full/item03-42.pdf).

6 "Management Mandate," chap. 2, section 2(3).

7 "Management Mandate," chap. 2, section 3(2).

8 It is called a "pension fund" insofar as the Fund's assets provide hypothetical financial backing for the Norwegian State's future pension obligations. As is, however, noted on NBIM's website "despite its name, the fund has no formal pension liabilities. No political decision has been made as to when the fund may be used to cover future pension costs, and the probability of large withdrawals from the fund is limited" (www.nbim.no/en/the-fund/about-the-fund).

9 The Fund's "capital inflow consists of all government petroleum revenue, net financial transactions related to petroleum activities, net of what is spent to balance the state's non-oil budget deficit … Fiscal policy is based on the guideline that over time the structural, non-oil budget deficit shall correspond to the expected real return on the fund, estimated at 3 percent" (www.nbim.no/en/the-fund/about-the-fund).

10 For sovereign wealth fund rankings, see www.swfinstitute.org/sovereign-wealth-fund-rankings. Kuwait's wealth fund would likely have been the largest in the world today were it not for the fact that much of its accrued capital was spent in 1991 to finance the coalition war-effort that ended the Iraqi occupation of the country.

11 For NBIM's mandate, see "Management Mandate," www.nbim.no/en/the-fund/governance-model/management-mandate.

12 www.nbim.no/en/transparency/submissions-to-ministry/2011-and-older/2008/the-consultation-on-the-ethical-guidelines-for-the-management-of-the-government-pension-fund–global.

13 "The Bank shall advise the Ministry on the investment strategy for the investment portfolio. Advice may be provided on the initiative of the Bank or on request from the Ministry," "Management Mandate," chap. 1 (1).

14 www.nbim.no/en/the-fund/about-the-fund.

15 "Management Mandate," chap. 2, section 2(2).

16 Apropos its fixed income holdings, NBIM does note that exclusions from the investment universe can be "established in the exceptional cases where the Ministry has barred such investments based on particularly large-scale UN sanctions or other international initiatives of a particularly large scale that are aimed at a specific country and where Norway supports the initiatives" (www.nbim.no/en/the-fund/governance-model/management-mandate). Similarly, with respect to "its management of the unlisted real estate portfolio, the Bank shall, within the environmental field, consider, among other matters, energy efficiency, water consumption and waste management" "Management Mandate," chap. 2, section 2(5)

17 The title of a report NBIM published in 2016. www.nbim.no/en/transparency/reports/2016/responsible-investment-2016.

18 "Indexing" is the process whereby a "portfolio [is] constructed to match or track the components of a market index, such as the Standard & Poor's 500 Index (S&P 500)" (*Investopedia*, www.investopedia.com/terms/i/indexfund.asp).

19 "Managing environmental, social and governance risks in the portfolio is an important aspect of safeguarding our investments" (*Responsible Investment Government Pension Fund Global/2016*, p. 13).

20 Ibid., p. 76.
21 Ibid., p. 81
22 Ibid., p. 89.
23 A representative sampling of rationales for this risk-based divestment appears in the 2016 report (ibid., pp. 80–81). Under the heading of "social and governance" the chart shows that in 2016 divestments 15 companies were excluded from the Fund on these grounds, 2 relating to "human rights issues in the seafood industry," 10 for "social and governance issues in the mining and metals industry," and 3 for corruption. Similar numbers (but without further differentiation within the category of "social and governance") are listed for the years 2015 and 2014. In the short discussion that follows we learn that the "social issues" (in distinction from "corruption") which can entail divestment include "health and safety, child labor and corruption" (p. 83). This is one of the few passages in the 2016 report that provides content to the "social issues" category.
24 Ibid., p. 77.
25 Ibid., section 4.3, pp. 84–87.
26 NBIM, *Return and Risk Report 2016*, p. 18 (www.nbim.no/contentassets/ 34b2d497426841208dbaadcc50c0d6f0/government-pension-fund-global—return-a nd-risk-2016.pdf). The losses in question are due primarily to the product-based exclusions (see below), which are calculated to have reduced the equity index by close to 1.9 percentage points; it is noted however that this reduction has been "mitigated by the positive contribution of the conduct-based exclusions, primarily the environmentally based exclusions of mining companies. In the same report it is further observed that "[t] he other exclusion criteria have had only a minor effect on the return on the benchmark index" (ibid., p. 18).
27 Ibid., "Where we have substantial investments in a company, dialogue may be a more suitable approach than divestment. Generally, we have better analytical coverage of, and contact with, our largest investments" (ibid., p. 76).
28 www.regjeringen.no/contentassets/7c9a364d2d1c474f8220965065695a4a/guidelines_observ ation_exclusion2016.pdf.
29 In 2016 a coal product criterion was added by the Finance Ministry. Unlike the other product-based criteria, the coal criterion is based on a proportional measure. Any firm that derives 30 percent or more of their revenue from thermal coal, or base more than 30 percent of their operations on thermal coal, will be placed on observation or excluded from the Fund.
30 *Return and Risk Report 2016*, p. 18.
31 www.ft.com/content/3ed3be5a-3d19-11e6-8716-a4a71e8140b0 and www.nbim.no/ en/transparency/news-list/2016/decision-on-exclusion-of-companies-from-the-go vernment-pension-fund-global/.
32 A representative of Kosmos has told us that the Council's rationale for excluding the firm, rather than placing it on observation, was that Kosmos represents too small an investment for NBIM to spend resources on verifying its progress toward compliance. But this account is contested by the member of the Council with whom we spoke. Kosmos has since withdrawn from exploratory drilling off the coast of Western Sahara (https://wsrw.org/a105x4080); this decision was made, we were told, because the fields in question are considered unprofitable to develop.
33 www.theguardian.com/business/2006/jun/07/supermarkets.asda and www.nbim.no/ en/responsibility/exclusion-of-companies/.
34 *Responsible Investment Norwegian Pension Fund Global/2016* (www.nbim.no/contenta ssets/2c3377d07c5a4c4fbd442b345e7cfd67/government-pension-fund-global—resp onsible-investment-2016.pdf), section 3.3 "Environmental investments," pp. 58–67.
35 http://norfund.no.
36 In the frequent repetitions this phrase, the expected "for Norwegians" does not appear. It is understood, however, given the Fund's official name, that its main purpose is to cover future pension liabilities for Norwegians, especially in view of the period, about 60 years ahead, when the oil/gas reserves run out.

37 To assure its independence from purely financial considerations (impact on the Fund's rate of return), the Council on Ethics was originally set up as a unit of the Finance Ministry apart from NBIM. More recently, however, to increase the sharing of research findings (which are highly relevant to NBIM's financial risk analysis), and to aide in NBIM's engagement with corporations, from 2015 onwards the Council has been housed within NBIM, as a unit with a special autonomous status. As before, in making its divestment recommendations the Council is not directly answerable to guidance from NBIM's leadership.

38 *Responsible Investment Norwegian Pension Fund Global/2016*, p. 24.

39 Ibid.

40 The original idea behind picking these focus areas, as seen by Henrik Syse, who was NBIM's Head of Corporate Governance from 2005 to 2007, was to address issues of obvious ethical import, that are of long-term significance (given the inter-generational perspective of the Fund), and that also are financially significant to the fund's holdings.

41 Ibid., p. 68.

42 Ibid., p. 25.

43 Ibid., p. 69.

44 Ibid., 69. These briefs are often written before the company reports, as most often it is a particularly troublesome incident that prompts a closer look at the company's wider operations.

45 Ibid., p. 25.

46 Ibid.

47 *Responsible Investment: Norwegian Government Pension Global/2017*, p. 48.

48 Ibid., p. 53.

49 Ibid., p. 41. No further breakdown of issues is supplied, thus the degree to which these meetings represent follow-up to the 2016 focus area assessments, or involve a wider set if social and environmental issues, is not disclosed.

50 Ibid., p. 41.

51 The 2016 report (ibid., pp. 54–55) relates that the ongoing dialogue with AngloGold Ashanti has two goals: tackling "the legacy of historical pollution stemming from mining in the Obuasi area" and adopting "generally accepted environmental standards" once the infrastructure has been modernized. NBIM notes that it has yet seen little "material progress" in this regard. We have learned from our interviews that the wider social impacts are not currently being monitored by NBIM, nor are they being taken up in its dialogue with the company.

52 Ibid., p. 44.

53 Ibid., p. 53.

54 This, we have been told, was the case for the human rights expectation document.

55 On a visit to PRIO, NBIM's chief executive officer, Yngve Slyngstad, was asked whether there is any indication that the expectation documents are being read by the target group (corporate board members). Admitting that this was the first time he had received the question, Slyngstad responded that he had received numerous letters attesting to the seriousness with which these reports had been read.

56 www.nbim.no/en/responsibility/risk-management/human-rights.

57 Ibid.

58 See www.nbim.no/en/transparency/features/2011-and-older/2009/childrens-rights–a-concern-for-investors/ and www.nbim.no/en/transparency/news-list/2011-and-older/2009/breakthrough-for-corporate-governance/. Henrik Syse, one of the authors, was himself directly engaged in this process from 2007 to 2009.

59 See Reichberg, Gregory M. and Henrik Syse (2004) The Idea of Double Effect – in War and in Business, in *Responsibility in World Business: Managing Harmful Side-Effects of Corporate Activity*. Tokyo: United Nations University Press (17–38).

60 PRIO's report *Business and Peacebuilding: Seven Ways to Maximize Positive Impact* (by Jason Miklian, Peer Schouten, Cindy Horst, and Øystein H. Rolandsen; Oslo: PRIO, 2018) outline these sorts of cases; see esp. pp. 25–26.

61 Ibid., pp. 18–20.

INDEX